Cinema Nation

Cinema Nation

The Best Writing on Film from

1913–2000

EDITED BY
CARL BROMLEY
•
INTRODUCTION BY
STUART KLAWANS

THUNDER'S MOUTH PRESS / NATION BOOKS
NEW YORK

Published by Thunder's Mouth Press/Nation Books
841 Broadway, Fourth Floor
New York, NY 10003

Nation Books is a co-publishing venture of the Nation Institute and Avalon Publishing Group, Incorporated.

ISBN 1-56025-286-3

Library of Congress Cataloging-in-Publication Data

Cinema nation : the best writing on film from the Nation, 1913–2000 / edited by Carl Bromley ; introduction by Stuart Klawans.

p. cm.

ISBN 1-56025-286-3

1. Motion pictures. 2. Motion pictures—Reviews. I. Bromley, Carl. II. Nation (New York, N.Y.)

PN1994 .C522 2000

791.43'75—dc21

00–056384

Distributed by Publishers Group West

Manufactured in the United States of America

Contents

2. FOUNDING FATHERS

3. Is that a pistol in your pocket?—Morality, influence and censorship

4. Einstein in Hollywood and other Probabilities

8. Going Underground: The Sixties

9. The World Is Not Enough: Hollywood and the World

11. OUR CRITICS SPEAK

Editor's Note

When JoAnne Wypijewski showed me an article by Sergei Eisenstein, from a *Nation* special issue on the Soviet Union from 1927, which she was excerpting in the magazine's special millennium issue, she probably didn't realize what sort of treasure trail she was sending me on. Naturally I was intrigued and wondered what other treasures from the world of cinema lurked in the *Nation*'s frail, deteriorating archives at 33 Irving Place? This book, and the irreversible destruction of whole decades of that archive, is the result of that hunt.

My own work on the two *Nation* Politics of Hollywood issues Peter Biskind edited exposed me to the long political and historical ties between Tinseltown's progressive community and *The Nation* (readers may be interested to learn that the magazine's subscriber base is higher in Los Angeles than New York City). And even though some readers were apparently appalled by *The Nation*'s decision to have a movie issue (further evidence of the dumbing down of our culture, eh?) my exploration of the archives confirmed my suspicion that the special issues were in fact a continuity of *The Nation*'s rich and ambivalent tradition of writing about cinema which Stuart Klawans (and this book, I hope), in his introduction, captures with his customary wit and intelligence.

Not all the results of my dig are exhibited. Space, alas, meant losing a number of valuable pieces: Akira Iwasaki on Japanese cinema, Daniel Singer on Wajda's Danton, Barbara Probst Solomon on "The Franglais Film" and novelist Julian Halevy on Disneyland and Las Vegas, are just a few examples. And fascinating curiosities such as *LOONY: A Modern Movie* by Robert L. Wolf, a strange screenwriting experiment from September 9, 1925 concerning a strike at a gasworks. This was the first movie-themed cover *The Nation* published, with constructivist graphics resembling early Soviet agitprop. A rather high-minded editorial note set the pace: "Writing for the movies, in any genuine creative sense, is a new art. In France Romain Rolland has written a 'Revolt of the Machines', in Germany Ivan Goll a 'Chapliniade'. Robert Wolf's scenario, printed in this issue, is a pioneer American effort in the same field." This was managing editor Freda Kirchwey's idea, who wrote editor Oswald Garrison Villard, "we are printing this week a dazzling, lively, futuristic movie scenario." Villard was furious because this wasn't the sort of thing *The Nation* published. Kirchwey replied "I think *The Nation* ought to be proud to lead in this sort of modernism." A turf war between Kirchwey and Villard broke out over who had the right to accept manuscripts. Villard eventually conceded Kirchwey's right to accept such material but such an experiment was never tried again. Neither did *LOONY* make it to the screen. There's a moral there somewhere.

In many respects this work has been a collective enterprise: I thank Ham Fish, Victor Navasky and Katrina vanden Heuvel (who has allowed me to borrow some of her editorial notes from her anthology *The Nation: 1865–1900*) for their help and encouragement. I am equally indebted to Ghadah Alrawi, Neil Orternberg and Daniel O'Connor from Thunder's Mouth Press. At various times I have received invaluable help, assistance, advice, love etc from Peter Biskind, Roane Carey, Sarah Chamberlain, Taya Grobow, Stephen Hyde, Stuart Klawans, Betsy Reed, Mary Taylor Schilling, Bruce Shapiro, Daniel Singer, and my wife Stefanie, who, when she gets round to reading this, will finally discover what I do with myself during the day. As we say in England, cheers mate.

Carl Bromley
New York, June 2000

Introduction by Stuart Klawans

LIKE LOVERS IN a screwball comedy—nut cases with complementary manias, bickering their way toward a happy ending—*The Nation* and the movies were made for each other. The marriage, in this case, is particularly unstable; but it's gone on for about a century, and the awful truth of it now lies in your hands.

In these pages, you will read evidence of how the movies—the 20th century's great popular entertainment—also aspired to be an art form and a force for social change. What kind of art? Change toward what end? The answers have been wildly various, and frequently at odds with the core impulse of the movies. Art-seekers and world-improvers sometimes settle for a small audience, but moviemakers want to reach us all.

The Nation, taking the Irene Dunne role to the movies' Cary Grant, neatly mirrors this self-contradiction. As an organ of the left, concerned with what used to be called the broad masses, *The Nation* keeps an eye on the movies. It even manages to like them, sometimes. But no one has ever accused this magazine of having the popular touch. Unmistakably elitist in tone and tastes, *The Nation* goes against its own core impulse every time it sneaks away from high art and good causes for a two-dollar matinee.

I write as one of the sneakers. Since 1988, I have served as film critic for *The Nation*, from which post I have signaled my enthusiasm for any number of pictures that baffled the magazine's readership, though not the public at large: *Bill & Ted's Bogus Journey, Mission: Impossible 2*, Howard Stern's *Private Parts, Babe, Men in Black*. You will be spared my opinions of these movies, since they lie beyond the scope of this volume. However, you may find similar pieces in this collection, of more historic weight: Mark Van Doren writing in praise of Walt Disney's *Snow White*, James Agee on *The Curse of the Cat People*. I imagine that when my predecessors published these reviews, they got the same response that's heard today from *Nation* readers: "Why waste your ink? Tell us about something important."

From principle and passion, *Nation* writers have done that, too. Again, you will be spared my thoughts on a lot of this higher-toned stuff: films from Iran and Senegal, gay and lesbian experimentalism, starless American features with all of two prints in distribution, documentaries on a world of political woes. But in this area, too, you will find evidence of *The Nation's* distinguished history witness, among other items, Susan Sontag's legendary defense of *Flaming Creatures*. For its support of the no-budget and non-commercial, *The Nation* has won a surprisingly large and loyal following in the film community, not only among those who make and exhibit these worthy pictures but among those who wish they did. These readers consistently express their gratitude for *The Nation*'s coverage, then add, "But tell us about something important. What about the threat to the republic represented by *Blow Hard 3*?"

Let us consider some of the threats to the republic addressed in this collection, and some of the people who have written about them.

The tremendous social and economic institution known as the movies—as distinguished from the older and broader field of film—became established definitively in 1915 with the release of *The Birth of a Nation*. At that moment, popular entertainment intersected with both artistic ambition and a strong social message; and since the movies' message-bearers were the Ku Klux Klan, *The Nation* responded with its first substantial commentary on motion pictures, written by the magazine's future editor, Oswald Garrison Villard. Looking back at the novelty of the situation—never before had so many people attended a spectacle of such blatant racism—we may excuse Villard for ignoring the picture's artistry. (James Agee would take up that subject many years later, in an obituary tribute to D. W. Griffith, adding the improbable claim that Griffith had gone "to almost preposterous lengths to be fair to the Negroes as he understood them," and that the picture had shown "the salient facts of the so-called Reconstruction years.") For Villard, the only salient facts were the distortion of history and the fomenting of hatred against ten million citizens—and so he launched *The Nation*'s movie coverage with a call for censorship.

The magazine soon reversed itself on this issue—see the gently worded 1922 editorial "Film Censors and Other Morons," as well as a multitude of pieces down to Diane di Prima's 1964 "Fuzz's Progress." I ascribe to enlightened self interest this wholly admirable love of free speech. *The Nation* may disagree with what the movies say, but it will defend to the death its right to disagree with the movies. And so, in this volume, you will find complaints about Hollywood's portrayals of black people, American Indians, gay people, and women, written (in tones ranging from high dudgeon to feigned amusement) by John Oliver Killens, Patricia Williams, David Seals, Paul Rudnick, and Katha Pollitt. And more: Here are Richard Condon and Marcel Ophuls, laying into the mass-merchandising of violence; and just about everybody having a say about the uses of history, when Oliver Stone brings out *JFK*.

So much for the bickering. What about the love?

You will have noticed, perhaps, that some of the complainers listed above have worked in the movies. Other contributors to this volume who have not yet been named—Nelson Algren, for example—narrowly escaped a term in Hollywood. (How was job recruitment managed during the last days of the studio system? Read Algren, and discover how even a tough case from Chicago went all starry-eyed, given enough booze, and the thought of meeting Sylvia Sidney.) Although some of the magazine's greatest movie-appreciators kept their distance from Hollywood—as you may see at one of the high points of this book, Lincoln Kirstein's farewell to Marilyn Monroe—much of the writing has come from people who were inside the industry and wanted to be there.

We come to the sections that are, for me, the heart of the book. First, from the period of the studio system, we have reports on the drive to unionize Hollywood. No one who throws around the term "Hollywood liberal" should miss these accounts of stars and bit players coming together in hasty living-room meetings, union negotiators breaking in on moguls at their poker game, picketers at the studio gate being bludgeoned by goons (while the Los Angeles police politely looked away). Whatever liberalism you might find today within the movie business, in whatever form—a useful update is included in this book—its roots lie within a labor movement long championed by *The Nation*.

After the labor struggle, and not unrelated to it, came the blacklist.

At the time, *The Nation* had the all-too-rare honor of speaking out against the Hollywood Red hunt. Subsequently, our long-time editor and publisher, Victor Navasky, wrote the standard work on the subject, *Naming Names*; and the magazine today keeps alive the memory of those times.

Memory is sorely needed. In our present era of post–Cold War triumphalism, it's become commonplace to borrow one of the most dunderheaded of Old Left slogans and dismiss the blacklistees as having been on the wrong side of history. The Soviet Union was bad, therefore the Red hunters were good; as if the blacklist had cut short by one day peoples' sufferings in the Soviet bloc, or prevented a Bolshevik coup led by the Screen Writers Guild, West. *The Nation* was always clear about the central issue of the blacklist, which was not the potential curtailment of liberties in a Red menaced America, but the actual curtailment of liberties in an American searching for Reds.

What did it feel like, to be threatened with the loss of livelihood unless you informed? Here's Sidney Lumet's unblinkingly honest testimony, in which he recalls facing the crucial moment as an improviser, waiting to hear what might come out of his mouth. And what was it like to lose your livelihood, go to jail, emerge into a shadow existence? Here is Dalton Trumbo, magnificent in scorn. Too smart a show biz professional to scare off his audience, Trumbo narrates his story as a string of crackling one-liners, which pop off three, four, five times per sentence. Only when his eloquence gets away from him, sending the clauses tumbling down a paragraph, do you sense the driving rage.

I can add nothing to these accounts; I probably shouldn't even praise them, since by doing so I take on a moral superiority I've done nothing to earn. But the blacklist is too big a subject to abandon just yet; so maybe a few words are in order about the Red hunts impact on my own little corner of the world, film criticism.

A few years ago, while trolling through the video store, I decided to waste an evening with a decidedly minor picture from 1953: *Salome*, directed by William Dieterle. I knew of it only as a relatively late Rita Hayworth vehicle, in which the boss of Columbia Pictures, Harry Cohn, got one last dance out of his aging sex goddess. Imagine my surprise when I started watching. The film's key event turns out to be a government hearing, in which John the Baptist, having been accused of subversion, is invited to clear his name and win release from jail. All he has to do is inform on Jesus. It seems that a committee of Roman officials wants to make an example of this Galilean and needs someone to finger him as a troublemaker. John refuses, of course. At this point, the man who is in effect John's defense attorney—played by no less a figure than Maurice Schwartz, prince of the Yiddish theater—appears in close-up, so he can address the audience face to face: "He is not a traitor! He is a man of peace!"

How many other allegories of the Red hunt did moviemakers turn out under the guise of sword-and-sandal epics, Westerns, gangster pictures, tales of strange visitors from other planets? There's no reliable tally. The Production Code had already whetted the ingenuity of moviemakers, who'd learned to sneak in all that sex that the characters weren't supposed to be having. With the onset of the blacklist and the accompanying black market in scripts, which Dalton Trumbo discusses, all sorts of political meanings began to sneak in, too.

This development did not escape the more alert moviegoers in the Fifties, who saw that hidden messages, some of them desperate, kept flashing through the surface of genre pictures. Some of these moviegoers also happened to be critics and to them we owe the revolution in taste and understanding that goes by the name of auteurism.

Of course, there have been many auteurisms, whose promulgators have not necessarily felt sympathy for the left. (Neither François Truffaut nor Andrew Sarris showed much patience with political pleading of any kind.) But one common trait of all these schools has been the notion that meanings might be stuffed into even the most formulaic entertainment.

Through a trick of history, auteurism took root in the United States in 1963, shortly after the blacklist was broken and shortly before the Production Code came to an end. In other words, people got wise to the possibility of commandeering genre vehicles just when it was no longer necessary to do so. The result, in the emerging movie-brat culture, was an overvaluation of genre, till we got to the point that Jean-Luc Godard announced he was no longer an auteurist, now that there was such a thing as "A Film by Chris Columbus." Meanwhile, too many filmmakers with artistic and political ambitions developed an overreliance on allegory and irony—one of the traits that has most put off the audience, and enforced the distinction between movies and films.

I offer this potted history, first of all, to suggest that the blacklist had very profound effects, for good and ill, on the merits of movies, and also on the way we judge those merits. (In the same good-and-bad way, by pushing professionals out of the business or driving them underground, the blacklist fostered that important but ill-defined tendency known as "independent film.") None of this seems to have reached the attention of *The Nation*, not for many years. The studio system collapsed, the New Wave came and went, the first generation of film school directors reached middle age, "independence" became a marketing category, and still in the front of the magazine and very often in the arts pages at the back as well, *Nation* writers carried on as if a tightly co-ordinated production facility known as "Hollywood" were in operation; as if movies were good or bad depending upon the literary qualities of their dialogue and (above all) the political affiliation of their makers; as if "small and artistic" automatically meant "progressive," and "Panavision" was the name of a fascist tool.

This, too, is part of the awful truth contained in the book you hold. But it is not the whole truth. *The Nation* has also featured some of the world's smartest, most influential movie criticism and to drive home the point, to bring this comedy to its climax, I will now introduce Manny Farber.

He comes on the scene in 1949 acting like a hybrid of two figures from *My Man Godfrey*: William Powell fused with Mischa Auer. The motions of his prose are abrupt, extravagant, parodic, nonchalant, like Auer throwing off piano arpeggios amid bites of an apple, or hopping around the drawing room like an ape. But listen to the sense that rattles around in those sentences: It's the sound of Powell talking straight, giving you the benefit of an aristocrat's sensibilities combined with a hobo's practical knowledge.

Cinema Nation gives you four years worth of these performances—four years during which Farber set a standard that the rest of us can only strive to attain. He seemed to know everything about the movies, and to see everything that was in them. He looked seriously at genre pictures, and catalogued the habits of their directors, years before the politique des auteurs was even named. He studied the frame with the eye of a painter; the actors, with the eye of a con man sizing up a mark. Many critics have tried to imitate him; but he remains an anomaly in this field, as he was an anomaly at *The Nation*, filling its pages with brilliant discussions of boxing movies and the works of Jerry Lewis at a time when our readers most needed to hear about something important.

I think it was important that *The Nation* gave him the berth. Farber's reviews are still news, half a century after he wrote them; you read them not for historical context, but for insight. Here they are: testament to the power of that screwball alliance summed up in the title, *Cinema Nation*.

FOREWORD BY PETER BISKIND

CALL ME DUMB, but I had forgotten or maybe never known that Manny Farber had reviewed movies for *The Nation* in the late 40s. Watching him spill the blood of pictures that are now revered as classics, *Sunset Boulevard*, *Body and Soul*, *From Here To Eternity* with his razor sharp prose in these (mostly) republished for the first time mini-masterpieces makes your breath catch, and right or wrong, he is one of the unexpected pleasures in an anthology of writing on film from *The Nation* that is filled with unexpected pleasures.

Although celebrated for opening its pages to the reviews of James Agee, *The Nation* is not the first magazine one might think of in this context, but then one would be wrong, as this collection amply demonstrates. It's all here, from Eisenstein, in his own right, yet, to Reagan, and beyond. *The Nation*'s remarkable 100 year plus run is roughly coextensive with the century of the movies, so it was up and running at the birth of the silents.

Just bearing witness along with the timeliness of the weekly format gives a you-are-there jolt to the writing, allowing us, for example, to read civil liberties crusader and *Nation* editor Oswald Garrison Villard perversely endorsing the censorship of *Birth of the Nation* in the May 6, 1915 edition, nicely book ended by Agee's tribute to D. W. Griffith some 40 years later in which with equal perversity he underplays the film's racism. Or a fresh-from-the-picket line account of the bloody clash between strikers and studio-hired goons in front of Warner Brothers in 1946 that was right out of Eisenstein's Strike, except the tinsel town version didn't have a happy ending.

In a wonderful meditation on the state of Hollywood published in 1997, the great Marcel Ophuls quotes his friend Francois Truffaut, who had grown increasingly conservative as he lived to see the *Nouvelle Vague* he helped to create become the new official cinema of France, saying, "Marcel, all our lives, we've been fighting censorship, and rightly so. And in our eyes, of course, the worst form of censorship has always been self censorship. But lately I've begun to ask myself: Just what is the difference between self-censorship . . . and a sense of responsibility?" Ophuls doesn't record his response, but he himself was never troubled by this question, never mistook self-censorship for responsibility, and neither did the writers collected in this volume who, as might be expected, speak out bluntly, often eloquently on movies and the larger cultural issues that swirl around them. Thus, we find Eisenstein pace *Cahiers du Cinema*'s *politique des auteurs* ranting against art: "I approach the making of a motion picture in much the same way as I would the equipment of a poultry farm or the installation of a water system. . . . Down with intuitive creation." And *Nation* editor Carey McWilliams speaking out in a 1935 piece called "Hollywood Plays with Fascism" against the vogue for America First–tinged military drill corps with names such as the Hollywood Hussars, the California Escadrille, and the Light Horse Cavalry organized by the likes to Gary Cooper, Victor McLaglen, and George Brent, apparently backed with Hearst money. Or Dalton Trumbo and Sidney Lumet on the blacklist, or Paul Rudnick on gays in Hollywood movies. Or Susan Sontag defending Jack Smith's *Flaming Creatures* when it was suppressed in 1964. It was Giuliani-time back then, too, and one of the lessons of this collection is *plus ca change, plus c'est la meme chose*.

But you'll find a lot more here than issues and politics; there is plenty of good, often funny writing, frequently from unexpected sources: James Thurber with tongue firmly in cheek urging Disney to make *The Odyssey*; a George S. Kaufman riff apparently spun off a news item reporting Freud had been invited to Hollywood to consult on a Bette Davis movie, *Dark Victory*; Nelson Algren looking back dourly on his adventures in the film trade; Ring Lardner, Jr. musing, amusingly, on the storied misfortunes of the screenwriter; Michael Moore on his "rules for success in the movies." Sample: "If you're going to attack a big bad corporation in your film, it will help to have another big bad corporation in your corner." (This may have worked in the late 80s for *Roger and Me*, his documentary thumping of General Motors distributed by Warner Brothers, but just a decade later with media mergers proceeding pell mell it is becoming nearly impossible to follow Moore's example. With *The Insider* and *Erin Brockovich*, we may have marked the high tide of business bashing business.)

And, not surprisingly, there's plenty of controversy, too: Ariel Dorfman on Constantine Costa Gravas's *Missing*, while the brouhaha surrounding Oliver Stone's *JFK*, featuring Alexander Cockburn at his polemical best, provides an excuse for an excursion into the bowels of the magazine's letters column, as outraged readers go mano-a mano with Cockburn who, as usual, has the last word. And wait there's more: opinion, reporting, and analysis from Nora Ephron, John Leonard, and current *Nation* regulars like Katha Pollitt, Christopher Hitchens, Marc Cooper, Patricia Williams, and David Corn—and even a piece of journalism from the Soviet formalist theoretician Alexander Bakshy about the "talkies". The critics section alone provides a surprisingly comprehensive and informative overview of the movies—American and otherwise—through the decades, from Gilbert Seldes writing in 1925, through Siegfried Kracauer in 1941, to Farber, Agee, Harold Clurman, and the present reviewer, Stuart Klawans.

All in all, this anthology provides a real service, putting between covers hard-to-find material that uncollected would have been—and has been—neglected. And perhaps best of all, the veritable Babel of voices and opinions here presented gives the lie to the oft-heard dismissal of left wing cultural reporting and criticism as boring and predictable. It's anything but.

1

Early Days

Fatty and the Wobblies

DECEMBER 18, 1913

THE WEEK

•

Paragraphs of (unsigned) comment on current affairs called "The Week" filled the first three or four pages of the magazine from 1865 to 1936. Items often reflected the editor's view that the function of a weekly was not to explain or report or celebrate national virtues but to take a consistently critical view of "the idols of the tribe." Despite the mirthful tone of the paragraph below—the earliest I managed to discover from *The Nation* archives on cinema—and the fact that the ideas proposed have found few, if any, takers, one can certainly detect a sense of wonder in its voice. "The Week" would soon explore (and agonize over) the nature of cinema as a mass entertainment form, thus beginning a century long obsession for cultural and social theorists of the left.

Members of society saw themselves in moving-pictures last night and enjoyed the novelty immensely.

Robert Burns's famous prayer has been answered. The gift has been given us to see ourselves as others see us. If society has enjoyed the revelation, it is to be congratulated. It is not always that the sight of one's own unfamiliar profile or the sound of one's unfamiliar voice is concducive to satisfaction. The motion film, in conjuction with the phonograph, thus directed to self-study, can be made of enormous educational value and a factor for the increase of human happiness. Take the after-dinner speaker. A cinematograph presentation of himself, erect above rows of heads bent in submission, reinforced by a phonographic reproduction of himself staggering on through a Serbonian bog of platitudes and imbecilities, would make an extraordinary impression in the cold light of the morning after. The swelling tide of oratory will experience a remarkable subsidence when a speaker begins wondering whether he could really have been so big an idiot as he looks and sounds.

DECEMBER 7, 1916

THE WEEK

•

NO DISCUSSION OF the "movies" as the art of the future can be complete without taking cognizance of the fact that prices in the neighborhood picture theatres are ten cents in the evening and only five cents at other times. The reason, of course, is the child. To busy mothers in crowded city sections Charlie Chaplin has come in the role of governess and traffic policeman. For the price of a nickel the nine-year-old is kept off the streets for an hour or two in the afternoon; and the afternoon audiences in poor or moderately comfortable neighborhoods are made up largely of little ones unattended. From this situation have arisen all sorts of evils with which child-welfare agencies are now contending. But it is the comparatively rare mother who stops to weigh such dangers against the usefulness of the "nickelodeon" in the way of taking the child off her hands, giving him amusement, and, most of all, keeping him out of the danger of street traffic. The small coin which formerly was devoted to candy to keep the child happy and give the mother freedom for her work, now goes to contribute to the support of an industry which ranks in importance with steel and coal.

Once the importance of the juvenile audience in the movie business is recognized, it becomes plain that the art of the movies must in large measure be shaped by that factor. The public, to which must be given what it wants, is now drawn from the primary school ages with a fair sprinkling of kindergarten upper-classmen. Obviously, the scenario writers are now busy upon an art that is democratic with a vengeance.

They must cater to an appeal infinitely broader than the playwright must keep in mind when he sets out to please at the same time Broadway and Kankakee. He solves the problem by going in for the elemental emotions which are the same on both sides of the Hudson, by appealing, as the phrase goes, to the child that is in all of us. The movie writer must go further. He must appeal to the infant that is in all of us. That the trick can be done is attested by the present state of the new art. It is all very simple. The infant cannot always understand and like what his parents do. It remains, therefore, to make the parents like what their youngest likes. The thing has been done before in the case of the newspaper "comic." Starting out as a Sunday device for keeping the children quiet while father was asleep, it has become the everyday necessity for father's sporting page and mother's home page.

OCTOBER 20, 1920

EDUCATION BY CELLULOID

•

The letter below was one of many to lament the deplorable moral and ideological content of early Hollywood cinema. Another letter-writer was horrified by an audience applauding German soldiers goose-stepping past German Field Marshall Hindenberg. Things changed though. In 1926 one letter writer was cheered by Cecil B. DeMille's The Volga Boatman: "No women are nationalized. The only indecencies committed against women are by the Czarist white forces. What a change since Norma Talmadge's excruciatingly anti-Bolshevik picture a few years since!"

TO THE EDITOR OF THE NATION:

Sir: Within the week I have seen two moving picture films. One was called *The Riders of the Dawn,* the other *The Flame of Hell Gate.* The acting in the first was clever, in the second, abominable, crude, and ludicrous. The effects of each, the ideas suggested to the mind of the spectator, were vicious in the extreme. In the first, a lynching-bee was applauded by the crowded house. A raid upon a labor-camp supposedly. IWW was cheered. The IWWs were chased out of town with bull-whips, much to the enjoyment of the spectators. For misrepresentation of the IWW, it would be hard to beat *The Riders of the Dawn.*

In the second film, outlawry was idolized. Extra-legal methods of securing justice, of getting revenge, were applauded. Government was held up to contempt. Due process of law was ridiculed as entirely inadequate and undependable in both films. Violence of the mob was pictured as the only means of punishing I.W.W.'s in the first film and of punishing a cattle-thief in the second. Thus do the movies teach Americanism!

Perhaps Freud would explain it in terms of the sadistic impulse. In the movies, people have a means of obtaining vicarious satisfaction for their suppressed desires. But the suggestions in such films do harm that is beyond the possibility of calculation. There was a boy in our neighborhood who having stolen a revolver and jewelry, set fire to several buildings. At each place he left a sign "The Black Mask." It is easy to see where he got the suggestion.

Berkeley, California, August 20 ALLEN OAK

FEBRUARY 14, 1923

ARBUCKLE AND THE I.W.W.

Catherine Hofteling

•

Catherine Hofteling was the pseudonym of a San Francisco journalist.

"Away with this man and release unto us Barabbas!"

The facts of their conviction are so raw and unjust that it is like telling a vulgar story to relate them. The papers said briefly that "ten self-admitted Industrial Workers of the World were found guilty under the State criminal syndicalism act." They didn't even mention their names.

Now, it almost seems as though the San Francisco papers might have mentioned the name of young Peter Beazley, born and brought up here in this city, a boy of twenty-one, educated in the public schools. As a sinner it would seem that he deserved that much publicity—especially when one considers that Fatty Arbuckle not only filled the papers but the drawing-rooms and club meets—and still does. All the hideous and salacious details of Arbuckle's alleged crime have been mouthed lingeringly and long. But if one were to mention the crime of Peter Seazley speculatively and as though it were discussable, one would be met with suspicion and a queer silence. Which goes to prove that sins have their standing just as people do and that a sin against the Decalogue is accepted but a sin against the *status quo* is unmentionable.

This, briefly, is the story of Peter and the nine others: Last March two men were on trial in Sacramento charged with criminal syndicalism and the call went out from the defense for witnesses to testify that the IWW does not advocate or practice violence. It seemed an orderly thing to do considering that the prosecution had their witnesses to prove that the IWW does advocate and practice violence. So the call went out and from all the countryside they came pouring in.

Three witnesses for the defense were called the first morning of the trial. Anita Whitney had just started to testify that in all her years of contact with the IWW boys she had never heard a hint of advocacy of violence among them, when her testimony was struck out because she was not a member of the organization. Peter was called next and having admitted membership was allowed to testify, and so was young LaRue, a sailor lad of twenty years.

When the noon recess came the jury was hustled out and then, before they left the courtroom, young Beazley and LaRue were arrested—because they were members. When the case went to the jury ten men were in jail for testifying in defense of their fellow-workers and their organization. I must emphasize it: The two laborers on trial were allowed no witnesses before this "bar of justice" but members of the IWW and any man who acknowledged membership in the IWW was immediately arrested and faced with a term of from one to fourteen years in the penitentiary.

The Sacramento "can" in summer time is, they say, as hot as hades. The bail was impossibly high and so during all the summer months they sweltered in jail. Then they went to trial and—heigh-ho I got a hung jury; which would never do. So the State disbarred their lawyer, Elmer Smith of Centralia, Washington, from practicing in the State of California. Then came the second trial and a second disagreement of the jury. By this time you might have thought that the State would have wiggled out of an embarrassing and costly trial by dismissing the case. But no. Ten Don Quixotes willing to go to the bat for their beliefs could not be tolerated. So during the holiday season, almost on the birthday of our blessed Lord, the ten were convicted and now they have been sentenced and presently they will go over the sun-kissed road that runs reluctantly through the winter-green meadows to where the gray walls of San Quentin wait to close them in. Beans for breakfast, beans for dinner, beans for supper, no green vegetables until they are free again, and one egg once a year, on Easter morning.

The diet, the confinement, the jute mill, the cell will be hard for young Edwards the lumber-jack from the North; and for Rutherford, a fine, clean young Scotchman, plumber by trade; and for O'Meaid, who has sold more wobbly papers under more noses of bulls than can be counted. Kayler and Zangler, seasonal laborers used to the open, will be clicked into a cell every night. "Whitey" Anderson will find the Pen different from the logging camp, and as for Walter Smith, he has already done a "jolt" for the organization in Leavenworth, so they'll probably bury him, a second-timer at Folson. Smith is also a member of the General Executive Board of the organization. And there is old Jack Nash. Some would say that after riding the rods, sleeping in hay mows or in the burks of the dirt camps, San Quentin would seem like a home. But it won't. It is hard to think of guards ordering that old rebel about.

So presently they will go over the road, and Coutts and Diamond and Townsend, the three stool-pigeons whose word sent them there, will go to their country homes, homes made fleecy by the salaries paid them by the people of the State.

And Fatty Arbuckle, it is very important to consider Arbuckle in this matter, for to understand the attitude toward him is to understand the apathy toward these others. Whether Fatty is guilty or not is not so important. The point is that those who are for him and those who are against still discuss him seriously. The women's clubs hear speakers pro and con on the subject of this Arbuckle, but never will they allow a discussion of the prosecutions under the criminal syndicalism act in their midst—not even a breath of it. Fatty's was a sin of the Decalogue; the IWW boys—theirs is a sin against the *status quo*. "Crucify him! Crucify him! Release unto us Barabbas:" The crime against these workers in dirt, these builders of the famed California highways, is met by a great bourgeois silence. California is no worse than other States. It is only richer, more golden, with a fatter *status quo*, against which a crime is greater.

That is all. What can be done about it? Handcuffed, these ten men will presently go over the road through the sunshine, past the flower beds that surround the prison; the waters of the bay will sparkle flippantly, the gates will click, and for years to come the young sailor lad, LaRue, and the old mule skinner, Jack Nash, and the eight others will never see the stars.

FEBRUARY 10, 1929

THE "TALKIES"

Alexander Bakshy

•

Alexander Bakshy was the first *Nation* writer to be given a regular beat as film critic. He also wrote regularly about theater, translated Gorky's plays, and authored a number of books on theater. In his last film column from January 18, 1933 he wrote: "If you do not like the kind of literature that is published in the so-called pulp magazines, you just do not like it, and that is the end of it. You do not rush into print to expose the pathetic ineptitude of these weekly or monthly outpourings. With films, unfortunately, the situation is different. Not only are there woefully few that are worthy of serious consideration, but if you happen to be a film critic you are obliged to stop and analyze the incessant flow of bilge issuing from the film factories of Hollywood and elsewhere as if it were really to be measured by the standards of intellectual and artistic achievement. The whole procedure becomes unspeakably grotesque, resembling in a way what the Russians describe as shooting sparrows with cannon balls. Worse still, it becomes wearisomely repetitious, for in the films originality is found in virtues, not, as in real life, in sins. Yet once more I have to devote this column to the exploration of motion-picture vices . . ."

IT IS A sad reflection on the limitations of intellectuals and artists all over the world to see history repeat itself in the contemptuous resentment with which they are greeting the arrival of the talking picture.

Just as twenty years ago when the silent movies began to stir the world, so today the patrons of art and the theater refuse to see in the talking picture anything but another vulgar product of our machine civilization. But so, too, does history repeat itself in the eagerness of the commercially minded not to miss their share in the windfall of the talking picture, however little they may understand the problems which arise from the use of the new medium, or be able to see where to look for their solution. Thus between the incompetence of the commercial entertainer and the superior self-righteousness of the intellectual, the talking picture is apparently doomed to grope blindly for several years before it reaches anything that may be properly described as an original form of drama. That it will reach this goal eventually does not seem to me in the least doubtful.

In the meantime let us consider the prospects of the talking picture. So far its greatest successes have been scored in a field which does not quite come under the definition of "talking." Pictures like *The Singing Fool* or *My Man* are really "song pictures." The fact, however, that they succeed in conveying their appeal to the audience is vastly significant. Lacking as they are in color and depth, they still capture something of the personality of the artist. No doubt Al Jolson and Fannie Brice are more intimately felt and radiate more genuine warmth when one sees them on the stage. At the same time even on the screen they are unmistakably their peculiar and likable selves. The loudspeaker, though still very imperfect, serves them much more loyally than it does the "talking" actors, since singing reproduces better than speech.

With the inevitable technical improvement in the production of human voice and in the effects of color and stereoscopic depth, the song picture of today will naturally expand into a full-blown musical comedy. So long as this *genre* of entertainment rests its appeal on the singing of popular stars and the gyrations of pretty chorus girls, the screen musical comedy will be able to depart little from the orthodox methods of the stage. In this respect it is in the same boat as the screen drama which would also take the stage for its model. For it has been laid down by our aestheticians that in copying the stage the talking picture would lose all claim to be regarded as a medium of art. Though why should it? A perfect copy is obviously as good as the original, and it is absurd to claim that no reproduction can be perfect. Besides, in the case of the talking picture one does not so much copy an original stage production as imitate the stage form—which, if a sin, is certainly not a cardinal one.

At present the trouble with the talking picture is to be found less in its attempts to imitate the stage than in its numerous technical imperfections. It is safe to predict that within the next ten years these will be removed. And it is only then that the real aesthetic problem of the talking picture will become apparent. The ability to give a perfect imitation of the stage or to create a new and completely original dramatic form means nothing unless it is inspired by the genuine spirit of art. It is here that one becomes seriously alarmed. In the coming fight between Hollywood and Broadway it is ten to one that the former will be victorious. But if the defeat of the Broadway journeymen can hardly be regarded as a great loss to art, the victory of the Hollywood robots will undoubtedly endanger the future of drama on the stage as well as on the screen. The talking picture is merely a mechanized tool; but the Hollywood manufacturers of films represent mechanized brains, and what this means to art we have already learned from the experience of the silent movies.

In this rather dismal picture of the future there are two important factors which have yet to be taken account of, and which are likely to counteract if not completely overcome the influence of Hollywood. The first of these is the remarkable growth in volume and quality of amateur production together with the rapid spread of little cinema houses. Before many years are past these developments will seize the artistic leadership in the movies and will force Hollywood to accept their superior standards. The second factor is the inevitable evolution of the talking picture in accordance with the laws of its own nature. This undoubtedly will exercise a far-reaching influence on Hollywood methods. When the talking-picture mechanism is made perfect the really important development will be along lines which are already beginning to reveal themselves and which will definitely direct the talking picture away from the stage and toward a new, authentic motion-picture drama.

This evolution is inevitable. It is dictated by the inner logic of the medium. Analogies between the stage and the screen assume that they deal with the same material. But they don't. The material of the screen is not actual objects but images fixed on the film. And the very fact that they have their being on the film endows these images with properties which are never found in actual objects. For instance, on the stage the actor moves in real space and time. He cannot even cross the room without performing a definite number of movements. On the screen an action may be shown only in its terminal points with all its intervening moments left out. Similarly, in watching a performance on the stage the spectator is governed by the actual conditions of space and time. Not so in the case of the movie spectator. Thanks to the moving camera he is able to view the scene from all kinds of angles, leaping from a long-distance view to a close-range inspection of every detail. It is obvious that with this extraordinary power of handling space and time—by elimination and emphasis, according to its dramatic needs—the motion picture can never be content with modeling itself after the stage. The fact that it has now acquired the power of speech will certainly not make it any more willing to sacrifice its freedom and individuality. Nor is there any need for such a sacrifice. Dialogue can be concentrated—reduced to a number of essential statements—as effectively as action, just as it is done now in the dialogue titles of silent pictures. Then, the talking picture will also develop the specifically cinematic method of "close up." It will be able to focus an individual utterance, and at the same time put out of focus all the other voices—a procedure unquestionably in advance of the method of the "realistic" stage which, in order that certain characters may be heard, enforces a most unrealistic silence among all the other characters. And such being its technique, the spoken drama of the screen will obviously and inevitably develop into something original and non-stagy—something that will be instinct with the dynamic spirit of the movies.

2

Founding Fathers

•

MAY 6, 1915

THE REGULATION OF FILMS

Oswald Garrison Villard

•

Oswald Garrison Villard was editor of *The Nation* from 1918 to 1933 and dedicated the magazine to the defense of civil liberties. Within months of assuming the editorship, Villard recalled: "The general belief among the war-mad, the reactionaries, the war profiteers, and the general public which did not read *The Nation*, was that we had gone violently 'red,' crazily pacifist, and openly pro-German, while the new adjective 'bolshevik' seemed expressly invented for the purpose of tagging the editors of this wicked sheet." Villard helped found the American Civil Liberties Union in 1920 and was on the board of directors of The National Association for the Advancement of Colored People. As Stuart Klawans tells in his book *Film Follies*, the NAACP "mounted a city-by-city campaign against [*Birth of a Nation*]; and a group of reform leaders, including W.E.B. DuBois, Lillian Wald, Rabbi Stephen Wise, and Oswald Garrison Villard gathered in the chambers of New York City's City Council to denounce it. None of this could halt Griffith's triumph."

WHEREVER IT GOES, the *Birth of the Nation* film arouses widespread indignation. In Boston the excitement has been at white heat, because of a series of hearings before Mayor, Governor, and a committee of the Legislature. A judge has been found with authority and courage enough to cut out the most objectionable scene. The press has been full of arguments for and against the film and the proposed legislation. Many clergymen have preached about the play; and ex-President Eliot, speaking in a Cambridge church, was one of those who protested against its falsification of history. Never before have the colored people of Boston been so united and determined, or appeared to better advantage, and their white friends have rallied in great force to their aid. Gov. Walsh, ex-Congressman McCall, and Lieut.-Gov. Cushing have spoken out emphatically against permitting the play to continue, though the Mayor sided with the producers—as the Mayor of New York has failed to recognize in his utterances the gravity of the situation, or to rise to the emergency, being content with the promise of certain slight evasions, which appear to be of little or no value. The play continues to do its devilish work of misrepresentation and of arousing race hatred.

That Mayor Mitchel has had little legal authority to deal with the play is admitted, though there are differences in opinion as to just what powers were available. But this alleged lack of authority is to be remedied by an ordinance now before the Board of Aldermen to empower the Commissioner of Licenses to revoke, suspend, or annul any moving-picture license "for cause after a trial." The ordinance further reads:

> Proof shall be taken before the Commissioner of Licenses upon notice of not less than two (2) days to the proprietor, manager, or person in charge of said place, to show cause why such license should not be revoked, annulled, or suspended. The Commissioner of Licenses shall hear the proofs and allegations in each case, and determine the same, and any place the license for which shall have been revoked, annulled, or suspended shall not thereafter be licensed again to the same licensee within one year, under the provisions of said sections. On any examination before a Commissioner of Licenses, pursuant to a notice to show cause as aforesaid, the accused party may be a witness in his own behalf.

This plainly constitutes the Commissioner of Licenses a censor of all moving-picture plays, precisely as the Mayor of every town in Massachusetts, except Boston, now has similar powers. That the plan has its defects is obvious, for a Commissioner of Licenses with bad judgment might work a considerable amount of harm.

But this risk is inevitable with any censorship, and no bill has as yet been suggested to the Massachusetts Legislature—which is bent on passing some measure before it adjourns—that is free from defects of one kind or another, save the proposal to put Boston on an equal footing with the other cities of Massachusetts. The truth is that this new means for public amusement and education has brought with it grave perils which we are only just beginning to realize, for side by side with its educational possibilities are the dangers of unrestricted propaganda. As the Rev. Dr. Crothers has pointed out, we have lulled ourselves into a sense of security by repeating to ourselves that the "past at least is secure." But along comes this play, which is not only designed to make large sums for its promoters, but is admittedly a deliberate propaganda to degrade and injure ten millions of citizens, besides misrepresenting some of the noblest figures in our past, Stevens, Sumner, and Lincoln, and perverting history, if only by the onesidedness of its portrayal. Now, let us suppose, as Dr. Crothers has also suggested, that others inspired by this shameful example turn to religious propaganda, and represent the horrible murdering of Catholics at Drogheda by Cromwell, or the massacre of Protestants on St. Bartholomew's night—what then?

Undoubtedly, the tortures of the Inquisition would make effective capital against the Pope at Rome; and if moving pictures had existed in 1898, we might have seen a still more vindictive anti-Spanish crusade by films of battle, or devastation, or reconcentrado camps. Pictures of Russian pogroms would make plenty of money, yet rouse bitter national and racial antipathies. Obviously, the feeling that would result from a religious film-propaganda might lead to most serious breaches of the peace. If a mild, gentle, humorous philosopher like Dr. Crothers admits that the offending film in Boston stirred his heart to mutiny and rage, the potentialities for evil in less-balanced minds need no stressing. What makes the matter worse is that it is not a question of dealing with a single theatrical production, for the film can be duplicated so that the objectionable performance may be going on in forty or more cities at the same moment. It is not surprising, in view of this power for evil, that the United States Supreme Court on February 23 last in three unanimous decisions upheld the laws of Ohio and Kansas creating official censors. "We would have," it said, "to shut our eyes to the facts of the world to regard the precaution unreasonable or the legislation to effect it a mere wanton interference with personal liberty." The Court plainly had in mind the difficulty of controlling by public sentiment alone a series of films scattered over the whole country.

Yet so excellent a newspaper as the Boston *Advertiser* feels that the proposed censorship may be a most dangerous infringement of our freedom of speech and of expression, on a par with the efforts to suppress Garrison and Phillips in anti-slavery days. The Boston *Transcript* and *Herald* appear to believe that if one bill proposed should become a law any citizens who indulged in a fight over a play could stop it, and that any play with a lesson to teach or one which undertook to dwell on the weaknesses of a group of our citizens might easily be driven off the stage. The plan of an official censor for whom the Mayor is responsible, with such a trial as is provided in the pending Aldermanic ordinance in New York, seems for the moment the best way out.

NOVEMBER 9, 1927

MASS MOVIES

Sergei Mikhailovich Eisenstein

•

Eisenstein wrote "Mass Movies" for *The Nation*'s special issue on the tenth anniversary of the Russian Revolution (other contributors included Lenin's widow Nadezhda Krupskaya and the writer Mikhail Zoshchenko). *Battleship Potemkin* was released two years later in America while in England it was banned for fear of its seditious effect on working class audiences until 1954. The film launched Soviet cinema internationally even though its reception in Russia initially was met with a lukewarm public response.

I AM A civil engineer and mathematician by training. I approach the making of a motion picture in much the same way as I would the equipment of a poultry farm or the installation of a water system. My point of view is thoroughly utilitarian, rational, materialistic.

When the little "collective" which I direct hits on a subject we do not draft plans in an office. Nor do I go and sit under an oak tree waiting for poetic inspiration. Our slogan is "Down with intuitive creation." Instead we wallow in life. Having chosen the village as the theme of our latest production, *Generalnaya Linya* (General Peasant Policy), we dip into the archives of the Commissariat of Agriculture. Thousands of peasant complaints are perused. We attend village soviet meetings and listen to village gossips. The picture—it will be finished on January 1—shows the power of the soil over man and aims to teach the town-dweller understanding and affection for the peasant. We took the actors from night-lodging houses; we picked them up on the road. The "heroine" must plow and milk a cow.

Our films do not center around an individual or a triangle. We want to develop the public, not the actor. This is a reflection of the spirit of collectivism which is abroad in the land. Nor do we attempt to excite vicarious participation in the lives of the persons of the drama; that is an appeal to sentiment. The cinema can make a far bigger contribution and a far stronger impression by projecting matter and bodies rather than feelings. We photograph an echo and the rat-a-tat-tat of a machine-gun. The impression is physiological. Our psychological approach is on the one hand that of the great Russian scholar, Pavlov, with his principle of reflexology, and on the other, that of the Austrian Freud—the principle of psychoanalysis.

Take the scene in *Potemkin* where the Cossacks slowly, deliberately walk down the Odessa steps firing into the masses. By consciously combining the elements of legs, steps, blood, people, we produce an impression—of what kind? The spectator does not imagine himself at the Odessa wharf in 1905. But as the soldiers' boots press forward he physically recoils. He tries to get out of the range of the bullets. As the baby carriage of the crazed mother goes over the side of the mole he holds on to his cinema chair. He does not want to fall into the water.

Our mounting method is a further aid in achieving such effects. Some countries in which the picture industry is highly developed do not use mounting at all. A sled rushes down a snowy toboggan and you merely see it sliding and skidding to the bottom. We photograph the bumps, and the movie goer feels them, and hears them, too, from the orchestra pit just as he did the throbbing of the engines when the armored cruiser "Potemkin" moved into battle. For this reason, probably, the movement of things and of machines in our pictures is not a part quickly to be passed over but one of absorbing interest. Mounting—the interlacing of close-ups, of side-views, top-views, bottom-views—is the most important part of our work. A picture is either made or unmade by it. Such methods cannot be adapted to the theater. I started in the theater, with the Proletcult, but left it for motion pictures. The theater, I believe, is a dying institution. It is the handiwork of the petty artisan. The movie reflects heavy, highly organized industry.

The scenic effect is calculated; so also is the ideological effect. We never start a picture without knowing why. *Potemkin* was an episode of revolutionary heroism calculated to electrify the masses. *Generalnaya Linya* seeks to encourage the bond between the city and the village—the outstanding political task of Bolshevism. "October," which will be shown all over the Union on November 7, depicts the ten days in the autumn of 1917 that shook the world. It shows history being made by the man in the street, by the worker from the foundry, by the lousy soldier from the trench. It identifies the common citizen of today with that history.

Conditions make our work easy. Night after night from four to five thousand Leningrad workers volunteered to participate in the storming of the Winter Palace which forms part of *October*. The government supplied the arms and uniforms, as well as the army. In addition to workers and soldiers, we needed a mob. But word was whispered about and the militia had to be summoned to keep away the tens of thousands.

In *Potemkin* the Black Sea fleet was put at our disposal. On November 7, 1917, the flagship Aurora of the Baltic squadron joined the Communists and proceeded up the Neva to bombard the Winter Palace. The state lent us the Aurora for the reenactment of this scene in *October.* We likewise had the use of tanks and artillery.

As we stick to life for our subjects so we stick to life for our scenery. We never build streets, or cities, or villages. The natural ones are truer. The detail of permission is easily arranged. No private owner or entrepreneur can object to the photographing of his premises or demand payment for the privilege. These things cheapen production.

Potemkin was a poster. *Generalnaya Linya* and *October* are subtler. They are nearer life. We are learning. We feel that our method is the only correct one and that its potentialities are unlimited.

Our method and America's highly developed movie technique ought to be a powerful combination. For this reason we are interested in an invitation to work in the United States during the next year. If our activities here permit, and if we are granted freedom of action in the United States, we may soon be there.

JUNE 27, 1928

THE SEASON IN MOSCOW
EISENSTEIN AND LUNACHARSKY

Joseph Wood Krutch

•

Joseph Wood Krutch was *The Nation*'s Drama Critic from 1924 to 1952 and an associate editor between 1932 and 1937. Renowned for his books on drama, literature, and especially natural history, his book *The Measure of Man: On Freedom, Human Value, Survival and the Modern Temper* won the National Book Award for nonfiction in 1955.

Moscow, May 24

EISENSTEIN (THE MAKER of "*Potemkin*") received me in his very modest lodgings littered with books and scraps of film. A large, heavy man, with a head of flying hair like that affected some years ago by the youth of Italy, his bearing and his conversation alike suggest very strongly the Italian futurists with whom, as a matter of fact, he was formerly allied; and they serve to prepare one for the fact that his communistic ideology is superimposed upon the futurism which was at its full tide in Russia when the Revolution broke. Lunacharsky, on the other hand, ensconced at his desk in the Commissariat of Education, might be any cultivated gentleman. Speaking excellent French, and carefully avoiding the paradoxes in which Eisenstein revels, he seems, indeed, the "good European" more than anything else. Both are friendly and accessible men, but it is evident that they do not think very highly of each other and they will stand conveniently as representative of two opposite tendencies in contemporary Russian art.

Eisenstein begins, like most people brought up in the futurist school, by sweeping nearly everything that is into the junk-heap with one wave of the hand. The theater, of course, is dead and done for. Art should strike with the direct impact of a physical blow, and only the cinema can do that. The only good play in Moscow is "The Humming of the Rails," and it is good only because it is killing the theater. As a matter of fact, its perfectly literal naturalism is not theater at all—it is merely inferior cinema. The people of the future will want only actualities and the movie is much more actual than the stage.

The legitimate function of art is a purely practical one: its purpose is solely to produce convictions and to lead to actions. During the Revolution, for example, its duty was to provoke revolutionary acts. People went from the theater or the cinema to the barricades. Now that the Revolution is accomplished it has of course other work to do; religion, for example, has not been completely destroyed and for that reason the thing which he likes best in his new film *October* (shown in Germany and probably to be shown in America under the title *Ten Days That Shook the World!*) is the attack upon religion. Since the purpose of art is purely practical there is no such thing as a "permanent aesthetic value" and every work must be judged according to its usefulness at a given time in a given place. He himself is no longer interested in *Potemkin* which is more or less passé and not as purely cinematographical in its methods as he would like it to be. One can get an idea of what he wants to do from certain scenes in *October* where dynamic ideas are translated into pictures. The scene, for instance, in which the overweening Kerensky is shown, all alone, mounting up and up the successive flights of stairs in the imperial palace which lead to the throne-room, or that in which the downfall of religion is suggested by a series of flashes beginning with a picture of the fully developed God on an icon and descending through a whole series of representations to the grotesque idol of a savage.

Warming to his theme, Eisenstein develops it to its simple logical conclusion. In the perfect state there will be no art. Bourgeois art is a vicarious fulfilment of unsatisfied desires; Communist art an instrument for social adjustment. But in the perfect state there will be no unsatisfied desires and no more social adjustments to be made. Art, therefore, will disappear. I remind him that in "Reason and Art" Santayana suggests that this is exactly what Plato meant when he said that poets would be expelled from the perfect republic; but Eisenstein, as one might guess, is not much interested in either Plato or Santayana. *The Nation's* Russian correspondent, Louis Fischer, who is acting as my interpreter, puts in a word: "The theater is already dead. Then I suppose you consider it your function to kill the cinema." Eisenstein smiles. The idea pleases him.

Though he is a brilliant director and the representative of one school of aesthetic opinion in Russia I doubt if that school is actually as important as it sometimes seems from the outside. To my mind his films are more impressive than his theories, and to assume that either he or a man like Meyerhold is truly representative of even the more extreme wing of the Russian masses is to forget the element of futuristic dilettantism which plays so large a part in determining the attitude of both of them. They were accustomed for so long to "épater le bourgeois" that it is hard for them to remember that it is now even less important than ever to do so, and it is to be feared that nowadays they sometimes merely "épater le prolétariat" instead. "Constructivism" (apparently less popular now than formerly) was the futuristic response to that enthusiasm for the machine of which I have previously spoken, and Eisenstein's theories are the futuristic response to that general tendency to socialize the arts which is, of course, fundamental in Communistic society. But neither the one nor the other is so deep, so genuine, or so significant as are the tendencies which they parody, and to my mind at least one gets much nearer to the real meaning of the whole Russian phenomenon in such relatively naive plays as "The Humming of the Rails" than one does in these sophisticated attempts to translate the impulses there expressed into somewhat dilettantish terms.

If, however, Eisenstein may (with the reservations just suggested) be taken as a representative of the extreme aesthetic Left, Lunacharsky will speak for those who are, on the contrary, anxious that Communist art should be a continuation of or logical development from the art of the past. As Commissar of Education he has all the state theaters under his control, and it is probably due more to him than to anyone else that the opera and ballet have survived. He has watched without enthusiasm the increasing tendency of the theater to devote itself to contemporary social problems to the exclusion of everything else, and he would certainly not look forward with pleasure to Eisenstein's perfect and therefore artless state. "I shall," he said, "be ready very soon to issue a protest against the growing neglect of the classics in the state theaters and against their tendency to produce no new plays except those which concern themselves with more or less minor details of social adjustment. What used to be called the 'eternal problems' were properly so called, and they are as important to the members of a Communist society as to those of any other. Sooner or later Russian art must return to a consideration of them.

"Of course," he continued, "I do not mean that I desire any return to 'art for art's sake.' From the standpoint of a Communist, art must have its social function, but that function is a broad one. It includes the widening of the intellectual horizon as well as the discussion of sociological problems, and it is particularly important in an industrial state. The life of the workman is inevitably narrow if his experience is confined to the factory alone. He more than anyone else has need of those aesthetic experiences which will expand his range of comprehensions and appreciations. It is for this reason that I am even more interested in the music drama than in the ordinary play. Unfortunately we have not at present any new composers equal to the task, but I look forward most eagerly to the time when some Russian shall arise who will express the hope of the Russian people in a form not dissimilar, perhaps, to that in which Wagner embodied his Schopenhauerian pessimism."

It is obvious that there can be no peace between the representatives of attitudes so opposed. To Eisenstein, Lunacharsky is only a half-assimilated bourgeois; and to Lunacharsky, Eisenstein is only a new barbarian. From the standpoint of fanatical logic there is, of course, no doubt that Eisenstein would have the better of the argument. His theory is based upon one of the fundamental Communist postulates—that in a communistic state the ordinary processes of life will be all-sufficient in themselves—while Lunacharsky's assumption that the life of a factory worker is "narrow" does constitute a sort of heresy. I am told that once when he was explaining his theories at a public meeting some one rose to charge him with defending a kind of art which was, in effect, only another "opium of the people." That charge embodies the substance of a complaint often made against him. A cultivated man with a strong love of the past, he wept when he heard the false report that the Kremlin had been fired upon by the Bolsheviki, and he is less anxious to destroy what the old society created than he is to put the new masses into possession of whatever may be salvaged from it.

It is not, of course, worth while for an outsider to venture any opinion concerning the probable outcome of a conflict as fundamental as this one is, though it goes without saying that the ideas of Lunacharsky are far more easily comprehensible to such an outsider and must seem to him more reasonable, even if less simply logical, than those of his opponents. But like all that concerns contemporary Russian art, the question has connotations not purely artistic, and the conflict is only part of a much larger conflict upon the issue of which the future of the whole communistic experiment will depend. If communism is essentially only a new form of political and economic organization—if, that is to say, it is merely a logical continuation of the evolution from absolute monarchy through constitutional government and democracy—then its task is to rule a humanity not in itself radically different from the humanity we know, and Lunacharsky is right. But if, on the other hand, the coming of communism is, as to its more fanatical proponents it seems, a phenomenon of an entirely different sort—a reconstruction not merely of the social order but of human nature itself—then of course we as yet unreconstructed souls can know nothing of its future and can only conclude that whatever seems to us most incomprehensible is that which the future will probably choose.

APRIL 26, 1947

IVAN THE TERRIBLE

James Agee

•

James Agee, author of *Let Us Now Praise Famous Men* (with photographer Walker Evans) and the screenwriter of *The African Queen* and *Night of the Hunter*, was *The Nation*'s film critic from 1942 to 1948 (he was also a film reviewer at *Time* magazine during the same period). Margaret Marshall, then literary editor, gave him free rein to cover what he wanted and to write as he pleased. His style was immensely influential. Manny Farber, who succeeded Agee as *Nation* film critic described him as "the most intriguing star-gazer in the middle-brow era of Hollywood films, a virtuoso who capped a strange company of stars on people's lips and set up a hailstorm of ideas for other critics to use." W. H. Auden, in a letter to *The Nation* in 1944, declared, "In my opinion, Agee's column is the most remarkable regular event in American journalism today."

WHEN HE MADE *Alexander Nevsky*, Sergei Eisenstein deprived himself of practically everything that had been most wonderful in his original style and developed a new and less exciting one—a kind of speeded-up, fluent, basically operatic style which was like watching a handsome, well-organized funeral cortège carry his free genius to its grave at a cheerful forty miles an hour. Relatively conventional as the film was, it was also highly charged, in nearly every shot, with Eisenstein's unique blend of poetic, intellectual, and purely animal energy.

In *Ivan the Terrible*, Part I, Eisenstein has deprived himself even of the speed, flow, and shape which helped give *Nevsky* grace, and most of his peculiar energy has become cold, muscle-bound, and somber. Yet *Ivan* is a bolder, more adventurous, more interesting film; for a while I felt even more admiration for it than grief over it.

Eisenstein's theme is more deeply involved in an individual and his development, and is in many ways greater, than any he has undertaken before. It is a study, on a scale as ambitious anyhow as that of Shakespeare in his political plays—and more politically knowledgeable and incomparably hotter to handle—of an able man in whom two obsessions collide and become all but identical: love for an idea (his country's strength) and, however discreetly suggested, love of power for its own sake. It is a study of what such a fanatic becomes, given unprecedented power and opportunity, under the impingement of constant danger, treachery, and intrigue. Ivan, as Eisenstein presents him, is a fair parallel to Stalin; but he is still more suggestively a symbol of the whole history of Russian communism. Eisenstein has, for Ivan, a magnificent looking actor, Cherkassov, who can handle the utmost grandiloquence of manner; he causes him to suggest some of the superhuman complexities of Stavrogin, and it may not be accidental that he makes him up with a chin and cranium which becomes ever more pointed, like John Barrymore as Mr. Hyde. He seems all but desperately absorbed in communicating political ideas and vindications, especially parallels to Stalin and his regime. Ivan's siege and defeat of Kazan, to choose one of the simpler examples, becomes an interesting text on dealing with a foreign enemy: while the enemy watches the army which threatens their walls, you tunnel beneath their city, roll in kegs of gunpowder, and blow it to kingdom come, meaning *your* kingdom. (It is made clear, moreover, that this stratagem is strictly Ivan's idea, that his lieutenants prefer the old-fashioned cavalry charge, and that his sappers never quite realize what they're up to.)

Eisenstein is very acute with his research, very excitable over architecture and decoration, costume and ritual, and very astute and forceful in his use of them. He is evidently much interested in finding out how little a movie can be made to move and yet move at all, and in giving each movement legendary grandeur—as in the marvelous shots, at once comic and sinister and full of glory, in which the kneeling Ivan's rising hands accept the orb and scepter. He goes boldly and successfully against naturalism and even simple likelihood: in his poisoning scene only opera singers could be so blind to what is happening in plain sight, and in one fine close-up Ivan's wife, his arch-enemy, and his treacherous best friend huddle their heads into the intimacy of one frame as they would never do in a court obsessed with intrigue and suspicion. Depriving himself of a good 99 percent of all he believes in and is capable of as a cutter, Eisenstein nevertheless demonstrates what exquisiteness and power can be accomplished, even conventionally, by rhythm and series alone. The film is already famous for its lavish use of prodigious close-ups and of exorbitance in gesture and in facial expression, and I would like to make a particularly unprintable gesture toward those who can feel that in his use of these one of the most sophisticated artists of the twentieth century has been naive.

I have only faintly suggested a few of the things about *Ivan,* and behind it, which make the film fascinating to watch; but I will have to move along. Interesting as the film is, the longer I reflect on it the unhappier I feel about it. I can't remember a foot of it which doesn't give evidence of a first-rate creative intelligence at work; but there is hardly a foot in which that intelligence is working on anything anywhere near sufficiently worthy of it. The picture is splendid to look at; yet there is little that is superior to, or much different from, Russian operatic and theatrical mannerisms which must have been over-rich and over-digested a generation ago. It is as if Picasso were to spend several years crowding all the sophistication that would fit within the conventions of nineteenth-century chromos. And considering the illusion Eisenstein manages to create of expressing many complex ideas, densely and continuously, it is remarkable how little actually gets expressed, and how commonplace most of it is.

I even have to wonder whether Eisenstein perversely or perforce intended this doubleness. I wonder, for that matter, whether he may not be split between a compulsion to choose the most dangerous theme possible, and virtual paralysis in its development: a paralysis which might be a natural effect of being unable, on pain of death, to say honestly, or even surreptitiously, what you really believe. There is a kind of frozen, catatonic deadness about the particular intensity and rigidity of style developed for this film—as if the intelligence, great as it is, could liberate only a very little of itself in the actual images of the film. The kind of liberation I mean occurs just twice in this picture, in the opening, coronation scene; a deacon's hair-raising intonation of a royal benediction (and his wonderful face as he sings), and the moment at which Eisenstein cuts from the ritualistic pouring of gold coins over the new Czar to the faces of young women, watching the sleeting gold and the monarch's tumescent face through it and blossoming into smiles of sexual delight. In their suddenness, beauty, and wildness, and in their ability to enrich the film with whole new trains of ideas and reactions, these two moments are of a different order from any others in *Ivan*. They would have been memorable in any of Eisenstein's early films; but there, ideas as good swarmed and coruscated upon his new-found, new-crowned poetry as abundantly as the anointing storm of gold itself.

For years, as everyone knows, Eisenstein has been working as if in a prison, under the supervision of jailers who are not only peculiarly dangerous and merciless but also as sudden to change their minds as minnows their direction. It goes without saying that this has interfered monstrously with his work. Just how, and just how much it has shaped his work and his mind, I see no use whatever in trying to guess, for I fear it is impossible to guess how much he agrees with his jailers, even in their treatment of him, and how much, quite aside from that, his own nature may have been predisposed to this sort of hardening and change. No mind and spirit stand still, least of all the mind and spirit of a great artist. Even discounting outside pressures, there is no guaranty that the development will be for the better, and heaven knows they cannot be discounted in Eisenstein's case. Everything that is meant by creative genius and its performance, and everything that that signifies about freedom and potentiality in general, is crucified in Eisenstein, more meaningfully, and abominably, than in any other man I can think of. I hardly know which seems the more tragic: the possibility that he is still essentially a free man, his own master, doing the best he can under annihilating difficulties; or the possibility that he accepts the crucifixion and has even helped drive such nails as, in that predicament, he could manage.

SEPTEMBER 4, 1948

DAVID WARK GRIFFITH

James Agee

•

Probably one of the more controversial of this anthology's entries, especially in reference to Agee's belief that *Birth of a Nation*—a film Stuart Klawans describes as having "coon-show melodramatics" and glorifying the Ku Klux Klan—wasn't racist. This was Agee's last film piece for *The Nation*.

HE ACHIEVED WHAT no other known man has ever achieved. To watch his work is like being witness to the beginning of melody, or the first conscious use of the lever or the wheel; the emergence, coordination, and first eloquence of language; the birth of an art: and to realize that this is all the work of one man.

We will never realize how good he really was until we have the chance to see his work as often as it deserves to be seen, to examine and enjoy it in detail as exact as his achievement. But even relying, as we mainly have to, on years-old memories, a good deal becomes clear.

One crude but unquestionable indication of his greatness was his power to create permanent images. All through his work there are images which are as impossible to forget, once you have seen them, as some of the grandest and simplest passages in music or poetry.

The most beautiful single shot I have seen in any movie is the battle charge in *The Birth of a Nation*. I have heard it praised for its realism, and that is deserved; but it is also far beyond realism. It seems to me to be a perfect realization of a collective dream of what the Civil War was like, as veterans might remember it fifty years later, or as children, fifty years later, might imagine it. I have had several clear mental images of that war, from almost as early as I can remember, and I didn't have the luck to see *The Birth of a Nation* until I was in my early twenties; but when I saw that charge, it was merely the clarification, and corroboration, of one of those visions, and took its place among them immediately without seeming to be of a different kind or order. It is the perfection that I know of, of the tragic glory that is possible, in war; or in war as the best in the spirit imagines or remembers it.

This is, I realize, mainly subjective; but it suggests to me the clearest and deepest aspect of Griffith's genius: he was a great primitive poet, a man capable, as only great and primitive artists can be, of intuitively perceiving and perfecting the tremendous magical images that underlie the memory and imagination of entire peoples. If he had achieved this only once, and only for me, I could not feel that he was what I believe he is; but he created many such images, and I suspect that many people besides me have recognized them, on that deepest level that art can draw on, reach, and serve. There are many others in that one film: the homecoming of the defeated hero; the ride of the Clansmen; the rapist and his victim among the dark leaves; a glimpse of a war hospital; dead young soldiers after battle; the dark, slow movement of the Union Army away from the camera, along a valley which is quartered strongly between hill-shadow and sunlight; all these and still others have a dreamlike absoluteness which, indeed, cradles and suffuses the whole film.

This was the one time in movie history that a man of great ability worked freely, in an unspoiled medium, for an unspoiled audience, on a majestic theme which involved all that he was; and brought to it, besides his abilities as an inventor and artist, absolute passion, pity, courage, and honesty. *The Birth of a Nation* is equal with Brady's photographs, Lincoln's speeches, Whitman's war poems; for all its imperfections and absurdities it is equal, in fact, to the best work that has been done in this country. And among moving pictures it is alone, not necessarily as "the greatest"—whatever that means—but as the one great epic, tragic film.

(Today, *The Birth of a Nation* is boycotted or shown piecemeal; too many more or less well-meaning people still accuse Griffith of having made it an anti-Negro movie. At best, this is nonsense, and at worst, it is vicious nonsense. Even if it were an anti-Negro movie, a work of such quality should be shown, and shown whole. But the accusation is unjust. Griffith went to almost preposterous lengths to be fair to the Negroes as he understood them, and he understood them as a good type of Southerner does. I don't entirely agree with him; nor can I be sure that the film wouldn't cause trouble and misunderstanding, especially as advertised and exacerbated by contemporary abolitionists; but Griffith's absolute desire to be fair, and understandable, is written all over the picture; so are degrees of understanding, honesty, and compassion far beyond the capacity of his accusers. So, of course, are the salient facts of the so-called Reconstruction years.)

Griffith never managed to equal *The Birth of a Nation* again, nor was he ever to strike off, in any other film, so many of those final images. Nevertheless, he found many: the strikers in *Intolerance*—the realism of those short scenes has never been surpassed, not their shock and restiveness as an image of near-revolution; the intercutting, at the climax of that picture, between the climaxes of four parallel stories, like the swinging together of tremendous gongs; the paralyzing excitement of the melodrama near the waterfall, in *Way Down East*; Paul Revere's ride and the battle of Bunker Hill, in *America*; Danton's ride, in *Orphans of the Storm*; most subtle and remarkable of all, the early morning scene in his German film, *Isn't Life Wonderful?*, in which the ape-like Dick Sutherland pursues Carol Dempster through a grove of slender trees. All these images, and so many others of Griffith's, have a sort of crude sublimity which nobody else in movies has managed to achieve; this last one, like his images of our Civil War, seems to come out of the deep subconscious: it is an absolute and prophetic image of a nation and a people. I will always regret having missed *Abraham Lincoln*, his last film to be released: a friend has told me of its wonderful opening in stormy mid-winter night woods, the camera bearing along toward the natal cabin; and that surely must have been one of Griffith's finest images.

Even in Griffith's best work there is enough that is poor, or foolish, or merely old-fashioned, so that one has to understand, if by no means forgive, those who laugh indiscriminately at his good work and his bad. (With all that "understanding," I look forward to killing, some day, some specially happy giggler at the exquisite scene in which the veteran comes home, in *The Birth of a Nation*.) But even his poorest work was never just bad. Whatever may be wrong with it, there is in every instant, so well as I can remember, the unique purity and vitality of birth or of a creature just born and first exerting its unprecedented, incredible strength; and there are, besides, Griffith's overwhelming innocence and magnanimity of spirit; his moral and poetic earnestness; his joy in his work; and his splendid intuitiveness, directness, common sense, daring, and skill as an inventor and as an artist. Aside from his talent or genius as an inventor and artist, he was all heart; and ruinous as his excess sometimes were in that respect, they were inseparable from his virtues, and small beside them. He was remarkably good, as a rule, in the whole middle range of feeling, but he was at his best just short of his excesses, and he tended in general to work out toward the dangerous edge. He was capable of realism that has never been beaten and he might, if he had been able to appreciate his powers as a realist, have found therein his growth and salvation. But he seems to have been a realist only by accident, hit-and-run; essentially, he was a poet. He doesn't appear ever to have realized one of the richest promises that movies hold, as the perfect medium for realism raised to the level of high poetry; nor, oddly enough, was he much of a dramatic poet. But in epic and lyrical and narrative visual poetry, I can think of nobody who has surpassed him, and of few to compare with him. And as a primitive tribal poet, combining something of the bard and the seer, he is beyond even Dovzhenko, and no others of their kind have worked in movies.

What he had above all, his ability as a craftsman and artist, would be hard enough—and quite unnecessary—to write of, if we had typical scenes before us, or within recent memory; since we have seen so little of his work in so many years, it is virtually impossible. I can remember very vividly his general spirit and manner—heroic, impetuous, tender, magniloquent, naive, beyond the endowment or daring of anybody since; just as vividly, I can remember the total impression of various major sequences. By my remembrance, his images were nearly always a little larger and wilder than life. The frame was always full, spontaneous, and lively. He knew wonderfully well how to contrast and combine different intensities throughout an immense range of emotion, movement, shadow, and light. Much of the liveliness was not intrinsic to the characters on the screen or their predicament, but was his own vitality and emotion; and much of it—notably in the amazing flickering and vivacity of his women—came of his almost maniacal realization of the importance of expressive movement.

It seems to me entirely reasonable to infer, from the extraordinary power and endurance in the memory of certain scenes in their total effect, that he was as brilliant a master of design and cutting and form as he was a composer of frames and a director of feeling and motion. But I cannot clearly remember one sequence or scene, shot by and rhythm by rhythm. I suspect, for instance, that analysis would show that the climatic sequence on the icy river, in *Way Down East*, is as finely constructed a piece of melodramatic story-telling as any in movies. But I can only venture to bet on this and to suggest that that sequence, like a hundred others of Griffith's is eminently worth analysis.

My veneration for Griffith's achievements is all the deeper when I realize what handicaps he worked against, how limited a man he was. He had no remarkable power of intellect, or delicateness of soul; no subtlety; little restraint; little if any "taste," whether to help his work or harm it; Lord knows (and be thanked) no cleverness; no fundamental capacity, once he had achieved his first astonishing development, for change or growth. He wasn't particularly observant of people; nor do his movies suggest that he understood them at all deeply. He had noble powers of imagination, but little of the *intricacy* of imagination that most good poets also have. His sense of comedy was pathetically crude and numb. He had an exorbitant appetite for violence, for cruelty, and for the Siamese twin of cruelty, a kind of obsessive tenderness which at its worst was all but nauseating. Much as he invented, his work was saturated in the style, the mannerisms, and the underlying assumptions and attitudes of the nineteenth century provincial theater; and although much of that was much better than most of us realize, and any amount better than most of the styles and non-styles we accept and praise, much of it was cheap and false, and all of it, good and bad, was dying when Griffith gave it a new lease on life, and in spite of that new lease, died soon after, and took him down with it. I doubt that Griffith ever clearly knew the good from the bad in this theatricality; or, for that matter, clearly understood what was original in his work, and capable of almost unimaginably great development; and what was over-derivative, essentially non-cinematic, and dying. In any case, he did not manage to outgrow, or sufficiently to transform, enough in his style that was bad, or merely obsolescent.

If what I hear is right about the opening scene in *Abraham Lincoln*, this incapacity for radical change may have slowed him up but never killed him as an artist; in his no longer fashionable way, he remained capable, and inspired. He was merely unadaptable and unemployable, like an old, sore, ardent individualist among contemporary progressives. Hollywood and, to a great extent, movies in general, grew down from him rather than up past him; audiences, and the whole eye and feeling of the world, have suffered the same degeneration; he didn't have it in him to be amenable, even if he'd tried; and that was the end of him. Or quite possibly he was finished, as smaller men are not, as soon as he had reached the limit of his own powers of innovation, and began to realize he was only repeating himself. Certainly, anyhow, he was natural-born for the years of adventure and discovery, not for the inevitable following era of safe-playing and of fat consolidation of others' gains.

His last movie, which was never even released, was made fourteen or fifteen years ago; and for years before that, most people had thought of him as a has-been. Nobody would hire him; he had nothing to do. He lived too long, and that is one of few things that are sadder than dying too soon.

There is not a man working in movies, or a man who cares for them, who does not owe Griffith more than he owes anybody else.

AUGUST 4, 1956

The Great Chaplin Chase

Ernest Callenbach

•

Ernest Callenbach admits to leading a double life. He was a founding editor of *Film Quarterly* where he published early pieces by Peter Biskind, David Denby and Pauline Kael, and author of *Our Modern Art: The Movies*. Callenbach, however, is also a noted ecological writer and activist—"my evil brother" he jokes—and the author of the cult novel *Ecotopia* and its sequel *Ecotopia Emerging*. He is also the author of the recent *Ecology: A Pocket Guide* and *Living Cheaply with Style*, Callenbach remembers that his editor on the following piece felt initially that he was a little too easy on Chaplin, complaining that Chaplin tended "to follow his cock around."

CHAPLIN FIRST ARRIVED in the United States in 1910, a twenty-one-year old music-hall comedian. He left September 17, 1952, probably for good and amid much acrid publicity, the "one universal man of modern times"—or, at the very least, the world's most famous comedian and one of the screen's few great men.

The intervening years were years of triumph for Chaplin in many ways; but they were also years of turbulence and struggle to a greater extent than many people remembered during the last uproar.

Relatively recent were the sensational headlines and legal hocus pocus of the Joan Berry case in 1943–44. Some readers may recall the court battles with Lita Grey in 1926–27. But there was much more, too, which provides the material for a study in the curiously bad public relations between the brilliant, controversial celebrity and the nation he lived in.

Many Hollywood figures flouted moral convention without arousing the same concerted hostility—John Barrymore, Wallace Beery, Errol Flynn, Robert Mitchum and others. Many have held irregular political views as well. Apparently Chaplin's leftish but naive political outlook earned him enemies who joined forces with domestic puritans and patriots; and thus sexual and subversive themes became coupled in the public image of Chaplin which his detractors promoted. The present story, in a way, is more about America than about Chaplin.

Chaplin came from England with a vaudeville company in which he learned much of the pantomime skill he later perfected in his films. He signed his first picture contract ($150 per week) with many doubts. At the Keystone studio he had trouble adapting his slower, subtler style to the fast-and-rough tradition of the Keystone Cops, Fatty Arbuckle, Mack Swain and the other Sennett clowns. With his thirteenth picture, however, Sennett gave him a free hand, and from then on he wrote and directed all his own work. Later he was also to produce and score his own films, becoming a unique individual creator in an "art-industry" characterized by extreme division of creative labor.

After a year at Keystone, making one comedy a week, Chaplin's growing popularity enabled him to switch to Essanay at a salary of $1,250 per week. In May, 1915, came the first of the headlines announcing legal combat over the Chaplin name and fame. Enterprising individuals had begun manufacturing Tramp statuettes, infringing (Chaplin's suit charged) on the costume to which Chaplin claimed exclusive rights.

The comedian's fame grew steadily. He appeared at benefits; fantastic reports circulated about his earnings. In 1916, Mutual offered him a guarantee of $500,000; he got $670,000. In 1917, estimates of his yearly earnings ran as high as $1,000,000, and First National offered him that amount. Such spectacular sums, together with his enormous screen popularity, kept Chaplin conspicuous even in the midst of growing him-colony extravagance.

When America entered World War I he began to have a new kind of trouble. Now working in his own studio, producing for First National, he started to receive oddly emotional letters demanding that he enlist. A physical examination showed him to be unfit, but the clamor continued even after he spent two months touring for the Third Liberty Loan.

In November, 1918, Chaplin married Mildred Harris. By the middle of March, 1920, the papers were carrying reports of domestic strife, and in August Chaplin filed divorce proceedings. Charges and counter-charges flew; in November, 1920, Mildred obtained a divorce, getting $100,000 and a share in joint property. The publicity over the case was damaging; Mildred appeared as a wronged but still devoted wife, claiming humiliation and cruelty and hurting about another woman. During this period Chaplin was making *A Dog's Life, Shoulder Arms* and *Sunnyside*—his apprenticeship was over and he had become the acknowledged master of screen comedy.

In 1921, just after the release of *The Kid*, Chaplin brought his mother to the United States. She had difficulties with the Immigration Service both that year and the next, when she was detained and investigated; the papers said she was "mentally deranged as a result of shell-shock." Chaplin himself went off on a triumphant tour. He was mobbed by enthusiastic crowds in London, Paris and Berlin; he was decorated by the French government. And he was sued for $50,000 by one L. Loeb, who charged that his ideas had been used in *Shoulder Arms*.

Then came the on-again-off-again affair with screen siren Pola Negri, and the ugly rumor that Marina Vega had killed herself by taking poison in the Chaplin home. Hollywood was now widely regarded as a hotbed of vice and wild living, and a "moral crusade" led to the formation of the Hays office in 1922. Chaplin went on working—*A Woman of Paris* appeared in October, 1923.

Mildred Harris had been only sixteen when she married Chaplin. Much prying speculation took place when Lita Grey, who married Chaplin in November, 1924, was also found to be only sixteen and therefore still subject to the school laws of California. By February lawyers were reportedly seeking a settlement for the bride.

Other public business continued: Chaplin sued Charles Amador (alias Charles "Aplin") for imitating him and managed to have his make-up ruled his private property (though a later decision reversed this). The immigration authorities next moved against Chaplin's mother, ordering her to leave the country. Chaplin fought the order and won a postponement. She remained here until her death in 1928.

The spate of printed material dealing with Chaplin increased to grotesque proportions. The *New York Times* reported solemnly on August 12, 1925, that Chaplin had a slight cold; on August 14 he was said to be better. The intricacies of Chaplin's possible influence on a proposed merger of M.G.M. and United Artists were explored. The Soviet movie trust publicly invited him to take part in a film based on a Gogol satire. The dying of his hair for film purposes aroused much comment. Imitators sprang up like weeds: Sober film critics and intellectuals made pilgrimages to his studio, and their praise helped create an impression that Chaplin was not only a great comic but a profound social thinker.

Late in 1926 Lita left him, taking the children, and initiated the second sensational court fight of Chaplin's law-beset life. Lita asked $1,000,000 alimony and separate maintenance; she announced that she had turned down a London theatrical offer to "attend her babies." Spurning a proposal that she and Chaplin each take one child, she filed for divorce.

Meanwhile Chaplin sued the *Pictorial Review* for printing a particularly damaging life story. Tension over the divorce case grew as an injunction was placed on Chaplin's property, preventing him from cashing checks or transferring or disposing of assets. And with this came the first signs of really widespread trouble. The mayor of staunchly Catholic Quebec barred advertisements of Chaplin pictures. Receivers seized his property. The mayor of Seattle asked the local censors to consider banning Chaplin pictures from the city. The League of Women Voters in Ottawa (Illinois) asked for a ban. But Mayor Jimmy Walker of New York, approached on the matter, said he would take no action. The Miami Beach (Florida) Woman's Club launched a counteroffensive, asking theatre owners to show all the Chaplin pictures available. In mid-January, 1927, Chaplin suffered a "nervous breakdown" and rumors began circulating that he might commit suicide.

The Lita court case included some inspired sequences of real-life comedy. Sam Goldwyn was summoned to tell of Chaplin's assets and business dealings. The federal government, following the testimony with interest, filed an income-tax lien. Three safes were drilled open in a vain attempt to locate Chaplin's assets. Private and government lawyers squabbled over priority of claims. Professional moralists grew more heated day by day. Pasadena (California), even gaining a reputation for municipal witlessness, banned Chaplin's films.

Suspecting the outcry was synthetic, however, the Theater Owners Chamber of Commerce sent out a questionnaire to 438 exhibitors, asking them to find out what their customers really thought. Assured that the *grand public* of the cinema not only wasn't prejudiced against Chaplin, but was if anything even more eager to see his films, the body adopted a resolution praising Chaplin's "clean and wholesome" pictures and affirming confidence in him "as an artist and as a man." Other defenders of Chaplin began to make themselves heard. The Motion Picture Theater Owners joined the TOCC in supporting Chaplin. The Green Room Club of New York presented him with a gold plaque.

Legal proposals went back and forth, minutely chronicled by the newspapers. Chaplin's funds were freed, but his work on *The Circus* was constantly interrupted. Lita asked police protection from death threats she claimed to have received by mail, and Chaplin began to take on an almost ghoulish aura in some press reports.

Chaplin's suit to restrain further numbers of the life story in the *Pictorial Review* failed. The Russians again invited him to work with them, this time "to escape pious hypocrisy." He agreed to pay $1,000,000 to settle the income-tax claim, and Lita finally got $625,000 for herself and $200,000 in trust for the children; a few days after the grant she was honored by an audience with President Coolidge.

After the divorce furor died down, other items kept cropping up. One A. Kopesky sued Chaplin for plagiarism, and lost. Chaplin refused a $1,000,000-contract offer; he was placed in the "Contemporary Hall of Fame." He entertained Professor and Mrs. Einstein. Going abroad again, he met MacDonald, Shaw, Lady Astor and denied a rumor that he had sent greetings to the Communist youth of Germany. He called financiers comic when they played economists in the sweep of a disastrous depression. He was Briand's guest; he hunted with the Duke of Westminster; he received the decoration of the *Légion d'Honneur*.

In 1933, after suing unauthorized "dupers" of his films, he took a trip to the Far East with Paulette Goddard. The gossip mills went full blast; at the end of 1936 it was revealed that they had been married over a year. Then *Modern Times* came out and Films Sonores Tobis sued Chaplin (unsuccessfully) charging plagiarism of René Clair's *A Nous la Liberté*.

With the Hitler regime moving toward war, Chaplin announced that the proceeds of his next film, *The Great Dictator*, would go to aid Jewish emigrants from Nazi persecution. After the German invasion of

Russia, he advocated an early second front and fullest cooperation with the Russians; this, in the minds of some, was later to facilitate an easy jump from the premise "satirist" to the conclusion "subversive."

In June, 1942, Paulette Goddard got a divorce—quietly, to her everlasting credit. But a year later Joan Berry opened another legal fracas by naming Chaplin the father of her unborn child and suing for expenses and support. Chaplin denied the charge, but agreed to pay Joan an allowance pending the paternity trial. A few days later he married Oona O'Neill, daughter of playwright Eugene O'Neill.

The law machinery turned again, with incredible barrages of publicity. At one point Chaplin testified that he thought 95 per cent of the papers were against him. Blood tests indicated that Chaplin could not be the father of the child. But instead of the paternity suit being dropped thereupon, as the stipulation provided, it was continued, various judges ruling that such a stipulation could not be binding on the possible rights of an unborn baby. The jury deadlocked, however, and a mistrial was declared. A new suit was then brought against Chaplin, with roughly the same evidence being introduced; Chaplin was convicted and became the legal father of the child. He was ordered to pay $5,000 to Joan's attorney and $75 weekly for the support of the child, which he is evidently paying still, since an appeal was denied in 1946. Justice rolled on, doubtless lubricated by Chaplin's admission that his fortune amounted to nearly $3,000,000.

Late in 1946, *Monsieur Verdoux* was released, and met a cool reception; after a short run Chaplin withdrew it and it has never been released since. With the advent of the cold war, outraged cries against Chaplin became more frequent and took on a specifically political tone. By April, 1947, he found it necessary to deny that he was a Communist and to explain why he never became an American citizen. Columbus (Ohio) threatened a boycott. Congressman Rankin demanded deportation. Chaplin was called before the Un-American Activities Committee. The Catholic War Veterans urged the State and Justice Departments to investigate him.

During 1948 the publicity front was quiet, and Chaplin worked on in his usual secrecy. But in 1949 he was labelled subversive by the Tenney Committee, California's bush-league McCarthyite group. Senator Cain urged deportation.

The year 1950 was again uneventful, marked only by the striking response of the American public to *City Lights*, reissued after nineteen years and reportedly the most profitable picture of the year. This box-office verdict did not faze the busy-bodies, however, and in 1951 and 1952 things picked up again. A hint of things to come was the news that Chaplin and Mary Pickford were selling their controlling interest in United Artists. Meanwhile Chaplin sued the National Broadcasting Company for libel in implying he was a Communist.

Then came the final crisis. With *Limelight* completed, Chaplin departed on a world cruise. Attorney General McGranery revealed that, sure enough, the Justice Department would now probe Chaplin's alleged subversive activities to determine his fitness for readmission to this country. The department ordered an investigation of the Paulette Goddard divorce, hoping to turn up evidence of "moral turpitude."

Chaplin's world tour continued, this time with a new dimension: in France he was treated as a martyr to hyper-Americanism, and the press all over Europe was hostile or suspicious toward McGranery. Chaplin was nominated for the Nobél Prize, redecorated in France and greeted by the new queen in London.

But McGranery, too, received honors—in the form of a plaque from the American Legion (California Department). Oona returned to the United States on business, reportedly withdrawing a cool $4,000,000 from the Chaplin funds. In January, 1953, Chaplin revealed plans to live in a newly acquired $350,000 Swiss chateau. He turned in his re-entry permit in April, issuing the following statement:

> It is not easy to uproot myself and my family from a country where I have lived for forty years without a feeling of sadness.
>
> But since the end of the last World War I have been the object of lies and vicious propaganda by powerful reactionary groups who by their influence and the aid of America's yellow press have created an unhealthy atmosphere in which liberal-minded individuals can be singled out and persecuted.
>
> Under these conditions I find it virtually impossible to continue my motion-picture work and I have therefore given up my residence in the United States.

If he had not been rich enough to employ himself, Chaplin would probably have been forced long before to join the numerous blacklisted movie people trying to work in foreign studios. His Hollywood employees, it was said, "regretted" his decision, but there was no tangible effect on his film enterprises. *Limelight* was withdrawn by the Fox West Coast and Loew's New York theatre chains under threat of American Legion picketing, but most exhibitors were less easily scared and the picture has made a good deal of money.

And this, we may surmise, is the end. Neither the Immigration Service nor the Justice Department has had anything more to say. Chaplin will probably make a few more films and will probably keep his recent embittered promise not to send them to the United States. But the strangely intense resentments of which Chaplin was the target will have to be directed elsewhere.

Looking back, their strength seems to have come from a rare concatenation of circumstances. On the simplest level, Chaplin's nonchalance toward the supposed glories of United States citizenship enraged patriots, as his sexual free-wheeling shocked moralists. Moreover, his almost unseemly earnings, and his dependence as an artist on public favor, made him a popular mark for gold-digging females and would-be scenarists with itchy legal trigger-fingers; both secured sympathy from a still widespread American puritanism. Also, his power as a screen artist aroused the natural resentments which many people pay as an unwilling tribute to genius.

Of the cross-currents of public conflict which flowed around Chaplin during his American career, however, the most interesting involve a less explicable brand of hostility—a kind which may unconsciously prove the true "subversiveness" of Chaplin's humor. His underdog comedies stirred the great movie masses; with a kind of folk-anarchism, Chaplin was constantly puncturing approved ideas and behavior. What further reason would powerful men need for a deep hatred of the clown who had made more people laugh than anybody else in history?

OCTOBER 12, 1964

CHARLIE'S CHAPLIN

John Houseman

•

John Houseman, a co-founder of the Mercury Theater, was a theater director and film producer whose films included *Citizen Kane, They Live By Night*, and *Julius Caesar*. He also had memorable roles in *The Paper Chase* (winning an Oscar as best supporting actor), *Rollerball*, and *Three Days of the Condor*.

I REMEMBER A winter in the early fifties when three well-known writers were biting their nails-around Beverly Hills, setting up interviews with Charles Chaplin, each trying to wring out of him some authentic account of his early years—to be used in books they were hoping to write about him. He was charming to them all, listened politely to the results of their painful research, which he neither confirmed nor denied, and bade them a smiling farewell.

"Writers are nice people," declares Mr. Chaplin in his autobiography, "but not very giving. Whatever they know they seldom impart to others; most of them keep it between the covers of their books." And as though to prove his point, after so many years of stubborn silence, here, finally, between the covers of his own book, is the wild, tragic and improbable drama of his life, consciously and unconsciously revealed in words which, for better or for worse, are unmistakably his own.

"To gauge the morals of our family by commonplace standards

would be as erroneous as putting a thermometer in boiling water." Charles Chaplin was born into a broken theatrical family—his father, a quiet, brooding man with dark eyes who looked like Napoleon, was a talented but alcoholic baritone on the Variety stage; his mother, a successful "soubrette," until she lost her voice in her late 20s, was herself the child of a broken home, the daughter of a half-gypsy and a cobbler from County Cork. The first and most affecting part of Mr. Chaplin's book is, in fact, a memorial to Lily Chaplin, his gay, spirited mother with the "violet-blue eyes and long, light-brown hair that she could sit upon," who through the years of their blackest misery managed, with her racy elegance and theatrical literacy, to make her sons Sydney and Charlie feel that they were "not the ordinary product of poverty, but unique and distinguished."

Yet the circumstances of her life and theirs were tragic, almost beyond belief: an unbroken decline from gentility to poverty and then, as her health gave way, to an indigence so complete that it drove them through the Lambeth Poorhouse to the Hanwell School for Orphans and Destitute Children and, later, when Lily had her first mental collapse, led the doctors to attribute it, in large part, to chronic malnutrition. These grim years are described in a style that is dramatic and largely unsentimental. There are scenes so brilliantly constructed for irony and pathos that one is inclined to suspect a certain artifice in their telling; others—like the story of their ten-hour truancy from the poorhouse, the sheep escaped from the slaughterhouse, and Charlie's association with the wood choppers—are told with a directness that leaves you blinking with amusement and pity. Few incidents in realistic fiction can compare, for bland horror, to the brief account of his father's death and funeral:

> Mother, being the legal widow, was told to call at the hospital for his belongings, which consisted of a black suit spotted with blood, underwear, a shirt, a black tie, an old dressing-gown and some plaid house-slippers with oranges stuffed in the toes. When she took the oranges out a half sovereign fell out of the slipper onto the bed. This was a godsend. . . .

Or the way in which, returning home from a guilty meal at a less impoverished neighbor's, Charlie first learns, from the children in the street, of his mother's insanity: "She's been knocking at all our doors, giving away pieces of coal, saying they're birthday presents for the children." Later, when he and Sidney were allowed to see her at the Cane Hill Asylum:

> . . . she just sat there listening and nodding, looking vague and preoccupied. I told her that she would soon get well. "Of course," she said dolefully, "if only you had given me a cup of tea that afternoon, I would have been all right."

When a man's art is as intensely personal as Chaplin's, the life and the work become inseparable. This gives the first part of his book the fascinating effect of double exposure. As he draws us back to the turn of the century, across Westminster Bridge to Lambeth and along the Kennington Road, we find ourselves following him with a strange recollection of having been there before. On page 65 are two fading photographs, one of "The garret at Pownall Terrace, Kempton Road and one of the back street "where we lived behind Kennington Cross, next to the slaughterhouse and the pickle factory . . ." It becomes clear, studying the production stills of Charlie and Jackie Coogan in *The Kid*, that except for the formal presence of an American cop (with a 1905 under the badge of his cap), the set which Chaplin created in his studio at the corner of La Brea and Sunset in Hollywood in 1920 not merely suggests but *is* the alley "behind Kennington Cross next to the slaughterhouse and the pickle factory." The corner where the sheep escaped on its way to death and the back street to which Charlie and the Kid return from their window-smashing expeditions are one and the same: so are the little room where they try to forget their hunger and the garret at Pownall Terrace ("a little over twelve feet square . . . and in the corner, snug against the wall, an old bed") where Lily Chaplin sat listlessly staring out of the window on the afternoon she became ill.

Once this correspondence is established it is a rare page that does not reflect some well-remembered episode from one or other of the films. The many odd occupations which Chaplin followed before and during his teens: newsboy, flower vendor, doctor's boy, glass blower, wood chopper, old-clothes peddler, page boy and operator atop a giant printing machine of whose innards he was totally ignorant—we have seen them all, in some form dramatized and transmuted by the richest comic talent of our time.

But those were interludes. With his heritage and environment there was only one way for Charles Chaplin to go—into the theatre. His professional debut (for wages of ½ crown a week and a "bread-and-jam breakfast") was as one of the Eight Lancashire Ladies a juvenile song-and-dance troupe managed by a devout Catholic couple. At 12½ (pretending to be 14) he played his first dramatic role as Billy, the Baker Street page boy in *Sherlock Holmes.* At 21, after years of touring with Fred Karno's comedy companies, he was a seasoned professional, in and out of work, having known triumphs and disasters, with a fair chance—if he played his cards right—of one day joining the ranks of Britain's leading Variety performers. The moment of decision came when Karno offered him an American tour as principal comedian of a foolishness known as "The Wow-Wows."

> The night before sailing I walked about the West End of London with the wistful feeling that it would be the last time I would see London. . . . In the morning I did not bother to wake Sydney but left a note on the table stating "Off to America. Will keep you posted. Love, Charlie."

Charlie's conquest of America was not instantaneous. There were many months of touring (with his violin, his cello, Bob Ingersoll, Ralph Waldo Emerson and Schopenhauer), two more Atlantic crossings and a 25th birthday, before he finally summoned up the courage to enter the Keystone Studio in Ellendale, Calif., and appear before his new employer, Mack Sennett, who had hired him to work in one-reel film comedies at a starting salary of $150 a week. From his first morning before the camera, Chaplin displayed that ruthless, egomaniacal self-assurance that distinguishes great men at the critical stages of their rise to fame—a fame so overwhelming that it made him, for a time, the best known and most beloved performer in the history of the world.

Mr. Chaplin gives us his version—which we might as well accept as definitive—of his creation of the Little Tramp, though one detects an element of hindsight in his elaborate and rather self-conscious analysis of the Tramp's personality at birth. Elsewhere he writes more simply of the figure who was.

> . . . unfamiliar even to myself. With the clothes on I felt he was a reality, a living person. In fact it ignited all sorts of crazy ideas that I would never have dreamed of till I was dressed and made up as the Tramp.

He also quotes a startled barroom acquaintance of his early California days: "The guy has baggy pants, flat feet, the most miserable, bedraggled-looking little bastard you ever saw; makes gestures as though he's got crabs under his arms—but he's funny!" And funny is what America, and then the world, found him—funny and affecting and irresistible.

By fiscal standards (to which Mr. Chaplin himself attaches great importance) his rise was astronomical. In twelve months his earnings rose from $150 to $1,250 a week; his next contract was for $670,000, the next for $1,250,000. It has always been a moot question whether it was the Little Tramp's special and fantastic popularity that lifted the American movie industry from Side Show to Mass Medium, or if he was just lucky enough to ride in on the crest of the public's sudden, ravenous and insatiable passion for movie entertainment. Either way, the Little Tramp did, without question, add a new and vital element to the mechanical virtuosity of the medium. Out of the acting tradition which he had absorbed with his mother's milk, and from the British Variety stage where he had practiced its techniques, Chaplin brought into movie comedy, for the first time, the concept of character, or as he prefers to call it—*personality*. His early conflicts at Keystone—and later at Essanay—were all on this theme. "We have no scenarios," Sennett explained to him that first morning. "We get an idea, then follow the natural sequence of events until it leads to a chase, which is the essence of your comedy." To which Chaplin replied that he hated a chase. "It dissipates one's personality; and little as I knew about movies, I knew that nothing transcends personality." The personality of Lily's boy Charlie developed freely in the heady sunshine of the new world and metamorphosed on tens of thousands of screens the world over into the mute, universal figure of the Little Tramp.

In the third and central part of his book he covers the quarter-century of his greatest renown: the period in which he made most of his most famous pictures, from *Shoulder Arms* to *Modern Times*. As the movies grew longer and their creator more sophisticated, certain inevitable problems arose:

> In the Keystone days the Tramp had been freer. . . . His brain was seldom active then, only his instincts which were concerned with the basic essentials: food, warmth and shelter. But with each succeeding comedy the Tramp was growing more complex. Sentiment was beginning to percolate through the character.

In *The Kid* and *The Gold Rush*, the new blend of slapstick and sentiment, drama and comedy was brilliantly achieved: in later works, with the coming of sound, the problem was to arise again, in aggravated form.

This period also witnessed two unsuccessful marriages, several celebrated-amours, the formation of United Artists with Doug and Mary, and a series of triumphal visits to New York, London, Paris, Berlin and Tokyo, which occupy the least satisfying section of the book. The urge to "cash in on this business of being a celebrity" was, in the circumstances, a natural and respectable one, but it makes for tedious and frequently embarrassing reading—especially when it is couched in a jargon that seems derived, in equal parts, from Cholly Knicker-bocker and Roget's Thesaurus:

> Having skimmed over the surface of New York society, I now desired to penetrate the intellectual subcutaneous texture of Greenwich Village.

Or again:

> It was an affluent potpourri: Prince George of Greece, Lady Sarah Wilson, the Marquis de Talleyrand-Périgord, Commandant Paul Louis Weiller, Elsa Maxwell and others.

Plowing through pages that are crammed with the names (and snapshots) of the world's most illustrious figures, bristling with cute faux pas and snappy quips ("And with this cryptic remark I said goodbye!"), I found myself unkindly recalling the words of the song with which Charlie had made his theatrical debut:

> I've no fault to find with Jack at all
> Not when 'e's as 'e used to be.
> But since Jack has come into a little bit of cash,
> Well, 'e don't know where 'e are.

At last Mr. Chaplin leads us back to California, to work, and to the fourth, most melodramatic act of his life. "A holiday is at best an empty pursuit; I had dallied around the resorts of Europe long enough . . . I knew why I was aimless and frustrated—I could not determine my future plans." With the reluctant but universal adoption of Sound in films, Chaplin faced serious aesthetic and commercial problems. Squeezed between the "depressing fear of being old-fashioned" and the conviction that "if the Tramp talked, the first word he ever uttered would transform him to another person," he took his dilemma so seriously that at one time he considered moving to China where he could "live well and forget motion pictures!" History, finally, provided a solution. In 1937 Alexander Korda had suggested a Hitler movie based on mistaken identity. Now, two years later, it suddenly struck him—"Of course! As Hitler I could harangue the crowds in jargon and talk all I wanted to. And as the Tramp I could remain more or less silent."

It came about that the film with which he had hoped to lay the bugbear of Sound ended by raising a whirlwind more devastating than anything Chaplin had yet encountered. At the time of its release, *The Great Dictator* got a mixed reception. It disturbed not only Bundists and isolationists, but also a number of passionate anti-Nazis who found it frivolous; among those of the Left it got caught up in the confusion of loyalties that followed the Nazi-Soviet Pact. But not until much later was it officially classed as a clear and flagrant example of "premature anti-fascism" and used, as such, to swell the case against Chaplin.

The complicated drama of the Red purge reached a virulent and spiteful climax in Hollywood during the late forties. Chaplin was one of its many victims. Marked from one high as the nation's most prominent and vulnerable fellow traveler, of whom an example must be made, his lynching was carried out over a period of several years, with weapons that included an organized press offensive, personal and professional blackmail, an economic boycott, the superannuated sex laws of the state of California and the direct intervention of the government of the United States.

Chaplin's main offense lay in three flamboyant, highly publicized speeches (one in San Francisco, one by telephone to Madison Square garden and one in Carnegie Hall) praising the Russian war effort and urging an opening of the Second Front. Though they were delivered at a time when every major Hollywood studio (not to mention the U.S. Signal Corps) was making "pro-Soviet" movies either for money or to promote the war effort it is difficult to understand what drove a resident alien, an avowed anti-nationalist, a war hater and a jealous individualist to involve himself in a spontaneous (but three times repeated) act of direct political pressure in favor of a military operation of which he was utterly ignorant and which unquestionably involved the risk of several hundred thousand human lives. Was he driven to it by "a genuine hatred and contempt for the Nazi system" and an overwhelming fury against those who blandly recommended that we "let them both bleed white"? In part, I'm sure he was; but now, after almost twenty years, Mr. Chaplin himself has attempted an objective and perceptive analysis of his secondary motives:

> Would I have entered this quixotic adventure if I had not made an anti-Nazi film? Was it a sublimation of all my irritations and reactions against talking pictures? How much was I stimulated by the actor in me and the reactions of a live audience?

Reading that final sentence, I found myself thinking back half a century and 200 pages to his account of those simpler and happier days of the First World War when he and Doug and Mary (all in the full flush of their success) were racketing around the country on their Third Liberty Bond tour; how Charlie "bounded onto the platform and let fly with a verbal machine-gun barrage: 'The Germans are at your doors! We've got to stop them! And we *will* stop them! If you buy Liberty Bonds!' "—to tumultuous applause and congratulations from the Assistant Secretary of the Navy, Franklin Delano Roosevelt. Now for appearing in a dinner jacket and addressing a cheering audience as "Comrades!" he was to be hounded out of the country in which he had lived and worked for forty years by those same legal devices which the government employs to get rid of murderers, dope peddlers and pimps.

All is well that ends well. As the curtain rises on the last act—but by no means the epilogue—of Mr. Chaplin's history, the old Maestro is discovered against the background of the Swiss Alps, surrounded by his beautiful, talented and ever-growing family. And the paradox of this astonishing life goes on: on the one hand, "we live relatively near the Queen of Spain and the Count and the Countess of Chevreau d'Antraigues, who have been most cordial to us"; on the other, "I am still very ambitious; I could never retire; beside having a few unfinished movie scripts, I should like to write a play and an opera—if time will allow." Of course it will.

SEPTEMBER 21, 1970

GRIFFITH'S RUSSIAN FANS

Robert Sklar

•

Robert Sklar teaches Cinema Studies at New York University and is a Contributing Editor to *Cineaste*. He is the author of *Film: An International History of the Medium* and *Movie-Made America: A Cultural History of American Movies*. This piece is a review of *Film Essays and A Lecture* by Sergei Eisenstein and *D. W. Griffith: The Years at Biograph* by Robert M. Henderson.

IN 1919, MIRACULOUSLY, a print of D. W. Griffith's *Intolerance* appeared in revolutionary Moscow. The film was enormously popular with Soviet audiences. According to legend, Lenin saw it and immediately cabled Griffith an offer to head the Russian film industry. Young Soviet film makers screened *Intolerance* again and again, absorbing Griffith's editing and camera techniques. The brilliant achievements of the Soviet silent film, as was freely acknowledged, were founded on the fortuitous influence of the great American silent film epic. Yet to most film critics and ordinary movie-goers the Soviet directors—Pudovkin, Davzkenko and particularly Sergei Eisenstein—are more securely rooted as major figures in motion-picture history than is the man whose example launched their careers.

The reasons why are not difficult to grasp. Griffith's films have been less readily available for public viewing. No biography of his life or even a comprehensive critical study of his films has yet appeared—nor did Griffith himself write on film technique or aesthetics as did the Russians, exemplified by this latest collection of Eisenstein's *Film Essays*. Moreover, Griffith's inactivity after the advent of sound encouraged the belief that his film-making powers had declined, or that his style and imagination had become obsolescent in the modern era—beliefs that would have been more readily disputed had he been accorded the biographical and critical attention his importance merited.

But at the heart of Griffith's ambiguous historical standing lies the very issue by which the Soviet directors were eventually to proclaim their independence of his influence. He was an intuitive director, they said, who attained his impressive effects as if by instinct; through systematic and rational application they had transformed his technique into an aesthetic far more comprehensive and powerful. Griffith lacked, in short, the theoretical equipment that might have enabled him to develop his methods to their full artistic and social significance.

Eisenstein himself put it most succinctly in his essay on Griffith in *Film Form*, still the most perceptive critical account of Griffith yet written: "In social attitudes Griffith was always a liberal, never departing far from the slightly sentimental humanism of the good old gentlemen and sweet old ladies of Victorian England, just as Dickens loved to picture them. His tender-hearted film morals go no higher than a level of Christian accusation of human injustice, and nowhere in his films is there sounded a protest against social injustice."

Anyone who has seen *Intolerance* knows that Eisenstein is quite wrong. Early in the modern story, one of four parallel episodes in *Intolerance*, a strike is called at a factory. With medium shots and close-ups, in the "switch-back" editing that was soon to be called *montage*, Griffith establishes the forces of conflict and confrontation: the strikers in one series of shots, heavily armed soldiers in the other. Then Griffith cuts suddenly to a long shot encompassing the two opposing forces in the same frame for the first time—the strikers at the lower left edge of the screen, the soldiers at the upper right, and between them, open space filling most of the screen. The shot has a stunning emotional impact, conveying through purely visual form the warfare between workers and the state. It is one of the great examples of true cinema, and also a brilliantly effective protest.

Yet Eisenstein was also right about Griffith, because Griffith never created a fully sustained social protest film in the manner of Eisenstein's great silent movies, *Strike, Battleship Potemkin, October* and *Old and New*. As the four parallel episodes unfold in *Intolerance*, the modern story of social injustice is subsumed by the theme of human injustice in universal form, ancient and modern. Even in his most effective social commentary films, like the neglected silent of 1923, *Isn't Life Wonderful?* Griffith includes love interests and other complications which, though perfectly proper by the canons of dramatic structure, inevitably tend to dilute the social message.

Eisenstein, in contrast, learned to be single-minded. In one of his earliest and most pointed essays, "The Method of Making Workers' Films," translated for the first time in *Film Essays*, he described his montage method as a technique to produce "a socially useful emotional and psychological affect on the audience." This, he said, was the film's content. *Strike*, thus, is "an accumulation of reflexes without intervals (satisfaction), that is, a focusing of reflexes on struggle (and a lifting of potential class·tone)."

What rescues such manifestoes from meaninglessness is Eisentein's artistry. Indeed his fundamental historical importance lies in the unity of his art and his ideology. Men who were ideologues without being artists—on both the capitalist and Soviet sides—hindered and frustrated his work. But he held on to his fundamental belief that artistry is the primary requirement for Socialist or revolutionary art. No essay in this new collection is more fascinating than "Problems of Composition," a stenographic transcript of one of his last lectures. Eisenstein leads his students through a passage from a Soviet novel, showing them how the author buries his significant detail in an excess of insignificant detail. It is an essay that artists in all media can learn from; and it applies directly to Griffith's case as well.

Robert M. Henderson's study of the director's early career provides an essential start to a full understanding of Griffith's place in film history. Griffith was a stock company actor in his mid '30s, with few prospects when he began directing films for Biograph in 1908. Over the next five years he was to make more than 400 one- and two-reel films for Biograph, developing at the same time the techniques that were to become the fundamental syntax of motion-picture aesthetics: parallel cutting for suspense, closer and more varied camera angles, multiple shots of the same scene, back lighting and many more. In 1913 he left Biograph because his employers were discouraging him from making longer films. Thereupon he went on to direct

The Birth of a Nation, *Intolerance* and the great silent features of the post–World War I years.

Henderson's valuable book is as much a source work as a critical study of Griffith's early films; like Griffith himself, Henderson leaves in too much—not only the names of every actor in the company but the names of the wagon drivers as well. The chief failing of the book is its slighting of the four-reel feature Griffith made in 1913 before leaving Biograph, *Judith of Bethulia*. *Judith* marks a great turning point in Griffith's career, focusing for the first time all his developing ability to make the motion picture a work of psychological and emotional force, and in a *concise* epic form. But it was Eisenstein rather than Griffith who perfected the short, direct epic as a vehicle of social purpose.

3

Is That a Pistol in Your Pocket?

Morality, Influence and Censorship

Current Nation *editor Katrina vanden Heuvel noted in her introduction to her anthology* The Nation: 1865–1990 *that "it is remarkable how many of the controversies that engaged the moral and political concern of* The Nation *twenty-five, fifty, or seventy-five years ago still do." Such is the case of free speech and censorship. Whether it was the 1999 Sensation exhibition at the Brooklyn Museum, or Piss Christ, Scorcese's* The Last Temptation of Christ, *or Godard's* Hail Mary *the magazine has been passionate and consistent in its fight against censorship. Probably its bravest hour was during the McCarthy period, when, as former editor Carey McWilliams noted, what readers particularly appreciated about the magazine's tone was that it "was neither apologetic nor defensive but indignant and defiant." The articles that follow, except Stuart Klawans's piece, are a small sample of the many editorial paragraphs and articles that were devoted to censorship, morality, the Hays Office, and the influence of the Catholic Church, during the pre-McCarthy period.*

DECEMBER 12, 1920

FILM CENSORS AND OTHER MORONS

•

A MAGNIFICENT FARCE could be written on the works and ways of the film censors in the various States, but their antics are important because they illustrate what an irresponsible and dangerous thing censorship is.

Let us give a few examples. In 1921 the Kansas State Board of Review ordered all scenes and titles dealing with the Tulsa, Oklahoma, race riots eliminated. Newspapers were printing pictures and stories about the riots every day, but the newspapers have waged a long and successful fight against censorship in peace time at least. The movies, afraid of their dollars, have yielded abject surrender, and the result is a fraud upon the public. Even Ku Klux Klan pictures were barred by the Kansas board, and other boards once ordered cut these words: "Probe of murders laid to Klan."

Accounts of the tricks of these censors read like a burlesque of the worst possibilities of censorship. One board ordered out the title, "Harvey Porter, an attorney to whom victory is more important than the honor of his profession," in its zealous respect for lawyers. Another board objected to the title "Kick the dog and Brulet will fight"—in *The Oregon Trail*—as "tending to incite to crime." Still another objected to a picture of a marriage by radio as "sacrilegious," although such a marriage had in fact been performed. From a Rupert Hughes comedy the title "In Sicily they challenge to a duel by biting off the tip of your ear" had to go. It was the Ohio board which would not let the International News Service say of Eugene V. Debs: "Leaving the White House after telling President Harding he has not changed his mind." In Illinois a picture was barred because a delegation of ministers who had never seen it protested that they had heard that it reflected upon the clergy. Texas barred a fantasy based on Aladdin's Lamp as "medieval, fantastic; absurd, and fit only for the dark ages." Pennsylvania would not even permit the word "anarchists" in a film, suggesting "fanatics" as an alternative, although the "anarchists" were pictured as wreckers of society. Ohio would not allow a parrot in an O. Henry story to say "Give him hell, Dickey," and here in New York filmgoers were not permitted to see these horrid words (in a scene showing the spanking of two children by their uncle): "This hurts me more than it does you!" "Yes, but not in the same place."

It sounds crazy. The movies sometimes try to defend themselves, but they are not permitted even to do that. A Pathé news reel pictured several sponsors of the censorship, with the caption: "The people who favor censorship of moving pictures will oftentimes argue the hardest in favor of letting the people rule," but Ohio ordered the caption out. We are subjected in the movies to irresponsible boards of morons, who cut anything which offends their individual prejudices. No wonder the potentialities of the film are slow in developing.

We can expect such censorship on every printed word if the New York Legislature passes the "Clean Books Bill." And now the busybodies are begging permission to extend their puerilities to the spoken stage. They cry that the country is in danger from licentious plays and theatrical performances. In New York City the hue and cry is at its height. Commissioner of Licenses August W. Glatzmayer tells us that the self-constituted moral jury of authors, actors, managers, and plain citizens which was instituted last season has been scrapped—that, indeed, no complaints have been received; but Acting Mayor Murray Hulbert is on the warpath. He wants every theatergoer to complain whenever his or her moral sensibilities have been wounded. He hopes thus, he says, to defeat the nefarious plans of those who "wallow in dirt that they might wallow in riches."

Who, we wonder, does he mean by "they"? The musical shows display a little more epidermis than of yore, but we are not sure that this is not as decent as the old fashion of lingerie at provocative intervals. We suspect that Major Hulbert has his eye not on the musical shows, however, nor on the plays which picture life with an indecent falseness, but on those which are really most moral in their piercing of conventional hypocrisies. He denounces plays which "make a laughing-stock of virtue and place vice on a pedestal." What does he mean? Does he mean virtue and vice according to the statute-books, or according to the churches that forbid dancing and call belief in evolution a crime, or according to the dictates of a delicate and enlightened conscience? We suspect that he objects to plays like *Rain* rather than to shows like *Artists and Models*. He lets the cat out of the bag when he denounces any play that "contains words or expressions doing violence to accepted standards." Like all censors he wants life petrified.

And it is just such a censorship that the "unco guid" and the pathologically angry sigh for. For to the arm of the state is about to be added that of the church. Bishop Manning vociferously brandishes the moral tomahawk. The Social Service Commission of his diocese, besieged with complaints, is about to start an investigation. According to these complaints the conditions of the New York stage are "terrible." The reverend bishop refuses so far to name plays. He insinuates that they are in fact nameless. Equally aroused are the New York Federation of Churches and the Society for the Prevention of Crime. The redoubtable Summer, strange to say, seems to be in a mild and placable mood. But the probable results of ecclesiastical "censure" can be studied from one priceless example. The Rev. Dr. S. Edward Young, president of the Society for the Prevention of Crime, and Mrs. Young visited in the course of their research the Knickerbocker Theater, saw *The Lullaby*, and "found no fault with it." Now we do not wish to see *The Lullaby* suppressed. We would fight such suppression tooth and nail because we believe that the hurt done the cause of liberty and tolerance infinitely outweighs of public amusement. But if there is one play in New York today that is morally false and misleading to the repulsive core of it, one play that is rancid in substance and meretricious in execution, that play is *The Lullaby*. But because it could be summed up in a copybook maxim the Rev. Dr. Young finds no fault with it. What he, alas, is after is not hypocrisy and meretriciousness but fresh notions of human life and an attitude of inquiry.

New York is fast becoming the first theatrical city in the world. It can manage Mr. Hulbert; let it beware of Dr. Manning and his cohorts—else they will reduce its great stage to the level of Hollywood.

April 16, 1930

Virtue in Cans

•

Mr. Will Hays, Moses of the Movies, has gone his illustrious prototype several better, for he has just descended from his own particular Sinai located at (469 Fifth Avenue) with no less than twenty-one commandments intended for the guidance of the Children of Hollywood. *Among other things* the new code provides:

1. That crimes against law shall never be presented in such a way as to throw sympathy with the crime as against law and justice. (Note. Law and justice are assumed to be inevitably the same. The Boston Tea Party is ruled out.)
2. Revenge in modern times shall not be justified as a motive. (Note. "Modern times" probably lets "Hamlet" in.)
3. The use of liquor in American life shall be restricted to the actual requirements of characterization or plot. (Note. Whatever that may mean.)
4. Scenes of passion shall not be introduced when not essential to the plot. (Note. Whatever you may mean.) Ministers of religion in their character of ministers of religion shall not be used as comic characters or as villains. (Note. The New Art of the Movies being what it is, it is obviously inadvisable to suggest that there may be such a thing as hypocrisy. Those who pretend to be good are good.)
6. The history, institutions, prominent people, and citizenry of other nations shall be represented fairly. (Note. We sell our films

almost everywhere. Bolsheviks need not be considered as "people." In case of war all citizens of the enemy country automatically become villains and sadists.)

Mr. Hays is so transparently simple-minded that it is hardly worth while to accuse him of deliberately using virtue for commercial purposes, but whether he happens to be in on the game or merely a tool in the hands of others the fact remains that he always manages to strike the proper attitude—the one, that is to say, which surrenders every right to every sincerity while promising to respect all the prejudices of every convention. Some years ago the industry discovered that suggestiveness and sensation were necessary to its profits but that truth and consistency were not. Accordingly it invented the perfect formula—five reels of transgression followed by one reel of retribution; it hired Mr. Hays to consecrate that formula; and Mr. Hays has been busy at his task ever since. Obviously it is now the job of the directors to stay within the letter of his law without ceasing to be as lurid, as salacious, and as tawdry as the audience demands. And to judge by their achievements of the past there is little reason to doubt that they will succeed magnificently.

We are willing to leave aside all questions of art and its duty to comment upon life as the artist sees it. We should, however, like to point to the results already achieved by Mr. Hays's method. He has proposed above all to keep the movies sexually clean, and yet there was never any form of artistic expression which was so completely drenched with sex. The suggestion of everything which he has attempted to suppress has diffused itself through every scene, and the mind of the audience is encouraged to play about every idea that cannot be stated. Perhaps if an occasional film "justified adultery" or admitted that otherwise respectable girls sometimes have illegitimate children it would not be necessary for every film to deal with seduction arrested at the bedside.

NOVEMBER 1, 1933

THE WEEK

•

IN HIS COMMENTS upon the provisions of the proposed motion-picture code Will H. Hays characteristically laid his emphasis upon the moral rather than upon the economic responsibility of the producers. Meanwhile, and under his auspices, Mae West is rapidly eclipsing the popularity of all other stars of the past or present. According to our energetic contemporary, *Variety*, papers from all parts of the country are clamoring for publicity material, and exactly 185 interviews with her have been published since April. In addition, *Liberty* has ordered a six-part serial story of her life, 1,200 newspapers have signed up for another serial biography of the same heroine, and *True Confessions* will publish a third. At the same time the Macaulay publishing house is having the finishing touches put to her new volume, "How to Misbehave"; *Cosmopolitan* is dickering for a novelette; and articles have either already appeared or are scheduled to appear in *Vanity Fair, Harper's Bazaar, Time*, and the *American Mercury*. Her last film is said to have earned about $3,000,000 gross, and we note from the trade-paper advertisements of the new one that Miss West is offering prizes to the exhibitor who puts on the best advertising campaign and to the one who plays the film the greatest number of times. One prize is "a personally conducted 'Come up and see me sometime' trip to Hollywood"; the other is "a diamond-studded watch with an intimate inscription in the back; it's got to be good for a man like that."

MAY 8, 1948

THE CHURCH AND THE MOVIES

Paul Blanshard

•

In his autobiography Carey McWilliams writes, "With the publication of Paul Blanshard's famous series of articles on the Catholic Church in 1948, which were primarily concerned with the politics of the hierarchy, the [New York City] superintendents of the Board of Education abruptly banned *The Nation* [from local public high school libraries] without notice or a prior hearing or so much of a formal announcement." The legal challenge to this ban "cost the magazine dearly," McWilliams observes, especially as the magazine was also under severe attack for its stand on the Cold War. But the ban was eventually lifted in 1963, fifteen years later. Paul Blanshard was a regular contributor for the magazine and his books included *American Freedom and Catholic Power; Some of My Best Friends Are Christians; Communism, Democracy, and Catholic Power*; and *Personal and Controversial: An Autobiography.*

MOST AMERICANS PROBABLY assume that the Legion of Decency, the Roman Catholic instrument for censoring films, is concerned primarily with what H. L. Mencken once called "translucent drawers." The legion's name implies that it is the guardian of purity and the logical heir to Anthony Comstock in the pursuit of the lewd, lascivious, and obscene. It pleases the Catholic hierarchy to have Americans take this view of the agency because if it were called the Catholic Political and Doctrinal Censorship it would immediately lose its usefulness to the church.

Nothing in the public pledge of the Legion of Decency, administered once a year to all Catholic congregations in the United States, indicates its underlying denominational and political objectives. The pledge says:

> In the name of the Father and the Son and the Holy Ghost. Amen.
>
> I condemn indecent and immoral motion pictures, and those which glorify crime or criminals.
>
> I promise to do all that I can to strengthen public opinion against the production of indecent and immoral films, and to unite with all those who protest against them.
>
> I acknowledge my obligation to form a right conscience about pictures that are dangerous to my moral life. As a member of the Legion of Decency, I pledge myself to remain away from them. I promise, further, to stay away altogether from places of amusement which show them as a matter of policy.

Actually the Legion of Decency, in its private censorship of nearly four hundred films a year, is far more concerned with Catholic dogma and Catholic social philosophy than with decency. It is well known that regular government and industry agencies censor too long kisses, recumbent petting, and suggestive figure displays. Many people believe that the industry is over-censored already by the government, the Johnston office, and a considerable amount of internal Catholic influence. The industry's Production Code was written by one of the most aggressive Jesuit pamphleteers in the country, Father Daniel Lord, and the Production Code Administrator, Joseph I. Breen, is a Catholic.

The Legion of Decency begins where the censors of the government and the industry leave off. It seeks to rate all films according to a kind of super-code which emphasizes distinctly Catholic taboos and to suppress all films which contain any material critical of the present or historical social policies of the Catholic church. It exerts pressure upon the industry in favor of films which treat the church in a flattering manner. Its value to the church in this respect is inestimable. *Going My Way*, *Boys' Town*, *Song of Bernadette*, and *The Bells of St. Mary* were probably worth more to the hierarchy in creating good-will than all the propaganda produced by the church's official proselyting agencies in a decade.

The legion's denominational bias is quite transparent and has been since the organization was founded in 1934. Last August it raised such a clamor against the British film *Black Narcissus* as an "affront to religion and religious life" that the producer was forced to withdraw the picture and make substantial changes to avoid a permanent "condemned" rating. *Black Narcissus* was a fair and realistic film about frustrated Anglican nuns, but the Roman Catholic church could not allow convent life to be exposed even indirectly to frank criticism. The legion did not dare to boycott completely such a charming family picture as *Life with Father*, but it refused to give the film top rating as "unobjectionable for general patronage" because "it presents certain concepts on the sacrament of baptism which are contrary to Catholic teaching and practice." The harmless and delightful *The Bishop's Wife* was likewise rated not suitable for the whole family because one of its characters, according to the film critic of *America*, was "a dictatorial widow who tells him [the bishop], among other things, that it was she who had him made bishop." Part of the duty of the legion, it appears, is to protect Catholic youth from the suggestion that bishoprics can be brought in *any* church. Occasionally the legion breaks out in a condemnation which is purely theological, as in its objection to *Repeat Performance*: "This film presents as a theory the inevitability of destiny despite the free-will of man."

Of the seventy films rated "objectionable in part" by the legion last year, only 40 percent were called suggestive; the objections to the rest were largely denominational—that is to say, the objections would not necessarily be accepted by good Protestants and Jews. About one-third of the "objectionable in part" films were given this low rating because of "light treatment of marriage and divorce." In Catholic parlance this does not mean what it means to non-Catholics. If a script writer assumes that divorce may be an unfortunate but practical way to terminate an unhappy marriage, that assumption is considered "light treatment."

In fact, the most common indictment of films marked "objectionable in part" by the legion in its last published review of judgments was the phrase "Reflects the acceptability of divorce." Some of the films so branded undoubtedly treated family life in a frivolous and irresponsible manner, but many others were in accord with the highest non-Catholic moral ideals. *Gentlemen's Agreement* was given a Grade III "objectionable in part" rating because the heroine, played by Dorothy Maguire, had once been divorced, and it was improper to imagine that a divorced person could ever be happily remarried. *Miracle on 34th St.*, was similarly rated for the same reason. Darryl Zanuck had refused to make the divorced lady of the story into a war widow to suit the Legion of Decency. William H. Mooring, the Catholic convert who writes the syndicated motion-picture reviews for the Catholic diocesan press of the United States, summed up in the Brooklyn *Tablet* of January 31 his reasons for failing to give "Miracle on 34th St." his blessing:

> Unfortunately, the people who adhere rigidly to Legion of Decency ratings and firmly refuse to patronize pictures that are classified as "objectionable in part" had to forgo the pleasure of seeing it. "Miracle on 34th St." introduced the subject of divorce.
>
> The reference was entirely gratuitous. The leading feminine character, nicely played by Maureen O'Hara, was a divorcee. She had a little daughter who proved a pivotal character, but the little girl could just as easily have been a niece, or a young sister, or a child adopted by an unmarried professional woman. Spinsters have been known to make admirable foster mothers, and there's no law against it.

The same type of demand for the doctoring of the facts of ordinary human relationship was made in the case of *Black Narcissus*, not because of indecency but because of possible anti-Catholic or anti-clerical inferences. In Italy the Pope intervened against the picture. When the producer, J. Arthur Rank, sent the film to Ireland for the approval of Irish censors, they expressed willingness to approve it if one change could be made, the addition of a sentence in the foreword making it clear that the Anglican nuns were not Roman Catholic.

But this was not enough for the Legion of Decency of the United States. When it reached this country, extensive changes were demanded on the ground that an inferential criticism of non-Catholic nuns was an attack on the Catholic church as "the custodian of the Christian religion." Dreams of a red dress and a love affair after the end of one year's service in the convent had to be severely pruned: it must not be implied that nuns have any sexual regrets. The final version sent out to American theaters was mutilated; the flashbacks into the previous lives of the nuns as ordinary young females were cut out; and even the scene in which a nun takes off her costume and reveals a street dress underneath was eliminated as improper.

It is not surprising that a figure in the film industry said recently:

"We are selling a phony morality in the movies. This is not the way life is. In spite of the excesses before the Breen office and the Legion of Decency came into existence, it was still possible to make an honest picture of life."

The obligation to make "an honest picture of life" does not disturb the conscience of the Legion of Decency when Catholic denominational values are at stake. It consistently fights any reference in the film to any person or fact in history which would reflect upon the church's character. Last year it attempted to force Metro-Goldwyn-Mayer to alter Dumas's *The Three Musketeers*, and according to latest reports it partially succeeded. Thomas Brady, writing in the *New York Times* of December 7, said that the Legion of Decency's Hollywood representative, Father John J. Devlin, suggested the complete elimination of Cardinal Richelieu because Dumas's characterization of the cardinal as a worldly and unscrupulous man was offensive to the church. Father Devlin was not satisfied to take the clerical garb off the cardinal and omit all religious functions. Latest reports indicate that Cardinal Richelieu will be transformed into "Duke Richelieu" to satisfy the legion's objection!

The distortion of famous literary works has become such a commonplace in Hollywood that it excites little attention. Brady's article in the *Times* described other changes forced in this picture and in other words of art. "Constance, the married mistress of D'Artagnan in the novel," it said, "will be unmarried on the screen, her unsympathetic husband becoming her cruel father." Milady de Winter may be eliminated altogether because of the "doubly adulterous connection." A new Columbia film on Lucrezia Borgia may be compelled to suppress the fact that she was the illegitimate daughter of Pope Alexander VI. And Geiger, the producer of the Berthold Brecht–Charles Laughton version of the play "Galileo," is doctoring it so that the film "will present Galileo's opposition as general scholastic authoritarianism rather than specific religious inquisition."

In the legion itself there is no "general scholastic authoritarianism." The decrees and methods of operation of the film censorship are all directed from Rome. The Legion of Decency is an organic part of the Catholic church, completely dominated by the clergy and administered since 1936 by the archdiocese of New York. The public pledge was ordered by Pope Pius XI in his encyclical "On Motion Pictures." Probably 7,000,000 to 9,000,000 persons have taken the oath, and all Catholic organizations are directed to enforce the boycott whereever possible. Boycotts are frequently spearheaded by the Catholic War Veterans, whose members make excellent marchers and aggressive pickets.

Local bishops are empowered by the Pope specifically to go beyond the censorship of the Legion of Decency and "censor films which are admitted to the general list," but usually local priests and bishops abide by the list printed each week in all diocesan newspapers throughout the country and posted at the doors of churches. The actual first-judgment reviewing of films is done in New York by a revolving committee of alumnae of Catholic women's colleges; difficult cases are referred to a committee of priests. The literature of the legion has never made public the special qualifications of the censors for their work.

What effect does the Catholic censorship have upon the success or failure of American motion pictures? Probably only the few films which are given the lowest (wholly objectionable) rating are injured commercially; there were three such American films last year—*The Outlaw*, *Forever Amber*, and *Black Narcissus*. Pictures rated partially objectionable seem little affected. In fact, these pictures have increased from 10 percent of the total output to 16 percent since the legion began operations in 1936. Apparently Catholic movie fans do not boycott a film unless they are told that it is wholly objectionable, and even then the lure of a banned film offsets at least part of the loss. There is no evidence that Catholic boycotts would have much effect if theater owners stood their ground.

One Hollywood producer, Howard Hughes, has recently defied the Legion of Decency without, apparently, suffering the financial loss which was predicted. His picture, *The Outlaw*, originally condemned both by the legion and the Breen office, was dropped by Twentieth Century-Fox, but Hughes refused to alter it. Catholic leaders predicted its complete failure, but Hughes offered it to capacity audiences on the coast for months.

Forever Amber, slightly doctored after legion protests, played five weeks to packed houses in Catholic Boston after it had been bitterly denounced by the hierarchy. The slight changes, of course, made a difference. A spoken prologue was added which explained that here was a bad woman who was punished for her sins. A line was added to the speech of the victor in a duel: "In heaven's name, Amber, haven't we done enough? First, a nameless child, and now a dead man. May God have mercy on our souls!"

When a picture is officially boycotted by the hierarchy, and when the Catholic Action groups begin their public demonstrations, most theater owners run for cover. It is easy for the hierarchy to give the impression of a great mass movement because the press accords generous space to priestly denunciations, and a few ardent. Catholic demonstrators are always available for a "religious crusade." The church often pursues such a crusade with great aggressiveness. "I shall direct all Catholics to boycott for one year," wrote Cardinal Dougherty to two theater owners in Philadelphia last March who ventured to show *The Outlaw* and *Forever Amber*; and the Cardinal added that if the owners did not submit within forty-eight hours, the boycott would be extended to all productions at both theaters for the entire year. The Duluth diocesan office of the Legion of Decency declared one theater "out of bounds" for six months for the same reason.

The legion's boycott prevented the public from seeing not only the unexpurgated version of "Black Narcissus" but a sober educational film on venereal disease which had been sponsored originally by the United States Public Health Service. At present this film cannot be exhibited outside the army. When the outstanding film *Juarez* was made, Catholic pressure caused distortion of the historical material so that Juarez's opposition to the Mexican church was not mentioned, although his battle against the priests and their superstitions was one of the major struggles of his career. "Blockade," the famous Spanish war picture, cautiously omitted any identification of Loyalists, but even then it was bitterly assailed because it did not compliment the church and the Spanish fascist forces. Incidentally, the church's concern for preserving Franco's reputation on the screen has been rewarded. The Spanish government's censorship regulations, announced last October, give the Roman Catholic church final veto power over all films.

Side by side with the Legion of Decency in censorship activities is a small organization, the Catholic Theater Movement, which has been functioning for many years in New York without gaining national notice. Dominated entirely by priests, it attempts to tell the faithful what they should not see in the theater if they wish to preserve their faith and morals. Its lists of approved and disapproved plays are published in appropriate Catholic weekly newspapers. For many months in 1947 the only play in New York which the Catholic Theater Movement approved without qualification was the performance now known as

"Icetime of 1948." It rated *Harvey* objectionable in part, even when Frank Fay was in the lead, because the drama's six-foot rabbit seemed by implication a little too flip for a Catholic angel.

When Catholic censorship of literature and motion pictures is considered in the larger perspective of American life, there seems little to recommend it. No one questions the *right* of the hierarchy to influence its people in matters of art and literature, and Catholic censorship has undoubtedly eliminated some unwelcome vulgarity from the lower reaches of pornographic commerce. But the censorship operations of the hierarchy have gone far beyond religion and decency. They have extended into the world of politics, medicine, and historical research, and have impaired the integrity of the media of information which serve non-Catholics as well as Catholics. Most serious of all, the hierarchy has stifled judgment among its own people by refusing them permission to read both sides of important controversies on matters of social policy. Such repression is directly contrary to a fundamental thesis of our democracy—that a good citizen is a man who has learned to think for himself. Because most Catholics in this country are good citizens and good Americans it seems inevitable that sooner or later they will recognize the censorship system of their priesthood for what it is, a survival of medieval coercion which has no rightful place in the American environment.

FEBRUARY 14, 1994

WARNER BROS. BEFORE THE CODE

Stuart Klawans

•

Current *Nation* film critic Stuart Klawans used the hysteria in the early nineties as a point of departure to examine and draw lessons from the lost cinematic treasure of pre-Code Hollywood.

AS OF THIS writing, seven bills are pending in Congress to regulate violence on television. On the streets of Harlem, activists protest against the outlaw manners flaunted in rap videos. In a banquet room in Beverly Hills, our First Film Fan implores movie executives to clean up their products and save their souls. Once again, it's time to ask how (and why) America polices the moving image.

Actually, America's first film censors *were* cops. Beginning in 1907, under the leadership of Deputy Superintendent Major Metellus Lucullus Cicero Funkhouser, the Chicago police banned some films outright but more often chopped and rearranged them to suit their own tastes, if not those of nickelodeon patrons. It's instructive to see what kind of material particularly offended Major Funkhouser. In his 1990 study *Behind the Mask of Innocence*, film historian Kevin Brownlow cites a list of one month's excisions: "the application of the third degree by police; the bribing of a policeman; brutal handling of prisoners by police; prison guards failing to preserve order; bribing of a detective;

theft of a police uniform; love scene between a married woman and an army officer."

What a useful figure he makes, the self-important cop with the comic-opera name! How unfortunate for civil libertarians that the world's censors do not all live down to Major Funkhouser. On Christmas Eve 1908, a less risible figure, New York Mayor George Brinton McClellan, wrote the next chapter in film censorship. He shut down all the nickelodeons, ostensibly to insure public safety. (By operating in filthy, malodorous buildings, nickelodeons endangered the working-class immigrants who crowded the shows.) McClellan's more likely motive, though, was to safeguard public morals, broadly construed. (By crowding into nickelodeons, working-class immigrants endangered a prime chunk of New York real estate, making it filthy and malodorous.)

What to do? A committee of Progressive Era reformers associated with the People's Institute quickly convened to protest the Mayor's ban. Clearly, there was no need to deprive poor people of their entertainment. The proper course was to *improve* the entertainment and through it the poor themselves. So, in March 1909, the People's Institute formed a Board of Censorship. It was a private initiative, without governmental authority or police powers; and yet the dominant organization of American movie producers, the Motion Picture Patents Company, readily volunteered to submit all new releases to the board.

The movie producers chose this form of self-censorship mostly to avoid a multiplicity of imposed censorships, with all their trouble and expense. Every state, every locality, had its own Major Funkhouser waiting to happen. Better, then, to seek the approval of a reasonably sympathetic and intelligent board, which (with luck) would function on a national level.

But the producers had more than one reason for their decision. The Motion Picture Patents Company, better known to film history as the Edison Trust, was a monopoly, which in 1909 was attempting to throttle all competition, domestic and foreign alike. The Trust's policy of self-censorship may therefore be compared to the policies of many other industries monopolies during Theodore Roosevelt's presidency; they came to accept some degree of friendly regulation rather than risk a breakup. Beyond that, the trusts, and the Trust, wanted to seem public-spirited. Soon, edifying views of world landmarks became common in the Trust's productions, along with advice on hygiene and informative tours of factories and farms. Good, hair-raising murders and hot-blooded love affairs became correspondingly more difficult to find. The Trust's producers were going upmarket in search of middle-class dollars—which happened to be the very strategy of some would-be competitors who just then were starting to take on the Trust, certain sleazy operators with names like Zukor, Mayer, Fox and Laemmle.

So a pattern took shape in 1909, one that has held ever since for all major attempts to control the moving image—in 1922, 1933–34, 1947 and now. Each time, the censorship (self-censorship, in fact) has coincided with a consolidation of power within the industry. Each time, at this moment of consolidation, the industry's bosses have sought in part to protect themselves from interference, in part to create a more respectable product and in part to dissociate themselves from a segment of the audience that is deemed to be not respectable enough. Reformers always seem to feel that moving images, with their magical power, have inspired bad behavior among one group or another—working-class immigrants, or single women with bobbed hair and access to motorcars, or black male teenagers with their caps stuck on backward. Note that in each of these cases—by a strange coincidence—the misbehaving group is *already* seen as dangerous and in need of control. The desire to improve (that is, restrict) the moving image thus merges with a desire to improve the members of the savage group, or at least to limit their damage.

In 1921–22, for example, a series of Hollywood scandals, most of them involving free-living women, led to the creation of a new trade-regulating organization, the Motion Picture Producers and Distributors of America, with its own in-house censor, Will Hays. Women such as Virginia Rappe, the would-be starlet who died in the vicinity of Fatty Arbuckle, would henceforth be protected from their own infatuation with the movies. Meanwhile, Hollywood's bosses were free to institute the studio system (as Irving Thalberg was doing just then at Universal), to create vertically integrated trusts and to colonize Europe with their products.

With all that accomplished, Hollywood settled down to a period of relaxed self-censorship through the Hays Office—a practice that needed no revision until the next consolidation of power, the next threat of subversion. First came a shake-up from within (caused in large measure by Warner Bros.' introduction of sound); then came the industrial regrouping, which was complete by 1934. Jack and Harry Warner, the newest partners in the oligopoly, signed a deal that year with William Randolph Hearst giving them access to story material from his magazines, as well as favorable treatment in the Hearst newspapers. At the same time, Upton Sinclair was scaring the bosses with his End Poverty in California campaign, and trade unionism was taking hold in the studios.

Trying to maintain a grip on the market with one hand while beating back insurgents with the other, the studio bosses proved to be sympathetic when they next heard calls for censorship. In April 1934, for all the usual reasons, the Catholic Church founded the Legion of Decency; a boycott of Pennsylvania movie theaters soon followed. In July 1934, studio bosses allayed the protests by establishing the Production Code Administration, an office within the Motion Picture Producers and Distributors of America. It would rule American filmmaking for the next thirty-four years.

Of course, none of this matters very much if you think of film merely as "a business pure and simple, organized and conducted for profit." (I take that language from Justice McKenna's opinion in *Mutual Film Corporation v. Ohio Industrial Commission*, the 1915 case in which the Supreme Court laid down a justification for the censorship of films.) But if movies are sometimes more than commodities, if they're also worth thinking about as a medium of expression, then no issue could be more vital than that of censorship, nor could any exhibition be more illuminating than "Warner Bros. Before the Code," a series to run at New York's Film Forum from February 4 through March 24. Here's a chance to replace abstract issues of law with the particulars of the films themselves, so you can feel what was lost when the Production Code went into force.

I feel as if the whole world was lost. The pre-Code Warner Bros. movies are renowned for their tabloid-journalism plots and hard-edged visual style, their breakneck pace and air of raffishness; but their most remarkable quality is the sense they project of being engaged with the life of their time. You feel these movies *are* the early 1930s in urban America, much as Dickens's novels are the England of the Industrial Revolution. Of course, you can watch these movies just for the mindless pleasure of cataloguing taboos. (How many times do you glimpse Joan Blondell's peekaboo nipples? How far will Cagney go *this* time?) But the great merit of Film Forum's series is that it allows you to escape this account-ledger way of looking at pictures, which jibes all too well with a censor's mentality. The real question is, What *else* disappeared from the movies, once Joan Blondell's nipples were removed?

Among the tarnished treasures to be shown at Film Forum (nicely shined up, I might add, in new prints provided by Turner Entertainment) you can find at least two no-holds-barred portraits of Depression-era capitalists—amoral workaholics who spend their days cutting the throats of competitors and their nights boffing the employees. In *Employees' Entrance,* the alluring monster runs a department store; in *Female,* the business is automobiles. The directors of these pictures (Roy Del Ruth and Michael Curtiz) probably didn't know much about department stores or Detroit; neither did the writers. But they undoubtedly had seen Jack Warner in action, which explains the films' irresistible combination of flamboyance *and* verisimilitude. On top of that, it's interesting to see how the boss in *Employees' Entrance* is played by Warren William (a missing link between John Barrymore and Liam Neeson), whereas the sharklike, sexually predatory star of *Female* is—Ruth Chatterton. Yes, the protagonist's gender makes a difference to the working-out of the plot; but no, the difference is not that big. At the end of *Female,* Chatterton retains control of her company and still gets her man. Maybe *he* believes her last-minute speech about retiring and having nine babies, but nobody in the audience will fall for it.

The lesson, for men and women both, is that it's a tough world out there. The Warner Bros. world allows for some slight indulgence in sentiment, and there's always room for humor; but the rewards in this not-entirely-fictional America go to whoever has the most energy, just as the audience's hearts go to the actor who most thoroughly burns up the screen. That spirit died when the production Code went into force, not only at Warner Bros. but throughout Hollywood. Before the code, at Columbia, Frank Capra was making pictures such as *The Miracle Woman,* in which Barbara Stanwyck, as a revival-meeting huckster, winds up going toe-to-toe with a lion. After the Code—nothing but blowhard populism and Jean Arthur acting winsome.

And today? Once again, we are witnessing a consolidation of power in the moving-picture business, this time in television (which has long been the dominant medium). Huge conglomerates are behaving like Ruth Chatterton and Warren William, trying to push one another out of an electronic oligopoly that doesn't quite exist. At the same time—no surprise—we hear a renewed sympathy for self-policing expressed by bosses such as Rupert Murdoch (proprietor of Twentieth Century-Fox and Fox Broadcasting and proud sponsor of media whiner Michael Medved). The old pattern holds—right down to its program of moral uplift and social control, redolent of the Progressive Era. This time, the most talked-about targets of the censors are black musicians. Their videos, my colleague Armond White has shown, come as close as anything you'll see today to the edgy, alert, free spirit of the old Warner Bros. movies.

When the picture business started censoring itself in 1909, there were gains as well as losses. Filmmakers started tackling classy material such as *Romeo and Juliet* and *Hiawatha*. They made hash out of the stories—and so the filmmakers also dreamed up more sophisticated narrative methods. We got the works of D. W. Griffith. The institution of the Code in 1934 has its upside, too—it spurred the ingenuity of Ernst Lubitsch and Preston Sturges.

When the moving-picture bosses give in to censorship this time, as they almost certainly will, we can expect a few comparable benefits—including, perhaps, rap videos with polyrhythums and polysyllables. Anything can happen. But I won't expect to see an art that's truly of my time—not until the next industry shake-up and the next longed-for rising of the rabble.

4

Einstein in Hollywood and Other Probabilities

•

March 28, 1934

The "Odyssey" of Disney

James Thurber

•

The writer, illustrator and humorist James Thurber was a staff writer at *The New Yorker* when he wrote this article. T. S. Eliot, reviewing Thurber's work, described it as "a form of humor which is also a way of saying something serious." Disney, as yet, has not taken up Thurber's excellent suggestion.

I HAVE NEVER particularly cared for the "Odyssey" of Homer. The edition we used in high school—I forget the editors' names, but let us call it Bwumba and Bwam's edition—was too small to hide a livelier book behind, and it was cold and gray in style and in content. All the amorous goings on of the story were judiciously left out. We pupils might, at that age, have taken a greater interest in T. E. Shaw's recent rendering, the twenty-eighth, by his count, in English; for bang-off in Book I the third sentence reads: "She craved him for her bed-mate: while he was longing for his house and wife." But there wasn't any such sentence in old Bwumba and Bwam. It was a pretty dull book to read. No matter how thin Mr. Shaw has sliced it, it is still, it seems to me, a pretty dull book to read.

The fact that the "Odyssey" is the "oldest book worth reading for its story and the first novel of modern Europe" makes it no more lively—to me, anyway—than does the turning of it into what Mr. Shaw's publishers call "vital, modern, poetic prose." There are too many dreary hours between this rosy-fingered dawn and that rosy-fingered dawn. The menaces in ancient Jeopardy were too far apart, the hazards prowled at too great distances, the gods maundered and were repetitious. Ulysses himself is not a hero to whom a young man's fancy turns in any season. The comedy of the "Odyssey" is thought by some students to be unintentional and by others to be intentional, and there must not be any uncertainty about comedy. But whatever may be said about it, the "Odyssey" will always keep bobbing up, in our years and in the years to follow them. The brazen entry into the United States of Mr. Joyce's *Ulysses* has most recently brought the "Odyssey" again into view; as the magazine *Time* points out to its surprised readers, "almost every detail of the 'Odyssey's' action can be found in disguised form in 'Ulysses.' " So, many a reader might naturally enough ask, what? So nothing—that is, nothing of real importance in so far as the "Odyssey" or "Ulysses" itself is concerned. The ancient story just happened to make a point of departure for Mr. Joyce. He might equally well have taken for a pattern Sherman's campaign in Georgia. Nevertheless, here is the old tale before us again not quite two years after Mr. Shaw went over the whole ground for the twenty-eighth time in English.

My purpose in this essay is no such meager and footless one as to suggest that it is high time for some other ancient tale to be brought up in place of the "Odyssey"—although, if urged, I would say the "Morte d'Arthur." My purpose is to put forward in all sincerity and all arrogance the conviction that the right "Odyssey" has yet to be done, and to name as the man to do it no less a genius than Walt Disney. A year or two ago Mr. Disney made a Silly Symphony, as he too lightly called this masterpiece, entitled "Neptune." Those who missed seeing it missed a lusty, fearsome, beautiful thing. Here was a god and here were sea adventures in the ancient manner as nobody else has given them to us. The thing cannot be described; it can be rendered into no English. But it was only a hint of what Mr. Disney, let loose in the "Odyssey," could make of it.

The dark magic of Circe's isle, the crossing between Scylla and Charybdis, the slaying of the suitors are just by the way; and so are dozens of other transfigurations, mythical feats of strength, and godly interventions. Mr. Disney could toss these away by the dozen and keep only a select few. For one: Ulysses and his men in the cave of the Cyclops. That would be that scene as I should like my daughter to know it first, when she gets ready for the "Odyssey," or when she is grimly made ready for it—I presume one still has to read it in school as I did, along with "The Talisman" and "Julius Caesar." Picture Mr. Disney's version of the overcoming of the giant, the escape tied to the sheep, the rage of Polyphemus as he hurls the tops of mountains at the fleeing ship of Ulysses and his men!

But I think my favorite scene will be (I'm sure Mr. Disney will do the "Odyssey" if we all ask him please) that scene wherein Menelaus and his followers wrestle with the wily Proteus on the island of Pharos. You know: the Old Man of the Sea comes up out of the dark waters at noon to count his droves of precious seals all stretched out on the beach. In his innocence of treachery or of any change in the daily routine, he unwittingly counts Menelaus and his three men, who are curled up among the seals trying to look as much like seals as possible. It doesn't come out, by the way, in any rendering I've read, and I've read two, just what the Old Man thought when he found he had four seals too many. Anyway, at the proper moment Menelaus and his followers jump upon Proteus. In the terrific struggle that ensues the Old Man changes into—here I follow the Shaw version—"a hairy lion: then a dragon: then a leopard: then a mighty boar. He became a film of water, and afterwards a high-branched tree."

How only for Walt Disney's hand and his peculiar medium was that battle fought! His "Odyssey" can be, I am sure, a far, far greater thing than even his epic of the three little pigs. Let's all write to him about it, or to Roosevelt.

AUGUST 6, 1938

EINSTEIN IN HOLLYWOOD

George S. Kaufman

•

Pulitzer Prize–winning playwright and theater director George S. Kaufman wrote frequently for *The Nation* in the 1930s. Many of his plays were filmed, including *Animal Crackers, Stage Door*, and *George Washington Slept Here*, and in 1936, with Morrie Ryskind, another *Nation* contributor, wrote *A Night at the Opera* for which MGM paid him the modest sum of $100,000. Apparently Kaufman hated working in Hollywood despite the huge amounts of money Sam Goldwyn waved in front of his face and stayed put in New York. He did, however, direct one feature in 1947, *The Senator was Indiscreet*, a political satire starring William Powell which James Agee described in *The Nation*, "Most of it would seem feeble in print or on stage, but because of the generally vapid state of the movies it seems quite bold and funny on the screen."

Warner Brothers have cabled Sigmund Freud, in London, asking him to come to Hollywood to assist in the preparation of the new Bette Davis picture, Dark Victory.

—NEWS ITEM.

SIGMUND FREUD HAD been in Hollywood about a year, and was engaged to marry Merle Oberon, when the studio got another great idea. Louella Parsons broke the story, and her papers gave it a two-column head:

WARNER BROS. TO FILM THEORY OF RELATIVITY

Prof. Einstein Signed to Write Screen Treatment of Own Story—Arrives in Hollywood Next Month

Einstein's arrival in Hollywood, of course, was the signal for a gay round of dinners and cocktail parties. The Basil Rathbones, who had given a party in Freud's honor to which everyone came as his favorite neurosis, gave one for Einstein in which the guests were got up as their favorite numbers. Needless to say, there were some pretty hot numbers.

The climax, however, was a dinner at the Trocadero, given by the film colony as a whole, at which Will H. Hays was the principal speaker. "The signing of Professor Einstein for pictures," said Mr. Hays, "is the greatest forward step that the industry has ever taken. American motion pictures appeal to people all over the world. I will be happy to okay Professor Einstein's contract just as soon as we get permission from Germany."

Next morning, on the Warner lot, Professor Einstein was assigned an office in the writers' building and a stenographer named Goldie. Promptly at twelve o'clock he was summoned to a conference. The producer received him with a flourish.

"Professor," he said, "allow me to introduce Sol Bergen and Al Jenkins, who are going to work with you on the picture. Now, I've been thinking this thing over, and we want this to be absolutely *your* picture. What you say goes. But of course we all want a hit, and I'm sure you're willing to play ball with us. Now, I've got some great news for you. I've decided to put Joan Blondell in it."

Sol Bergen let out a war whoop. "Gee, Boss, that's great. Her name alone will put it over."

"I want the Professor to have the best," said the producer, "because I'm sure he's going to give us a great picture. Now, Professor, here's the problem: how can we treat this theory of yours so as to keep it just as you wrote it—because this has got to be *your* picture—and still make it entertainment? Because first and foremost a motion picture has got to be entertainment. But of course we want your theory in it too."

"I'm not sure that I've got the Professor's theory exactly straight," said Al Jenkins. "Would you mind, Professor, giving me just a quick summary of it, in a sort of non-technical way?"

"I don't think we have to bother the Professor about that," said the producer. "I've been thinking it over, and I've got a great way to work it in. And here it is." He leaned back and looked at them. "The scene is a college where they *teach* this theory of the Professor's. Only it's a very *tough* theory, and there's never been a *girl* that's been able to understand it. Of course it's a co-ed college. And finally along comes a girl, attractive, of course, and says, '*I* am going to understand it.' "

"Blondell!" said Sol Bergen.

"Right!" said the producer. "So she pitches in and goes to work. She won't go to parties or dances or anything, and she wears horn-rimmed glasses, and the boys think she's a grind and hasn't got any sex appeal. Underneath, of course, she's a regular girl."

"There's got to be one guy in particular that falls for her," said Jenkins.

"Sure!" said the producer, "and I'll tell you who'd be great in the part. Wayne Morris. How's that, Professor? How'd you like to have Wayne Morris in your picture?"

"Let's make him the captain of the football team," said Bergen. "It'll give us a great finale."

"Fine!" said the producer. "Now, Blondell has got a girl friend that goes to college with her, only she's a different type. Flighty, and never does any studying, but a smart little kid when it comes to handling the boys. Knows 'em from A to Z. Now, there's a millionaire, an old grad that's just presented the college with a stadium, and his son is going to the college. Lots of money, and a racing car, and this kid sets her cap for him. We could have a crack-up on his way back from the roadhouse."

"Or else he could lead the college band," said Bergen. "That way you get your music in."

"Great! And we have a kid playing the girl that can handle a couple of numbers. Here's an idea, Professor. How about Warren and Dubin for the score? How would you like that, huh?"

"And how's this?" asked Jenkins. "She has another girl friend that sort of likes the older boys—with dough, see? And she sets out after the rich father."

"I've got it!" said the producer. "I've got the title! 'Gold Diggers at College.' Yes, sir, 'Gold Diggers at College,' by Albert Einstein, Sol Bergen, and Al Jenkins, based on the Theory of Relativity, by Albert Einstein. Professor, you've done a great picture!"

JULY 25, 1953

HOLLYWOOD DJINN

WITH A DASH OF BITTERS

Nelson Algren

•

Nelson Algren, the author of *Man With a Golden Arm*, *The Neon Wilderness*, and *Walk on the Wild Side*, was a frequent contributor to *The Nation* and regularly sent his clippings to an appreciative Simone de Beauvoir. During the period he wrote the following article, Algren was apparently undergoing post-marital depression and was pining for de Beauvoir and Paris (his passport application to travel there was turned down due to his former Communist associations).

"LIFE," PEER GYNT decided, "is a matter of passing safe and dryshod down the rushing stream of time." When, not long past, I discovered myself to be not only passing safe and snugly shod but downright lavishly set up, I felt, though there was no Anitra near, that I agreed with Gynt all the same.

The downright lavish setup was called exotically enough, the Garden of Allah. But the only exotic thing about it was that the rent was free. Free because I was being accorded the ten-day-Hollywood-hospitality treatment, which is prescribed on the assumption that half a grand allotted from a producer's budget toward the comfort and entertainment of any writer from the hinterland is certain—with the help of that Yogi sun—to arouse such slavering gratitude in the hinterlander that he'll sign for whatever sum the producer deigns to name. That if the latter doesn't deign to name a sum, said hinterlander will come to feel so guilty about the advantage he is taking that ultimately he'll sign anything, just to be able to fool other men in the eye once more, and the producer can fill in the figures.

"Don't worry about price," I had been comforted over long distance; "you can trust me. I *like* taking care of writers. I'd especially like to take care of you."

I was touched. Even from a distance the man liked me. I could not know that he was applying the first stage of the treatment, wherein the party of the first part can afford nothing less than affection for the party of the second. Even from a distance. For I had not yet felt that sun.

Driving from the station, the producer's flunky assured me that the apartment I was to occupy had been vacated by a name star only a few hours ago.

"You'll be sleeping in *his* bed tonight," he promised. How lucky, I thought dreamily, that the train had been late. Living in such a place, I gathered, rent or no rent, was in itself an event, one to make a trip from Chicago well worth any hinterlander's while.

But I didn't myself consider the place any particular great shakes until the flunky appointed the star's pantry with a case of good scotch, a case of fair rye, and a case of cheap bourbon, then lowered his lids to indicate we weren't even to talk about money. "Don't mention it," he reassured me the moment I stopped shaking.

I chose to mention it all the same. What I mentioned specifically was, "For God's sake where's the gin?" He must have thought I said "djinn," for in a moment there appeared—precisely as in a story by John Collier—a real Hollywood djinn, an honest-to-God Guru looking as if he'd slept in a bottle with the cork in it. He was fresh up from Malibu, and his toes stuck out of his sandals like amputated thumbs. With the rest of him stuffed hurriedly into something that looked like a cast-off tattersall of the late Laird Cregar's.

It was of course, the producer himself. And we were off to Romanoff's.

I dined with him unaccompanied that first evening, a bit self-conscious of my closed-in toes. The next, I took the liberty of inviting a new-found friend. The next I took two liberties, and by the time we made the Brown Derby we were blocking traffic. With my senses by now a-whirl with the wonder and hurry of it all, I had no time for the appropriate gratitude.

In the faint hope of fanning a spark in that direction, the djinn inquired softly, during the course of some feverish carryings on at the Beverly-Wilshire, and the wind whisking every which way, whether I'd care to meet Miss Sylvia Sidney.

The entire course of my life having been determined by the 1931 version of *An American Tragedy*, it seemed of no importance at the moment that my eyes weren't focusing. Indeed, I bowed so low from the waist, in the direction I judged the lady to be, that I had a bit of trouble straightening up. It wasn't till the following forenoon that I learned that Miss Sidney was in Brussels.

When I confronted Guru with his betrayal he didn't so much as redden. He was just hurt. The party to whom he'd introduced me, it turned out, was a highly effective writers' agent—so why did I always have to get so salty when somebody tried to do something for me? "We'll get along better when you begin trusting others," he counseled me like a father—and topped the bit off with the hollowest laugh I'd yet heard in the Land of Hollow Laughter.

Then he put a contract before me and confessed, "I'm not a business man at heart"—placing one hand over the heart to indicate precisely where he wasn't a business man—"I'm just another frustrated writer."

I looked around for the other frustrated writer. Seeing none, I placed Bernard Shaw's hand over my own valentine-shaped ticker and confessed in turn, "I'm not a writer at heart. I'm just another frustrated business man. And don't even trust myself."

Again in a matter of moments, but now more as in something by Howard Fast, I was evicted from the Garden of Allah where no Anitra was near. And presented with a bill, *per diem*, which Guru just happened to have in his hand. Itemizing, among other small comforts, one case of good scotch, one case of fair rye, and one case of cheap bourbon. Nothing was free after all.

"Is there any relationship between my refusal to sign and my eviction?" I had just time to inquire.

He never so much as cracked. "What kind of a business man do you think I am?" he demanded.

"What kind of a writer do you think *I* am?" was all I could think to reply.

Whereupon we locked, the terrible djinn in the open-toed shoes and I in my watertight ones, in a life-and-death struggle to determine, once and for all, who was the greater jerk.

I very nearly won. But I was scarcely a ranking contender and I was up against the champ. Smart money would have said he wouldn't even have to extend himself. Yet on the morning he phoned to say, "After all, I *do* like you," I really felt I had him.

"I like you too," I assured him.*

We had now reached that stage wherein the party of the second part can afford nothing less than affection for the party of the first. I needed to buy a house in Indiana as much as he needed to make a million dollars.

So though the very sight of me caused his features to be suffused by a disgust matched by nothing earthly save the revulsion in my own breast, we clung passionately each to each in a friendship based on the solid rock of utter loathing.

He showed up with a flute of Johnny Walker on one arm and a male friend on the other. By the stardust in the friend's eyes I immediately recognized an autograph hunter, one who inquired my name so shyly that I laughed lightly, "You got me." Whereupon he put a packet of blue papers bound with a red rubber band into my hand, and the only process-server in the world with stardust eyes excused himself.

Riffling hurriedly through the packet, I realized that Guru was charging me with everything from piracy on the high seas to defrauding an innkeeper. I was secretly relieved to note that he didn't have anything on me for the theft of the Stone of Scone. "You see," he explained with that smile which succeeded so wondrously in being at once abjectly shamefaced and haughtily self-satisfied, "every time I talked long distance to you I had a lawyer on the extension."

O Great Guru from Malibu, I knew then how much you liked me.

And as if struck abruptly by the injustice of everything, he strode to the middle of the room, literally beating his breast with one hand and still clutching the bottle fervidly with the other, to turn the awful accu-

*To illustrate further the operation of affection in The Land of Hollow Laughter: While I was waiting in the office of a medium-sized bigshot to be introduced to a king-size bigshot, the latter entered and went directly into conference with the medium-sized one without indicating awareness of a third party in the room except by a palm over his mouth and an occasional jerk of a thumb in the general direction of that party. Whispers, chuckles, thumb jerks, a final back slap—and he had left quite as unceremoniously as he had entered. Whereupon the medium-sized one assured me: "He *likes* you." And meant it.

sation upon me—"I'm a nice guy! *Why do you make me act like a jerk?*"

Overwhelmed by what I had done to this kindly soul, I followed him to the room as hysterical as he was: I don't know *why* I make you act like this, I broke down completely; "that isn't the real me! Back home people *like* me!"

Whereupon the party of the first part gently placed the bottle in the left hand of the party of the second and evermore gently, a pen that writes under water in his right.

That Yogi sun had done me in at last.

FEBRUARY 7, 1981

GOODBYE TO MR. STARK

Ring Lardner Jr.

•

Ring Lardner, Jr. worked as a reporter in New York before leaving for Hollywood to work with David O. Selznick where he allegedly advised Selznick against making *Gone With the Wind*. At 28 he won an Oscar for writing *Woman of the Year*, the first on-screen pairing of Spencer Tracy and Katherine Hepburn. An active member of the Hollywood branch of the Communist Party (the highest paid communists in the world outside of the Kremlin he quipped), he was one of the Hollywood Ten flung in front of the House Un-American Activities Committee and one of the first writers to be blacklisted. When asked, "Are you now or have you ever been a member of the Communist Party?" Lardner memorably replied "It depends on the circumstances. I could answer it, but if I did, I would hate myself in the morning." One of the lucky few to resume their careers, he won his second Oscar for *M*A*S*H* in 1970. His memoir, *I'd Hate Myself in the Morning*, has just been published by *Nation* Books.

I AM INDEBTED to Ray Stark for giving me the final push into retirement from screenwriting after forty-five years. When he telephoned me last May, I was already planning to claim my Social Security benefit and a Writers Guild pension as of my 65th birthday in August, and to start work on a novel. Stark, one of Hollywood's richest and most powerful executives, suggested that I do one last screenplay: a new version of *Pal*

Joey, the 1940 Broadway musical, with Al Pacino as star and Herbert Ross as director. I would be free, he told me, to start afresh with the original John O'Hara stories, but we would have the benefit not only of the superb score but also of any other Rodgers and Hart number that suited our needs. "And in my setup," he promised, "you won't have to talk to any studio. You won't even have to talk to me. Just to Herb Ross."

Now, one of my reasons for getting out of movies was a run of unproduced screenplays. This has always been an occupational hazard, but several aborted projects in a row had left me more frustrated than usual. In this context it was a positive factor that both Stark and Ross had been having a lot of commercial success lately, especially as producer and director of a series of Neil Simon films. How much more satisfying to quit the scene with a hit in the can than a script on the shelf. I agreed to meet with Ross in New York to see if our attitudes toward the material were congenial.

That first discussion was encouraging enough for me to say I would give another week's thought to the project. Stark called during that period to say how heartened he had been by Ross's report of our meeting and how much they both hoped I would undertake the assignment. My next conversation with Ross, who had proceeded to California, was on the phone. Again we felt we were making progress, but I at least was still not ready to make a commitment. After another few days, however, I had some more specific ideas to propose, and he responded to them with so much enthusiasm that I said I would be willing to take the job. He said it only remained for terms to be agreed upon between Stark and my agent, and Stark confirmed this in a call just before I left for Italy on a ten-day vacation. By the time I returned, he predicted, there would be a contract for me to sign.

That was the last I ever heard from either of them. No proposal was made to the agent; instead, he was told they needed a week to clear up "a technicality" concerning the rights to the material. That was the last word he ever had on the matter.

I cannot reveal to you what caused the sudden switch in this case because I don't have a clue myself. I can only report that it belongs to a class of phenomena that no longer surprise me after more than four decades. I don't even know whether Stark controlled the rights to *Pal Joey* when he approached me about it. If he didn't it was a serious breach of ethics to enlist my time and effort for two weeks without so advising me, and in any case it was a breach of common courtesy not to explain the technicality directly to me when it arose.

I am not so ambitious, however, as to want to reform Stark's character or his manners. What I am concerned with is the familiar blend of flattery and contempt with which writers have always been treated in the American motion picture business.

I was barely 22 years old when I turned in the first screenplay I had written without a collaborator. I could hardly wait for the producer's reaction, but I wasn't ready to hear it before he even opened the script. "I'm sending this right over to Wald and Macaulay," he said, referring to a well-paid writing team on the lot. "I gave it to you so you could break ground for them while they were finishing another job." It was hard to believe he was going to pass it on without reading a word, but that is just what he did. And on what grounds could I object? I had been paid for my work, almost $1,000, as I remember it.

It is the fact rather than the amount of payment that counts. Three years later Michael Kanin and I were paid $100,000, the highest price to that date for an original screenplay. We also received an Academy Award for the script, but in a transmutation so prodigious it could only be achieved by contract, Metro-Goldwyn-Mayer "became" the author of the work. If anyone remains skeptical about this process, let him take note that when a musical based on that 1942 movie, *Woman of the Year*, is produced on Broadway this spring, MGM, not we, will be collecting authors' royalties.

My career in Hollywood was divided into two parts by a hiatus of fifteen years during which my name was barred from the screen and my presence from the studios. By coincidence it was in those blacklist years that a basic change took place in control over the screenplay. In the old days a writer was subject to replacement for no more substantial reason than "getting a fresh viewpoint." Changing writers was about as significant to Irving Thalberg and David Selznick as sending in an alternate wide receiver with the next play is to a modern football coach. But if yours happened to be the final script approved by the man in charge, you knew no one else had the authority to make changes from then on.

My first experience with the new system came when another blacklisted writer, Ian McLellan Hunter, and I wrote a screenplay for a British company under a pseudonym. After meeting with the producers and the director on the Caribbean location, we made some changes to conform to what we found there. Just before filming began we were startled to receive a "final shooting script" that was quite a drastic rewrite of ours, with the added defect of being, in our opinion, decidedly inferior. Sidney Poitier told me later that he and John Cassavetes, who had agreed to do the picture, *Virgin Island*, after reading our script, had shared our surprise and disappointment in the new one. The producers' only response to our protest was that standard British practice entitled the director to final revision after the writer was through.

By the time I was able to write under my own name again in the 1960s, this inflation of the director's authority was already taking hold in Hollywood although the time was still years off when one of them could single-handedly change the whole purpose and thrust of a picture in mid-production, or spend twice his authorized budget without any effective restraint.

The whole *auteur* theory, as imported from France in the late 1950s, was actually quite incongruous with an American system in which the director usually appeared on the scene after the second or third draft of the script. It is true, nonetheless, that the most impressive film-making talent of the last twenty years has emerged among the younger directors who see themselves as creators as well as interpreters. Unfortunately, their egos have generally developed faster than their self-critical faculties, and their best efforts have been followed by such anticlimaxes as *New York, New York, 1941, Heaven's Gate, Images, At Long Last, Love, Buffalo Bill* and the apocalyptic part of *Apocalypse Now*.

I had the good luck to come in contact with one of the most original of these new talents when Robert Altman undertook my screenplay of *M*A*S*H* after its rejection by sixteen other directors in a row. In my partisan judgment, he discarded values that could have made it a better movie, but he added so many more that I remain in his debt for my share of the acclaim, including my second Oscar in 1970.

Three years and five unproduced screenplays later, I tried to cheer up my agent, a mercurial Sicilian, for our lack of success in advancing my career. "George," I said, "you know the old Hollywood saying: 'You're only as good as your last picture.' Well, what better strategy could we think up than keeping *M*A*S*H* as my last picture?"

In reality, though, it hurt—all that construction and action and dialogue that was not being recorded on film. One of the times I can recall hurting most was when a man named Michael Ritchie refused to speak to me. I had done, for David Merrick, a couple of drafts of an adaptation of the book *Semi-Tough* by Dan Jenkins. Merrick liked my script; Jenkins liked it and, most significant of all, United Artists liked it enough to say they were taking the crucial step from "developing the property" to making it as a starring vehicle for Burt Reynolds.

The one missing element was a director, and this was supplied in the person of Ritchie, who, it turned out, had one reservation. Even after I had conveyed to him indirectly my willingness to consider a major revision, he said he didn't care to talk to the writer of the script; he wanted to talk to a new writer. Merrick and the U.A. hierarchy at the time regarded this demand as arbitrary but not excessive. They displayed their adaptability by transferring their entrepreneurial endorsement from the book and screenplay they had bought to whatever Ritchie and his new writer might devise to take its place. What they had bought was a satirical comedy about professional football; what Ritchie felt like making that season—and did—was a satirical comedy about consciousness-raising groups. (The new writer was my friend Walter Bernstein, who called me when he was offered the job and received my dispensation and blessing, just as I would have had his in a reversal of the situation.)

So many factors over which he has no control contribute to the eventual fate of a screenwriter's work that he can ease the pain by persuading himself he has no control at all—that it really doesn't matter how hard he tries. To fortify himself against this delusion, he has to remember that while good scripts have been turned into bad films, no good film was ever made from a poor script.

Another temptation is to fantasize that his unshot scripts would have become more original and provocative movies than the ones that ran the gauntlet to theatrical exhibition. A sober review of the files exposes this, too, in my own case at least, to be a piece of self-delusion. Among the unproduced scripts are a sizable number that were poor ideas to begin with, undertaken for misguided or unworthy motives, including the classic cop-out of the indentured artist: "If they're dumb enough to pay all that money for this crap, who am I to object?" In the end, "my best scripts are on the shelf" has to be amended to "my best and worst scripts are on the shelf."

There still remain just enough of the former, however, to put together a small festival of respectable unshot films. The picture that opens this festival was definitely ahead of its time. It concerned the disease of alcoholism and its ravaging effects on a woman played by Carole Lombard. I can see no one else in the role because it was Carole who took the story from one studio to another, to be told by all of them that the subject was unacceptable. Five years later, Charles Brackett and Billy Wilder made *The Lost Weekend*.

Next is a historical epic from 1943, produced and directed by Otto Preminger and dealing with the Nazi takeover as seen by the daughter (Martha Dodd) of Franklin Roosevelt's ambassador to Germany. Even as we were preparing that script, we knew its fate depended on the box office results of one starring Alexander Knox as our twenty-eighth President. *Wilson*, Darryl Zanuck had declared, was his favorite project, but if it failed he would have to send history back to the printed page.

The most lively and enduring of all my defunct creations was an original comedy written that same year called *The Great Indoors*. I sold it the year I went to prison as one of the Hollywood Ten to an enterprising producer named Bob Roberts, whose payments went for family support while I was away. Then he was blacklisted and moved to London, where he has let few years go by in the last thirty without a statement of his intention to produce *The Great Indoors*.

From the year 1945 comes the first Hollywood movie to deal with the subject of anti-Semitism, a screenplay based on Gwethalyn Graham's novel *Earth and High Heaven*. My adaptation provoked a memorable reaction from its first reader, the Samuel Goldwyn of life and legend: "Lardner, you have defrauded and betrayed me!" Defrauded, he explained, by writing scenes that were more explicitly on the theme than they had seemed to be when I described them in synopsis. "And one of the reasons I hired you, just one, was the fact that you're a gentile. You have betrayed me by writing like a Jew." (That same year, William Cagney, brother of James and head of the family production company, complained about my only Western screenplay: "Lardner treated the Indians like a race of oppressed Jews.")

Skipping to the decade just past, I did an adaptation of an entertaining and cogent novel by Tom McHale called *Farragan's Retreat*. A reactionary family of Roman Catholics in Philadelphia assigns one of its members to liquidate his own son, who has disgraced them all by fleeing to Montreal instead of taking his patriotic place with our troops in Vietnam. Paramount Pictures cheerfully paid for the book and the script of this black comedy, then abruptly decided Vietnam might become a forgotten issue during the year it would take to get the picture out. Actually, just fourteen months later, Nixon and Kissinger were keeping the issue fresh with their Christmas bombing.

Another comedy was *Cedarhurst Alley*, based on a novel by Denison Hatch. It is the story of a family, plagued by noise and vibration, that raises a barrage balloon over their house and into a main approach corridor to Kennedy Airport; it was a fine setting for a lone-individual-versus-the-system movie. But what makes it especially memorable to me now is how urgently I felt the obligation to get that script ready for shooting. When asked to write the pilot episode for the proposed

*M*A*S*H* television series, with a piece of the action for however long that speculative venture might last, I had to say no because I couldn't do it without losing some of my concentration on *Cedarhurst Alley*.

Completing the festival week is an original screenplay, *The Volunteers*, about the Americans in the Spanish Civil War. The main character is a correspondent who went to Spain as my brother Jim did in 1938 to cover the war, joined the Abraham Lincoln Brigade in the last terrible months and was killed, as Jim was, the night before the Internationals were withdrawn. On this one, Hannah Weinstein, the producer who originated the project, and I ran into the problem that the top jobs in Hollywood these days are the least secure ones. The head of production at Columbia Pictures, who liked the idea and contracted with us for the script, had been replaced, when we returned with a first draft, by a head of production who announced for starters that he hated the idea. That meant Hannah had to look elsewhere for financing. She's still looking, but you don't find investors readily for an expensive production with debatable box office appeal.

They all still sound like good ideas for pictures, but I guess I have to admit that the great appeal of every one of these films is not so much the strength of the original concept as the brilliant fidelity of its execution. In what other festival has each entry been photographed with faultless taste, accented with an unassuming yet telling musical score, directed with imaginative respect and played up to the hilt and not an inch beyond by inspired and selfless actors?

In the real world, unfortunately, the screenwriter faces the constant, inescapable truth that nothing ever quite comes out the way it was conceived. He can be rewritten by one of his colleagues, or by a director, producer, actor or cutter, or in a final affront called editing for television. Occasionally, a marvelous moment will emerge on film that could only have come from such promiscuous collaboration. But the results far more often fall somewhere short of the intention. And the most binding reality of all is the finality of those results.

Books have been published decades after they were originally written; a current Broadway hit, *Morning's at Seven*, was a failure when it was first produced forty years ago. Mature writers have thought anew about an early novel, then revised and republished it. It is a regular part of an out-of-town tryout of a play for the playwright to test various versions of a scene before a paid audience. A publisher, a magazine editor, a theatrical producer, may all make suggestions to a writer, but it is the writer who decides whether to change his work or find another sponsor.

For the screenwriter, 99 percent of the time, there is no control over the transition from concept to frames of exposed film, and once that transition has been made, no previous versions retains any significant reality. How can I match my paper draft of a scene against what is now implanted on celluloid? Even if I could spend millions to shoot my rejected script, how could I put together enough of the same components to make a valid comparison with the version they released?

I recall the only time I ever thought I won an argument with Darryl Zanuck. We were discussing (quite soberly; all such discussions seem important at the time) his proposal to cut from the script of *Forever Amber* a scene that I felt was essential to the leading character's motivation. Although motivation scenes were a prime Zanuck target (he preferred to strip down to pure action), he finally conceded that I might have a point and instructed Otto Preminger, the director, to go ahead and shoot the scene. A couple of months later we sat in a projection room watching a rough assembly of the picture, and the scene in question, which I never did see on film, was now out. Zanuck directed a comment at me over his shoulder: "Humoring you on that one cost us $20,000."

That closed the subject for good, and properly so. If I had pointed out that I found the new transition confusing, I would have been ignoring the several facts he had incorporated into that one short statement. It was a fact that I had wanted to retain the scene; it was a fact that he had made the irrevocable decision to eliminate it; therefore, it was equally a fact that I had made a mistake costing the studio $20,000.

If I added up the various drafts of the scripts in my fantasy festival and multiplied that by four to approximate the total number of unshot screenplays I have written since 1936, and then added all the preliminary drafts and unused versions of scenes in the scripts that did get produced, I would be talking about tens of thousands of pages filled with characters and scenes, dialogue and description that served little or no function in the past and are not likely to be put to any use in the future.

I am not saying by any means that I regard all that as wasted effort. For a young writer every discarded page is a step in mastering his craft. At my age, however, it is natural to think more about immediate results and to return to a medium in which I can hope to expend my energy more frugally.

NOVEMBER 4, 1996

THE MOVIES AND ME

Michael Moore

•

Michael Moore is the author of the best-selling *Downsize This*! and the director of *Roger and Me, Canadian Bacon*, and *The Big One*. He was the host and producer of two TV series, *Michael Moore's TV Nation* and *The Awful Truth*.

AS I WRITE this I am sitting in the Mall of America in Minneapolis, No. 27 on my forty-seven city tour across the country on behalf of my first book, *Downsize This! Random Threats From an Unarmed American*. In a couple of hours I will speak to another gathering of fellow citizens who are anxious to tell me about how their American Dream has gone up in smoke. But as I sit at the table afterward signing my book, the question I will be asked the most is, "How the hell did *THEY* ever let *YOU* in the movies or on TV?" This week I would like to share with you my rules for success in the movies.

1. *If you're going to attack a big bad corporation in your film, it will help to have another big bad corporation in your corner*. I figured the only way to protect *Roger & Me*, a satirical documentary about how General Motors destroyed my hometown, Flint, Michigan, was to have Time Warner distribute it. The strategy worked. The people at Warner Bros. defended the film against twenty lawsuits and a full-scale disinformation campaign. G.M threatened to cancel its

advertising on any station that carried my appearance on *Donahue*.

Then, on the evening of January 16, 1990, I was sitting in my dressing room at NBC in Burbank waiting to go on *The Tonight Show*. (Unbeknownst to me, across town in Los Angeles someone was distributing G.M's "*Roger & Me* truth packet" at a closed meeting of the Academy Award nominating committee for Best Documentary.) Suddenly Jay Leno walked into the room carrying a manila envelope and looking a little peeved. He emptied the contents of the envelope, which contained articles I had written for my paper, *The Flint Voice*, an article I had written for *The Nation*, a piece from *In These Times* and a few other "documents." Anything sounding remotely pinko in these clippings was highlighted in, appropriately, Day-Glo pink.

"A guy who said he was responsible for G.M. in Southern California stopped by here today to try and convince us not to have you on the show and gave me this," Jay said, referring to the packet, which also included a picture of me from the mid-seventies—WITH LONG HAIR! Jay was amused at this interference and said we should "go out there and try to mention Roger's name at least a dozen times!" I agreed and we had a lot of fun ridiculing G.M. for a full ten minutes on network television.

General Motors responded by pulling its ads from *Time* for nearly a month, costing Time Warner millions of dollars; Warner Bros, mean while had announced it was reserving a seat for Roger Smith in every theater where *Roger & Me* played. And, to drive home the point it had life-sized cardboard cutouts of Smith made and placed in an empty seat in each of those theaters. I'm still not sure why Warner did this. Maybe one of its executives had a bad experience with Mr. Goodwrench after his Corvette caught on fire.

2. If you want to make a movie attacking the actions of the U.S. government, get a big name to star in it.

Back in 1991, I was so appalled at how quickly the country got behind President Bush when he announced that Iraq was the new "evil empire" that I wrote a screenplay based on the premise that the President could go on TV and pick any country—even Canada—and get everyone whipped into a big enough frenzy that we'd send our kids off to fight them. This became the movie *Canadian Bacon*, which thirty-nine production companies and studios turned down. Then John Candy said he wanted to be in it and suddenly the film got a green light from PolyGram—one of the thirty-nine companies that had said the script was "too political"! PolyGram thought John Candy would get me to soften the script, but just the opposite happened. John, who had started out on the Canadian satire show *SCTV*, told me he wanted to do something with a political edge.

Unfortunately, John died two months after the completion of filming, and within hours the vultures from Hollywood descended on me, first trying to find out if they were due any "insurance money" because of John's death, and then trying to gut the film. After months of fights with the studio in the editing room—without my friend John to protect me from "the suits"—I succeeded in editing the film the way I wanted it. I then slipped a print to the Sundance Film Festival. The selection committee loved it and wanted to show it in one of their "gala" evening presentations. But PolyGram refused to allow *Canadian Bacon* to be shown, and over lunch at a trendy Beverly Hills bistro (two days after the 1994 Congressional elections), one of their P.R. people informed me they were not sure if they were going to release the film at all.

"The mood of the country has shifted to the right and this film just doesn't fit in with where the public is at these days," he told me. I couldn't believe what I was hearing. To prove their point, they tested the film in front of an all-white audience near, of all places, Simi Valley, California (site of the infamous Rodney King verdict and the Ronald Reagan Presidential Library). Guess what? THE AUDIENCE HATED IT!

PolyGram showed the film in two cities for three weeks (in order to claim a "theatrical release" and thus be able to charge more for home-video), then dumped it. The company made only 40,000 videos, or about one per store nationwide. That was a major underestimation. One week before the video release of *Canadian Bacon*, PolyGram had received more than 100,000 orders. The video factory worked overtime for the next seven days to meet the demand. The film has been one of the most rented videos in the country, with more than 15 million people seeing it this year.

So the country hadn't turned to the right. The only wrong turn was the one made by PolyGram, a company owned by Philips of the Netherlands, makers of weapons and, by honest coincidence, one of the Corporate Crooks listed in *Downsize This!*

I'm sure John Candy is getting a kick out this somewhere.

5

Hollywood Goes to War

Fascism and World War Two

•

MAY 29, 1935

HOLLYWOOD PLAYS WITH FASCISM

Carey McWilliams

•

As a lawyer, journalist and historian, "for most of the twentieth century, whenever and wherever social justice flourished, Carey McWilliams was there," reads the dust wrapper of *The Education of Carey McWilliams*. McWilliams was *The Nation*'s editor from 1955 to 1975 though he joined the New York office in 1952 when he edited its special civil liberties issue, "How Free is Free?" and became a de facto editor soon after that. Before this he had been *The Nation*'s California correspondent. During this time he authored such classics as *California: The Great Exception* (which University of California reprinted in 1999 with a new introduction by Lewis Lapham), *Southern California: An Island on the Land, Factories in the Field, Ill fares the land*, and *Brothers Under the Skin*, that have influenced the likes of Cesar Chavez, Joan Didion, and Mike Davis. McWilliams was intimately familiar with Hollywood and often wrote about it. He also represented a group of rank and file studio workers in a suit against the then mobbed-up International Alliance of Theatrical and Stage Employees and in 1936 he spoke, along with actor Lionel Stander, and the writers Lewis Browne and Manchester Boddy, at the first meeting of The Hollywood Women's Club in support of the Spanish Republic. The article below which linked Gary Cooper with the antics of such Hitler fanciers as the Hollywood Hussars obviously had its effect because a month later McWilliams wrote "I have been advised by Gary Cooper that he has withdrawn from that organization. Mr. Cooper told me that the character of the Hollywood Hussars was grossly misrepresented to him at the time he consented to be "founder."

HOLLYWOOD HAS SUDDENLY become a fascist recruiting station. No one knows precisely how it happened or who began it or what it means, but the evidence of flamboyant militarism is incontrovertible: flags decorate the night clubs, bugles trumpet from the lodge halls, and the roll of drums is audible along the boulevards. Since the first of the year the Light Horse Cavalry, the Hollywood Hussars, and other saber-rattling gangs have been conducting intensive recruiting campaigns. Almost any actor one meets in Hollywood nowadays is apt to be a clandestine major or a night-time once-a-week colonel. Such brilliant militarists as Gary Cooper, distinguished as a movie-lot Bengal Lancer, and Victor McLaglen, whose military prowess is known in all movie places, and George Brent, whose cinematographic gallantry is notorious on the sets, have permitted their names to be used as sponsors for fascist groups in Hollywood. Such have been the success and popularity of these groups that other stars will unquestionably join in the business of promoting fascism.

Within a short period of time Messrs. Copper, McLaglen, and Brent have promoted three successful fascist units: the Hollywood Hussars, the Light Horse Cavalry, and the California Esquadrille. When Mr. McLaglen pioneered in this business, it was the fashion to wisecrack about his light horsemen. But now that three such-groups have been definitely established as profitably operated, permanently organized armed forces, it is time that the joke was given its proper name. To be sure, there is nothing alarming about the spectacle of slapstick Hitlers parading about Hollywood in dress uniforms. But when these warriors-in-make-up are financed by powerful interests, backed by civic organizations, blessed by the local ministry, and drilled by army officers, their burlesque of fascism warrants careful consideration.

The first of these organizations in the field was Mr. McLaglen's Light Horse Cavalry Troop. Originally restricted to Canadian and British ex-service men, the troop has suddenly developed an amazing concern over American politics. The Light Horsemen, it seems, are to "save America." Pictures of these dashing Hollywood cavalrymen in their weekly drills and assemblies have appeared frequently in the newspapers, and the society columns have carried items about their numerous social festivities. From the start the Light Horse unit was a successful business venture. As a well-trained cavalry unit, it has been rented to motion-picture studios, and its various athletic teams regularly compete with professional and semi-professional groups. Quite recently Mr. McLaglen began the construction of a $20,000 stadium in Los Angeles with an auditorium of 700 seats, and with recreation and dressing-rooms in the basement. This clubhouse is designed "for the use of members of a new club which McLaglen has organized to promote Americanism, membership in which already numbers about 1,000." The "new club" is really an amplification of the original Light Horse unit. Mr. McLaglen was recently quoted in the Los Angeles "*Post-Record* to the effect that the new unit has offered its services to city, state, and federal authorities at any time it might be needed." In their public meetings the Light Horsemen listen to speakers who specialize in the fanciest variety of red-baiting.

But McLaglen's organization, successful though it is, is not in the same category with the Hollywood Hussars. Organized early in March, Mr. Cooper's little army has created a great furor. The advertising columns of the Los Angeles *Times* and *Examiner* carry full-column recruiting notices for the Hussars. The Hussars, it seems, were founded by Mr. Cooper to "uphold and protect the principles and ideals of true Americanism"; they have "pledged themselves to make their regiment the model to inspire other communities to organize similar bodies of trained Americans throughout the nation.

Membership in the Hussars is limited to "American citizens of excellent character and of social and financial standing, who are physically fit, not under five feet seven inches in height, and between the ages of eighteen and forty-five." In order to become "a soldier and a gentleman," the recruit must pay an initiation fee of $5 ($20 if he wants to be a charter member), dues of $5 monthly (payable in advance), rent a horse for $1 per drill, and purchase a nifty service uniform at $39.75. Incidentally, the uniforms were specially designed for the Hussars by Montagu Love. The shirt of the "service or field" uniform is of "yellow gabardine, the breeches of dark blue elastic material trimmed with broad yellow stripes, similar to those used by the United States cavalry of post-Civil War days." The full-dress uniforms are of blue, yellow, and white, "a composite of those used by the original Hungarian Hussars, the English Hussars, and the German Uhlans."

At present Troops A, B, C, and D of the Hussars are being enrolled. When organized, the units will have a medical and first-aid detachment, a signal-communications troop, a signal photographic section, a motor-cycle detachment, a military police and intelligence detachment, and buglers and a mounted band. The recruiting slogans are fetching: "A military-social organization with good fellowship and community spirit"; "Excellent social opportunities"; "Strictly disciplined! Smartly drilled! Colorfully uniformed!" The recruiting notice stresses that "we particularly desire young men of accredited military academies, universities, schools, ROTC and ORC." The troops drill one night a week and are trained by veteran officers.

The Hussars have an imposing array of officers. Gary Cooper, the Bengal Lancer, is founder-sponsor. Colonel Arthur Guy Empey ("Over the Top" Empey) is commanding officer. There are three regimental captain-chaplains: Father George G. Fox, a Jesuit whose boasted distinction it is to have instructed Edmund Lowe, the movie star, at Santa Clara University; the Reverend Neal Dodd, popular pastor of St. Mary of Angles, Hollywood; and, oddly enough, Rabbi Isadore Isaacson, of Temple of Israel, Hollywood. (Incidentally, when I inquired of "Regimental Headquarters" whether Jews were eligible for membership, I could not get a definite answer.) On the regimental staff are four advisory colonels, all retired United States army officers; ten majors, many of whom are former army officers; fourteen captains, seven of whom are former army officers; ten first lieutenants; and three second lieutenants, one an ex-marine, one an Austrian of the Seventh Uhlan Regiment, and one—for glamour—a former member of the Royal Northwest Mounted Police.

The organization reaches deep into local politics. Judge Marshall F. McComb, of the Superior Court of Los Angeles County, is listed as a major (he was formerly of counsel for the Los Angeles *Examiner* and was backed for judicial appointment by William Randolph Hearst); and Judge Joseph Sproul of the local Superior Court, prominent as an officer in the marine reserve corps, appears likewise as a major. Both of these men, of course, have occasion to pass upon the rights of workers and organizers charged with violating California's numerous laws for the maintenance of the status quo. Sheriff Eugene W. Biscailuz is listed as an officer. "Major" James E. Davis is none other than the notorious "Jim" Davis, chief of police, who recently confessed that the tear-gas bombs his policemen hurled at the striking employees of the Los Angeles Railway Company were the gift of that corporation to the police. Davis, according to the announcement, is "an internationally recognized pistol shot and instructor, who is assisted by his competent staff," that is, the Los Angeles red squad.

The third group, George Brent's California Esquadrille, is similarly organized. Members are recruited; they pay an initiation fee and get a uniform; they pay for flying instructions; and finally they are commissioned as air pilots and do formation flying. It is relatively inconspicuous. The slogan reads, "if you want to be a birdman, you can be a Brent one at a nominal cost."

Why, it may be asked, should Hollywood suddenly become so militaristic? It seems that Mr. Hearst was deeply impressed with Victor McLaglen's success in organizing the Light Horse unit, Mr. Hearst then induced Gary Cooper to try his hand at the game, promising liberal backing and support. It will be recalled that Mr. Cooper is friendly with the Hearst ménage, having recently appeared as leading man for one of Hollywood's most charming actresses. Mr. Hearst, so the story goes, is quite alarmed over the growth of "radicalism" in the motion-picture industry. Not only has Hollywood had labor trouble in the past, but such stars as James Cagney and Dolores Del Rio have been known to contribute to liberal causes—an unpardonable offense. The Screen Writers' Guild, a fairly strong organization, has shown liberal tendencies. Then, too, the scenario and reading departments are suspected of various heresies. The primary purpose of these fascist units in the industry was therefore to counteract the agitation and influence of the liberal groups.

But the Hussars and their allies have other uses. They are designed to advertise the charms of fascist organization to the American public. Through the publicity medium of the industry, the most powerful propaganda machine in America, these gaudy units sponsored by popular and well-known stars can be advertised to millions of Americans as the latest and snappiest fascist models. It is even rumored that a motion picture will be made, presenting the Hollywood Hussars in the act of suppressing a radical uprising in California. Also these groups have all volunteered their services to the authorities "in case of trouble." They constitute, in other words, a threat and a warning. Nor should the business aspects be overlooked: these units serve to advertise the stars, to make money for the actual promoters, to attract commercial careerists— that is, dentists, lawyers, insurance salesmen, and others—in quest of valuable "contacts." Moreover, they have the added value to their sponsors of being self-supporting. And there can be little question of the identity of the forces that are giving the Hussars their moral support. The meetings of the organization are held in the Hollywood Chamber of Commerce.

To observe the antics of the Hussars is amusing; the very idea of such an organization in Hollywood is down-right funny. But a moment's reflection is sufficient to dispel the illusion of mirth. This is clowning, but it is crazy clowning; this is silliness, but it is organized silliness; this is foolishness, but it is armed foolishness. Will America laugh or step up to shake hands with Colonel Cooper?

MARCH 4, 1936

No Soap-Boxes in Hollywood

Morrie Ryskind

•

Playwright and screenwriter Morrie Ryskind often wrote for *The Nation* during this period. He was also George Kaufman's co-writer on a number of successful Broadway comedies and the Marx Brothers classic *A Night At The Opera*, as well as a screenwriter in his own right. Incidentally Ryskind's concluding prophecy—"Hollywood is so unpolitically minded that the boss doesn't give a damn what you think as long as you do your work. If Irving Thalberg ever fires Groucho Marx, it won't be because Groucho subscribes to *The Nation*, but because the next picture isn't a money-maker."—proved to be horribly wrong and Ryskind himself eventually drifted to the political right.

Hollywood, February 21

THERE ARE TWO fair indictments to be lodged against Hollywood: one is, to use the industry's favorite adjective, its colossal ignorance of current political happenings; the other is the shocking cowardice to be found in high places. What I hope to do in this article is explain the first of these, for which there is a reason; and to argue against the second, for which there is no reason at all.

Let me start by telling you there are no soap-boxes in Hollywood. That is a significant and dismaying fact to a born New Yorker, whose first wails do not interrupt the political argument against the doctor who is delivering him and the attending nurse; who grows up watching the crowd heckling the Socialist speaker on the corner; who, in his maturer years, can get a hot discussion on the merits of Tammany from his lawyer, his broker, his barber, and his wife. I do not contend, mind you, that any of this talk has any intrinsic merit, but I do contend that it is better than no talk at all.

Not—heaven knows!—that you can't get talk in Hollywood. Everybody can tell you what *Mutiny on the Bounty* did in its third week in New York; and anybody can tell you who is to be the new head of Paramount now that Lubitsch is out; further, if you're interested, everybody has a good tip on the races. Well, not a good tip exactly, but a tip. But, very definitely, Hollywood is not politically minded. Of current events it knows practically nothing. It knows that the Prince of Wales is now Edward VIII, and that Italy and Ethiopia are at war; that, however, about sums it up. Mention the California criminal syndication act, the pending Tydings-McCormack disaffection bill, or the Kramer sedition bill (the latter introduced by California's own contribution to Washington), and you will get but a blank look. Not even a dirty look—just plain blank. Once—this was before I had learned—I mentioned the Scottsboro case to my hostess, and she wanted to know who was playing in it.

Now there's an explanation for this, and it isn't the old, convenient bromide that Hollywood is made up of morons. I have met directors, writers, stars, supervisors, producers, and even song writers whose intelligence is not to be questioned. But they're in Hollywood. And Hollywood is essentially a summer resort—an all-year summer resort.

You know what happens in a summer resort. People check their thinking caps and go in for some fun. They relax. Everybody relaxes—even strict Marxists, I am reliably informed, relax at summer resorts. Walter Lippmann relaxes. The editors of *The Nation* relax—and a pretty sight it is, too, they tell me. Even Morris Ernst relaxes. If such people can't help relaxing, how can Hollywood avoid succumbing to its climate? Especially when it is compelled, against nature, to produce an enormous number of pictures for the public? From nine to five, writers write against time, directors direct against time, producers produce against budgets. If you're a writer under contract to turn out six scripts a year, or a director who gets on the set at eight in the morning, or a producer who has to worry about six pictures at once, you do not at the end of the working day rush to find out how the ship of state is faring. You go home and take a shower, you have a cocktail and eat your dinner, and you are ready for an evening of intensive relaxation.

The only chance you would have to get any news would be from the newspapers. But the newspapers here are small-time, summer-resort newspapers. There are three days that are important—the two Hearst papers and the Los Angeles *Times*. I can describe their editorial policies only by telling you that, compared to them, the New York *Herald Tribune* is edited by Mike Gold, and the New York *Sun* by John Strachey. I find them invaluable then I decide to look at the stock market. For my daily news I get, three days late, the New York *Times* and *Herald Tribune*.

So, ladies and gentlemen of the jury, I hope I have made it clear to you why Hollywood is not politically minded.

I had another point. About the people who do read the news and therefore know what's going on. Ever so many of them will discuss things with you and then add, "Of course, you won't quote me." If you ask them to serve on a committee for a cause they profess to be devoutly interested in, they hastily beg off. They are afraid.

I am constantly amazed that people earning between $25,000 and $100,000 yearly can be afraid. I can understand the poor devil with just enough each day to pay for his meals and his roof being afraid for his job. The thing I cannot understand is cringing and cowardice from people who have enough and more than enough; but if ever I met a wage slave, it was not in the lodging-houses of the poorly paid but in the luxurious palaces of Beverly Hills.

And the pity of it is that their fear is so unnecessary. They are not only cowardly but stupid in their fear of a fascism that doesn't exist. Hollywood is so unpolitically mined that the boss doesn't give a damn what you think as long as you do your work. If Irving Thalberg ever fires Groucho Marx, it won't be because Groucho subscribes to *The Nation*, but because the next picture isn't a money-maker.

MAY 13, 1936

HOLLYWOOD FIGHTS BACK

Herbert Kline

•

Herbert Kline was one of the first Americans to arrive in republican Spain and his film *Heart of Spain* documented the travails of the Civil War. He made similarly themed anti-fascist documentaries about the Nazi invasion of Czechoslovakia and the outbreak of World War 2.

IN HIS ARTICLE a, Soap Boxes in Hollywood in *The Nation* for March Morrie Ryskind indicted the entire film colony on two major charges: first, "its colossal ignorance of current political happenings," and, second, "the shocking cowardice to be found in high places." According to Mr. Ryskind, Hollywood is hopeless, most film people are ignoramuses, and the few intelligent ones are too cowardly to stand by their private opinions. In a later article, in the May 6 issue, Mr. Ryskind gave Hollywood people credit for participating in a mass-meeting to raise funds to combat the reactionary Russell-Kramer bill, but he overlooked many happenings that took place both before and after his charges of "ignorance" and "cowardice" were preferred against Hollywood.

Three weeks before his first article appeared almost a thousand prominent members of the Hollywood community paid $10 a ticket to hear Lord Listowell deliver a lecture on Nazi Germany. The proceeds went to help suffering anti-fascists. The majority of the audience were disappointed with the unexpected mildness of the Englishman's criticism of the Nazis. Hollywood was far ahead of this particular soapboxer in its feelings about current political happenings in Germany.

And for the past three years, despite Mr. Ryskind's charges, a struggle between the screen workers and the producers has been taking place that tops any other trade-union activity in the theatrical profession since the 1919 strike. Ernest Pascal, Ralph Block, OHP, Garrett, James Cagney, Edward G. Robinson, Dudley Nichols, Frances Faragoh, Sidney Howard, Kenneth Thompson, John Howard Lawson, and Fredric March, among others, took the lead in a successful movement to pull the majority of screen writers and actors out of the producer-controlled Academy of Motion Picture Arts and Sciences. Today the screen workers have their own actors', writers', and directors' guilds to protect them against unscrupulous practices and to gain every possible fair concession for their members. Since the leaders of these guilds have been subjected to every kind of producer pressure, including of course the usual charges of radicalism, I trust Mr. Ryskind will be willing to add guild activities to his future listings of important Hollywood events.

Most New Yorkers think of Hollywood as the Land of Boy Meets Girl. But three weeks before "Bury the Dead" opened on Broadway twelve hundred members of the film colony crowded into the Hollywood Women's Club auditorium to hear Fredric March, Florence Eldridge, and John Cromwell give a public reading of Irwin Shaw's macabre anti-war play for the benefit of the local Contemporary Theater and the magazine *New Theater*. Basil Rathbone, James Cagney, Groucho Marx, Donald Ogden Stewart, and Lewis Milestone sponsored the performance, signifying their interest in seeing this blast against war staged in the heart of the community that specializes in grinding out such messages as "No Greater Glory" and "Professional Soldier."

According to Hollywood reports, there never was a more unusual or more stirring opening in this town of colossal world premières. Not only did Shaw's play about "the war that is to begin tomorrow night" receive an ovation from the nation's leading entertainment specialists, but many of them used the discussion period that followed to declare publicly their sentiments about war, fascism, working conditions in the industry, Scottsboro, Hearst, and other current political issues that concern Hollywood's high-salaried screenworkers.

In his introductory speech as chairman of the reading Donald Ogden Stewart said:

As I remember it we writers were very, very bitter, we were very, very disillusioned, and we were above all determined to tell the truth about life. That was twelve years ago. I don't know whether or not any of you have seen my two latest contributions to the screen. One was a vehicle for Marion Davies entitled "Going Hollywood" and the other was Miss Crawford's "No More Ladies." That isn't exactly what I meant twelve years ago. It isn't as funny as that . . . and I am not really blaming the movies for my downfall. Nobody came to me with a revolver and said, "You've got to take this big salary and have three automobiles and live in this goddam sunshine." It's my fault and I simply want to say a few words about my present situation and particularly why I am here to night.

I am here simply and directly because the movies aren't good enough. And this Hollywood happiness isn't good enough in the face of the misery that there is in the world today. . . . You know what Hollywood's answer is to that entertainment . . . pictures are made for entertainment.

That's a lot like seeing a man who is starving to death and saying, "Maybe if we make funny faces he won't notice it." We are making funny faces while people are starving to death . . . ten million men are out of work, but the movies say nothing about that. Five innocent colored boys are going to be sent to the electric chair in Alabama, but the movies are concerned only with whether Dick Powell gets his girl.

Now I say that isn't good enough. And I am here on behalf of the Contemporary Theater and the New Theater League because they offer something better than Hollywood. They don't want people to go into the theater to get away from life . . . but to have them realize that there is a way out of their troubles that they can take part in themselves. It is not charity they want—it is hope . . . and the New Theater can give them hope. I think that even with the small productions . . . that one flash of hope and truth against a plain white canvas wall is more important than all the entertainment that Hollywood and its million- and two-million-dollar productions can ever give.

Mr. Ryskind wrote, "You can't get talk in Hollywood, people are afraid," but Mr. Stewart and Arthur Kober got up after the reading had ended and spoke openly against Hearst's jingoism and against both the Russell-Kramer bill, "which makes meetings such as this a horrible thing," and the Tydings-McCormack bill, "which makes any talk against the military an offense"; while Dudley Nichols, speaking "as an ex-officer in the United States army," declared himself in favor of strong anti-war plays like "Bury the Dead." At the same session Lionel Stander, the young comedian, wasn't being funny when he spoke of "the significance of this play to those of us who are against war but who are puzzled as to just what we as individuals can do about it." And James Cagney, Onslow Stevens, Egon Brecher, John Cromwell, Dorothy Tree, J. M. Kerrigan, Clifford Odets, and others offered their services as actors and directors for the pending Hollywood production of *Bury the Dead.*

It is certainly true that there are a great many people in Hollywood as there are in every American community who are indifferent to current political happenings, I fully sympathize with Mr. Ryskind when he declares "The thing I cannot understand is the cringing and cowardice of people who have more than enough." But when he says, "They are not only cowardly but stupid in their fear of a fascism that doesn't exist," he simply isn't talking about the movie-company town controlled by the Warner Brothers, Hearst, Louis B. Mayer, and so on, or the reactionary state machinery that has turned loose its propaganda and political power against every manifestation of progressive thought or action from Upton Sinclair's Epic movement to the strike activities of the Imperial Valley agricultural workers and the Pacific Coast seamen and longshoremen. He isn't talking about the studio set-up that was powerful enough to force 99 percent of the Hollywood screen employees to contribute to Governor Merriam's campaign chest regardless of their political opinions. He isn't talking about the Hollywood where the Hines "red squad" was used to terrorize film stars "communistic" enough to believe in the innocence of Tom Mooney. He isn't talking about the monopoly-controlled movie center which has produced reactionary "Riff-Raffs" and "Red Salutes" but never a single progressive picture such as "It Can't Happen Here" might have been. He isn't talking about the town where liberals like the leaders of the screen guilds are labeled dangerous radicals, and where anybody who treads on the toes of Louella Parsons or Marion Davies or Norma Shearer or Will Hays is liable to get it where the chicken got the ax.

Is there any hope that the brave but sporadic activity recorded in this article indicates a definite break with the popular conception of Hollywood as an intellectual Sahara? I think there is. One hope. The screen guilds. They have the power to stand up for the right of their individual members to free speech and free assemblage whether William Randolph Hearst, Governor Merrian, and Louis B. Mayer like it or not. Personally, I think Mr. Mayer, Mr. Thalberg, Mr. Warner, and others should consider the plight of the former heads of the German film industry before giving further support to the type of fascism that greets every progressive thought or action in the great state of California.

Not dealing directly with the war but reflecting current problems are Leo McCarey's *Once upon a Honeymoon*, a comedy-drama with a European setting, and *Talk of the Town*, which finds its climax in a lynch scene and trial. The latter is directed by George Stevens, who made *Woman of the Year*. Stevens will next do a film version of Kaufman and Hart's *The American Way*. Franz Werfel's *The Song of Bernadette* is in preparation as a parable on modern intolerance. "The success of *Yankee Doodle Dandy*, based on the career of George M. Cohan, and *Pride of the Yankees*, about Lou Gehrig, has turned the attention of producers to indigenous American themes and personalities, and *The Adventures of Mark Twain* and *The Ox-Bow Incident* are receiving lavish production.

The studios are avidly purchasing stories dealing with such subjects as Bataan, the underground movements in Europe, army nurses, and the paratroops. The enthusiasm accorded *Mrs. Miniver* has confirmed Hollywood's belief that moviegoers want either bold and forthright films about things that matter today or pictures completely divorced from current events. The public has indicated its apathy toward productions that take vital themes and reduce them to the level of vapid entertainment. "Escapist" film fare is, of course, still being produced; musicals, comedies, and spectacles fill out the production programs. One of the pictures doing the biggest business at the moment is Cecil DeMille's *Reap the Wild Wind*, a Technicolor spectacle of the Florida keys, and such musicals as *My Gal Sal* and *Holiday Inn* and excursions into romantic fiction like *Tales of Manhattan* are extremely popular.

The activity at the studios is spurred by the executives' recognition that no one knows what the next few months may bring in the film industry. Raw film stock, which uses many elements that go into explosives, is now under government priority regulations, and the use of film has been drastically restricted. The ceiling for the cost of construction of a set is $5,000, and much ingenuity is being exercised in adapting standing sets to new stories. It is practically impossible to obtain any new cameras, lights, or other mechanical equipment. Location trips are being eliminated to save tires. Realizing that future production may be still more restricted or even suspended, Hollywood is trying to accumulate a backlog of completed pictures.

By making bold and courageous pictures about the war the film industry is demonstrating its emergence from its mental shell. It still has a long way to go. It has yet to realize the essential seriousness of the war as a theme; it has yet to remove the last blonde from the bombers. England, Russia, and China are far more skilful than Hollywood in using the screen as a weapon of persuasion and propaganda, but the propaganda pictures of today when compared with those of the last war, "The Beast of Berlin," for example, show that there has been progress. The screen can be a most effective medium for creating understanding between the peoples of the United Nations and for affirming the democratic ideals that we are fighting for. It is a responsibility that Hollywood cannot afford to shirk.

JANUARY 27, 1945

HOLLYWOOD GOES TO WAR

Dorothy B. Jones

•

The following article was from a series devoted to the future of Hollywood. The writer's bio note reads: "Dorothy B. Jones served for more than two years as head of the Film reviewing and Analysis section of the Office of War Information Bureau of Motion Pictures. The opinions expressed in her article, however, are her own." Jones's "Communism and the Movies: A Study of Film Content," which was originally published by The Fund for the Republic in 1956, was an in-depth examination (and refutation) of the allegation that Hollywood movies were infested with communist propaganda. She also noted that of the more than thirty-five anti-Communist movies made between the late forties and mid fifties—films like *I Was a Communist for the FBI*—none of them made money.

AMERICANS AT HOME know little about the actualities of war. Our cities have not been bombed. Our existence as a nation has not been threatened. Consequently, it has been necessary to find a means of bringing the realities of the war home to people, and the motion picture, with its substitution of visual for actual experience, has proved the best device. Films have also found new uses overseas. Nazi propagandists have long characterized America as a decadent democracy, ruled by gangsters and thugs, its people softened by easy living. Our own gangster pictures bore them out. There was a need for films which gave foreign audiences a true projection of American life.

Immediately after the outbreak of the war the motion-picture industry established a War Activities Committee. This committee recommended that the President appoint a single agency or individual to coordinate the government's and the industry's film production. Accordingly, early in May, 1942, the office of Coordinator of Government Films was set up, with headquarters in Hollywood. This office, which later became the Motion Picture Bureau of the Office of War Information, has, since its inception, interpreted the government's needs and policies to the motion-picture makers, supplied them with the special information required for the production of certain war films, and at the request of the studios has analyzed short subjects and feature scripts for their potential effect on the war effort. The functions of this office have been purely advisory. In accordance with the wishes of both the industry and the Administration, final responsibility for the films made in Hollywood during the war has rested with the motion-picture industry.

1942: Spies and Comedy G.I.'s

America's first year of war saw the desperate losing struggle for the Philippines, the uncertain days when the enemy threatened Australia, the long-drawn-out battle for Guadalcanal. Through all this the American public, psychologically as well as materially unprepared for war, groped for some way to meet the crisis effectively.

The feature pictures produced by Hollywood in this period did little to help solve the nation's most pressing problem, that of mobilizing the public for an all-out war effort. American home-front activities were usually given comedy treatment. Red Cross work, the role of the air-raid warden, and civilian-defense activities generally were ridiculed in several films. Such presentations, belittling the seriousness of civilian war activities, may very well have made more difficult the recruitment of volunteer workers. Also, at a time when Britain and other nations were suffering under heavy enemy bombing, it was poor taste to distribute them overseas.

The films made about the enemy were likewise inappropriate. At a time when the public needed above all else a sober evaluation of the strength of the enemy, then far greater than our own, spy pictures were the order of the day in Hollywood; even some of the westerns wove the spy theme into their usual formula. Some films went so far as to ridicule the enemy.

A few of the 1942 pictures attempted to tell the story of the conquered countries: the best among these were *Paris Calling* (Universal), starring Randolph Scott and Elisabeth Bergner, and *Joan of Paris* (RKO), with Michele Morgan and Paul Henreid. However, the big United Nations picture of the year, and unquestionably one of the best war films produced during this early period, was *Mrs. Miniver* (Metro-Goldwyn-Mayer). Although this film was assailed by some as an unrealistic, Hollywood version of war-time England, it furthered British good-will toward this country by its tribute to the fortitude of Englishmen under the blitz.

Not many other war films in that year were worthy of note. An excellent why-we-fight film was *Joe Smith, American* (MGM), which in its presentation of the life of an average American production worker dramatized the values of our way of life. One of the best was *Wake Island* (Paramount), a tribute to the marines who held out there against overpowering odds. This was the first Hollywood film to attempt a documentary approach to a war story.

Of 486 features released by Hollywood during 1942, more than one-quarter dealt primarily with the war. Of course many of the films released during the first half of the year were written, and in some instances produced, prior to America's entry. In its new productions the industry by and large took the easy way out, capitalizing on the war with stories about spies and fifth columnists and the lighter side of army life; 65 percent of the war films and more than 15 percent of all films turned out were spy pictures, comedies, or musicals about camp life. Thus the bulk of Hollywood's 1942 product gave foreign audiences a poor picture of America's understanding of the war and must have caused much resentment.

1943: More and Better War Pictures

During America's second year of war the proportion of the total product devoted to the war increased, and at the same time the character of the war films underwent a considerable change. For example, many more films—twice the number in 1942—attempted to tell why we in America were fighting this war. Pictures about the United Nations almost trebled in number, with thirty productions in this category. On the other hand, films dealing primarily with enemy activities dropped off to less than one-half of the number put out in 1942. Most important of all, the number of films of value to the war effort increased.

Among the pictures about conquered Europe were *The Moon Is*

Down (20th Century-Fox), *Tonight We Raid Calais* (also 20th), and *Edge of Darkness* (Warner Brothers). Though well-intentioned, these films were Hollywood versions of conditions and peoples about which the producers, writers, directors, and actors knew little. One of the most unfortunate efforts was *The Chetniks* (20th), which mirrored American ignorance in its heroic portrayal of Mihailovich, the Yugoslav two-timer. The films about Britain included *Journey for Margaret* (MGM) a story about the children of England during the blitz, and *Thumbs Up* (Republic), about Britain's war production, both useful to the war effort. *Corvette K-225* (Universal), portraying the Canadian navy's convoy system, was one of the best war films of the year. Among the films about the Soviet Union the most talked-about was *Mission to Moscow* (Warner), which adapted the documentary form to a dramatization of Ambassador Davies's book of the same title. While this picture was criticized for the dramatic license which it took with certain facts, it was an extremely useful film in that it gave a fundamentally sympathetic portrayal of our Soviet allies, who had for several decades been ridiculed on the screen and maligned by the press of this country.

The cycle of melodramatic stories about enemy espionage and fifth columns pretty much spent itself in the first half of the year. With films like *Hitler's Children* (RKO) and *This Land Is Mine* (RKO) the industry began to examine enemy ideology more seriously. In Hollywood films generally the enemy came to be less often identified merely as a slant-eyed Japanese or guttural-tongued German and more clearly characterized as fascist. This change was reflected in several efforts to portray American fascism on the screen, as for example *Pilot Number 5* and *Keeper of the Flame* (both MGM). Run-of-the-mill pictures about our armed forces continued to be highly melodramatic, with the swash-buckling American hero so deeply resented overseas, but a more realistic and more dignified portrayal of American fighting men was introduced in such films as *Air Force* (Warner), *Bataan* (MGM) *Guadalcanal Diary* (20th), *Sahara* (Columbia), and *Gung Ho* (Universal). After *Air Force* the documentary influence became stronger.

Thus 1943 as a whole was distinguished by a more realistic and more seriously intentioned screen treatment of the war. Other outstanding films useful to the war effort were *Watch on the Rhine* (Warner), Lillian Hellman's story of an anti-fascist, and *The Ox-Bow Incident* (20th), which turned the camera spotlight on the question of civil liberties. Also worthy of note was *Power of the Press*, a Columbia "B" picture, which undertook to dramatize the responsibility entailed by freedom of the press. Finally, *The Human Comedy* (MGM), in its homely portrayal of American small-town life, told the world something about what Americans feel they are fighting for.

1944: The Decline of the War Film

The third year of the war saw the war film begin to decline. Since most studios had large backlogs of films about the war which were released as the year wore on, the proportion of war films to the total product was only slightly less than that of the previous year, but there was a definite swing in interest away from the war feature. Fearful of being caught on V-Day with a stock of war films, Hollywood groped uneasily for post-war themes. Uncertain where to find them, it swung back to known pre-war formulas, and scores of light musicals, murder mysteries, and other escapist films unrelated to present events were put into production.

Films about the enemy continued to decrease in number, and spy melodrams became almost extinct. In May Paramount released *The Hitler Gang*, a film with a documentary-like quality which examined the Nazi ideology and the history of the rise of the party in Germany. Films about the American armed forces were numerous, but with few exceptions were of poorer quality than those of the previous year. There was a tendency to return to the musical-comedy treatment of army life. One notable exception was *Destination Tokyo* (Warner), which dramatized the hazardous life of our submarine crews in enemy waters. Several films relating to the post-war period were released. Among these were *None Shall Escape* (Columbia), which dealt with the necessity for punishing war criminals, and *Wilson* (20th), which examined some of the mistakes of the last peace—the latter a very exceptional film.

On the whole, there were fewer films of value and significance to the war effort than in the preceding year. At least three other 1944 releases, however, should be mentioned: *The Sullivans* (20th), *Dragon Seed* (MGM), and *North Star* (Goldwyn). *North Star,* while presenting what is obviously a Hollywood version of the Soviet Union, made an important contribution both at home and abroad by its moving dramatization of the impact of the Nazi invasion on the lives of Russians.

Hollywood's War Score

Certain Hollywood producers have pointed out that the industry has fulfilled its primary war function by providing entertainment for weary production and home-front workers, as well as for our fighting men.

Although this contribution has its value, the fact remains that the film's real opportunity to further the war effort lies in providing information about the war or increasing our understanding of some aspect of it. In general, the Hollywood "movie" is not the best vehicle for conveying information, since it is fundamentally a fantasy form, but some efforts have been made to use the form for information purposes by giving it a documentary flavor (*Wake Island, Mission to Moscow, Wilson*, and the like). Unfortunately, such films, though about real people and real happenings, retained their story-like quality, and this led to confusion as to what was fact and what fantasy and greatly lessened their information value.

On the other hand, many of the films mentioned in this article did aid in increasing the public's understanding of war problems. By its very freedom from factual details, the feature film achieves a clarity of theme which enables it to make its point more easily than the documentary. Even more important, audience identification with imaginary characters is a valuable asset in developing audience understanding of a problem. Films like *This Land Is Mine* or *Corvette K-225* which conveyed the spirit of reality without tying themselves down to a specific set of facts, demonstrated that the movie form is well suited to the difficult task of increasing understanding of the war.

Hollywood's actual contribution to the war effort through its feature pictures may be summed up as follows: From December 1, 1941, to December 1, 1944, the industry released 1,321 features. The main story of three in every ten of these films revolved around the war. Yet of a total of some 370 war pictures, only a few dozen can have accomplished anything of significance for the war effort at home or abroad. What is behind this failure of the motion-picture industry to fulfill its obligations to the nation at war?

To begin with, the movies, like most other American industries, were unprepared for the important work they had to do. For years Hollywood had been producing six or seven hundred films a year, the vast majority of which were musicals, domestic comedies, westerns, and murder mysteries based on well-worn formulas. For years the producers had stoutly maintained that the American public wanted, above all else, to be "entertained." It is small wonder, then, that faced with the task of making films which would educate the public about the war, Hollywood movie makers did not know where to begin. They lacked the experience. They lacked the know-how. And, like the rest of America, they themselves lacked real understanding of the war.

There were in Hollywood, however, a number of sincere, progressive individuals who for years had been fighting a losing battle against the viewpoint of the average Hollywood producer. Among them were producers, directors, and story editors, but the majority were writers. In pre-war years the more successful members of this group had occasionally been permitted to make a film or two of social significance. By and large, however, though some of them earned weekly salaries that ran into four figures and were expert craftsmen in film-making, they had developed a feeling of hopelessness about what they could achieve in Hollywood. These were the men and women who saw immediately the important role which the industry could play in the winning of the war. They saw, too, a new opportunity to overturn the Hollywood tradition. To these men and women Hollywood owes much, for they have been the writers, directors, and in some cases the producers of the most significant and useful of Hollywood's war films. The recognition given their films in the press and at the box-office has lent new prestige in Hollywood to such names as Dudley Nichols, Dalton Trumbo, Mary McCall, Jr., Dory Schary, Henry Koch, John Howard Lawson, Emmett Lavery, Sidney Buckman, and others.

Though the industry as a whole, through its feature films, has contributed relatively little to the war effort, important changes have taken place in Hollywood as a result of the war, changes which will leave a permanent mark on the Hollywood product.

6

Rhapsody in Blue and Black

Scene from the Struggle in Company Town

•

JULY 17, 1929

Revolt in Hollywood

Somerset Logan

•

Somerset Logan was an actor, writer, and director based in Hollywood.

Hollywood, June 23

EQUITY WILL PREVAIL in Hollywood. The embattled thespians of this city, members of the Actors' Equity Association, are girding up their loins for combat with the motion-picture producers and their wealthy backers. The producers have doggedly refused either to negotiate with the actors, or to recognize their union in any way. If the present uncompromising attitude is maintained, there is only one effective weapon available for the actors—the strike.

During the first week of June of this year, Frank Gilmore, president of the Actors' Equity, notified all members of the association residing in Los Angeles that on June 5 and thereafter only the new Equity basic agreement was to be accepted by Equity members from producers of talking or sound pictures—which virtually meant *all* pictures. Contracts signed before that time were to be scrupulously observed, but upon their expiration nothing but the Equity agreement was to be signed.

Mr. Gilmore and the Equity Council considered this action mandatory on their part, since six months ago, in response to a questionnaire sent to all Los Angeles members of Equity, 1,087 votes were cast in favor of all-Equity casts for talking pictures, and only 98 against. Therefore, after a close study of the local situation, Mr. Gilmore, who is now in Hollywood leading the fight, fired the first gun.

The struggle promises to be an interesting one, for more than 70 percent of the people in talking pictures are members of the Actors' Equity, many of them commanding the highest salaries. Several actors who ignored the edict of their organization and signed non-Equity contracts on or after June 5 have been promptly suspended from their union.

The producers are receiving the powerful assistance of intrenched privilege, including the local commercial organizations and the newspapers. Behind the actors are the Central Labor Council of Los Angeles and the American Federation of Labor. J. W. Bussel, secretary of the Central Labor Council, to which Equity is now allied has pledged the unqualified support of the federated unions—the strongly organized camera-men, the operators, the electricians and carpenters, and allied crafts. President Green of the American Federation of Labor, in a telegram to Mr. Gilmore, has promised his heartiest support.

The courageous move of the Actors' Equity is the result of the picture actor's determination to have a union of his own, capable of correcting obvious abuses and instituting much needed reforms. With the advent of the talking picture came the necessity of employing many legitimate theater actors with trained speaking voices. The local forces of Equity were increased, and a crisis became inevitable.

The abuses and maltreatment which the picture actors—particularly the small-part players—have suffered can scarcely be overstated. Actors are sometimes forced to accept contracts offering a lump sum for their part in a picture. In these contracts there is no stipulation as to the length of the working day, or the length of the entire engagement. An actor, upon engagement, must take the casting-director's word. Actors are quite frequently paid nothing for rehearsals. There are instances of players being required to work from sixty to eighty hours a week. When on location, any hours, from eight to twenty, have constituted a day—sometimes with an additional bonus, sometimes not. The entire working schedule is hopelessly vague and inequitable to the actor. The new Equity contract would correct such flagrant abuses.

Of course, the individual star can insist upon his own terms—and his price, but the character actor and the small-part player—and that includes the overwhelming majority of players—are frequently victimized. If they speak their mind, they are seldom reemployed at the same studio. With the recent amalgamation of so many of the picture companies, and the antagonism of the producers' association, this is no slight matter.

Actors' salaries in motion pictures may appear exorbitant to the outsider. But for every fabulous amount pocketed by some star of the first magnitude, there are a hundred modest salaries meted out to the small-part player. Moreover, the motion-picture actor, like so many of his legitimate theater confreres, is seldom sure of continuous employment. There are many weeks in each year when the actor is waiting about or looking for another transient engagement.

The producers are resorting to every conceivable device to break the spirit of the actors. As soon as Equity's ultimatum was received, one player after another was called to a studio—where he had never worked before—and was offered a tempting non-Equity contract. If he refused, he was told it was regrettable, and such a good part too! In one instance, a studio stock company was suddenly organized, offering long-term non-Equity contracts. Casting-directors are looking over files of players which have not been touched for a year. Lists of actors, including a few Equity people who signed the standard non-Equity studio contracts after the designated time, have been published in all the local press.

Every few days, the local papers, completely ignoring the essential decency of Equity's demands, and refusing to print any pro-Equity statements, publish reputed interviews with this or that prominent actor or actress, condemning the stand of Equity and highly commending the producers for their habitual sweetness and light. Both the *Times*, with its notorious anti-union proclivities, and the *Examiner*, with its owner a picture producer in his own right, have had lengthy editorials against Equity. In order to offset this propaganda, the local Equity Association is publishing, semi-weekly, the *Actors' Equity News*.

The tone and general attitude of the little paper are well exemplified in the following excerpt. The *Times*, in a recent issue, said: "Instead of remaining an association of artists, it (Equity) placed itself in line and agreement with stage-hands, ditch-diggers, janitors, iron-molders, and such." To which the *Actors' Equity News* responded:

> Why not? Walter Damrosch, Victor Herbert and others found such alignment no bar to their art nor their dignity. Why should you? And, after all, what's the matter with a ditch-digger . . . or a janitor, or a stage hand? A ditch-digger may not always be a ditch-digger. He may become a

producer, or even a director. Just as much chance as shirt salesmen, clothes peddlers, waiters, or saloon-song pluggers.* That you once followed a lowly trade is no disgrace. Rather the reverse.

Oh, *Times*, you got off on the wrong foot, for—There was a Railsplitter. . . . And once there was a Carpenter.

On June 17 the Actors' Equity Association called a general meeting of its members at the Writers' Club in Hollywood. More than 1,200 actors thronged the hall. George Arliss was in the chair, and Frank Gilmore addressed the gathering. There has never been such a display of genuine enthusiasm in Hollywood. Both speakers were given an ovation. The entire assembly stood up and cheered lustily for several minutes.

Mr. Gilmore read a resolution passed by the Central Labor Council of Los Angeles, pledging unstinted support. He then reviewed the present situation in the studios, emphasizing the necessity for Equity shop. He described the few members who had issued statements in the daily press against the organization as "selfish egotists, indifferent to the welfare of their fellow-players." When the players' names were mentioned they were greeted with a storm of boos and hisses. In concluding, Mr. Gilmore said:

> This uprising of the motion-picture actors is no passionate gesture of the moment. It is the result of eight years of striving to get the producers to meet us in a friendly conference, and because of their indifference to our efforts this move was the only possible thing to do, if we intend to remedy the flagrant injustices which are now so common. . . . We must win because our cause is just, and because in the offing there lies the sympathy and the association, if we need it, of the great American Federation of Labor.

The meeting adjourned with the actors singing the song first used in the theatrical strike of 1919, "All for one, and one for all." Other meetings are scheduled. The local office is a hive of activity. A strike? Perhaps. But with a resurgence of the indomitable spirit which characterized the struggle of 1919 and 1924, Equity is bound to prevail in Hollywood.

*A gentle reminder of the humble antecedents of a number of our directors and producers.

APRIL 2, 1938

HOLLYWOOD IS A UNION TOWN

Morton Thompson

•

Morton Thompson was a screenwriter, columnist and best-selling novelist. He once described Hollywood as a "state of mind surrounded by Los Angeles." His books include *Not as a Stranger, The Cry and the Covenant*, and *Joe, The Wounded Tennis Player* which included a turkey recipe (now known as the "Thompson Turkey recipe") which was lauded by the likes of Robert Benchley and Craig Claiborne and is posted on the Internet.

Culver City, California, March 14

HOLLYWOOD IS A union town. Its actors are union men. Its pickets are union pickets. Its scabs are mobbed with union thoroughness and dispatch. Its stars are as labor conscious as its carpenters. And the stronghold of unionism in Hollywood is the Screen Actors' Guild.

Five years ago a gag about a Hollywood actor being a union man would have been good for a ripple of horror in Hollywood's drawing-rooms and for a derisive laugh along the embattled labor fronts of Eastern and Midwestern America. Stars were artists. Featured players were artists. The least conspicuous extra was an artist. The hem of Hollywood's epicene skirt was lifted gingerly and superciliously as Hollywood walked over the mud puddles of its labor problems.

But Hollywood is a town where the least likely things happen. The incredible has now become commonplace. The Screen Actors' Guild rules the roost. It is probably on its way to becoming the richest and most powerful labor union in America. The stars have stepped down into the ranks to fight for the extras, the bit players, the masses. Their victories have been crushing and complete. What the S. A. G. dictates, the producers do. The result has been a startling betterment of working conditions, somewhat increased pay, and the discovery that the iron heel of the studios is still a heel, but that it is not iron and that it is not, in fact, any more impressive than any other heel.

The Screen Actors' Guild really started in 1929. It started with a strike. Most Hollywood actors belonged to Equity. Equity called a strike, it wanted better working conditions than the producers were willing to grant. Equity wasn't daring enough. It told its Hollywood members who had contracts to refuse to sign new contracts. It told members with pending contracts to refuse to sign. It told members without contracts not to go to work. The brunt of the blow fell, of course, on the little fellow, the chap without a contract. The strike collapsed in twelve weeks without having accomplished much more than keeping a few hundred actors out of work.

In March of 1930 the producers, a little worried by the abortive Equity affair, decided to organize the actors in their own way. The Academy of Motion Picture Arts and Sciences was thrust forward as an arbitration board. Actors got a few assurances that conditions would be bettered and a method of lodging complaints, in return for a signed agreement not to strike for five years. Most of the actors signed.

In 1932 the Eastern banks began to send out efficiency experts to stop money wastage at the studios in which they had investments. They couldn't do much about actors with contracts, but they slashed terms for pending contracts, and by one ingenious dodge after another proceeded to snip almost in half the salaries of many a free-lance player. There were other grievances. California state labor laws stipulate that women may not work longer than sixteen hours a day. But it was pretty general knowledge that the major studios were able to control the state labor bureau. Chorus girls were worked twenty-four hours straight. Extras were kept shivering in the rain for endless hours. Stunt men risked their necks; and when they broke them the studios wouldn't pay the repair bills. Actors had no place to go to complain. True, they had the Academy established by the producers. But they were afraid to go there. They were afraid they might become known as trouble-makers and be put on the studios' famous black list. As a matter of fact, almost all who did appeal to the Academy received unfailing courtesy and fair treatment. Nine out of ten of the cases brought before the Academy were decided in favor of the actors. But not many brought cases.

While Hollywood's famous parties raged, little coteries of sober-minded actors conferred furtively. Their deliberations were dangerous. Any hint of them, reaching the ear of a producer, unquestionably would have meant the black list—bad pictures, bad roles, joblessness. The studios had a bland one-for-all and all-for-one policy by which unruly actors were disciplined by universally shut doors. But out of these deliberations was born the S. A. G. The original members deserve mention. They included Alan Mowbray, Ralph Morgan, Kenneth Thomson, Alden Gay, Morgan Wallace, Leon Ames, James and Lucille Gleason, Bradley Page, Claude King, Ivan Simpson, Boris Karloff, Richard Tucker, Reginald Mason, Arthur Vinton, Clay Clement, Charles Starrett, C. Aubrey Smith, Willard Robertson, Tyler Brooke, and Noel Madison. At first they fared rather badly. Many persons asked to join were shocked at the thought of joining a labor movement. Then 1933 came along. That was the year in which the studios, pleading poverty, cut the salaries of every actor in Hollywood squarely in half on the plea that the cut would avert tremendous lay-offs. When the cut was accomplished, the studios proceeded to effect drastic lay-offs anyway. And virtually every studio in Hollywood declared bonuses that same year. This was a little too much even for blithe actors. In June the S. A. G. was quietly incorporated. In July it invited every actor in Hollywood to a big mass-meeting. Only a few turned out. It got sixty members. The big shots wouldn't come in. Most of the stars were still members of the Academy. Then the NRA motion-picture code was adopted, and the Academy promptly assumed the right to represent the actors.

The producers now made a code of their own, which consisted mainly of an agreement not to bid competitively for talent. A $10,000 fine was established as a penalty for competitive bidding. It was this competitive-bidding agreement that smoked out the big names. A meeting was called at Frank Morgan's house. The Marx brothers and Charlie Butterworth spent the entire day calling every actor and actress in Hollywood. The newly-founded S. A. G., shaky and pitifully small, was invited along with the rest. One of the big shots made a small speech. The gist of it was that the group gathered at Morgan's should hire someone like Arthur Garfield Hays to go to Washington as their representative. There was a considering silence. Eddie Cantor stood up. "I've apparently come here," he said, "under a misconception. If this organization isn't one that's going to help every man, woman, and child in the industry, I'll say good night!" He didn't have to say good night. Some of them sheepishly, some of them angrily, every star and featured player in the room fell in with Cantor's demand.

The S. A. G. unit was asked to stand up and give its views on the situation. Its proposals, explained by Ralph Morgan, its first president, were so sound and its organization so ready for use that the meeting resolved to join the group, reorganize it, elect new officers, and proceed under the S. A. G. banner. Unionism had invaded Hollywood. The battle had begun. When it became known that the stars were joining the group, the membership jumped in three weeks from 81 to 4,000.

Almost immediately the new union sent its famous two-thousand-word telegram to President Roosevelt, who countered by inviting Eddie Cantor to Warm Springs. As a result, the actors won every point on which they had attacked the producers' code and the suggestions made by the producer-managed Academy for an actors' code.

Next the problem of extras was tackled—the most serious problem before the union today. In 1934 the Senior Guild voted the creation of the Junior Guild to be composed of extras and bit players and to give it its own council and governing board. The demands of the Junior Guild are made known to the Senior Guild, which then decides whether to give them its support. Overwhelmingly the Seniors have sustained all demands of the Juniors.

The abuses heaped on bit players, extras, and stunt men had always been great. They were the victims of a stupid and lazy system which originated at Central Casting, a bureau where the name and qualifications of every extra in Hollywood are filed. Rank favoritism still flourishes at Central Casting—the same extras can be seen in picture after picture—but the extras are no longer helpless. They have bargaining power now. In the old days, when a studio called Central Casting and asked for 400 roller skates, the lazy wretch who took the call refused to go to the trouble of digging 400 roller skaters out of the files. Instead, he drove down to a roller-skating rink, lined up 400 skaters at random, and sent them off to the studio. They were paid a top of $10 a day for their work. And they kept 400 legitimate extras out of work. That wasn't the worst of it, though. Those 400, a studio paycheck hot in their hands, began to ask one another: "How long has *this* been going on? Let's be regular extras! Let's get in on some of this gravy!" And they became extras, thousands of them.

Now the studios rarely spend more than two and a half million dollars a year for extras. And the S. A. G. suddenly discovered that there were 23,000 extras in Hollywood. If the work had been spread out evenly, an extra could have earned only $109 a year! Perhaps 5,000 extras could make a living wage—if there were only 5,000 extras. Today by imposing dues the S. A. G. has cut down the Junior Guild population to 6,600, and of that number 500 are dancers and 800 are bit players. If an extra doesn't belong to the S. A. G. he can't get work in Hollywood. And he doesn't belong if he can't pay his dues, which are $18 a year in addition to an initiation fee of $25. Two weeks ago the membership books were closed. The Junior Guild asked that dues be high; it asked that its membership list be closed.

In 1934 the S. A. G. affiliated with the A. F. of L. through Equity and the A. A. A. A. From 1935 to 1937 it cemented its relations with labor, mended its fences. In 1937 the producers still wouldn't negotiate with the S. A. G. The Wagner Act was validated. The producers negotiated.

The Painters' Union called a strike. Actors passed through the painters' picket lines and were called scabs. The S. A. G. called a mass-meeting. It was evident that the producers were stalling in negotiations which demanded a guild shop and that the time was ripe for a show-down. The officers informed the meeting that they would bring back a contract signed by the producers in a week or call a strike. Afterward they realized that it was necessary to obtain a 75 percent vote of the membership before any strike of the Senior Guild could be called. At a meeting held at his house Robert Montgomery opened without preamble: "Ladies and gentlemen, you are here to sign a strike ballot. If you sign, you may be called out on strike. You will strike—if you do strike—on behalf of the extras. We are not asking for any privileges for the Senior Guild." By the end of the week 600 Seniors had voted for the strike and 18 against. The union began to make plans to open coffee houses and restaurants to feed those who would be hard hit. Everyone figured the strike was four days off. The tension was grave.

On Sunday morning Franchot Tone, Kenneth Thomson, Aubrey Blair, and Robert Montgomery went to Louis B. Mayer's house. Joe Schenck was there. The four told Mayer and Schenck flatly that they had to have something in writing to take to the members at a mass-meeting that night or else the strike was on. They interrupted a bridge game. Mayer was a little petulant. Schenck said it was impossible to get all the studio executives together on such short notice. Then he called Harry Cohn, who was playing the races at Agua Caliente. Cohn told him what was good enough for Schenck was good enough for him and got away from the phone in time for the fifth race. Mayer next refused to call in a stenographer. "It's Sunday!" he objected. "I've got 200 guests here!" So Kenneth Thomson wrote the historic surrender in longhand. The terms were guild shop; and Mayer and Schenck signed.

The four went back to Fredric March's house, where the S. A. G. board was waiting. Now that the agreement was signed, they were a little worried about some of the terms. The mass-meeting that night ended their worries. The crowd tore the roof off. In another week the handwritten surrender was reduced to formal legal *phraseology* and formally signed, sealed, and delivered. Hollywood is a closed-shop town, now. When the Brown Derby's union waiters walked out on strike, actors refused to go through the picket lines.

There is many a Communist in the union, for the S. A. G. doesn't care what a man's politics are so long as he doesn't bring them into the guild. A minority thinks that the Senior Guild "sold out" the extras and disagrees violently with almost everything either the Junior or the Senior Guild proposes. It is a very vocal minority and even a rather welcome one. Its latest proposal, that the Junior Guild be given equal voting powers with the Senior Guild, was voted down by the Juniors, 4,500 to 50.

The guild has obtained almost everything it has asked for. Ninety-nine percent of all Hollywood actors belong. The battle is now definitely over, though a few minor objectives are still being discussed. Producers are walking the straightest of straight lines. The victories have been victories for the rank and file. For themselves the stars have asked and won next to nothing.

The important thing is that the highest stars, like the lowest extras, are vigilantly labor conscious. They are anxious to identify themselves with any and all labor movements on behalf of the underdog. They are lending their names and their talents and their time, with unabating enthusiasm. It would be unfair to single out any individual actor as the greatest contributor. For his personal courage and incisive strategy Robert Montgomery, present president of the S. A. G., has won the respect of the producers and unstinted praise from the union and the public—a public, incidentally, which not so long ago thought of him as a movie playboy. Joan Crawford, second vice-president, has been of invaluable aid in enlisting the support of actresses. Alan Mowbray, when the organization was being planned in secret, financed the embryo S. A. G. with his personal check of $2,500. Kenneth Thomson, executive secretary, has given nearly five years of hard work and health-straining devotion. Ralph Morgan, a member of the board for five years, Chester Morris, third vice-president, Franchot Tone, James Cagney, first vice-president, Boris Karloff, assistant secretary, Noel Madison, treasurer, Murray Kinnell, assistant treasurer, and directors Edward Arnold, Humphrey Bogart, Dudley Digges, Lucille Gleason, Porter Hall, Paul Harvey, Jean Hersholt, Russell Hicks, Frank Morgan, Claude King, Fredric March, Jean Muir, Erin O'Brien-Moore, Irving Pichel, Edward G. Robinson, Edwin Stanley, Gloria Stuart, Warren William, Adolphe Menjou, Robert Young, Dick Powell, Gene Lockhart, and George Murphy are only a partial list of those who might be nominated for a labor Hall of Fame in Hollywood.

Rhapsody in Black and Blue

Gates Ward

•

The bio note described Gates Ward as "an employee of Metro-Goldwyn-Mayer now on strike."

Hollywood, October 11

A FOURTH OF Hollywood's 30,000 motion-picture-studio employees have been locked out since March 12 in a dispute over a single issue—the right of employees to belong to unions of their own choice. For seven months the 7,500 men and women involved have peacefully picketed the nine major studios by day and local theaters by night, generally in groups of ten to a hundred. Save for a few clashes between individuals there has been no violence; the picket lines have been gay and good-humored, pretty girls in the white-collar unions marching with young men from the crafts.

On Monday, October 8, the situation had changed. At six o'clock in the morning nearly a thousand pickets formed a peaceful line at the Warner studio in suburban Burbank. At once two hundred goons engaged by I. A. T. S. E. (International Alliance of Theatrical Stage Employees), a notorious company-sponsored A. F. of L. organization, came toward them, swinging chains, clubs, and other weapons. Behind the goons came about four hundred non-strikers, mainly scabs from rump-chartered I. A. T. S. E. unions. The unarmed pickets fell bleeding in the street, but the line held until two hundred suburban police and deputy sheriffs rushed out from the studio and used their clubs recklessly. Then the line parted, letting in the strike-breakers and a few dozen employees from uninvolved unions. Hundreds of other workers, including many I. A. T. S. E. members, refused to cross the picket line. From the safety of a sound-stage roof, studio executives watched the bloody battle and by loud speakers invited reluctant workers to come inside.

The violence had begun at Warner's the previous Friday, when strike-breakers vainly tried to run down the pickets in automobiles, and company cops, aided by the Los Angeles and suburban police, sought to break up the line with fire hoses and with tear-gas bombs thrown from the studio roofs. About seventy pickets were injured—a dozen seriously—in the two days of rioting instigated by the studio, I. A. T. S. E., and the law-enforcement agencies. The strike leaders—but no studio chiefs—were arrested, charged with inciting to riot. A number of pickets were arrested for carrying concealed weapons, which they had picked up or seized from goons, but so far as is known no thugs were arrested. However, their weapons were unconcealed.

At the height of Monday's battle four police officers walked off the job in disgust when they saw what they had been sent to do, and joined the pickets. When it was announced on Monday night that Warner's, supported by other major studios, would meet the pickets in a showdown battle on Tuesday, such a wave of protest swept the community that hundreds of respectable citizens—doctors, lawyers, businessmen, housewives, even some I. A. T. S. E. members—rushed to join the picket line at dawn. Nothing happened. Warner's apparently had had enough. Not an employee crossed the picket line.

On Tuesday the producers visited Sheriff Biscailuz. The strikers' original plan was to move the mass picket line to each studio in turn, but when Warner's reacted violently to its first appearance, they decided to keep it there until the violence subsided. On Wednesday morning as about four hundred pickets, a third of them women, almost all of them locked-out employees from Warner's and other studios, were circling peacefully before Warner's main gate, two hundred deputy sheriffs advanced on them carrying teargas bombs and machine-guns. They forced the pickets to put up their hands and then marched them into the studio, where they held them for several hours, refusing to let them see lawyers and even denying them toilet facilities.

Finally all the pickets were taken to the Burbank jail and held on $500 bail each, on the charge of illegal assembly and rioting. Many, including a number of women, refused to accept freedom on bail. I saw all this and can state that there was no violence of any kind by the pickets. On Thursday ten thousand A. F. of L. Lockheed workers joined the picket line, twenty-five hundred at 6 A.M. and the others in later shifts.

These mass demonstrations by the strikers were the result of the long run-around they had been given by the producers and of the Washington NLRB's mysterious delay in rendering a decision in the dispute.

Hollywood is completely organized now, from office workers to directors, in some thirty-four A. F. of L. and ten independent unions. And of course there is the Association of Motion Picture Producers. Engaged in the present strike are fourteen A. F. of L. locals and an independent extras union. Nine are craft locals—the painters, molders, carpenters, machinists, electricians, janitors, blacksmiths, plumbers, sheet-metal workers; and five are white-collar and technical workers' unions—the cartoonists, office employees, publicists, story analysts, and the key union of the strike, Local 1421, of set designers, decorators, and illustrators. The producer-backed I. A. T. S. E. has twelve regular locals, among which are the progressive, sympathetic camera men, film technicians, sound men, and costumers. Controlled by dictatorial top leaders, they have been unable to avoid their misuse in the present conflict.

Equity has taken no stand in the strike, but it would have been won over long ago if the Screen Actors' Guild, which escaped I. A. T. S. E. seizure only after a bitter fight a few years ago, would support it. Despite a substantial progressive element, the guild is under reactionary leaders and as a union has taken a neutral, hands-off stand. Its president is George Murphy, a conservative Republican, and its treasurer is Russell Hicks, who knocked a girl picket down with a blow to the nose in Monday's battle. The equally powerful Writers' Guild, unaffiliated but progressive, vigorously supports the strikers but has been prevented from joining them by its peculiar contractual relations with the producers. Even so, the producers have been severely handicapped; insufficient and incompetent replacements have caused serious delays and the cancellation of many scheduled productions, at a cost of millions of dollars. Some five hundred I. A. T. S. E. scabs are sleeping in the Warner studio. But no pictures are being made because the rebellious I. A. T. S. E. camera men refuse to cross the picket line. The picketing of local theaters has brought a 25 percent drop in box-office receipts, and theater owners are privately begging the producers to settle the strike. Most of the independent producers privately or openly favor the strikers and have long been trying to persuade the major producers to settle.

The present strike is the climax of the all-out, ten-year-old effort of certain producers, a powerful minority in the A. M. P. P., to put all studio labor under the control of a company-dominated labor organization that was set up in Hollywood by two racketeers with the producers' help. In 1934 two Chicagoans with police records, George Browne and Willie Bioff, took over the International Alliance of Theatrical Stage Employees and with it control of the projectionists in picture theaters. In 1935 Bioff came to Hollywood and told the producers—so it was asserted in court—that he and Browne would close up the theaters unless they were paid off.

Not only did the producers start paying off, but in January, 1936, through the Hays Office, they gave to these crooks and their union a closed shop in the studios. At that time I. A. T. S. E. had only seventy-six members in Hollywood, but the producers ordered all their organized employees to join it or risk losing their jobs, and the membership rose to 12,000 in less than two years. Here was an obvious answer to the Wagner act and the rise of labor in the mid-thirties—an industry-wide organization controlled by the producers, who found it more convenient to make deals with dictatorial and crooked labor chiefs than to bargain with free unions.

Several studio locals resisted the producers' effort to herd them into I. A. T. S. E. until the pay-off scandal exploded and Bioff and Browne, together with an important producer, were sent to prison in 1941. A dozen or more free unions then seized the opportunity to form a progressive group called the Conference of Studio Unions (C. S. U.) with the purpose of protecting and promoting free unionism. This group made rapid progress in improving wage and working conditions, and in consequence a revolt broke out in the ranks of the twelve I. A. T. S. E. locals. It was smashed, however, by Richard Walsh, a vice-president of I. A. T. S. E. during the Browne-Bioff regime.

A truce reigned until October, 1943, when a small independent union of seventy-seven set decorators voted to join Local 1421, one of the C. S. U. unions, and to designate it as their bargaining agent. For almost a year the producers avoided official recognition of Local 1421 as the decorators' agent while actually treating it as such. Then the trap was sprung. In August, 1944, the producers suggested that, "merely as a formality," Local 1421 should be certified by the NLRB as the decorators' representative. Although this action was unnecessary, since the decorators had the right to join any union they chose, the local complied. Two weeks later, on the instigation of the producers, a I. A. T. S. E. local filed a cross-petition claiming exclusive jurisdiction over the decorators—although not a single decorator, as such, had ever been a member of an I. A. T. S. E. local. Of course, the NLRB could not hold an election to decide the claims of two rival A. F. of L. unions except upon the employers' petition. Instead of petitioning, the producers suddenly announced that they were "caught in the middle of a foolish quarrel between brother A. F. of L. unions."

Local 1421 withdrew its petition in disgust, for jurisdiction was not an issue, and gave the producers proof that it represented 100 percent of the decorators by their own free choice. The producers flatly refused to recognize the local or to negotiate with it as the decorators' agent. In December the local filed a strike notice in accordance with the Smith-Connally act; in January, 1945, the producers having made no move to heal the breach, it voted overwhelmingly to strike. Now the WLB intervened, and in February its arbitrator awarded the decorators to Local 1421, pending final decision by the NLRB. The producers refused to obey the WLB order and filed a petition, at last, with the NLRB to resolve the "jurisdictional dispute." In March Local 1421 went out on strike.

The producers' plot was transparent. The war was still on, and the no-strike pledge was sacred. The producers thought they had the local over a barrel. If it was faithful to the no-strike pledge and refrained from striking, after having voted to strike, its integrity and strength as a union might be fatally compromised. If it struck—which was apparently what the producers wanted it to do—and was joined by other unions in the hated C. S. U., the producers hoped to see them all discredited through their violation of the no-strike pledge.

When the unions defied the producers' ultimatum to return to work by April 4, contracts were canceled and members fired. Richard Walsh ordered his men to take over the strikers' work, but they refused. When the producers announced that thousands of jobs were open to all comers, he issued rump charters wholesale for strike-breakers, declaring it was his duty to "keep out communism and keep the studios running in war time." Oddly, the heads of the A. F. of L. international failed to support the strike until the regional NLRB decided in June that it was legal and justified.

In August the C. I. O. came to the support of the strikers, "to help defeat company unionism, labor's menace in the post-war era," and began to help picket theaters in various large cities.

Although an NLRB election was held in May, the Washington board did not resolve the "jurisdictional" issue until Tuesday, October 9. It then decided in favor of the strikers. 'According to reliable reports the producers will defy the decision on the pretext that if they accept it, I. A. T. S. E. will strike. In any case, the strike may be hard to settle, for the local and its allied unions insist not only on recognition by the producers but also that machinery be set up to prevent and settle jurisdictional disputes and that all union contracts and jobs be restored as of the date the strike began. The situation is tense; the strike may last a long time.

November 3, 1945

The settlement that ended the strike in the motion-picture industry represents a complete victory for, and vindication of, the position taken by the Conference of Studio Unions. The contracts of these unions will be reinstated and all striking members returned to their jobs as of the date the dispute started. Recognition of the Set Decorators' Union follows as a matter of course from its recent certification by the National Labor Relations Board, and a procedure has now been established with the American Federation of Labor for the settlement of so-called jurisdictional disputes in the motion-picture industry. All this represents a decided setback for the International Alliance of Theatrical and Stage Employees (I. A. T. S. E.), whose dictatorial methods started the trouble. Thus *The Nation's* prediction of ultimate victory, made at the start of the strike, has been fulfilled. Under the honest and courageous leadership of Herbert Sorrell, the 7,000 members of the fourteen unions on strike waged a fight with few parallels in recent labor history. For thirty-three weeks they held out in the face of extreme violence by goons, thugs, and employer-minded police and of mass arrests. To continue a struggle of this kind, not for a matter of wages and hours, but for a principle—the right of men to belong to a union of their own choice—shows an understanding and integrity which the whole labor movement should salute.

SEPTEMBER 20, 1965

HOLLYWOOD IN BLACK AND WHITE

John Oliver Killens

•

John Oliver Killens was a novelist, TV and film writer, playwright and essayist. He wrote two films, *Odds Against Tomorrow* (fronting for the blacklisted Abraham Polonsky) and *Slaves*. His classic novel *Youngblood* was recently reissued by the University of Georgia Press. He was a founder of the Harlem Writers Guild.

IN THE BEGINNING was the Word, and the Word was God, and the Word was with God, but somewhere along the line Hollywood preempted God's dominion.

My first trip to Hollywood occurred when I was twenty and impressionable. I thought at the time that Los Angeles, especially the Hollywood-Beverly Hills part of it, was Paradise Regained with glamorous moving picture stars thrown in for good measure. I had driven with three friends of mine across the vast and varied country. My friend who owned the car in which we made the trip was a Negro American Legionnaire, and his reason for making the trip was to attend the Legion's convention. My reason for going was the actual going and the seeing. We saw a huge hunk of America that summer and fall. We drove from Washington, D.C. through Maryland, through Pennsylvania, through Ohio, through Illinois, through Indiana, over the muddy rutty roads of Nebraska. And we "Americans" were perfectly willing to "give Nebraska back to the Indians," which was a rather masochistic pun on our part, coming as it did from four black men who never owned Nebraska or any other of the Forty-Eight. I shall never forget one of the billboards on a Middle West highway outside a great industrial complex:

EVERY WORKER WITH HIS TOOL IS AN AMERICAN CAPITALIST

This made us feel better about the whole thing.

We went through gorgeous, luxuriant Wyoming, through Lusk and Cody and on and up into Yellowstone National Park where nature runs amuck in all her naked shameless beauty, and then two days later down out of the mountains to Salt Lake City where we spent the night in a "chinch harbor" (which is Afro-Americanese for all the dinky colored hotels with hot and cold running roaches and bloated bed-bugs and a public, alligator-legged showerless bath at the end of the dark and dingy hall). It seemed that our money did not spend at the white hotels of that fair city. The next afternoon we followed the Okies in hapless trek across the hot Mojave Desert and on and on to sunny California, where the earth is lush and glistening green and breathing with fertility. We also stopped in a chinch harbor in Los Angeles, but we told ourselves it had nothing to do with our color this time, but was because our money was not long enough for the fancy white hotels. We also noticed, but overlooked, the discrepancy between Central Avenue and Wiltshire Boulevard, which was even more glaring than the difference between Lenox and Madison Avenues.

The next occasion for visiting the City of Angels was years later when I flew West on a lecture tour. I was older and had been to a great World War to fight against fascism and to make the whole world safe for democracy. I had come home and quit Washington for New York, had written a novel, and had been published. I was wiser and I should have been wise to L. A. and to Hollywood. I should not have been taken in a second time. Probably because I came to the city that second time as a "celebrity" it was difficult for me to see the city, realistically, through all that smog and adulation. The weather, the people, the cleanliness, the expanse, life slower-paced, the glowing landscape, all that pretty superficiality. And, of course, the inevitable stars all over again. I was going to New York, I told a couple of my California friends, and bring my family out there to live. "Fine! Great!" they said. "This is the place for an artist like you to live and work. And you can write scenarios for Hollywood while you're at it." There was one dissenting voice. Almena Lomax, editor of an angry incorruptible newspaper, the regrettably defunct *Los Angeles Tribune*, told me: "The worst thing someone like you could do would be to move out here. Los Angeles is moribund. Most of the people are empty, a legion of lost souls. The town is a deadly poison to the creative spirit." I have been back several times since to do film work and I found out, painfully, how right Almena was.

By "Hollywood," I mean the film industry and its comparatively younger brother, television. And anything we say about Hollywood may be said of Madison Avenue—*in spades*. Hollywood just happens to be *where* it is. Madison Avenue determines *what* it is. Hollywood is Fake-town, the great city of make-believe. Here are the culture-makers of our society, many of whom are the most uncultured of men. Here are the true head-shrinkers and the brainwashers of America. I was out west working on a screen treatment once, when my producer, who had a reputation for being the most sensitive of the Hollywood species, got that far-away wistful look in his eyes and said longingly: "Ah, John, if I could only come across just one good 'monster' script to put on my schedule for this season. I don't ask for much in this life." He sighed. I shuddered.

Hollywood, moreover, is a Southern-oriented city, as is all of Greater Los Angeles. This statement should surprise no one, since Hollywood, more than any other institution, has been responsible for the glorification of the South, past and present, and for creating the image of black inferiority. It created the lying, stealing, childish, eyeball-rolling, feet-shuffling, sex-obsessed, teeth-showing, dice-shooting black male, and told the world this was the real Negro in the U.S.A. It invented the Negro "mammy" whose breasts were always large enough to suckle an entire nation, and who always loved old massa's chilluns more than she loved her own. The men of Fake-town have brainwashed America and the entire world with the brush of white supremacy.

I accuse Hollywood of being the most anti-Negro influence in this nation in the 20th century. With *Birth of a Nation*, Hollywood fired its first big gun in its war against the black American, and the gunfire has continued unabated ever since. Hollywood has ever glorified the Confederates' and slavery's cause, with such magnificent monstrosities as *Gone With the Wind*, *Virginia*, *Kentucky*, ad infinitum. Oh, how many oceans of bitter tears have been shed for the likes of Rob Lee and Jeff Davis? How much weeping and nostalgia for the good old days down on the plantation with the pretty, white and Southern-hooded ladies and the handsome white colonels in the Big House at their grand and gracious parties, replete with dancing and live (and sometimes black) musicians? What kind of distortion of history has made Grant and Sherman anti-heroes and Lee and Stonewall Jackson men of unblemished character and unquestioned loyalty and heroism?

I was seated in a Hollywood movie house with a friend in 1959 watching a ridiculous version of slavery entitled *Band of Angels*, based on a novel by Robert Penn Warren. In one particular scene, Clark Gable, who was Sidney Poitier's good massa, was coming from New Orleans via the Mississippi River back to his plantation. When the boat neared the shore, all of his happy faithful slaves were gathered there singing a song of welcome to old massa. White people in the theatre were weeping, some slyly, some unashamedly, at the touching scene, when suddenly my friend and I erupted with laughter, because we thought that surely, in the time of Montgomery and Little Rock, this must have been put into the film for comic relief.

The other great myth created by Hollywood was the "good" cowboy and the "bad" Indian, again standing truth and history on their heads. Again white folks were inevitably cast in the role of supermen. Surrounded and outnumbered by wild and screaming Indians, the gallant whites crouched with their women and children behind a barricade of broken-down covered wagons, and they somehow always managed to break out. . . . Either that, or they held the bloody bastards off till the Cavalry arrived. The only good Injun was a Gunga Din type, who sold out his tribe to the whites, or one like Tonto who was the white man's lackey. The pity is not so much that Hollywood distorted history, but that most Americans, black and white, accepted the distortion as truth.

Once upon an afternoon in the middle fifties, I got a phone call from a friend. He was in Hollywood and I was in Brooklyn, and the conversation went something like this: "John, what do you think of *Emperor Jones?*"

"*Emperor Jones?* What do you mean?"

"I mean—making a movie of *Emperor Jones*. I've been meeting most of the day with the executive producer of a major studio, and they want me to do *Emperor Jones*, and I told them you were the only writer I would trust to do the screen-play, because that way I would be certain that the dignity of the Negro people would not be violated."

I said, "But, Harry, crap-shooting, razor-toting, all the tired stereotypes—who needs it in 1957?"

Harry said, "The man assured me we could do anything we wanted with the script, make any changes, so long as we called it *Emperor Jones,* based on the play by Eugene O'Neill."

I said, "But—"

He said, "Look, why don't you come out here for a few days at their expense and we'll sit down with them, and if you don't like what you see or hear, I don't like it either. All you can lose is a couple of days."

I agreed. During my flight to the coast, I did a hasty three- or four-page outline in which I rewrote O'Neill's *Emperor*. I took the studio at its word. Instead of Jones being a train porter, I made him a slave on a Southern plantation. Instead of his getting into a fight with another Negro in a dice game and slashing him to death with a razor, I had Jones hit his white whipping boss in the head with a hoe and escape to an island in the West Indies, where he meets Smithers and so forth and so on, change after change after change. When I arrived in Los Angeles, I found that the studio had set me up in a suite across from Belafonte's at the Hotel Ambassador, where he was appearing nightly at the Coconut Grove. I went over to Harry's suite, and Sidney Poitier was visiting, and we had a lengthy bull session about what we were going to do in Hollywood to change the Negro's image of himself. I remember Sidney saying very excitedly, "I will never make a movie that will reflect against the dignity of Negro people." As sophisticated as we three deemed ourselves, we naïvely thought we could set jaded Hollywood on her uppers.

The next day Harry and I sat for hours with the executive producer and staff members of the major studio. After I read my outline with a straight face, Mr. Executive Producer said, "Well, Mr. Killens, you will admit that this is hardly what Mr. O'Neill had in mind."

I said, offhandedly, "You can still call it *Emperor Jones*."

What we tried to get them to do was to tell the real story of Henri Christophe, the magnificent Emperor of Haiti, upon whose life O'Neill apparently based his story. Belafonte talked to them as if he had just stepped out of Haitian history. We would make a movie that would include not only Christophe, but Toussaint L'Ouverture and all the other Haitian heroes who made history in the war against Napoleon. As we depicted it, it would have involved all of the major Negro actors as well as white ones. A spectacular. I could almost hear the sound of the cash register clanking in the producer's head. He agreed. Forget about *Emperor Jones*. This is the movie we would make. And in the epic tradition. A week or so later the studio changed its mind, with this explanation: "We paid one hundred and fifty thousand dollars for the rights to *Emperor Jones*, and this is the movie we will do. If Mr. Belafonte doesn't do it, we will get a Negro star who will." Thanks to the rising consciousness of black Americans as reflected in leading. Negro actors, this movie has not been made. Decades before, the great Paul Robeson, who is a hero-symbol to every black artist with a heart or memory, played *Emperor Jones* on Broadway and in Hollywood. An era ended when Mr. Robeson denounced the film capital after making *Tales of Manhattan*.

In 1959, I spent five months in Hollywood writing a screenplay of my novel, *Youngblood*. When my family (which consisted of my wife and two children) were ready to spend five weeks of the summer with me, I had to look for larger living quarters. This was when I came to know Hollywood for what it really was. I spent two frustrating weeks trying to find a vacancy in the hotels and motels of that city. My producer would call a motel and ask about accommodations for his writer and his writer's family, and of course, "We have just the thing you're looking for; come right over." We would drive to the spacious motel, but as soon as the manager realized what the deal was, the vacancies would disappear mysteriously. One proprietor took my producer aside and told him: "I sympathize with the colored people, especially the kind that's made something out of themselves, like your writer. I'll take a chance and take him and his family in, provided they agree not to use the swimming pool." Imagine how ungrateful he must have thought I was, since I would not agree that my family would not use his old lily-white swimming pool. Fortunately, a friend of mine came to the rescue. His family was visiting in the East, and he offered us the use of his house.

I do not, cannot, care for Hollywood because it has ever been my arch enemy, even with its enlightened films like *Lost Boundaries* and *Home of the Brave*. If the latter one says anything at all, it says that the American Negro is a "nigger" not because of white America but because he, the Negro, believes himself to be a "nigger." And if all American Negroes could be psyched by the white man out of looking upon themselves as "niggers," all their problems would be solved. For, after all, Jim Crow and racial prejudice and lynching are only psychological states of the Negro's mind and have no bases in reality. Thus it is the victim's fault that he is the victim. Following this "logic," history would blame the Jews and not the Nazis, the Algerians, not the French. Thanks particularly to Hollywood, it has already blamed the American Indians and made heroes of the men who practiced genocide against them.

World, Flesh and the Devil, starring Harry Belafonte, Inger Stevens and Mel Ferrer, was another movie of the new "Era of Hollywood

Enlightenment." The big hang-up in this one was: Which of the men would get the girl at the end of the story? The story's logic, its artistic integrity, and dramatic necessity dictated that Inger go for Harry. There were only three people left on the earth after an atomic holocaust. Harry was handsome and the good guy. Ferrer was the embodiment of evil. Notwithstanding, one of the first versions of the script gave Inger to Ferrer. After much debating between New York and California, they arrived at a compromise that satisfied nobody at all. In the final scene of the film, Harry and Inger walk up a deserted Times Square together, and that is how the movie should have ended. But no. Just as we are about to believe that justice has triumphed and that love will conquer all, including racial prejudice, we reckoned without the racial fears of Hollywood. At the final moment, Belafonte turns around and gestures for Ferrer to join them, and the three go off together toward a stone-and-steel horizon.

I remember Ruby Dee commenting once: "I'm not concerned with interracial love and kisses on the movie screen. I'm just looking forward to the day a Negro man can kiss a Negro woman." She noted that with all the roles she had played, as wife and lover, she had never been kissed. It seems that Hollywood is very self-conscious about Negroes being in love and kissing, carrying on like other humans. *A Raisin in the Sun* made history in this respect. Sidney Poitier was probably the first Negro man ever to kiss a woman in a love scene on the movie screens of America. The woman, of course, was Ruby Dee.

Why is Hollywood the most backward of mass media as far as black Americans are concerned? An obvious reason is that more money is involved in making a film than in producing a play, and, consequently, more money is likely to be lost in case of box office failure. In its turn, Broadway is far more backward than book-publishing. The hard facts are: the more money involved, the less likelihood that the truth about the black man will achieve an audience. And thus black voices, stilled for centuries, are yet committed to oblivion at a moment in history when America needs most desperately to hear black voices. What else is new besides the new Negro? All else is repetition, a gross redundancy. What else is dynamic in this homeland of the brave? The Negro is the nation's mid-century protagonist.

That is why there's never been a crop of black writers for film or television. If you don't work in these two media, you do not reach the multitudes. Hollywood makes great pretensions of doing controversial movies. But the great debate in America today is *Negro freedom*. This is the fundamental controversy. How does the Negro artist break through this wall of censorship? We black writers and performing artists are ready to pool our creative strength to make our statements to our country. Where are the big-talking liberals?

Television is such a powerful persuader, hidden and overt, it could saturate the Southland with democracy, spreading the word to every nook and corner. Why has not the sunny Southland been sold a democratic image? In the November 14, 1964 edition of the New York *Amsterdam News*, Jesse Walker wrote: "Of the 35 new television shows this season, none has a Negro on a regular basis." How is that for getting the "real" image of America across? In the entire history of Hollywood, less than a half dozen screenplays have been written by Negroes. In that time not a single black screenwriter has been developed. If he has, it has been kept a deep dark secret. As for television, not a single Negro star has ever had his own weekly TV show (with national hook-up), except the late Nat Cole, who did a very very abbreviated stint. Why? Why is the Negro star forever relegated to the role of "guest in the house"? Why is he never the host? Where are the black news commentators? Sports announcers? Weather "experts"?

Of course, the brainwashers have never in history become the unbrainwashers. The slavemaster has never freed the slave. If a slavocracy had to wait for the slave-holders to overthrow it, it would surely last forever. Slave-masters cannot create free societies, even if they are of a mind to do so. The chains—economic, social, sentimental, psychological—that shackle the master to his slave are unbreakable, as far as he is concerned. On the other hand, the slave's fundamental aim is to break these chains. He awaits the day, the hour, the moment. The Nazis would never have freed the Jews. America has not yet freed the Negro, one hundred years after the word was given.

Ironically, the American Negro, at whom Hollywood has eternally aimed her fire, has been the least vulnerable of all Americans, the least brainwashed. We have never been completely taken in by the hypocritical culture, by film or television. Our belief in our innate inferiority has been, at most, superficial. Yes, the black American is a believer, but not a True Believer in the Word according to Saint Hollywood. That is why we will be the basic folk to free this country. We'll need a great deal of help from you, but we cannot, shall not, wait while you procrastinate.

APRIL 3, 2000

RUNAWAY SHOPS

Marc Cooper

•

Marc Cooper is a *Nation* contributing editor and host of the weekly show *Radio Nation*. Two earlier pieces of his on the impasse of Hollywood's labor unions were published in the late 1980s in *American Film* and *Premiere*.

REMEMBER THOSE GREAT scenes in *Blues Brothers 2000* that evoked the urban grit and soul of southside Chicago and Joliet? Well, sorry. Those scenes were actually filmed in a city that doesn't know an el station from Wrigley Field. *Blues Brothers 2000* was shot across the Canadian border, in Toronto.

The same goes for a rapidly increasing number of TV movies and feature films. Production is migrating, principally to Canada, to take advantage of labor costs that are on average 20 percent lower than in the United States. This runaway globalization of production has thrown Hollywood—and its unions—into a full-scale alert. "This issue is at the very top of our legislative and organizational agenda," says Catherine York, director of government relations for the Screen Actors Guild.

Last summer SAG and the Directors Guild issued a joint report measuring the extent of runaway production. The report revealed that between 1990 and 1998 the percentage of US film and TV production occurring overseas doubled, to more than 27 percent of the total. A full

45 percent of generally lower-budget TV movies of the week were being shot overseas by 1998. Canada not only offers lower wages; a clause in the NAFTA treaty allows the government to give film producers a hefty tax credit subsidy for films shot on Canadian soil.

The result: a mini-recession among Hollywood craft and technical workers in the midst of the celebrated economic expansion, with an estimated 60,000 full-time–equivalent jobs lost in three years, and a cumulative economic loss of more than $10 billion.

"I started feeling the squeeze about two years ago," says Mike Everett, an activist in IATSE Local 728, which represents lighting workers and electricians. "It's a sort of crash. All those middle-ground movies of the week and commercials, all the bread-and-butter work, has taken off to Canada and some to Australia." One recent press report described a monthly meeting of a set decorators' local. Of the thirty people who showed up, only three claimed full-time employment. All were fully employed three years ago.

So the unions and other entertainment-industry groups are fighting back. At the national level, SAG, the motion picture academy, the Association of Imaging Technology and Sound, the Directors Guild, the Producers Guild, some IATSE locals and an association of state film commissions have formed the FILM US Alliance. Working with a bipartisan group of Congress members who represent districts dependent on film production, it is fashioning legislation that would offer to companies a 20 percent federal tax credit on wages paid to workers employed in domestic production. Proponents claim this would fully equalize the playing field with Canada's cheaper labor rates. "We are taking a methodical approach to this legislation," says SAG's York. "We are working with the Congressional leadership, with the Ways and Means Committee, to come up with the best approach, the best solution, the best legal vehicle."

In California, the state hardest hit by foreign production, union activists came together to form the Film and Television Action Committee. The FTAC has been pressuring the California legislature to pass a similar wage-credit bill—a caravan of honking Teamsters semitrailers encircled the state Capitol—but it has so far met the resistance of Democratic Governor Gray Davis. A tax-credit bill died in last year's session.

Some union activists are uncomfortable with the tax-credit approach. "It's really just about countering Canadian subsidies with our own subsidies and offering even more corporate welfare to the media giants," says Mike Everett. Along with other more politicized activists, Everett has formed the Hollywood Fair Trade Campaign—a group fighting to strike down NAFTA's Canadian subsidy clause. So far, that's a long-shot strategy. But the Fair Trade Campaign is committed to working within the FTAC alliance toward solutions that go beyond corporate welfare.

As part of that strategy, Hollywood unionists plan to show up at the protest demonstrations now being planned to welcome the Democratic convention to Los Angeles this summer. "Last month we were already able to bring out some Hollywood workers to protest at both the Republican and Democratic debates here in LA," Everett says. "And you can be sure we will be at the convention. I compare this to an issue like Vietnam—an issue that both parties agreed upon. So we need to light a fire under their feet. And until we do, we are not going to go away."

7

Honor Bright and All That Jazz

The Blacklist and After

•

NOVEMBER 8, 1947

THE GRAND INQUISITION

I. F. Stone

•

One of America's most celebrated independent journalists, "Izzy" Stone earned a place as the conscience of American journalism through his incisive intelligence and his investigative zeal. At *The Nation*'s Washington correspondent from 1941 to 1946, and founder of the legendary *I. F. Stone's Weekly*—the independent, iconoclastic newsletter of opinion that he edited for nineteen years (1953–1971)—Stone specialized in publishing information ignored by the mainstream media.

Washington, October 31

IT WOULD BE easy to be cute about the pratt-fall with which the House Committee on Un-American Activities ended two weeks of hearings on the movie industry. No such inquiry is complete nowadays without the disclosure of some attempt to steal the atom bomb. By sophisticated standards the atom-bomb sensation produced by the committee was a dud; the ties between it and the film industry were of Rube Goldbergian tortuousness. Unfortunately, relatively few readers of newspapers will get beyond the flaring headlines which link Hollywood with atom-bomb spying.

It would be difficult to imagine a more far-fetched example of slander by association. A Soviet consul in San Francisco is alleged to have "offered" money to an oil-company scientist in 1942 to obtain information on some secret radiation work at the University of California. This scientist went to a faculty member, who in turn approached J. Robert Oppenheimer, later but not then in charge of the atom-bomb project at Los Alamos. Oppenheimer is said to have declared that he regarded such attempts to obtain information as treasonable. There is no allegation that any information was supplied. All this occurred in San Francisco.

How was it linked to the film industry? At this point the plot, as told by Louis J. Russell, a committee investigator, really thickened. The first scientist in the chain was a dinner guest two years later of Mrs. Louise Bransten, who stands accused of having helped to get Gerhard Eisler out of a concentration camp in France, of having aided many Communist causes, and of having given a dinner for Manuilsky, chief delegate of the Ukraine, during the San Francisco conference. Mrs. Bransten is alleged to have been helped in the Eisler rescue by a former State Department employee who knew John Howard Lawson and Herbert Biberman, two of the film writers cited for contempt in the film inquiry. The presumed clincher is that both these writers had also been dinner guests of Mrs. Bransten.

Even the committee investigator, Russell, who is not paid to be judicious, did not charge that anyone in the film industry had any part in trying to steal atom-bomb secrets, if any such attempt actually was made. That it was made is highly doubtful, unless the FBI and the Department of Justice are also in cahoots with Moscow. Russell said he gave this story to the Justice Department more than a year ago, and it took no action. Certainly it must have made an investigation, but scientist no. 1 in this Charlie Chan chain was allowed to leave for England recently to work for the Shell Oil Company. Would he have been allowed to leave if he had tried to obtain atomic secrets for the Russians? But for every newspaper reader who examines the dispatches closely enough to ask himself that question, there will be ten thousand who glance at the headline "Film Reds Linked to Atom-Bomb Plot," and turn to the sports pages with the feeling that something will have to be done about these reds.

The literate and the thoughtful must not deceive themselves. The committee is succeeding in its objectives: to build up an impression that Communists have penetrated everywhere; that they menace the prize national possession, the atom bomb; that something drastic will have to be done about them; that the peril warrants dismissal of appeals to constitutional rights as legal pettifogging, if not treasonable jesuitry. The state of mind being created is a kind of plot-and-persecution system akin to paranoid obsession and like paranoia impervious to correction by rational argument. The creation of this state of mind is the necessary preliminary for the emergence of a full-scale fascist movement garbed as militant Americanism. It is in this perspective, and not as some kind of unfortunate Congressional aberration, that one must view this latest in the long series of "hearings" by the Thomas committee and its predecessors. What the committee needs above all is attention, and the attention-getting potentialities of the movie star and the film industry are so much richer than anything else in American life that if there were no reds in Hollywood the committee would have to plant some.

As sheer spectacle, whether for the sophisticated or the unsophisticated, the movie hearings were the most superb performance yet put on by the committee. Outside the huge marble-walled caucus room of the old House office building on Capitol Hill a long line waited daily for a glimpse of the glamorous folk in attendance. "My wife," I heard a poorly dressed man plead with the policeman on duty downstairs, "wants to have a look at Humphrey Bogart." Within the guarded hearing-room the scene matched Hollywood's best in productions. On the right sat the ponderous moguls of the industry, with their handsome gray-haired counsel, Paul McNutt. A million dollars in movie names were scattered through the intent audience. In the front rows left sat perhaps the most affluent-looking looked group of alleged "reds" in modern history: earnest men, mostly young—only rich America could provide its alleged revolutionaries with such sleek clothes and Sulka ties. On the aisle, out-dazzled both by their clients and by McNutt, sat Bob Kenny and Bart Crum, the determined counsel of the accused screen writers. The rows of press tables in front of them were crowded with stellar by-lines, hemmed in by Klieg lights. And on the high bench presiding was the Grand Inquisitor himself—the bald, stout, red-faced apoplectic looking J. Parnell Thomas. One could not imagine a more perfect piece of casting for his role.

The first week's hearings were largely taken up with the lunatic fringe of the right, Hollywood's Liz Dillings, male and female. The second week was different. From the moment strong-faced John Howard Lawson hitched up his pants over a rather capitalistic paunch as he strode to the witness stand, it was clear that the committee was in for a fight. Lawson's stentorian voice, aided by a microphone, out-shouted both Thomas, no dulcet tenor, and Thomas's gavel, which broke the first day under the pounding he gave it. The committee is accustomed to quiet crucifixions and docile answers to loaded questions. One screen writer after another declined to give Thomas the pleasure of watching the victim squirm, and ten were finally cited for contempt. The key question, "Are you a Communist?" brought neither denial nor affirmation nor even a flat refusal to answer, but an insistence on shouting the committee down. At one point Thomas asked a witness almost pleadingly, "Can't you answer yes, no, or maybe?" and two witnesses were even allowed to read their statements.

"The committee is determined," Thomas said at the beginning of the inquiry, "that the hearings shall be fair and impartial. We have subpoenaed witnesses representing both sides of the question." But the nearest the "accused" got to presenting their side, except for the reading of the two statements, was the chance to answer "yes" or "no" when they were asked about membership in the Screen Writers' Guild and the Communist Party. Their counsel, laying the groundwork for what will be a crucial test of the right of Congress to investigate in the sphere of ideas, were given no chance to cross-examine witnesses or rebut charges against their clients, and at one point were threatened with indictment for conspiracy if they had advised their clients not to answer. On each of the ten cited for contempt the committee released a voluminous dossier. These dossiers showed that the committee's investigators are constant readers of the Communist Party press: most of the information in them came from the *Daily Worker*, the rest from other party papers. That few of the "accused" could qualify as Republicans is hardly news. The dossiers were made up of numbered counts like an indictment; each purported to represent an "affiliation" with the Communist Party, but many of them could be brought forward against other leftists and liberals who are by no means party-liners. Aid to Spain, defense of one of a long list of leftists from Tom Mooney to Gerhard Eisler, a 1931 speech against the criminal-syndicalism laws, praise of Marx and Engels, membership in Consumers' Union or the P.C.A., showing "an active interest in the Soviet Union," and signing an ad in 1945 calling for breaking relations with Spain were among the "counts" in these indictments, which could set precedents for wider dragnet proceedings.

But the most striking feature of the hearings and the dossiers was the almost complete absence of allegations concerned with what was supposed to be the business of the inquiry—Communist propaganda in the films. The committee claims to have a list of complaints but seems hesitant to make it public. The hesitancy becomes clear when one notes the character of the only two films to which the "dossiers" object as communistic. One is *Blockade*, the Lawson film about the Spanish civil war, which was covertly pro-Loyalist; the other, *The Brotherhood of Man*, which Ring Lardner, Jr., helped to write for the Automobile Workers' Union. This was based on the pamphlet "The Races of Mankind," by Ruth Benedict and Gene Weltfish. It is significant that among those cited for contempt are men who have written or produced those few movies which give the Negro a break and attack anti-Semitism: for example, Edward Dmytryk and Adrian Scott, who were responsible for *Crossfire*.

This inquiry must be fought by all men of good-will. The constitutional issues go to the very fundamentals of what may truly be called Americanism. If a Congressional committee can investigate ideas in the movies, it can investigate them in the press. The purpose is to terrorize all leftists, liberals, and intellectuals; to make them fearful in the film, the theater, the press, and any school of advanced ideas the Thomas committee can stigmatize as "red." In the films, as the transcript shows, the committee is out to give the moguls of the industry no rest until they not only take from the screen what little liberal and social content it has, but turn to making films which would prepare the way for fascism at home and war abroad. There were two revealing moments in the producers' testimony. Jack Warner, explaining the "subtle" methods of "red" screen writers, said, "They have the routine of the Indians and the colored folks. That is always their setup." And when Louis B. Mayer said he was going to start making some "anti-Communist films promptly," Thomas leaned forward with a grin and asked, "These hearings haven't anything to do with the promptness, have they?"

NOVEMBER 19, 1949

HOLLYWOOD GRAY LIST

Carey McWilliams

•

Carey McWilliams knew many of those called by the HUAC, including "friendly" witnesses like Edward Dmytryk, who, in an article for the *Saturday Evening Post*, claimed that McWilliams as well as Thomas Mann were being "used" by the defendants. McWilliams wrote vividly about the Hollywood Ten in his book *Witch Hunt: The Revival of Heresy* and in his memoir *The Education of Carey McWilliams*.

Los Angeles, November 9

IT HAS ALWAYS been difficult to take Hollywood seriously, and an observer of the scene today can scarcely believe that the familiar surface gaiety conceals currents of real fear. Fear of the black list is strong, but a more widespread and probably better-founded fear is that of the gray list.

Mr. X, a famous actor whose services were once in great demand, is now hard up. During Hollywood's vociferous "anti-fascist" phase he was active in political affairs, and at that time the studios did not appear to be annoyed by his extra-curricular interests. Today, although he gets work occasionally, he feels he is on a black list. His agent, friends "on the lot," the gossip columnists, and others tell him, however, that he is only on the gray list—the list of those political offenders who are, so to speak, on probation.

Every relationship in the industry is affected by people's awareness of the gray list. No one is sure where he stands or whom he can trust. Fear determines the proper warmth with which to greet an old friend, the proper line to take on a story, with whom it is wise to be seen having lunch. A social boycott reinforces the graylisting of workers.

One deplorable result is the great decrease of political interest and political activity in Hollywood. The Film Division of the Council of the Arts, Sciences, and Professions was once the most active division; today it is the least active. At political meetings in Los Angeles Hollywood figures used to appear on the platform as a matter of course; today it is almost impossible to enlist the services of a star for any political affair. A few big names, so-called, came out for Dewey in 1948, and a handful of stars sought to rehabilitate themselves in the eyes of their employers by supporting Truman, but in general the collapse of the left in Hollywood has meant the end of political activity. The talent groups, by and large, have not gone over to reaction; they have simply disintegrated as a liberal force.

Even the extreme right-wing organizations are quiescent. The Motion Picture Alliance for the Preservation of American Ideals has done practically nothing since its spokesmen "fingered" the ten Hollywood writers in the Washington hearings except sponsor poorly attended meetings for Robert Stripling, Hedda Hopper, and Elizabeth Bentley. The extreme right, in fact, seems to be riddled with dissension. Some directors of the Alliance are convinced that other directors are secretly sympathetic to "the welfare state." One director is even suspected of being a Democrat. Those who remember the effective role that Hollywood played in the Roosevelt campaigns must regret the present gray doldrums. In one sense, the situation is highly paradoxical, for Hollywood has ceased to be interested in politics precisely when politics are exercising an extraordinary influence on everyone connected with the motion-picture industry.

From 1920 to 1940 the production of motion pictures occupied a largely marginal position in American industry and finance. Although the bargaining power of the workers was atomized by a pattern of crazy craft unionism, the profits of the industry were so enormous that wages remained high. In the last quarter of this period the craft unions tended to merge, as was shown by the formation of the Conference of Studio Unions; even the weakest talent groups were organized; and Hollywood became intensely political. The moguls of the industry were beginning to feel the "discipline" of New York finance, but they remained fairly tolerant of politics and trade-unionism during most of the war years, when it was almost impossible to lose money in film-making.

In March, 1945, the producers manipulated the Conference of Studio Unions and its affiliates into calling a disastrous strike which lasted through November, 1945, and was resumed in 1946. The result was the complete destruction of the conference and the disintegration of many of its affiliates. Thousands of workers lost the savings of a lifetime; literally hundreds of strikers were placed on trial. The names of persons in the talent groups who supported this strike form the nucleus of the present gray list.

After this debacle about all that remained of the left wing in Hollywood was a group of articulate and influential members of the Screen Writers' Guild. The pocket of resistance they formed was quickly wiped out. The Motion Picture Alliance raised a clamor about "communism in Hollywood," which was quickly picked up by the Hearst press and eventually by the House Committee on Un-American Activities. At first the industry was reluctant to discharge and blacklist the ten writers cited for contempt for refusing to answer the committee's questions, but at a meeting held, appropriately, in New York its representatives were reminded that Hollywood no longer occupied a marginal position in the general scheme of American business. The gray list acts as a phantom Un-American Activities Committee in Hollywood today.

There is also, of course, a gray list for themes. One of the finest directors in the industry, an Academy Award winner, told me the other day that the studios have rejected almost every idea he has suggested in the last two years with the remark, "Can't you find a good love story?" The only bright spots in Hollywood's recent production record are a few pictures like *The Champion*, *Pinky*, and *Home of the Brave*. The last two deal with the race question and, significantly, have been highly successful. Racial tolerance is apparently the one controversial theme that they may be presented from the liberal or progressive point of view. On the other hand, *The Red Menace* and *I Married a Communist* have been dismal failures.

Faced with a shrinking world market, the industry is rapidly narrowing the domestic market by its slavish adherence to tepid themes and silly plots. People are treating Hollywood pictures as Hollywood treats its finest talent, patronizing them "occasionally" and putting most of them on a gray list.

JUNE 28, 1952

HOLLYWOOD MEETS FRANKENSTEIN

"X"

•

"X" was the pseudonym for a group of top-flight writers who had important positions in major Hollywood studios. That's what the magazine reported in its "How Free is Free?" special issue, edited by Carey McWilliams, devoted to the McCarthyite onslaught on civil and political liberties.

Unfortunately we have been unable to discover who the author or authors were, despite contacting remaining survivors of the Blacklist and the valiant effort of archivists going through the magazine's archives at both the Houghton Library at Harvard University and the special collections of UCLA.

Hollywood, California

ON OCTOBER 24, 1947, three of Hollywood's top directors sent a telegram to scores of key figures in the film industry. The wire read:

> THIS INDUSTRY IS NOW DIVIDED AGAINST ITSELF. UNITY MUST BE RECAPTURED, OR ALL OF US WILL SUFFER FOR YEARS TO COME, YOUR AID IS REQUIRED IN THIS CRITICAL MOMENT. THIS IS MORE IMPORTANT THAN ANY PICTURE YOU EVER MADE. SIGNED,
>
> JOHN HUSTON, WILLIAM WYLER, BILLY WILDER

"This critical moment" was an investigation of Hollywood by the House Committee on Un-American Activities, and the issue of "The Ten," then still this side of prison.

In those first days of the committee's onslaught, a broad group of film people stood up and fought back. More than fifty stars appeared on two nationwide broadcasts. Others made a junket to Washington to watch the shabby circus in action. Several top studio executives, among them Dore Schary and L. B. Mayer, said brave words. Both insisted that what mattered in the case of talent was performance, not politics.

But in the hierarchy of the film corporations, men like Schary and Mayer are less than kings. The overlords of the industry are the New York executives who control financing, distribution, and the theater chains. The motion-picture business is primarily a real-estate operation, and the real estate is in the hands of men like Loew's Nick Schenck, Paramount's Barney Balaban, and Fox's Spyros Skouras. It was these big boys who, at the close of the committee hearings, whistled the studio heads to a meeting at the Waldorf-Astoria. The high-priced hired help were given a brisk caning and a lecture on the facts of life. They emerged from the meeting to issue a statement announcing the firing of "The Ten." A portion of that document is worth quoting, for it has become a Pike's Peak of irony:

> In pursuing this policy, we are not going to be swayed by any hysteria or intimidation from any source. We are frank to recognize that such a policy involves dangers and risks. There is a danger of hurting innocent people, there is a risk of creating an atmosphere of fear. Creative work at its best cannot be carried on in an atmosphere of fear. We will guard against this danger, this risk, this fear.

Actually, with the firing of "The Ten," Hollywood created for itself a monster that was to grow as gruesome as any that ever frightened the wits out of children at a horror matinee. Since that day, the film industry has been in panicky retreat before every attack on civil liberties. It is now a hapless pushover for any witch-hunting outfit that seeks to collect blood or blackmail.

The spectacle of a giant monopoly gibbering with fright may seem curious until one recalls a bit of Hollywood history. The film executives (not unlike those in other industries) have always had an abiding faith in "the fix." They would rather buy off a racketeering union boss than sit down with an honest labor leader. It was this policy that led to the B-picture episode, a few years back, when the studio heads left a satchel of green-backs in a hotel room to buy off Willie Bioff. It was this faith in the fix that (when a cog slipped somewhere) led to the landing of 20th Century's Joe Schenck in the federal pokey for income-tax evasion.

Hollywood is a company town, and beneath the fancy publicity it is not so different from a coal town in Kentucky or a cotton town in Alabama. When a strike broke out in 1946, the studios smashed it by using tear gas, fire hoses, and gun-toting deputies.

A few final details to fill in the background. Nineteen fifty-one was a rocky year for motion pictures. The Supreme Court had handed down an anti-trust decision ordering the divorcement of theater chains from production facilities. The public, hit by high prices, began to cut down on money spent for entertainment. Television antennae darkened the sky. In Los Angeles, movie attendance dropped 30 percent. Hundreds of neighborhood theaters shut their doors. 20th Century's Skouras asked his 130 highest-priced personnel to take salary cuts, some up to 50 percent. Warner Brothers (showing a comfortable profit for the fiscal year) fired five department heads, one of them with twenty-three years' service.

The film industry, following a national pattern, was searching for a way to slash employee's paychecks and intimidate their unions. Many movie executives looked upon the investigations of Hollywood as a faintly noxious blessing. True, they created nasty publicity. But they also made workers fearful and reluctant to press wage demands. They also kept the unions from becoming militant. Hadn't the conviction of "The Ten" knocked off half a dozen leaders of the Screen Writers Guild?

Meanwhile, the witch hunters were busy. After "The Ten" came the hearings of last year, which used Larry Parks for a burnt offering. Then the Hollywood subcommittee session at which Sidney Buchman turned out to be the main event. Each of these investigations was regarded by the employer element as the big crisis which, once past, would get everybody off the hook and permit a return from panic to Hollywood's normal condition of twittering nervousness. A spokesman for the Un-American Activities Committee actually told an interviewer on TV that last year's hearing would definitely wind up the investigations of "Red influence" in films.

Early in 1952 there seemed to be some easing of the pressure against studio personnel. Studio heads were no longer (or less often) making rousing speeches against The Menace. (One top executive, at a *compulsory* meeting of the entire staff, from producers and stars to grips and messenger boys, demanded that every one of the workers become an informer and report immediately anything of a suspicious character in the words or actions of fellow employees.) But this sort of thing decreased and a numbed weariness settled over Hollywood. The monster had been fed, it seemed, and for a while would be content to digest its victims.

This prediction turned out to be wishful thinking. A new quarry was marked for the hunt—liberals and "fellow travelers." This meant attacks on more than isolated writers, directors, actors, and a few producers. It meant the impugning of certain top executives themselves, no matter how fervid their protestations of anti-communism, no matter how many anti-Communist pictures they had produced.

Dore Schary (in charge at Metro, the biggest studio of them all) became a prime target. So did Paramount's chief of production, Don Hartman. So did Stanley Kramer. The Wage Earners Committee, a local nuisance group, picketed theaters throughout the Los Angeles area and paid its respects to Schary and Kramer with placards, on one of which their names dripped blood.

Neither Schary nor Kramer took it lying down. Both filed suits for more than a million dollars against the Wage Earners, and these actions are now pending in the courts. Schary took a big ad in the movie trade papers and the Los Angeles dailies, defining his suit as "a challenge to all those who recklessly and viciously peddle the tawdry wares of defamation and personal slander." Even the right-wing Producers Association came out in behalf of the libel suits.

The picketing did not stop. But for a moment, there seemed to be a stiffening of resistance. The worm turned, ever so slightly. People who had long ago resigned themselves to a relentless and inevitable McCarthyism crawled up from their cyclone cellars. There even seemed to be a ray of sunlight. When the Republican faction on the Un-American Activities Committee released a report denouncing Hollywood for having failed to purge itself of Communist influence, elements of the Producers Association blasted the report. So vigorous was this reaction that the Democratic members of the committee later dissented from the Republican stand.

Had Hollywood had enough? Had the loss of talent and revenue and the acres of damaging publicity finally exasperated the studios? Had they glimpsed, in the light of events, the shadowy reflection of a lost principle, the principle of civil liberties? It almost seemed as though the saturation point had been reached when, as in the Salem witch hunts, the fanatics started to go after the higher echelons.

Perhaps by coincidence, perhaps by design, but at this moment—at a time when Schary and Kramer found themselves on the barricades lately manned by people who are now for the most part jobless—Howard Hughes joined battle with the Screen Writers Guild over the issue of monies and credit due screenwriter Paul Jarrico. The latter, a Fifth Amendment casualty, demanded both credit on a finished picture and $5,000. Hughes galloped into the fray, Sir Galahad in tennis sneakers, doing the noble thing to defend free America. That is, it began to be noble after $3,500, for which sum Hughes was originally willing to settle with Jarrico. The Guild, whose contract with the entire industry stipulates that it alone shall arbitrate credits, tried to force Hughes to honor a contract which he publicly and blandly renounced. So far, two courts have upheld Hughes, or at least relieved him of the obligation to fulfill his contract with the Guild.

And since we've come to the courts: recently a jury in federal court awarded Adrian Scott (one of "The Ten") $80,000 due him under an unfinished contract with RKO. Judge Ben Harrison, acting on the appeal of the studio, reversed the decision on the ground that the jury didn't know everything it should have known about the case. In announcing his decision, Judge Harrison also made a pejorative statement concerning what he thinks of a man who refuses to answer a question at a Congressional hearing. At the same time, it is only fair to say that in the case of another member of "The Ten" the judge allowed a verdict for a smaller amount to stand.

The Hughes controversy broke at just about the time that Elia Kazan (with a juicy new contract pending) confessed all to the Un-American Activities Committee and published an advertisement in which he urged "liberals" to "speak out" and inform on associates. The blasts from Hughes and Kazan sent a good many liberals scuttling back to their cyclone cellars to sit it out in what they hoped would be silence.

Then came a development that reached down into the cyclone cellars.

The American Legion for some time has had a proscribed list which feeds the hungry maw of the *American Legion Magazine* whenever that publication feels the need for more red meat in its diet. About three months ago, the Legion's Americanism experts found a brilliant new way of harassing the studios and getting them to lop off reddish pinks and pinkish whites. The method: picketing.

One or two pictures were picketed in one or two cities, and immediately Representatives of the Industry (run when you hear that phrase) rushed to the Legion experts with a view to arranging some kind of truce. The idea was to arrive at a formula whereby the studios would get a guarantee that pictures would not be picketed. What was dreamed up was a clearance mechanism that may well become Exhibit A in the evidence of this era's corruption of the American tradition. The mechanism works something like this:

Actor or writer finds himself on the list. He is called in by the chief in charge of such matters at the studio which employs him and is given a dossier of "charges" against him. These range from parlor gossip to hearsay quotes from the Tenney Committee reports, to scuttlebutt from the pages of "Red Channels," to data from state and county volunteer committees. Mention in the *Daily Worker* other than outright attack, is considered a charge.

Out of the "appeasement" meeting between the Legion and industry representatives came a preliminary list of some 300 names, furnished by letter to each studio. The letter stated that if the studio employed any of the listees, picketing on a national scale would ensure when the picture involving the person's services was released.

To meet this, the studio now calls the listee, presents him with the charges, and asks him to write a letter "to the head of the studio" answering, by what is known as an Affidavit of Explanation, the following questions:

1. Is this so?
2. The reasons for joining organizations cited in the charges.
3. The people who invited you to join.
4. Did you invite others to join?
5. Did you resign? When?

The letter or affidavit (copies of which go to various agencies and organizations, and to certain individuals, including, so it is said, George Sokolsky, Howard Rushmore, and Freddy Woltman) is then submitted to a vague "central committee" for "clearance."

What makes this of particular interest, even among the exhibits of atrocities against civil liberties that are so plentiful these days, is the unblushingly investigative character of the questions, as revealed in the third and fourth items. This goes beyond the Un-American Activities Committee in asking liberals or "sympathizers" to name other liberals or "sympathizers."

In addition to Hollywood's troubles with the Legion, the Un-American Activities Committee has announced a new round of hearings for this coming autumn. Its process-servers are as busy as ever. Throughout the spring, deputy marshals sought out Los Angeles physicians, lawyers, radio, and television artists. Film folk were not ignored. One of the latest to be subpoenaed is a screen writer who received his summons on the floor of a Screen Writers Guild meeting—a meeting presumably open only to members in good standing. Considering the fact that the writer's address and phone number appear in the local directory and that no attempt was made to serve him at home, so far as he knows, the choice of time and place was clearly a calculated intimidation. Fear, suspicion, and wild rumor can be kept at fever pitch without the necessity of formal hearings. All the committee needs is an unlimited supply of pink subpoena forms.

As matters stand today, Hollywood is using half a dozen blacklists, as well as supplementary graylists based upon the vaguest sort of innuendo. The assumption that a person is guilty until proved innocent has become standard operating procedure. A weedy growth of professional witch-hunting outfits has sprung up. Fingermen are doing a brisk business, hourly supplying additional names. In an effort to protect themselves from the cruder forms of blackmail, the studios are hiring their own investigators. Quite likely the talent scouts who once signed up young starlets are now combing the country for promising ex-FBI men.

All this has its effect on the kind of films that are being made. A fair cross-section of the pictures now in production includes the following: *Time Bomb, Tribute to a Bad Man, Apache Trail, Flat Top, Road to Bali, Pleasure Island, Something for the Birds, Springfield Rifle*, and *Bela Lugosi Meets the Gorilla Man*—plus two others whose titles seem uncomfortably autobiographical: *Panic Stricken* and *Tonight We Sing*.

It is the opinion of the seasoned if not shell-shocked observers out here that if the industry goes all the way with appeasement of the Legion or any other pressure group on the setting of standards for employability, it will finally deliver itself to the Sokolskys, the McCarthys, and the Wage Earners Committee. After that there can only be darkness and television.

MAY 4, 1957

BLACKLIST = BLACK MARKET

Dalton Trumbo

•

It was Dalton Trumbo, more than any other writer, who broke the blacklist by exposing its absurdity, and its unworkability in the face of an industry's appetite for moneymaking talent. In 1959 the Motion Picture Academy rescinded its bylaw prohibiting awards to those who refused to cooperate with the House Un-American Activities Committee and, after more than a year's hesitation, Universal Studios announced in August 1960 that Trumbo would be credited as the writer of *Spartacus*. That same year director Otto Preminger revealed that Trumbo had written the screenplay for his film *Exodus*. Trumbo won an Oscar for the 1956 film *The Brave One* under the pseudonym of Robert Rich.

The original editorial note to this article read: "The presently known works of screenwriter Dalton Trumbo—which include *Thirty Seconds Over Tokyo, A Man to Remember* and *Kitty Foyle*, among many others—may one day be revealed as his least important and least successful. Since his blacklisting as a member of the Hollywood Ten in 1947, Mr. Trumbo has become a prolific and anonymous contributor to Hollywood's black market in scripts, and for all anyone knows (other than Mr. Trumbo and his producers, who aren't saying), he may have won more Oscars in the last ten years than Walt Disney."

Hollywood

AS THE YEAR 1957 lurches toward its mid-point, Hollywood finds itself celebrating, willingly or unwillingly as the case may be, the tenth anniversary of a blacklist which began in 1947 when a producers' delegation composed of Messrs. Dore Schary, Walter Wanger and Eddie Mannix appeared before the Screen Writers' Guild to plead for acquiescence in the blacklisting of the Hollywood Ten.

Mr. Schary, who is probably the most civilized and certainly the most literate man ever to achieve executive leadership of a major motion-picture producing company, acted as reluctant spokesman for the producers: reluctant because some of the doomed men were his friends; reluctant because he had worked with others of them in the various Roosevelt campaigns; reluctant because he was and is a liberal who hated the idea of a blacklist and probably hates it even more today.

Despite assurances that ten heads would appease the gods, the guillotine has since claimed some 250 other artists and technicians. The most powerful man in Hollywood today is an inconspicuous, pleasant-mannered fellow named William Wheeler, who works as investigator for the House Committee on Un-American Activities. Upon his modest shoulders has fallen the glory that was Zanuck's and the power that was Mayer's.

The paradox of the tenth anniversary of the blacklist lies in the fact that while it finds most surviving members of the Hollywood Ten busily engaged in the practice of their professions, Mr. Schary, amidst a hideous outcry from avaricious stockholders, has just been ejected from his producership at MGM and presently, as the euphemism goes, is at liberty.

The reason for his discharge, Mr. Schary wrote in *The Reporter* of April 18, 1957, was "that I made too many speeches and wrote too many articles, and that my participation in the 1956 Presidential campaign on behalf of the Democrats had made for irritation and enmity." Mr. Schary, in a word, fell victim to the blacklist his own eloquence had inaugurated; the decade ends, as it began, with an absurdity.

The truth, of course, is that the blacklist was openly called for in 1947 by the House Committee on Un-American Activities (". . . Don't you think the most effective way is the payroll route?" ". . . Do you think the studios should continue to employ these individuals?") and that the producers opposed the idea. Eric Johnston, president of the Motion Picture Association of America, told the committee that for producers "to join together and to refuse to hire someone or some people would be a potential conspiracy, and our legal counsel advised against it."

Louis B. Mayer testified that "They have mentioned two or three writers to me several times. There is no proof about it, except they mark them as Communists, and when I look at the pictures they have written for us I can't find once where they have written anything like that. . . . I have asked counsel. They claim that unless you can prove they are Communists they could hold you for damages." Jack L. Warner declared under oath that he "wouldn't be a party with anyone in an association, especially where you would be liable for having a fellow's livelihood impaired; I wouldn't want to do that."

They did it, however, a few days later at a famous meeting in the Waldorf-Astoria. Depositions taken from persons present reveal a long and stormy session during which the Hollywood executives strongly opposed demands of the "Eastern people" for a blacklist. The "Eastern people" unfortunately, controlled the film corporations involved and the source of investment capital with which production is maintained. It was no contest. The meeting ended with a sullenly unanimous proclamation of the first blacklist in the history of motion pictures.

The Hollywood Ten, blacklisted and cursed with the worst press since Bruno Hauptmann, stood trial for contempt of Congress, drew maximum fines and sentences, wrangled their way through skeptical courts and finally were distributed throughout the federal penitentiary system. Ring Lardner, Jr., and Lester Cole landed in Danbury, Connecticut, where they renewed an old acquaintance with ex-Congressman J. Parnell Thomas, chairman of the 1947 hearings which had done them in. Thomas had been caught with his hand in the wrong cash drawer.

Jack Lawson, Adrian Scott and this correspondent, incarcerated under heavy guard in the grand old state of Kentucky, were thrown into intimate contact with its favorite son, ex-Congressman Andy May, who had celebrated the glory of American arms by snatching a few wartime defense bribes. Almost every jail in the country during that curious time found Congressman and contemptee standing cheek by jowl in the chow line, all their old malignities dissolved in common hunger for a few more of them there beans.

Meanwhile, sustained by an Appellate Court decision which confirmed its right and even its duty to investigate artists and their works, the committee embarked on a permanent career in Hollywood. Francis Walter, his chariot drawn by captive starlets, passed like Caesar through the lots attended by a chanting host of the repentent. Under the yelping attack of this stream-lined, sharp-toothed wolf pack, Communists, near-Communists, neo-Communists, proto-Communists, non-Communists and a few friends of anti-Communists fell like tenpins.

And then, imperceptibly at first, the uproar began to diminish. It faded off, about a year ago, into a stunned and terrible silence. There wasn't anybody left to investigate. The silence continues to this day, broken only occasionally by the contemplative licking of old wounds.

A blacklist, far from being a funny thing, is an illegal instrument of terror which can exist only by sufferance of and connivance with the federal government. The Hollywood blacklist is but part of an immensely greater official blacklist—barring its victims from work at home and denying them passage abroad—which mocks our government in all its relations with civilized powers that neither tolerate nor understand such repression. The shock of the blacklist produces psychic disorders among sensitive persons, from which result broken homes, desolate children, premature deaths and sometimes suicide.

It is not alone the loss of income or of property that hurts: the more terrible wound is the loss of a profession to which one's entire life has been dedicated. A director must have the facilities of a studio: denied them, he sells real estate. A violinist must appear in person for the concert: barred from admittance, he becomes a milkman and practices six hours a day against the unrevealed time when his music once more may be heard. The actor's physical personality, which is his greatest asset, becomes his supreme curse under the blacklist; he must be seen, and when the sight of him is prohibited he becomes a carpenter, an insurance salesman, a barber.

A writer is more fortunate. Give him nothing more than paper, a pencil and a nice clean cell, and he's in business. Dante, Cervantes, Rousseau, Voltaire, Ben Jonson, Milton, Defoe, Bunyan, Hugo, Zola, and a score of others have long since proved that in jail or out, writing under their own names or some one else's or a pseudonym or anonymously, writers will write; and that having written, they will find an audience. Only fools with no knowledge of history and bureaucrats with no knowledge of literature are stupid enough to think otherwise.

And so it chanced in Hollywood that each blacklisted writer, after swiftly describing that long parabola from the heart of the motion-picture industry to a small house in a low-rent district, picked himself up, dusted his trousers, anointed his abrasions, looked around for a ream of clean white paper and something to deface it with, and began to write. Through secret channels, and by means so cunning they may never be revealed, what he wrote was passed along until finally it appeared on a producer's desk, and the producer looked upon it and found it good, and monies were paid, and the writer's children began contentedly to eat. Thus the black market.

In the meantime, quietly domiciled nearby with his stunningly beautiful wife and two infant daughters a young man of Irish descent named Michael Wilson sat down at his typewriter and went furiously to work writing scripts. By 1951 he had risen to a position of such prominence that he was subpoenaed by the committee. Appearing before it in good form, Wilson took the Fifth Amendment, ending his career at the very moment it seemed ready to flower. Four months later his screenplay of *A Place in the Sun*, adapted from *An American Tragedy*, was nominated for an Academy Award. He thus became the first American screenwriter to be nominated for an award after being blacklisted. A month later he chalked up another first for the blacklist by winning the Oscar.

Wilson apparently had a number of unproduced scripts lying around the studios, for the following year his screenplay of *Five Fingers* was produced, and once again he received the Academy's scroll of nomination for the Award. With two nominations and one Oscar under his belt, Wilson continued the quiet life of a blacklistee until some two years later, when Allied Artists decided to produce another of his old scripts, this one an adaptation of Jessamyn West's *Friendly Persuasion*.

When the time rolled around for screen credits, Wilson discovered that Miss West and Robert Wyler, brother of the film's director, were credited as sole authors of the screenplay. Wilson appealed to the Writers' Guild arbitration committee, which ruled in his favor. Allied Artists thereupon released the picture without screenplay credits of any kind.

The academy of Motion Picture Arts and Sciences was now confronted with the horrid possibility that the picture might bring Wilson, who had been dead professionally for five years, still another Oscar. The man seemed to be getting out of hand; God alone knew how many more of his unproduced manuscripts were lying in studio files. So twenty-two members of the Academy's Board of Governors passed a by-law which was to remain secret unless "*Friendly Persuasion* receives a writing nomination as the best screenplay." It provided that no person who behaved as Wilson had before a Congressional committee was eligible for an Academy prize. That is why, when the screenwriters did nominate Wilson for *Friendly Persuasion* there was appended to the listing the sad little note: "Achievement nominated, but writer ineligible for Award under Academy by-laws."

Wilson, who during World War II served as a Captain in the Fifth Amphibious Corps, US Marines, under Major General Holland (Howling) M. Smith, doesn't scare too easily, and appears to take a dim view of secret by-laws designed to celebrate his professional demise. He is presently bringing suit against the Academy, in the course of which the patriots on the Academy's board who barred his work will be given an opportunity to explain under oath just, how their unanimity was achieved.

With *Friendly Persuasion* barred, the Academy for the first time in its history offered four instead of five candidates for its Best Screenplay Award. The Oscar, shabby and compromised but quite as golden as its twenty brethren, went almost by default to James Poe, John Farrow and S. J. Perelman for the screenplay of *Eighty Days Around the World*, The Oscar for the Best Original Story, glowing with the virtue of a fair contest, went to Robert Rich for *The Brave One*. The remaining writer's Oscar, for Best Original Screenplay, fell into the foreign hands of Albert Lamorisse for the French film, *The Red Balloon*.

And then something happened. A young man named Robert Rich (but not the Robert Rich for whom a proxy had picked up the Oscar), thinking no doubt to make sport of the Academy, pretended to be the *real* Robert Rich and sought to receive from the Academy those courtesies and distinctions that seemed to lie without visible claimant. In some fashion not yet known he got tangled up with Miss Margaret Herrick, executive director of the Academy, or George Seaton, its president, or some other Academy factotum yet undiscovered, and confessed his deception.

The Academy, giddy by now with patriotism, flushed with its victory over Wilson, anxious to proclaim itself Cerberus of the blacklist and sensing that a second barbarian might have breached the defenses and profaned the sanctuary, rushed at once into print with the most disastrous publicity release of its twenty-nine year history. "Robert Rich," it announced ominously, "credited by the studio which produced *The*

Brave One with authorship of the motion-picture story and winner of the Academy Award in this category, stated today he was not the author of the story."

There followed a series of dire warnings from Mr. Seaton and his underlings. The original story, it was hinted, wasn't original at all, or if so it was very likely a plagiarism, and the Academy would probably withhold the award, or punish the King Brothers by giving it to the owners of another story who were suing the Kings, or even declare Robert Rich, like Wilson, a nonperson, and turn the Oscar over to the next highest man in the vote, or maybe shoot craps for its custody.

Engrossed in its fierce pursuit of the infidel, the Academy had overlooked the fact that there are literally hundreds of valid, free-born, no-Amendment Robert Riches scattered through practically every country in the Western world. The King Brothers said theirs was a goatéed young photographer-writer from whom they had purchased the story in 1952 in Munich, and no one has yet disproved their claim. Overnight the New York *Post* turned up five Robert Riches. From San Francisco the nephew of a deceased Robert Rich announced he was arriving shortly to claim the trophy for his uncle. The large vacuum which now surrounded the Oscar was quickly filled with claims, counter-claims and disavowals on behalf of such disparate characters as the late Robert Flaherty, Orson Welles, Jesse Lasky, Jr., Willis O'Brien and Paul Rader.

The search even penetrated those cavernous depths wherein dwell the blacklisted and the anonymous. Among those flushed for questioning was this correspondent, who cannily refused to affirm or deny authorship. Suspicions then skittered like a starling from Albert Maltz to Michael Wilson, from Wilson to Carl Foreman, from Foreman to Paul Jarrico to others of the damned.

As the fourth day of turmoil dawned, the Academy took rueful stock of its coup. Someone with more perspicacity than president Seaton began to comprehend what had happened to the Immortals. First, they had flatly declared that Robert Rich wasn't the author of *The Brave One*, whereas there was a very good suing chance that Robert Rich was. Second, they had revealed themselves somewhat too nakedly as chief advocates and policemen of a blacklist that everybody else was fed up with. And third, they had cast a fatal shadow over the only other Oscar won this year by an American writer, the first having already been dishonored by the *ex post facto* annihilation of Michael

Wilson. The Academy, retiring behind its own version of the Fifth Amendment, announced that "on advice of counsel we are going to keep out of this situation." Since then there has been nothing but blessed silence.

Meanwhile William Stout, a brilliant young news commentator for Los Angeles Station KNX-TV, casting bemused eyes at Mr. Seaton and his cohorts, began to have a funny feeling. He telephoned me suggesting lunch, and we discovered that we both had a funny feeling. There was a stillness over Hollywood that seemed to call for a little noise. We decided on the spot to make our feelings known to the world via a filmed interview about the blacklist and the black market it produces.

The next evening Mr. Stout put part of the interview on the Emmy-winning program called *The Big News.* The following day four more minutes went coast-to-coast on the Douglas Edwards CBS-TV news show originating in New York. Later that night Mr. Stout wrapped it up with a second interview over KNX-TV.

What I said during the interview was what everyone in Hollywood knew but no one had ever mentioned: that I had been working steadily since the blacklist began; that others of my kind had also been working; that the major studios were openly in the black market, purchasing plays and other material and releasing them without their authors' names; that the Academy had become official guardian of the blacklist: that it had launched against the producers of *The Brave One* an attack it would never have dared make against any major producer; that I myself had been nominated for Academy Awards and would not tell whether I had won any Oscars; that I intended to keep right on working, and that I assumed others would continue also.

Five years ago, two years ago, perhaps even six months ago, such an interview would have brought down upon my head maledictions from the committee, outraged denials from the producers and parading delegations from the American Legion.

But in this pleasant April of 1957 I heard not one yelp of anger nor a single denial. All over town publicity departments worked furiously and overtime at the job of saying nothing and making sure nobody else said anything either. For the first time in ten years I was the only man in Hollywood who could be heard. Feeling that my personal charm alone couldn't explain such amiable treatment, I glanced cautiously about for the real reason, and came across a legal action called *Wilson vs. Loew's, Inc.*

On three different occasions, members of the Hollywood Ten have won jury decisions in contract cases against the producers; but each victory has been reversed by higher courts who found little merit in the opinions of twelve good men and true. Thus when *Wilson vs. Loew's, Inc.* was filed, it seemed only another futile and expensive attempt to attack the impregnable structure of the blacklist, and was presumed doomed to fail like all the others.

The suit, filed by Michael Wilson, Ann Revere, Gale Sondergaard, Guy Endore and nineteen others, charged that the plaintiffs had been blacklisted and demanded $52,000,000 for the losses and damages inflicted upon them. Loew's, Inc., while not admitting the existence of a blacklist, argued from the assumption that if a blacklist does exist it is justified and therefore legal. The district court ruled that even if everything alleged were true, the defendants were not entitled to judgment, and hence there was no reason for a trial. The Circuit Court of Appeals sustained the lower court. And then, quite suddenly and without warning of any kind, the Supreme Court granted certiorari, indicating the suit involves more substantial questions of law than the lower courts suspected.

Wilson vs. Loew's, Inc. will be argued before the Supreme Court next autumn. If the court rules for the plaintiffs—and there is just as much reason to believe it will decide for them as against them—the ruling will declare, in effect, that if the facts charged are true the plaintiffs are entitled to judgment. Then the lower courts will be compelled to accept for trial an issue which juries thus far have invariably decided in favor of plaintiffs. Pondering the possibilities, I am inclined to believe that *Wilson vs. Loew's* accounts for a great deal of the silence that has settled over Hollywood. It might even be the reason why the Motion Picture Association of America, ordinarily so greedy for space, denied to readers of *The Nation* answers to the questions propounded by their correspondent (see page 188).

There is, of course, another reason, which lies in the fading power and the growing disrepute of the committee itself. Only a few weeks ago the Board of Governors of the eminently conservative State Bar of California charged that "the proceedings of the committee and the conduct of the committee's counsel . . . were improper and lacking in dignity and impartiality which should govern the conduct of agencies of the United States . . . and they were of such a character as to pose a threat to the right to appear by counsel and to the proper independence of the Bar."

Rumblings now are heard from another quarter. *The Hollywood Reporter,* a trade paper which has been the committee's staunchest friend, carried on March 14 an item by its leading reporter, Mike Connelly, to the effect that "The House Un-American Activities Committee plans holding executive sessions to probe a report that one of its members received money to clear a show-business personality of suspicions of being a Red."

Thus far no member of the committee has denied the report. The committee's own standards of evidence would seem to require that each of its members take the oath and swear that he isn't receiving bribes—or to tell how much and from whom. It seems inconceivable that future witnesses won't demand such testimony in return for their own.

In the meanwhile there is a stillness at Appomattox, broken only by an occasional crack in the blacklist. The committee has no clothes, no honor, small power and practically no remaining candidates for oblivion. Far from being able to sell indulgences, it can scarcely give them away in the present declining market. The black market flourishes and the producers know it and dare not deny it and pray each night for a court decision, please God just one decision, that will give them an excuse to shake young Mr. Wheeler off their backs and regain control of the organizations they head. The "Eastern people," cocking a thoughtful eye at the Supreme Court and *Wilson vs. Loew's, Inc.*, begin to recall the glories of free enterprise, and to wonder whether those plaintiffs would really want $52,000,000 if they were given a chance to return openly to their professions.

Only George Seaton and twenty-two Immortals still like the blacklist; but even they, with the shadow of *Wilson vs. Academy Board of Governors* darkening their little patch of sky, may find it in their hearts to decide that ten years is punishment enough for any crime—especially when you can't be sure the criminal isn't anonymously undercutting you in the financial department.

There may come a time in this country when blacklists turn popular, and inquisitors are invited to dinner, and mothers at bedtime read to their children the story of the good informer. But just now the current runs in an opposite direction.

All things, as the man said, change.

The Crash of Silence

Along with his manuscript, Mr. Trumbo sent us the following brief diary which records his attempts to get the Motion Picture Association of America to answer some pointed questions. —Editors

Hollywood

Thursday, April 18. Telephone C. H. (Duke) Wales, popular and capable press relations man for Motion Picture Association of America. Explain mission re *Nation*, et al, read him following list of questions:

1. Would the MPAA deny that major studios are purchasing material from Fifth Amendment writers and removing their names from the screen?

2. Would the MPAA say there is no blacklist in Hollywood except that which applies to the Hollywood Ten?

3. Would the MPAA have any objections if a major studio openly hired a Fifth Amendment writer or a member of the Hollywood Ten?

4. Does the MPAA deal with the Committee on Un-American Activities, or any representative of that committee, in determining the employability of artists or other persons in the motion picture industry?

5. If there is a blacklist in the industry, to what persons or organizations does the MPAA attribute it?

Wales copies list, reads it back. Hell of a copyist. Everything checks out. I suggest he may want a little time. Wales agrees. Will be in office from 2:30 P.M. on, call him then. Call at 2:40 P.M. Wales not back yet. Call 4:00 P.M. Wales gone for day. Troubled by this, but still have faith in Wales.

Friday, April 19. Call Wales 9:34 a.m. Not in yet. Send fast straight wire reminding him of situation and giving phone number. Call Wales 1:50 P.M. Not back from lunch. Three P.M., no call from Wales. Send following straight fast wire 3:02 P.M.

C. H. WALES

MPAA

8480 BEVERLY BOULEVARD

HOLLYWOOD, CALIFORNIA

HAVE ACCURATE RECORD OF OUR TELEPHONE CONVERSATION AND OF MY

SUBSEQUENT CALLS. I DON'T BLAME YOU FOR DUCKING, BUT UNLESS I HEAR FROM YOU BEFORE MY DEADLINE SIX P.M. TONIGHT I SHALL NOTE THE EXTENT OF MY EFFORTS AND THEIR FAILURE AND ASSUME MPAA HAS TAKEN THE FIFTH. ALTHOUGH I HAVEN'T HAD THE PLEASURE OF INVOKING THE FIFTH, IT'S A GRAND OLD AMENDMENT AND I SHOULDN'T WISH TO DEPRIVE ERIC JOHNSTON OF ITS PROTECTION. CORDIALLY,

DALTON TRUMBO

Call Wales 5:14 P.M. Young man says Wales not available. Chill touches my heart: first time word "unavailable" has been used. Tell young man I'll stay by phone till 7 P.M. Wales doesn't get through. Sorry about Wales, but console self with Eric Johnston 1947 statement, "As long as I live I will never be a party to anything as un-American as a blacklist." Feel certain Eric's heart still in right place. Satisfied Wales will call tomorrow.

Saturday, April 20. No call from Wales. Hope he isn't ill. Mission uncompleted.

—D. T.

APRIL 3, 2000

Honor the Blacklistees

Victor Navasky

•

Victor Navasky is the Publisher and Editorial Director of *The Nation*. He was editor of *The Nation* from 1978 to 1994. He is the author of what many regard as the definitive account of the Hollywood blacklist years, *Naming Names*, which is to be republished next year.

AFTER LAST YEAR'S brouhaha surrounding the presentation by the Academy of Motion Picture Arts and Sciences of a Lifetime Achievement Award to Elia Kazan, one member of the academy had an idea. Samuel Gelfman, a literary and theatrical consultant and a member of the academy's producers branch, contacted its president, Robert Rehme, and made a suggestion: Next time around why not devote a segment of the evening to the blacklist?

The proposal was not received with glee. In a December 28, 1999, letter to the officers and governors of the academy Gelfman reported, "As several of you—to whom I spoke earlier—know, when I suggested the idea to Bob Rehme, he explained that the Academy's policy is to remain totally non-political and, after last year's events, any mention of the motion picture industry cooperation with the House Unamerican Activities Committee constitutes a political statement."

Gelfman respectfully demurred: "In a millennial overview of our industry's first hundred years, the political climate that led to the Black

List and the exclusion of these awards [to blacklistees] from public mention is a legitimate part of our history." He might have added that the academy, which had collaborated with the blacklist system in the first place, had already made its political statement. The question now is whether to revise that statement to let the public know that it regrets this stain on its institutional history.

The academy's desire to avoid recriminations about something that happened half a century ago is understandable, if not particularly admirable. But lest the academy forget, when those who were called went to prison, lost their jobs, were blacklisted and/or denied their screen credits—all for refusing to cooperate with opportunistic Congressional investigating committees—they were not protecting themselves. By resisting the demand that they confess, recant, inform, sign loyalty oaths, they were the latest in a long line of men and women down through the centuries who have been pressured by church and state to declare their allegiance to God and king (or, in the seventeenth century, official science, which held that the earth is at the center of the universe). Most of those who refused to bow to such pressures did so as a matter of conscience.

Back in the days of the domestic cold war it was part of the civic religion, the official mythology, to deny the existence of the blacklist. Indeed, as late as 1980 when Ronald Reagan ran for President he told journalist Robert Scheer that "there was no such thing as a blacklist in Hollywood." The academy knows better, and surely fifty years later, it's time to set the record straight.

As a general proposition it doesn't pay for outsiders to advise membership organizations on how to conduct their business. But where the academy is concerned, we are more than outsiders. We go to the movies. We stay home and watch the Oscars. We are the audience, the customer, and as such, while we may not always be right, we deserve to be heard.

Gelfman has proposed that the academy fill in some missing history. We suggest that it go him one better. Here, members of the academy, is our idea. Why not instruct your branch representatives on the board at their next meeting to pass a simple resolution honoring the anonymous blacklistees, those who were denied work and recognition at the time? The question is not whether such a resolution may constitute a political statement. It's the decent thing to do.

8

Going Underground

The Sixties

•

AUGUST 25, 1962

MARILYN MONROE: 1926–1962

Lincoln Kirstein

•

As well as being a regular *Nation* contributor, Lincoln Kirstein was *the* impresario of American dance and theater, co-founding with George Balanchine the American Ballet and general director (1948–89) of the New York City Ballet from 1948–1989. His many books include *Dance; Movement and Metaphor; Nijinsky Dancing; Mosaic; Memoirs*; and the essay collection *By With To & From: A Lincoln Kirstein Reader*. At the time of writing Kirstein was vice president of the American Shakespeare Festival and Academy. His brother George was publisher of *The Nation* from 1955 to 1966.

THE DEATH OF someone who has given you intense pleasure, even if you never met, amounts almost to the death of a personal friend. Having heard the news on the radio and knowing how I felt about Marilyn Monroe, an artist friend wrote me from Indonesia: "I liked everything about her; mainly her power that outwitted the hungry weak for so long."

Extravagant claims need not be made for her capacities as the complete actress; she never had the chance to develop them. But as a classic comedienne of grace, delicacy, and happy wonder, she certainly has had no peer since Billie Burke or Ina Claire. The lightness, justness and rhythm in her clowning often held hints of something more penetrating. Her comic tone was sometimes disturbingly ironic; her personal style was more lyric than naturalistic. Irony and lyricism are two prime components of the grand manner. Whether or not she could have succeeded as Lady Macbeth, which she solemnly said she wanted to play one day, after what she had done to herself with the aid and abetment of most of us, we cannot know. But it is possible that her gifts were far more in the scale of the proscenium frame than the camera-frame.

Imagination boggles at the overtime that would have been loaded onto the rehearsal schedule of any Shakespearean repertory company placed at her tender mercies. But her notorious tardiness or procrastination (it never bankrupted any body except herself) which so irritated the manipulators for whom she grossed only forty-three million dollars—not, alas, the two hundred million that was first reported—may not have been merely compulsive behavior. Does it never occur to the producer, director and investor that a performing artist at the peak of her craft may always want to give a peak performance; and that often, for reasons physical as well as psychological, she may not feel up to the peak she knows she can attain? In the theatre, a star is prepared by weeks of New York rehearsals, months of provincial tours, before settling into the final pattern of the Broadway run. Some seductive movie directors manage to get peak performances out of their stars faster or oftener than average, but by and large the American film industry rarely provides working conditions comparable to the comfort of a successful run in our commercial theatre (and we cannot even make comparison with what prevails in more cultivated countries, able to afford institutional theatre: the theatre of Stanislavsky, of Brecht, of Barrault or Olivier). Everything shot in Hollywood, or planned there, is geared for hysteria and the bet on lucky, improvised takes and type casting.

So Marilyn Monroe paralyzed production by demanding retakes; maybe she took sixty of a single scene and had them all printed. Maybe the sixtieth wasn't as good as the third. And maybe, at the same time, she had a conscience about the cash she was costing her partners and manipulators. She knew what money was about, since she was born with none, died with little and valued it chiefly for the pleasure of giving it to people poorer than herself.

Perhaps such things qualified her art—nothing qualified her life as the material of tragedy. It has been hard for novelists or dramatists to canonize the performing artist. Sarah Bernhardt inspired Proust and Henry James; Colette drew on her own fascinating life; Sartre worked hard at Kean. But whatever these triumphs were between covers, they have never given great actresses great roles. The performing artist is a complex mechanism, and in the most powerful of them the urge for self-exposure, the shame of an inadequate performance—even the continual racking desire to be rid, once and for all, of the very desire to risk such hazard—often exist in an almost intolerable balance. Marilyn Monroe was used in her own lifetime as the basis of a shoddy commercial film which failed, among other reasons, for its superficiality. The resemblance was duly publicized but no one really believed it or cared. *The Goddess*, cheap as it was in conception and execution, may well become a monument of taste and talent compared to the doubtless inevitable *Marilyn Monroe Story*, starring some as yet unborn replica of the best features of Jeanne Eagels, Jean Harlow, Carole Lombard, Bette Davis, and Greta Garbo, with a supporting cast of Joe DiMaggio, Jr., when he gets out of the Marines, and Clark Gable, Jr., when he gets out of the cradle.

But let us assume that one day Marilyn Monroe's story will find that poetic dramatist who can capture its tragedy—not as Norma Jean Mortenson turned into Marilyn Monroe, not as MM, but rather as the Performing Artist in our country, in our time. Such a dramatist, reading Maurice Zolotow's admirable biography (Harcourt, Brace; 1960), will see that the denouement is indicated from the first chapter. Zolotow's study, which comes up to *The Misfits* and her death, is courteous, humane and extremely perceptive. In it, only Monroe's wisecracks are funny. It is a book that can serve someone as North's *Plutarch* served Shakespeare: everything is there save the choice of scene and the grandeur of words.

Lacking a Shakespeare, who often breathed immortality into far less absorbing originals, we shall look long for someone to encompass her griefs. Her playwright-husband gave her her most serious script, and if it was a flawed masterpiece it is still a masterpiece. But *The Misfits*, unlike her other films, is not essentially about her performance, or about an artist performing. It is about the almost pornographic horror of a famous man who is actually dying and a famous woman who is having a nervous breakdown. Arthur Miller knew her as no one else: "If she was simple it would have been easy to help her. She could have made it with a little luck. She needed a blessing." Had she enjoyed that blessing, she certainly could have played magnificently Doll Tearsheet, Katharine the Shrew, Mistress Page, Portia. And if she had been granted another chance, in another life, in another society or culture, she could have played Cleopatra—not Shaw's kitten-queen, but the Alexandrian princess, the serpent of old Nile. Yet, in our time, who could have encompassed her character? Tennessee Williams naturally springs to mind, since he knows our movie industry well and has what passes for passion and compassion; but judging by his last two and possibly best plays, his largest gifts are for comedy. He writes comedies of manners, more mannerist than tragic. Brecht might have made a cartoon, but Monroe was not grim; O'Neill was almost humorless; neither had the innocence and gaiety which assert Monroe's aura.

However, there is one playwright, and evidence has just come to light that he is far more "modern" than many now living in the flesh. Oscar Wilde might have triumphed with Marilyn Monroe's material, since it was so much like his own. When the thousand and more pages of his collected letters appear here in the fall, so magnificently presented and annotated by Mr. Rupert Hart-Davis, we shall enjoy not only one of the greatest of English autobiographies; we shall also learn to know, for the first time, a marvelously funny, generous, profoundly decent man, who in his whole short life (he died at forty-six) never harmed a living soul, save himself, the wife he adored and the two very young children who meant more to him than anything in the world. His personal tragedy is certainly one of the most terrible and moving about which we have absolutely complete information. And he was a performing artist in his public as well as in his private life.

Monroe was a woman of considerable importance and Wilde would have known, as few others, just wherein her importance lay. She belongs in the fairly large company of tragedians in life who also performed for money in a broader theatre. Not all of them were stage actors, and in the cases of Oscar Wilde and Marilyn Monroe, some of their greatest scenes were not played on stage. Like Wilde, she often reserved her talent for her art and her genius for her life.

The essence of the star performer's individual contribution is the development of a tone, style and rhythm which make legible his private morality. The intensity of the distillation has an inflammatory effect on the whole world, high-brow, low-brow and middle-brow, because it seems a revelation, at least in part, of their own divine or monstrous qualities. The genius-performer, whose compelling, or "compulsive," problem is the editing of a private identity into an intoxicating icon, has a long line of saints and martyrs: Beckford, Byron, Kean, Baudelaire, Booth, Rimbaud, van Gogh, T. E. Lawrence, Nijinsky, Dylan Thomas, James Dean, Jean Harlow and her legitimate daughter, Marilyn Monroe. The stupendous question: "Who am I, really?"—unless it is answered to one's own satisfaction at about the age when one achieves an end of technical apprenticeship—generates an endless seesaw energy of frustration disguised as brilliant nervous energy, which is no less predictably fatal than cancer. By no means all great performers are martyrs, though some approach the saintly. Many of the best have had the power to solve their own questions of identity, and have heard the lovely music at the end. One thinks of Garrick at home; Walt Whitman, the arch-impersonator, receiving Oscar Wilde in Camden; Sir Henry Irving and Ellen Terry; Victor Hugo, whom Cocteau said was a madman who thought he was Victor Hugo; Duse, Pavlova, and Cocteau himself, who has played the various disguises of Harlequin for seventy years, surviving all the spiritual and physical exercises that are credited with killing so many of his juniors.

The "healthy," the "wholesome" performers, as opposed to the "compulsive" ones, have been able to balance or employ their compelling behavior in public, usually supported by a technique and a tradition of craft. And in the old days, no matter how horrifying their infancies or adolescences, performers could almost call their souls their own. Edmund Kean, the greatest Shakespearean of his time, had no easier a human apprenticeship than Marilyn Monroe; psychic shocks from his youth certainly killed him sooner than if he had been a nobleman and rich (in which case he could not have been an actor at all). But Kean, in spite of his hysterical behavior, had the final satisfaction of appearing in a great repertory. He himself controlled every element of its production, presentation as well as exploitation. His reputation and body belonged to himself to do with as he pleased, and he pleased to drink. However, he was not both president and partner of Edmund Kean Productions, Inc., a corporation manipulated by a cartel of hopeful wolves, who were treacherous always, and who could yet howl about their property's final, desperate, treachery. There was publicity-seeking in Kean's day and probably in Shakespeare's too. But in Shakespeare's time, repertory troupes were protected by royal patent or noble patrons, and the actors wore their responsible masters' livery. Now we have no repertory companies, except in a few interstitial or putative institutions, and it is highly unlikely that they will ever again dominate our theatre. Our only true repertory houses are the chains of small art-film houses, where *Bus Stop, The Blood of the Poet, Ten Days That Shook The World, Some Like It Hot* and *The Misfits,* will be shown for generations.

Certainly, Marilyn Monroe was victimized, but one must study Maurice Zolotow's book to understand the crafty uses she made of her own adversity, and the legends she helped augment as weapon, protection and blackmail. We all know how juvenile delinquents feed back quite adequately Freudian jargon to their interrogators, who then check off the predictable causes: guilt, rejection, alienation, insecurity, etc. Lacking a Shakespeare, it would take a Bernard Shaw—who understood T. E. Lawrence as Pvt. Shaw, Ross, the Bastard, the Poet, the Adventurer, the Failure, the Success—to utilize all of Monroe's maniacal procrastination, her treacheries to those who "helped" her—that wolf-pack and rat-pack, agents and instructors, who of course expected only a kind word for their investment.

Dance and song, unlike the spoken word or the use of classic diction, have absolute techniques. Virtuosity is the salvation of the singer and dancer; the actor has no such luck. Of course it is true that Nijinsky went mad, that Callas behaves badly (or astutely), and that Dylan Thomas wrote very good verse, read it very well, and drank too much. But the greatest performers of institutional theatre, singers, dancers and those actor-managers of the last century, by and large provide a picture of almost bourgeois domestic simplicity. That is also true of many excellent film actors who have come to their own satisfaction with a becoming modesty: James Cagney, Gary Cooper, Burt Lancaster, Katherine Hepburn, and many others. But these are fine character actors, which is different from a blazing star: a Garbo, who does not die, except to the screen; a Marilyn Monroe.

Hollywood has always been a supermarket of personality. As in most supermarkets, the comestibles come packed with additives, preservatives, detergents; and while not immediately lethal, such nourishment hasn't the savor that nature intended. Very little has issued from Hollywood that has any claim on the most transient memory. Naturally there is in Hollywood no museum devoted to the motion picture; it is a phenomenon without a real history, in which only the freaks, the exceptions, the tragedies are memorable. The one academy it ever sanctioned is suitably enough an annual racket. It is a climate providing less chance for healthy work than even downtown Los Angeles, for all its smog. But it's not the only villain; Hollywood has its conscious and unconscious accomplices.

It doesn't help the performing arts much that Harvard University, having some decades ago exiled George Pierce Baker to teach at Yale, finally erected a fantastically equipped theatre with the proviso that acting is not to be instructed for credit, and that there be no graduate school of drama. The Loeb Theatre is thus only a clean play-pen for the young gentlemen. It helps less to have Congress grant a land-site for a national cultural center with the proviso that the nation never be called upon either to erect the building or maintain it. It helps least of all that the Kennedy Administration, after a canny survey, has discovered no political mileage in culture, and is cloaking that bit of intelligence with tasteful interest in interior decoration, good cooking and polite literary conversation. Sure, lots of culture centers are going up all over the country. If one wants a fair idea of what happens when they are built, regard the situation in Seattle, which thanks to the planners of a successful World's Fair has an excellent facility. There is a dog-fight as to how the buildings will be used; and there is no plan for any future use, except the pious promise that expensive cultural events should be prudently pruned.

Marilyn Monroe was supposed to be the Sex Goddess, but somehow no one, including, or indeed first of all, herself, ever believed it. Rather, she was a comedienne *impersonating* the American idea of the Sex Goddess, just as she impersonated Hildegarde, the "chantoosie," in *Bus Stop.* When people paid their forty millions to see Monroe, it was for an aesthetic performance, not a simple provocation. And she, perhaps even consciously, exemplified a philosophy which had come to her pragmatically and which a lot of American women don't like very much—a philosophy at once hedonistic, full of uncommon common sense, and, even to some intellectuals, deeply disturbing. Her performances indicated that while sex is certainly fun, and often funny, it is only one of many games. Others include the use of the intelligence. Sex has a certain importance, indubitably, but the messianic role which has been assigned it in the first half of the twentieth century may have been overplayed, just as it was underplayed in the second half of the nineteenth century. It seems to have been played about right in Greece, Rome, Japan, and eighteenth-century France. Marilyn Monroe just played right around it. Her act was fantastic, uproarious and daft. Not the least ironic part of a life so crammed with irony was that someone made so dependent on the shaky therapies of contemporary post-Freudian philosophy should have portrayed to the public the very picture of bumptious sexual normaley.

A Hollywood gossip columnist, who should know if anyone does, said that Marilyn Monroe's life was an absolute waste; one wonders what he, in the brief watches of the night, thinks of what he does with his time. Radio Vatican proclaimed that a person should have the courage to face life without turning to the easy way out of suicide. It seems to have been a relatively difficult way for a woman who tried it some half-dozen times without success. Marilyn Monroe turned to Christian Science and let herself, as a good daughter-in-law, be instructed in the Reformed Jewish faith. There is evidence that she believed in divine providence, but its councilors on earth have not proceeded far enough in the ecumenical movement to help miserable performing artists whose God-given talents bring them more burdens than their God-given flesh can bear. More than predictably, the filthiest footnote appeared in *Time's* anonymity. Recapping every detail which could exude a faintly diapason pornographic whiff, its final diapason rolled: "All the same she was a star; it hardly matters she never quite became an actress." Get that "*quite.*" Marilyn Monroe's life was not a waste. She gave delight. She was a criterion of the comic in a rather sad world. Her films will continue to give delight, and it is blasphemy to say she had no use. Her example, our waste of her, has the use of a redemption in artists yet untrained and unborn.

DECEMBER 28, 1963

MANCHURIAN CANDIDATE IN DALLAS

Richard Condon

•

Richard Condon is the author of *The Manchurian Candidate* and many other books, many of which have been filmed including *Winter Kills* and *Prizzi's Honor*. He wrote this piece a few days after President Kennedy was assassinated.

Paris

I WAS READING about how Senator Thruston Morton of Kentucky absolved the American people from any guilt in the assassination of the President when a reporter from a South African press association telephoned from London to ask if I felt responsible for the President's killing, inasmuch as I had written a novel, *The Manchurian Candidate*, on which had been based a film that had just been "frozen" in the United States because it was felt that the assassin might have seen it and been influenced by it. I told the reporter that, with all Americans, I had contributed to form the attitudes of the assassin; and that the assassin, and Americans like him, had contributed to the attitudes which had caused me to write the novel.

The differences between Senator Morton's views on this and my own are vast. The man who shot John Kennedy, Senator Morton said, "was a stranger to the American heritage" and "his mind had been warped by an alien violence, not by a native condition."

Brainwashing to violence and assassination is the line taken in my novel. On its melodramatic surface, the book is a study of the consequences of "a mind warped by alien violence," but I had also hoped to suggest that for some time all of us in the United States had been brainwashed to violence, and to indicate that the reader might consider that the tempo of this all-American brainwashing was being speeded up.

I meant to call attention, through example, to the proved brainwashing to violence shown by the increased sale of cigarettes after they had been conclusively demonstrated to be suicide weapons. I meant to show that when the attention of a nation is focused upon violence—when it appears on the front page of all newspapers, throughout television programming, in the hundreds of millions of monthly comic books, in most motion pictures, in the rhythms of popular music and the dance, and in popular $5 novels which soon become 50¢ paperbacks, when a most violent example is set by city, state and federal governments, when organized crime merges with organized commerce and labor, when a feeble, bewildered set of churches cannot counteract any of this and all of it is power-hosed at all of us through the most gigantically complex overcommunications system ever developed—we must not be surprised that one of us bombs little girls in a Sunday school or shoots down a President of our republic. We can feign surprise, as we did with the murder of President Kennedy, but none of us seemed either surprised or moved by the murder of Medgar Evers, who was also a brave leader of his people, also a man who had a young wife and children, and whose assassin most certainly matched the basic, American psychological pattern of the killer of our President.

I was not surprised at the similarities between the two American products, Lee Oswald and Raymond Shaw, one all too actual, the other the fictional leading character of *The Manchurian Candidate*, Oswald's wife has said she married him because she felt sorry for him: absolutely no one had liked him, "even in Russia." The novel says, "It was not that Raymond was hard to like. He was impossible to like." Oswald spoke frequently of the hardships his mother had experienced in the depression, before he had been born, and his mother had been quick to say that "they" had always been against her boy. In the novel, I quoted Andrew Salter, the Pavlovian psychologists, ". . . the human fish swim about at the bottom of the great ocean of atmosphere and they develop psychic injuries as they collide with one another. Most mortal of these are the wounds gotten from the parent fish." The Associated Press dug up a truancy report on Oswald which said his resentment had been fixed on "authority." On the surface he was calm, but inside there was much anger. "'The resenters,' says the Chinese brainwasher in *The Manchurian Candidate*, "those men with cancer of the psyche, make the great assassins." Raymond Shaw's account of his past was confusingly dramatic, as was Oswald's. It all seemed to revolve around his mother, as did Oswald's.

The brainwasher who was describing Raymond Shaw to an audience in an amphitheatre might have been describing the murderers of John Kennedy and Medgar Evers. "It has been said that only the man who is capable of loving everything is capable of understanding everything. The resentful man is a human with a capacity for affection so poorly developed that his understanding for the motives of others very nearly does not exist. They are men of melancholic and reserved psychology. They are afflicted with total resentment."

Lee Oswald's indicated murder of Mr. Kennedy seems motivated only by his resentment against the most successful man in the world; resentment against a wonderfully intelligent, puissant, healthy, wealthy, witty and handsome man who was so rich in spirit that he made no effort to conceal his superiority, who dominated the world and outer space, and who had an inexpressibly fine wife and two lovely children. From the view of this resentment, as long as this fellow stayed out of Lee Oswald's path he would be all right, but when he came laughing into Dallas, and the newspapers printed a map that showed he would drive right past where Lee Oswald worked for a lousy fifty bucks a week, it was more than this classical resentment could bear.

It takes time to achieve such resentment and to fire it there must be careful nurturing by constant, unrelenting conditioning to violence. Oswald was not the only violence-packed American who was capable of murdering President Kennedy. The assassination was a wasteful, impersonal, senseless act, but the United States has undergone such a massive brainwashing to violence that such a senseless waste is *à la mode*.

Ralph Gleason wrote in the *San Francisco Chronicle* after the President's murder: ". . . we bred his murderer, our society produced him and he is, in one sense, a part of us all." Then Senator Morton said: ". . . let us not mourn the American soul . . . let the blame be on him who actually committed the crime . . . what happened was not America's fault."

John Hay Whitney, publisher of the New York *Herald Tribune* and thus a leading figure in the overcommunications industry, most hotly denied that the American people must share the guilt for President Kennedy's murder. He amplified his defense by saying: "It's true that there is hate in America, and violence, and brutality. There always has been. But violence has not been and is not now a dominant strain in our character."

To me, it seems certain that Mr. Gleason is right and Senator Morton and Mr. Whitney are mistaken. Neither saints nor assassins appear among us fully grown and wholly developed. All of us are nothing more than the result of our conditioning.

When the fanatic is a ruler, rather than the assassin of a ruler, the people who permitted him to take power must be blamed—whether they be the Germans of 1933–35 for Adolf Hitler, or the people of Chicago, Illinois, for their local government. But when the fanatic is the assassin, he emerges from the very fabric of the people. In answer to Senator Morton: if the American people are encouraging a mass educational system—the overcommunications industry—which instructs for the production of the highest crime rate and the most widely shared violence dependencies of any country in the world, it is not time to say, most particularly by our government, that each American is responsible for that state of affairs because he does nothing to change it? We are not, as some well-meaning European newspaper put it, a violent and unstable people because such "toughness" was required to tame the wild frontier 125 years ago. We are violent and unstable because we have been so conditioned to these responses that civilized, thoughtful conduct has become impossible for us.

It is a hell of a spot for a country to be in. Who, the least brainwashed among us, will cast the first redemptive thought?

APRIL 13, 1964

A Feast for Open Eyes

Susan Sontag

•

Flaming Creatures was one of two films seized in 1964 by the NYPD on the grounds of obscenity. The other was Jean Genet's *Chant D'amour*. Jonas Mekas, editor of *Film Culture* and one of the leading figures in the New York Underground film movement was arrested at these showings. Susan Sontag at the time of writing had just published her first novel *The Benefactor* and was teaching philosophy and theology at Columbia University. Perhaps her most memorable essays about cinema were about Jean Luc Godard, collected in *Styles of Radical Will*.

THE ONLY THING to be regretted about the close-ups of limp penises and bouncing breasts, and the shots of shots of masturbation and oral sexuality, in Jack Smith's *Flaming Creatures* is that it makes it hard simply to talk about this remarkable and beautiful film; one has to *defend* it. But in defending as well as talking about the film, I don't want to make it seem less outrageous, less shocking than it is. For the record: in *Flaming Creatures*, a couple of women and a much larger number of men, most of them clad in flamboyant thrift-shop women's clothes, frolic about, pose and posture, dance with one another, enact various scenes of voluptuousness, sexual frenzy, romantic love, and vampirism—to the accompaniment of a sound track which includes some pop Latin favorites (*Siboney, Amapola*), some rock-'n-roll, some scratchy violin playing, bullfight music, a Chinese song, the text of a wacky ad for a new brand of "heart-shaped lipstick" being demonstrated on the screen by a host of men, some in drag and some not; and the chorale of flutey shrieks and screams which accompany the group rape of a bosomy young woman, rape happily converting itself into an orgy. Of course, *Flaming Creatures* is outrageous, and intends to be. Even the very title tells us that.

As it happens, *Flaming Creatures* is not pornographic, if pornography be defined as the manifest intention and capacity to excite sexually; Smith's depiction of nakedness and various sexual embraces (with the notable omission of straight screwing) is both too full of pathos and too ingenuous to be prurient. Smith's images of sex are alternately childlike or witty, rather than sentimental or lustful. But even if *Flaming Creatures* were pornographic, that is, if it did (like the film Jean Genet made in 1950, *Chant d'Amour*) have the power to excite sexually, I would argue that this is a power of art for which it is shameful to apologize. Art is, always, the sphere of freedom. In those difficult works of art, works which we now call *avant-garde*, the artist consciously exercises his freedom. And as the price the *avant-garde* artist pays for the freedom to be outrageous is the small numbers of his audience, the least of his rewards should be freedom from meddling censorship by the Philistine, the prudish and the blind. Apart from the wrongness of censorship itself, there is no need to worry what will be the social consequences if *Flaming Creatures* ever plays at Radio City Music Hall because it won't. Smith's film, involving as it does certain esoteric assumptions about experience and beauty, is obscure, precious, intimate. It would be as lost on today's mass audience as a puppet theatre is on a huge stage.

The police hostility to *Flaming Creatures* is not hard to understand. It is, alas, inevitable that Smith's film will have to fight for its life in the courts. What is disappointing is the indifference, the squeamishness, the downright hostility to the film evinced by almost everyone in the mature intellectual and artistic community. Almost its only supporters are a loyal coterie of filmmakers, poets and young "Villagers." *Flaming Creatures* has not yet graduated from being a cult object, the prize exhibit of the New American Cinema Group, the Underground Cinema, whose house organ is the magazine *Film Culture*. Everyone should be grateful to and come to the aid of Jonas Mekas, who almost single-handedly, with tenacity and even heroism, has made it possible to see Smith's film and a number of other new works. Yet it must be admitted that the pronouncements of Mekas and his supporters are shrill, and often positively alienating. Mekas is wrong to argue that this new group of films, of which *Flaming Creatures* seems to me by far the most successful, is a totally unprecedented departure in the history of cinema, and makes everything else, in comparison, worthless. Such truculence does Smith a disservice, making it unnecessarily hard to grasp what he has accomplished in *Flaming Creatures*. For *Flaming Creatures* is a small but very important work in a tradition, the great tradition of the *avant-garde* cinema—along with Bunuel's *Le Chien d'Andalou* and *L'Age d'Or*, Cocteau's *Le Sang d'un Poete*, Artaud's *Le Coquille et le Clergyman*, parts of Eisenstein's first film *Strike*, some of the recent Polish and Czech shorts, the films of Kenneth Anger (*Fireworks, Les Eaux d'Artifice, Scorpio Rising*), etc., etc.

The older *avant-garde* film makers in America (Maya Deren, James Broughton, Kenneth Anger, et al.) turned out short films which were technically quite studied. Given their very low budgets, color, camera work, acting, and synchronization of image and sound were as professional as possible. The hallmark of one of the two new *avant-garde* styles in American cinema (Jack Smith, Ron Rice, et al., but not Gregory Markopolous and Stan Brakhage) is its willful technical crudity. The newer films—both the good ones and the poor, uninspired work—show a maddening indifference to every element of technique, a studied primitiveness. This is a very contemporary style, and very American. Nowhere in the world has the old cliché of European romanticism—the assassin mind versus the spontaneous heart—had such a long career as in America. Here, more than anywhere else, the belief lives on that neatness and carefulness of technique interfere with spontaneity, with truth with immediacy. Most of the prevailing techniques (for even to be against technique demands a technique) of *avant-garde* art express this conviction. In music, there is aleatoric performance now as well as composition, and new sources of sound and new ways of mutilating the old instruments; in painting and sculpture, there is the favoring of impermanent or found materials, and the transformation of objects into perishable (use-one-once-and-throw-away) environments or "happenings." In its own way *Flaming Creatures* illustrates this snobbery about the coherence and technical finish of the work of art. There is, of course, no story in *Flaming Creatures*, no development, no necessary order of the seven (as I count them) clearly separable sequences of the film. One can easily doubt that a certain piece of footage was indeed intended to be overexposed. Of no sequence is one convinced that it had to last this long, and not longer or shorter. Shots aren't framed in the traditional way; heads are cut off; extraneous figures sometimes appear on the margin of the scene. The camera is hand-held most of the time, and the image often quivers (when this is wholly effective, and no doubt deliberate, is in the orgy sequence).

But in *Flaming Creatures*, amateurishness of technique is not frustrating, as it is in so many other recent "underground" films. For Smith is visually very generous; at practically every moment there is simply a tremendous amount to see on the screen, a density of images, of different types of textures. And then, there is an extraordinary charge and beauty to his images, even when the effect of the strong ones are weakened by the ineffective ones, the ones that might have been better through planning. Often today indifference to technique is accompanied by bareness; the modern revolt against calculation in art often takes the form of aesthetic asceticism. (Much of Abstract Expressionist painting has this ascetic quality.) *Flaming Creatures*, though, represents a different aesthetic: it is crowded with visual material. There are no ideas, no symbols, no commentary on or critique of anything in *Flaming Creatures*, Smith's film is strictly a treat for the senses. In this it is the very opposite of a "literary" film (which is what so many French *avant-garde* films are). It is not in the knowing about, or being able to interpret, what one sees, that the pleasure of *Flaming Creatures* lies; but in the directness, the power and the lavish quantity of the images themselves. Unlike most serious modern art, this work is not about the frustrations of consciousness, the dead ends of the self. Thus Smith's crude technique serves, beautifully, the sensibility embodied in *Flaming Creatures*—a sensibility based on indiscriminateness, without ideas, beyond negation.

Flaming Creatures is that rare modern work of art: it is about joy and innocence. To be sure, this joyousness, this innocence is composed out of themes which are—by ordinary standards—perverse, decadent, at the least, highly theatrical and artificial. But this, I think, is precisely how the film comes by its extraordinarily moving beauty and modernity. *Flaming Creatures* is a lovely specimen of what now, in one genre, goes by the flippant name of "pop art." Smith's film has the sloppiness, the arbitrariness, the looseness of pop art. It also has pop art's gaiety, its ingenuousness, its exhilarating freedom from moralism. The great virtue of the pop art movement is the way it blasts through the old imperative about taking a *position* toward one's subject matter. (Needless to say, I'm not denying that there are certain events about which it is necessary to take a position. An extreme instance of a work of art dealing with such events is *The Deputy*. All I'm saying is that there are some elements of life—above all, sexual pleasure— about which it isn't necessary to have a position.) Pop art really transcends the old nonsense of choosing between approving or disapproving of what is depicted in art—or, by extension, experienced in life. (This is why all sociological sneering at pop art as a symptom of a new conformism, a cult of acceptance of the artifacts of mass civilization, is so obtuse.) Pop art lets in wonderful and new mixtures of attitude, which would before have seemed contradictions. Thus *Flaming Creatures* is a brilliant spoof on sex and at the same time full of the lyricism of erotic impulse. Technically, too, as I have suggested, it is a wonderfully inventive contradiction. Very studied visual materials (lacy effects, falling flowers, tableaux) are introduced into disorganized, clearly improvised scenes in which bodies, some shapely and convincingly feminine and some scrawny and hairy, tumble, dance, make love.

It is easy to see Smith's film as having, as its subject, the poetry of transvestitism. *Film Culture*, in awarding *Flaming Creatures* its Fifth Independent Film Award, said of Smith: "He has struck us with not the mere pity or curiosity of the perverse, but the glory, the pageantry of Transylvestia and the magic of Fairyland. He has lit up a part of life, although it is a part which most men scorn." The truth is that *Flaming Creatures* is much more about intersexuality than about homosexuality. Smith's vision is akin to the vision in Bosch's paintings of a paradise and a hell of writhing, shameless, ingenious bodies. Unlike those serious and stirring films about the beauties and terrors of homoerotic love, Kenneth Anger's *Fireworks* and Genet's *Chant d'Amour*, the important fact about the figures in Smith's film is that one cannot easily tell which are men and which are women. These are "creatures," flaming out in intersexual, polymorphous joy. The film is built out of a complex web of ambiguities and ambivalences, whose primary image is the confusion of male and female flesh. The shaken breast and the shaken penis are interchangeable with each other.

Bosch had a strange, aborted, ideal nature against which to situate his nude figures and androgynous visions of pain and pleasure. Smith has no literal background (it's hard to tell in the film whether one is indoors or outdoors), but instead the thoroughly artificial, invented landscape of costume, gesture, and music. The myth of intersexuality is played out against a background of corny songs, ads, clothes, dances, and above all, the repertory of fantasy drawn from corny movies. (Another beautiful recent work, this time for the theatre, the play *Home Movies*—written by Rosalyn Drexler, music by Al Carmines—has this same delicious range.) The texture of *Flaming Creatures* is made up of a rich collage of "camp" lore: a woman in white (a transvestite) with drooping head holding a stalk of lilies; a gaunt woman seen emerging from a coffin, who turns out to be a vampire and, eventually, male; a marvelous Spanish dancer (also a transvestite) with huge dark eyes, black lace mantilla and fan; a tableau from the *Sheik of Araby* with reclining men in burnooses and an Arab temptress stolidly exposing one breast; a scene between two women, reclining on flowers and rags, which recalls the dense, crowded texture of the movies in which von Sternberg directed Dietrich in the early thirties. The vocabulary of images and textures on which Smith draws includes pre-Raphaelite languidness; Art Nouveau; the great exotica styles of the twenties, the Spanish and the Arab; and the modern "camp" way of relishing mass culture.

Flaming Creatures is a triumphant example of an aesthetic vision of the world—and such a vision is perhaps always, at its core, epicene. But this type of art has still to be understood in this country. The space in which *Flaming Creatures* moves is not the space of moral ideas, which is where American critics have traditionally located art. What I am urging is that there is not only moral space, by whose laws *Flaming Creatures* would indeed come off badly; there is also aesthetic space, the space of pleasure. Here Smith's film moves and has its being.

MAY 4, 1964

FUZZ'S PROGRESS

Diane Di Prima

•

Diane Di Prima continues the saga of *Flaming Creatures*. Diane Di Prima is a poet and playwright whose *Memoirs of a Beatnik* was published recently.

THE TERM "HARASSMENT of the arts" is relatively new but it has already become a byword in New York and other cities of this country. Four theaters alone have been closed; writers and painters are spending more time in the courtroom than at the typewriter or the easel. The current outbreak is merely an acceleration of a process which has been building for some time. One of the more publicized cases from that earlier phase was the federal government's seizure of the Living Theatre for back taxes on October 17, 1963. Contrary to popular impression, co-director Julian Beck stated that he had been paying these taxes in small installments; the action was taken arbitrarily and without the customary period of grace in which the theatre might have raised the necessary money.

The following chronology of more recent cases is by no means complete and is limited to the New York area (except where otherwise stated), but it indicates certain patterns as well as the manner of persecution. To fully explain the legal complexities would be impossible here, but it may be useful to point out that the three main law-enforcement agencies at work are: New York City's Department of

Licenses; the New York State Division of Motion Pictures (under the Board of Education) which licenses films; the New York City police and occasionally fire, building or other municipal authorities.

December 1963: The City administration broke its 1961 agreement with the Artist-Tenants Association and began denying applications for Artist-in-Residence permits—which allow artists to live in lofts—on the basis of the new zoning code. That agreement specified that if certain safety standards were met, and if there were no more than two artists to each building, the city would not deny Artist-in-Residence standing merely on the basis of zoning or occupancy regulations. At present over 2,500 Manhattan artists are registered as living in lofts (the zoning term defining premises normally—or formerly—occupied by a light manufacturing business, and desirable to artists because of the large inexpensive space they offer).

On April 3, 1964, the ATA staged a demonstration for which 1,400 people turned out. On April 6, they had a meeting with city officials. The compromise plan which was unofficially offered would, by not allowing new application in manufacturing areas, slowly establish a few ghettos of loft areas available to artists. There is very little hope that ATA and the City will reach an agreement. If all else fails, the artists feel they must go ahead with the general boycott which they threatened in 1961.

December 7, 1963: A performance of Jack Smith's film *Flaming Creatures* was scheduled at the Tivoli Theatre. A crowd of 600–800 people was kept waiting and finally dispersed: the manager had been warned by a phone call from the Bureau of Licenses not to open that night.

February 2, 1964: Maurice Margules of the Metro Coffee Shop received a summons for presenting "entertainment"—poetry readings—without a coffeehouse license (in March, 1961, a statute was enacted redefining the coffeehouse and requiring it to be licensed for the presentation of certain forms of entertainment). The Metro has no admission charge or minimum; the readings are attended by a few dozen writers. After the readings, contributions are collected from the audience and turned over to the poet. The COP (Committee on Poetry) was formed, including poets Paul Blackburn and Allen Ginsberg, among others. The case was tried and the Metro was acquitted. COP's attorney interprets the acquittal as a sign that the statute involved is recognized to be unconstitutional, since this was the only ground on which a defense was made. However, the presiding judge made no statement at the time of acquittal, and since the decision came from a lower court, it does not set a precedent. Negotiations are being conducted between COP and the Department of Licenses in an attempt to revamp the coffeehouse law.

February 14: Lou Lloyd, operator of the Pocket Theatre, received a summons for showing unlicensed films. The Pocket Film Society, an experimental film group, had provided the works presented. Mr. Lloyd's theatre license was suspended for thirty days; he did not appeal the sentence. The plays by Harold Pinter which were being performed there moved to another theatre, and the Pocket Dance Series, a series of seven concerts by young choreographers (James Waring, Fred Herko, Yvonne Rainer and others) was canceled.

February 17: The owner of the Gramercy Arts Theatre—where the Film Makers Cooperative had been showing experimental films for some time—received a similar summons. His theatre license has been suspended for ninety days. The producers of *Diary of a Madman*, which was scheduled to open there on April 16, are appealing for a postponement of the suspension. (We had heard that something similar had happened at the Gate Theatre, but upon calling the theatre were informed that nothing of the kind had occurred there. The theatre owner said that the Gate Film Club had been "thrown out" as soon as the theatre had received a phone call from the License Department. However one interprets this statement, it clearly suggests that intimidation is at work.)

March 3, Flaming Creatures was seized on the grounds of obscenity at the New Bowery Theatre. Jonas Mekas, president of the Film Makers Cooperative, and three others, were arrested: the police also confiscated their movie projector and screen. The trial has now been set for May 18.

March 7, Los Angeles: Kenneth Anger's film, *Scorpio Rising*, was seized by the vice squad at the Cinema Theatre. Anger had received an award from the Ford Foundation just a few days before.

March 13: Police interrupted a showing at the Writers' Stage of Jean Genet's film *Un Chant d'Amour*. The film was seized on the grounds of obscenity; Jonas Mekas and Pierre Cottrell were arrested, and another projector and screen were impounded. Some days later, the owner of the Writers' Stage received a summons for showing an unlicensed film.

March 14: Theodora Bergery, owner of the New Bowery Theatre, attempted to cancel her lease with the American Theatre for Poets, Inc., the lessees of her premises. She stated that on March 9, she had received a summons from the License Department; on Friday, March 13, she had received a phone call from the same department and was told that if the performances of the American Theatre for Poets were allowed to go on that weekend, her license would be suspended, but that if she "got rid of" her tenant they would forget the matter.

March 17: Kenneth Jacobs of the Film Makers Cooperative received a summons from the City License Department for operating a motion picture theatre (the New Bowery again) without a license. That night the Fire Department also attended the screening, and set a match to the curtain and stage hangings to see if they were fireproof. Joel Markham, a painter, was hanging a show in the lobby; as the fire inspectors were leaving, one of them said to Mr. Markham in a threatening tone, "This theatre is going to burn down." (The Metro Coffee Shop mentioned above had an unexplained fire that month.)

March 18: Theodora Bergery successfully locked the American Theatre for Poets out of the New Bowery Theatre by means of a court order which was later upheld. The New York Poets Theatre performances of one-act plays by Diane di Prima, Le-Roi Jones and Frank O'Hara went on that Friday at midnight at the Writers' Stage, and twice the following weekend in a loft. But the theatre's new program of plays by Michael McClure, James Schuyler and Kenneth Koch, which had been scheduled to open on April 3, has been indefinitely postponed. The film showings, readings and concerts of new dance and music scheduled for April also had to be canceled. The license of the New Bowery Theatre has been suspended for thirty days.

March 18: New York State's Division of Motion Pictures served Alan S. Marlowe of the American Theatre for Poets and Kenneth Jacobs of the Film Makers Cooperative with summonses for "exhibiting an unlicensed motion picture in a place of public amusement for pay." The summonses were based on the show of the previous night. On that night, no tickets had been sold; at the entrance to the theatre a cigar box had been placed on a table, and a sign requesting that the audience "contribute to the Coop's anti-censorship fund" had been taped to the table. At the trial, the two groups will raise the question of whether this kind of voluntary contribution constitutes "pay."

March 22: The Committee for Freedom of the Arts was formed with the purpose of holding demonstrations informing the public (via a newsletter and other means), providing legal aid. Its headquarters are at 35 Cooper Square, New York, and its membership includes prominent American writers, painters, theatre artists and film makers.

April 3: Lenny Bruce was arrested at the Cafe Au Go Go for "giving an indecent performance." Howard Solomon, owner of the Au Go Go was arrested at the same time. At the police station, Solomon found a member of the License Department waiting for him with a summons based on another charge. On April 7, Lenny Bruce was arrested again, this time with Ella Solomon, Howard's wife. A License Department inspector issued another summons on this occasion, although the official policy of this department is that it is *not* a censorship agency and will not act as such.

The week of April 6, San Francisco: A showing of Kama Sutra sculpture's by Ron Boise was seized for obscenity at the Vorpal Gallery. The police carted away eleven metal statues and arrested Ed Muldoon, the gallery owner.

We have not mentioned the harassment of the Cafe La Mama and the Cafe Cino, both coffeehouses which present plays; the fifteen summonses issued by the Department of Buildings to village coffee shops on the day after the Metro won an acquittal; the closing of the Washington Square Theatre, whose owner has received and fought eleven summonses since he opened; the harassment of the Hardware Poets Theatre (a loft theatre which finally solved its licensing problems by becoming a private club), of the Bread and Puppets Theatre (another loft theatre which subsists on donations), and of Mort Lewis, whose tiny theatre in his own apartment held seats for only sixteen people, all invited.

There is almost nowhere in New York where one can now go to see the new cinema or the new theatre. Downtown Manhattan, where all the New York incidents took place and which has been the heart of young *avant-garde* work, is growing dark.

What has happened? Are the arts in America running amok? Is the harassment an attempt to "clean up New York for the World's Fair"? Are real estate interests, greedy for expansion, trying to drive out the artists? Or has the range of human consciousness so widened, the area, which concerns "art" so extended, the mores of the society so changed, that officialdom has become alarmed?

Perhaps it is simply that after the war one generation of artists arrived at their maturity, broke new ground and then grew respectable, as is the way of the world. Another generation has now come of age. All they ask is to do their work for whoever loves it or has need of it. But they are determined to utilize fully materials which their elders readied for them; among these are politics, drugs, homosexuality and what Susan Sontag has termed "intersexuality." For the artists, these are all means to an end: expanding human consciousness. The shape of man is changing, and the change is picking up speed.

FEBRUARY 22, 1965

ANDY WARHOL, MOVIE MAKER

Howard Junker

•

Howard Junker is the editor of *Zyzzyva*, a literary magazine based in San Francisco. A documentary filmmaker and essayist he has edited the following collections: *Lucy Break; Roots and Branches; Contemporary Essays by West Coast Writers*; and *Strange Attraction: The Best of Ten Years of Zyzzyva*.

UNTIL NOW, ANDY Warhol, high priest and elf of Pop Art and ascendant spirit of the Underground Cinema, has usually made his movies in his loft, which is sometimes referred to as his factory, and in which there are cases of Andy Warhol silvered Coke bottles, Andy Warhol Brillo boxes, Andy Warhol corn-flakes cartons, and multi-image, silk-screen canvases of Liz, Jackie, and flowers. All this, along with a couple of desks, clutters around a cutting table, the silvered lower half of a manikin, a hi-fi (for Pop music), a yellow (detached), toilet, and a curving, red divan, from which I was greeted by Warhol's assistant; Gerry Malanga, and by John Palmer and his wife, the international model, Ivy Nicholson.

An underground film maker in his own right, John was working with Andy because "Andy is the only, because a step back to the beginning of movies is the only possible kind of step forward." In brief, summed John, "Andy's a genius, therefore he makes genius movies."

(*Film Culture* gave Warhol its Sixth Independent Film Award, explaining that Warhol, by recording "in the plainest images possible in the plainest manner possible . . . almost obsessively, man's daily activities . . . takes cinema back to its origins, to the days of Lumière, for a rejuvenation and a cleansing.")

After mentioning that Andy loves movies, John suggested that Andy likes to make them because they're easy. For example, Andy never moves the camera because that's hard to do. Andy's main idea in filming what he does, the way he does, says John, is that the idea doesn't matter. Everything is the same. Who or how doesn't matter.

At this point John and Gerry compiled a Warhol filmography for me.

Sleep, Andy's first film, was shot in midsummer, 1963, and runs eight hours. It shows a man's abdomen, face, backside, etc., while the man is sleeping.

Eat shows Bob Indiana eating two mushroom's for two hours.

Kiss shows numbers of kissers. Each couple kisses for three minutes, which may be a world screen record.

Empire watched the Empire State Building from a top floor of the Time & Life Building from 7:30 P.M. to 8:00 A.M. It will premiere soon at a Film Makers' Cinematheque showing at the City Hall Cinema.

Also: *The Rose without Thorns (Dracula)*, *Tarzan and Jane Regained—Sort of, Henry Geldzahler, Thirteen Most Beautiful Girls, Thirteen Most Beautiful Boys, Personalities, Roller Skate, Soap Opera, Taylor Mead's Ass, Harlot* (award, Los Angeles Film Festival), *B. J., Dinner at Daley's, The End of Dawn, Salome and Delilah, Haircut Dance Movie* and *Newsreels.*

Considering this body of work, John stated that Andy would be just as happy if 2,000 other guys were to think up, make, sell and distribute Andy Warhol movies. "As long as they were in his idiom," said John, "I'd say he'd like that more."

John cautioned me on two counts: 1." Andy doesn't come on with much verbal magic; therefore, no one has the right to expect editorial conceptions in his movies. Andy achieves what he is; his theories constitute the product . . . they're all beautiful." "Andy says a lot of things to enflame people. He's very ironic."

In addition to not moving the camera, Andy shows what he shoots. That is, although to beef up *Sleep* to its full eight hours, Warhol had some shots repeated several times in the printing, he doesn't edit. He doesn't even cut away the leader at either end of a camera roll; he merely splices the film as it comes from the lab. Andy said later that seeing the leader run by in the midst of such boring other material was in itself quite a dramatic event.

About the time I was asking how Andy began making movies, Warhol himself came in. He wore a black Wagner College sweat shirt with a seahawk on the front, paint-flecked black chinos, and black shoes and socks. Plus mild green sunglasses.

Andy listened for a moment to the story of his film debut, then went to the telephone. When he came back John handed him a Quaker Oats magazine ad which showed the man exclaiming in a balloon, "Oh Mama, what are you doing to your kids?" Andy said he had already seen it. John said advertisers were finally learning from Pop artists.

While Andy returned to the phone, John and Gerry filled me in on Andy's possible films-in-progress:

Couch will examine anyone who sits or does anything on the curving, red divan. A climax, perhaps sexual, is expected in this film.

Trim will be a short version of *Haircut*.

Strip Poker, with eight or ten people, will also show post game play.

Building will be a major, major, major work and it is hoped with longest film ever made. It will watch the destruction of an old building, the erection of a new. Anticipated running time: six months.

An Open Letter to Barbara Rose will show gossipy John Bernard Meyers (Tibor de Nagy Gallery) gossiping for an hour and a half, by implication, to gossipy art critic Barbara Rose. (This would have to be a sound film.)

Messy Lives—Joey Le Sueur, who came in about this time, is making plans with Andy for a real feature. Joey loves plot and feels there's not enough in most movies. Therefore he's lined up a dozen script writers who will use roughly the same set of characters, each writer setting up a different story. A score or more well known poets have been approached to write dialogue.

Living Portrait Boxes, which might sell for $1,000 or $1,500 each, would be 8 mm. loops of the sort that showed four Warhol films at the New York Film festival. The LPB's would be just like photographic portraits except that they would move a little. Someone suggested that a sound track could be added: "I love you, give me a hug." Andy agreed.

Now arrived a Belgian television crew, eager to finish up their film on the School of New York, into which they had enrolled most of the other top Pop artists. For their benefit and for mine, Andy went through all the motions of shooting typical Andy Warhol movies.

Gerry was sent out for a dozen bananas. The Bolex was set up before the curving, red divan. John asked if Ivy could eat an apple in the *Banana* sequence.

"Yeah, do we have an apple?"

At this point I overheard a visiting dignitary from a provincial museum, who had dropped by, explain to a youthful colleague something about a "full range from white to black."

Joey Le Sueur mentioned that he had to be at a cocktail party in half an hour, but Andy assured him it would only take three minutes to do a roll of *Banana*. Therefore Joey, John, and Ivy, and Gerry arranged themselves on the divan, were rearranged by Andy, and urged not to unpeel their bananas before the start.

Andy turned the camera on, telling his cast, "You're on."

For a while he looked into the view finder. Joey, John and Ivy and Gary ate bananas. Andy watched. They continued. Andy walked away from the camera. He encouraged what they were doing.

"That's really beautiful," he would say. After two and a half minutes he looked at the footage counter and announced, "It's almost over."

A little later, Andy decided the film had run out. The participants, except for the Belgian TV crew, stopped. Someone complained that the hi-fi had been turned too low. "Music is half of it," admitted Gerry, who looks like Ringo when he frugs.

After another roll of *Banana*, John and Ivy began to rehearse for *Kiss*. Joey said he wanted to go. Andy told him to wait. The Belgians enjoyed *Kiss*. So did John and Ivy.

After a "take-five," Joey was persuaded to sit down on the small stool in the corner portrait gallery to pose for a stillie. He was filmed looking glum and puckish. John was filmed looking like Belmondo. Ivy sat down. She preened, the assistants nibbled on fish and chips.

Andy looked through the view finder. Ivy looked very good. Andy said she was glorious. He said she was fantastic. An assistant took a look and suggested a two-hour film of Ivy looking the way she was. It was a beautiful look. Ivy sat motionless while the camera ground through 100 feet.

Now the Belgians were shown a reel of *Dracula*, with Jack Smith resting his head on the shoulder of Beverly Grant while she eats a banana and he eats a Hershey bar. The Belgians watched politely.

I joined Andy at the loft's far end, by the telephone. Andy said it was all right to be doing something else during a projection of one of his movies. (He once told critic Andrew Sarris that "I make movies to read by, to eat by, to sleep by." I think Andy was being ironic.)

Dracula ran out. The Belgians prepared to leave. Gerry, John and Ivy began to frug on the curving red divan. And Ivy said, "We've just invented chair dancing."

Some weeks later I saw Andy shoot his first sound film, a remake of award winning *Harlot* with superstar Mario Montez in the title role. In attendance were a New York producer, the owner of a London gallery, an ex-CBS sound man, and a Magnum photographer, as well as Gerry, technical consultant Philip, and a trio of Tangiers-type poets who huddled out of camera range preparing to speak the sound track.

As soon as Mario had finished dressing, and Philip had figured out how to thread Andy's new Auricon sound-on-film camera, and as soon as Andy had learned how to turn it on, production went smoothly.

Andy had arranged Gerry and Philip leaning over the back of a straight, green divan, on which lounged Mario and superstarlet Carol, playing Harlot's friend.

Andy again used permissive enthusiasm as his major directorial device. Gerry smoked. Philip looked toughly at the camera. Mario ate bananas and fluttered her eyes. Carol restrained a white pussy.

Andy remained close to the camera throughout and frequently watched through the view finder, though, of course, he didn't touch the camera self.

Andy wanted to keep his actors in position while the magazine was changed, but they rebelled and complained about having to work under professional conditions.

9

The World Is Not Enough

Hollywood and the World

•

The century-long battle for the control of world cinema—a conflict which has transformed from being a war over profits and market share to one about culture and national identity—is also the hidden history of Hollywood's collusion with Capitol Hill to make the world a safer place for its product. The essays and articles that follow reflect this century of virtual warfare but also the role international cinema, especially in the post–World War 2 era, has played as a countervailing force. To the extent that during the glory, glory days of the New Hollywood of the 1970s—as Peter Biskind recounts in Easy Riders, Raging Bulls*—young Hollywood studio executives would while the days away watching the latest Antonioni, Bertolucci, and Godard films on the studio screening rooms, hoping that the genius they absorbed would be replicated in the movies they made.*

JANUARY 6, 1945

HOLLYWOOD INTERNATIONAL

John Grierson

•

This article was the first in a series of four published in early 1945 until the title "Tomorrow the Movies." John Grierson was head of the Canadian Film Board during the time of writing. Soon after he would resign and move to the US where he formed a company to produce movies that promoted international understanding. In 1947 he was appointed director of Mass Media at UNESCO.

Scottish by birth, Grierson was one of the founders of the British documentary film movement. According to Ephraim Katz, Grierson was the first person to use the term documentary (from the French *documentaire*) while describing Robert Flaherty's *Moana* in a film review in the *New York Sun*. Grierson went on to set up a film unit at the (British) Empire Marketing Board where he explored the possibilities of making government-sponsored education and propaganda films. Among the many documentaries produced by his unit was the classic *Nightmail* which has a hypnotic verse commentary written by W. H. Auden.

IF, AS MANY believe, the basis of international relationships is in course of drastic alteration, industries trading in foreign parts must examine the nature of this change. I am told, for example, that Bretton Woods must inevitably revolutionize the fishing industry in Canada because multilateral agreements preclude bilateral agreements and we can no longer "sneak behind," say, the back of Newfoundland: meaning, I take it, that the race is no longer exclusively to the strong or the smart. In the case of the fishing industry the situation calls, it is said, for a revolution in production and distribution methods which, by improving the product and meeting a real and not spurious taste, will give it greater international validity.

The analogy between films and fish should not be lightly dismissed. I could cite the case of the people of London, whose taste has been so perverted over the years that if they ever tasted a fresh fish they would certainly reject it as rotten. Both films and fish are obviously fields of illusion where standards, however widely accepted, may yet be false. The test, however, should not be the taste but the well-being of the consumer. What is called for in fish I shall now forget and consider instead, the economic relations of the film industry, the nature of its past bilateral and even unilateral arrangements, and the effect of the multilateral pressure which will presently be put upon it by nations with their own standards of nutrient.

The film has always been an international traveler. It had no trouble with national barriers when it was silent, and even now titles, dubbed in voices, and foreign-language versions can give it an extensive market outside its country of origin. Where, as in the case of American films, the home market takes care of the cost of production, the costs of conversion are not a considerable obstacle. In any event, the English-speaking world provides an international market in itself. Of all films, those of American origin have been the most widely circulated, partly because of their style and the enterprise of their salesmen, but mostly because of the economic advantage of their very large home market. The American producer has been able to command directors, actors, and writers from all over the world and so to provide pictures with international appeal. Even when he has been most American, he has had large enough funds to produce a highly polished, chromium-plated account of his country's material progress; and this, in the years gone by, had its special attraction for less privileged peoples.

Trade Follows the Picture

To what extent this American film empire can be maintained is another matter. Great Britain has always envied the strength of the American film industry, not least because of the vast propaganda support it gave to the sale of American products. The persistent champion of English film production has not been the industry itself, which in the distribution and exhibition fields does very well out of American films and is allied at many points to American companies, but the British Board of Trade, which is concerned with the trade that follows the picture. England's protective policy has therefore been different in kind from that of countries like Germany, Italy, Spain, and the Soviet Union. These latter had specific political ideas to protect from the anarchic impact—as they no doubt conceived it—of Hollywood values. England, however, has been primarily concerned with building up an exportable product which would share screen space abroad with American films and fly the flag of England over incidental automobiles and bathtubs. Sir Alexander Korda, Carol Reed, Michael Powell, and other good British producers would of course hardly think this a sufficient account of their production motives; but it would be safe to say that the clerks of Whitehall have had more to do with the formulation of long-time film policy than the producers.

The relationship between the government and the industry is different in England from here if only because the industry is coming from behind in international competition and has needed government help. Britain has for a long time required American operators in the United Kingdom to carry a specific proportion of British product. And the government has entered boldly into an analysis of the kind of British film most likely to serve British interests abroad. As a result it has given special encouragement, not to the small budgeted film, which on the whole tends to be very English, but to the sometimes denatured million-dollar type for which international markets are an economic necessity. It has observed with great equanimity the expenditure of very large sums during the period of experimental growth, on the good ground that only by trial and error can the larger showmanship be learned. Even in the midst of war, large quasi-experimental sums are being found.

The relative strength of the British film industry is certainly greater today than it has been for years. A very large proportion of British buying power has been for years combined under Arthur J. Rank, a miller of great wealth who has only recently gone into the film business; and the same group of interests has announced its intention of progressively buying into theater and distribution systems across the world, particularly in the dominions and colonies. A different official attitude toward the industry might not so easily have allowed the large combination of buying power in the hands of one man or approved such expensive production schemes at the present time; and public opinion might be unfavorable if there were not good assurance that Mr. Rank's great venture was going to be in every sense a national one.

The strength of this new buying power is reflected at present in new and more effective arrangements for the distribution of British films in the United States. The fact that, in general, the British market constitutes the margin of real profit in American film production has at last been turned into a strong bargaining weapon. This is not to say that British films will be any more successful than before—that depends on the drawing power of the films, themselves—but it is important that the distribution machinery of the United States is being increasingly engaged for films other than American.

This development is only one among many likely to affect American policy in the international field. The old days of easy monopoly have gone: in England, because of its special need for markets, but also in every country which has come to appreciate the power of the screen and has its own national interests to serve. There is a growing tendency everywhere to encourage home production. Increasing attention is being paid to the effect of American films on the mind of the people and their relation to native philosophies and needs. On the one hand, foreign countries want Hollywood to include more native themes in its schedules of production; on the other hand, they are becoming more sensitive about the handling of such themes. In nothing is the spectacular growth of propaganda consciousness better demonstrated.

Obviously, Hollywood will require a new approach in its international operations. In the past its salesmen have done very well for it. The need tomorrow may be for representatives who can go behind the mere problem of sales to the problem of international relations and build up, as statesmen try to do, those genuinely good relations which are based on common interests.

Relations with Canada

One might generalize in this regard from the situation in Canada, a country of 12,000,000 people which provides as great returns to the American film industry as all of South America with a population of 75,000,000. The tastes in entertainment of Canadians are much the same as those of people south of their border; because of the connection with England an English film will perhaps do 5 per cent better in Canada relatively, than in the United States, but this is a small difference. By and large, Canadians like the same stars, the same story line, and the same evaluations of character and issue as other Americans; Canada's own share of Hollywood stars, directors, and writers is considerable, and no one there or here knows the difference.

It might seem, therefore, that the American film could circulate as easily and happily in Canada as in its own country. But such an assumption on the part of the American film industry would be lacking in foresight. Canada is an up-and-coming nation. It feels that it has a tremendous future. It is already, it thinks, one of the greatest of the "middle" nations, and its huge agricultural and industrial output during the war and its contribution in fighting power support its claim. Inevitably, therefore, Canada is giving consideration to its place on the international screen. It certainly cannot leave its reputation entirely in the hands of the newsreel editors in New York and the producers in Hollywood, who might be so shortsighted as not to think of Canada at all.

Canada's attitude toward American films may well be an example to other countries, especially those whose native film industries are of limited strength. The natural good-will existing between Canada and the United States has made it possible for Canada to secure from cooperative discussions as much as if not more than a protective system and a competitive film industry could have given it. The Canadian content of American newsreels in Canada has been increased in recent years to a point near to satisfactory, and, just as importantly, the Canadian content in American and world newsreels has also been increased. American distributors in Canada are not only cooperating well with the government in the presentation of the nation's war effort but making it a matter of policy to obtain for Canada its measure of film representation. As a result one series of Canadian-produced short films, "The World in Action," enjoys worldwide circulation—incidentally, it is the only foreign series now shown regularly in American theaters. American companies, moreover, include numerous Canadian films in their travel talks, science films, and the like.

In addition to this cooperation in the matter of newsreels and short films, Hollywood has over the war years produced three major Canadian films and I used Canadian backgrounds for others as part of an earnest attempt to provide a quid pro quo for a very useful market. Like the Hollywood productions for South American markets encouraged by the State Department, this marks the beginning of a new and responsible policy toward foreign fields. The development of such a policy would be facilitated if countries like Canada would not only bring political pressure to bear on Hollywood and London but establish machinery for the encouragement of stories and plays that would of themselves command the attention of producers.

Of course in every country there will always be some who want to see a native feature industry established and who consequently demand protective quotas. But the international field tends to be kept clear for Hollywood and London by the fact that feature production imposes tremendous financial burdens, especially for a country with a small population. It is all the more difficult for a country which is not protected by the barrier of a different language and which lies within easy reach of the pull of American salaries and other attractions.

It seems clear that the American film industry has come to the most difficult period in its long international career. Its problems reflect the foreign problems of statesmen and demand a new and high degree of international knowledge and good-will. Concessions here and lobbyings there, such as the cruder exponents of international commerce may propose, will not suffice. Hand-outs, however well-intentioned, do not please sovereign peoples, and there is a sure law of diminishing returns on political pressure when applied by great nations. International success in a sphere of influence so extensive as that of films will demand finally, as in the political sphere, considered and creative cooperation in the pursuit of common values and common ideas. Great nations with superior means of production must be expected to take the lead in this matter.

It is not certain whether Hollywood and London have gone far enough in equipping themselves for this new and considerable task, although progress has been made. Hollywood is more politically conscious today that it ever was. Many of its principals are engaged in war duties of importance and know what it is to serve the state. But this may not be enough. Closer contact needs to be established with the body of international knowledge in Washington; and it is the best of news that this is now being deliberately furthered by a scheme for installing government film specialists abroad. There is certainly room for a diplomatic force which will not just support Hollywood sales power but will supply systematic information to Hollywood producers on the larger considerations governing their foreign trade. It may be that Hollywood needs an institute of international affairs through which producers, directors, and writers can study the relationship of their films to the wider and more difficult world in which they will operate after the war. There are clearly other levels of consideration than those of buying and selling, and neither Hollywood nor London will be able to ignore them.

MARCH 19, 1960

LETTER FROM ITALY

William Weaver

•

ONE EVENING LAST month, as the film director Federico Fellini was coming out of the Milanese theatre where his new picture *La dolce vita* had just had its premiere, an elegantly dressed man stepped up from the crowd and shouted at him: "You are dragging Italy in the mud!" With that, the stranger spat on the director, while other shouts arose, attacking Fellini or defending him. The next day he received something like 400 telegrams, the majority of which accused him of being a traitor, a Communist, an atheist, or things unprintable.

The film (which will no doubt open in New York shortly) is a series of long episodes, giving a rather grotesque view of the corruption of the Roman idle classes, from the film world to the aristocracy, mixed with sensation-seeking journalists and defeated intellectuals, actors and café society. Many starchy *Milanesi,* after witnessing the picture, said in effect that, though such things may very well go on in Rome, they could never happen in serious-minded, hard-working Milan. The answer to this came the next day, when the Milanese police announced that they had finally broken up a huge call-girl organization, which had been furnishing relaxation to tired industrialists of the city (at upwards of 100,000 *lire* a night).

In Rome itself, audience reaction to the picture was calmer, and so far no Roman has spat on Fellini, though he has been denounced in the local press, or at least in its right wing. And the Vatican organ, *L'Osser-*

vatore romano, devoted a long editorial to the film, un-hesitatingly calling it "obscene" and "disgusting," and demanding that the authorities withdraw it from circulation at once.

As this is written, *La dolce vita* is still playing at two Roman first-run houses, standing room only, four shows a day. And observers believe that it will survive even the Vatican's pummeling, especially because the director has some ecclesiastical authority on his side. When his preceding film, *Cabiria*, was about to appear, Fellini and his producer were afraid that its touchy subject matter (prostitution) might arouse Italy's censors. So Fellini took a print to Genoa and there had a private showing for Cardinal Siri (one of the church's smartest prelates and a Papal candidate at the last consistory). The cardinal gave the film his approval. He has also seen *La dolce vita* and has apparently expressed satisfaction at the work's moral viewpoint.

La dolce vita's troubles began long before it opened. The producer originally scheduled to make it took one look at the long, rambling script (much of which was left in the cutting-room) and turned Fellini down. Several other producers flirted with the idea, then backed out. When at last a producer was found and the shooting began, it took weeks longer than planned.

Those were entertaining weeks for the Romans. Rome really is a small town (far more provincial than *La dolce vita* might lead you to believe), and everybody knows or knows *about* everybody else. Last summer, while the film was being shot, half the city turned out to watch Anita Ekberg wading in the Trevi fountain or Lex (former Tarzan) Barker slouching around outside the Excelsior Hotel. And what seemed like the other half of the population played bit parts in the picture: members of aristocratic families played aristocrats (a Ruspoli, for example, and a Rodd), abstract painters played abstract painters, Miss Iris Tree, actress and poet, played a poet and read one of her poems. *La dolce vita* was a godsend for foreign actors passing through the city, and in need of a little cash.

"I'm in *La dolce vita* this week . . ." was a commonplace remark at the outdoor cafés of the Via Veneto last July.

"What scene?"

"The orgy."

"Oh, I'm in the night club. . . ."

So Fellini has made a kind of family album of Rome (with some of the portraits touched up and brightly colored, as they often are in albums), and the Romans are flocking to look at it. Though not all of them come away indignant, few come away without some kind of opinion. And in reply to the *Osservatore's* attack, the left-wing papers are devoting columns to Fellini's defense. Long interviews have appeared in *La voce repubblicana* (of the center Republican party) and in all the illustrated weeklies, while *Paese Sera* (more or less Communist) has twice in the last three days dedicated its entire back page to quotes from leading Roman literary and intellectual figures. *L'Unita* (out and out Communist) has had a front-page editorial attacking Fellini's detractors. And while an association of Rome's parish priests demanded the film's withdrawal, a public meeting of writers and filmmakers (presided over by Alberto Moravia) was called to discuss the work and express solidarity with the director.

The uproar of the Fellini opening has shadowed another event of last week, also concerned with Rome and the film world. This was the publication of a little volume entitled *The State as Filmmaker* by the economist Ernesto Rossi, a leader of Italy's small, intellectual and pugnacious Radical Party.

Rossi has written in the past some fierce and acutely documented works on Fascist economy and government and its hangovers in the Italy of today. In the new study he discusses the incredible amount of state support given the film industry in Italy and, at the same time, the marked reluctance of official or quasi-official organizations to discuss or itemize the amounts of these pump-priming contributions, now that the pump is flowing merrily.

The Fascist regime heavily supported the budding Italian film industry through its infamous Ministry of Popular Culture, and the industry repaid the support by making films like *Scipio Africanus* to glorify the dictator; or else the old "white telephone" comedies, to stultify the movie-going masses.

Immediately after the war, in the glorious period of *Open City* and *Shoeshine*, the film-makers of Italy were on their own. But the producers—and with them, the directors and actors—were soon pestering the new republic for handouts. At a mass meeting in Rome's Piazza del popolo, Miss Anna Magnani put her hands on her chest and shouted: "Save the Italian film" to an applauding public.

The Italian film was saved, and has been ever since—handsomely. The government took steps to protect it against the invasion from Hollywood (in those days, Italian films were not popular with the Italian public), and at the same time instituted a system of "prizes" to be given to locally made pictures. As Dr. Rossi points out, the prizes have got larger and larger, as the industry has grown and prospered; but while government censorship exists, there is no control of the artistic worth of the films to which money is given. Obscenity is condemned, but not vulgarity. So that films like *The Labors of Hercules*, which took in 630 million *lire* at the box office in its first year, was given 101 million by the government. And this was not the government's largest contribution nor, alas, the worst film of that year.

Movie-making in Italy is booming. Shady characters in small offices speculate on big names, counting on the prize money. They plan super-colossal productions; some of them are really made, others end only in a rain of unpaid bills and drawn-out Italian law suits.

The *Hercules* films have been a huge financial success in Italy and (to our shame) in America. Dozens of imitations now glut the Italian market, and dozens more are being prepared, on Biblical or classical themes: *The Battle of Marathon, Sappho, The Venus of Lesbos, Constantine the Great, Sodom and Gomorrah, Carthage in Flames*—these are the titles of films recently released or currently being cast. Producers gloomily predict that the classical craze can't last but all of them are desperately trying to slip in under the wire.

Meanwhile, the government's generosity continues. Directors, like Rossellini and Fellini, chafe at government censorship, but few of them (and still fewer producers) want to give up government money.

Rossi compares the film industry in Italy to a kept woman. "If she wants to make love where she likes, then she will have to give up her allowance." Or, she can always go out and work. The box office success of *La dolce vita*, for one example, indicates that, if she once tried it, the kept woman could do very well on her own.

JANUARY 24, 1968

FILMS FROM THE VIETCONG

Peter Gessner

•

At the time of publication Gessner had been working in Manhattan as an assistant film editor for several blacklisted filmmakers who had formed their own production company. As he recalls, "One day a nervous Venezuelan student wandered into the office with raw footage of the nascent guerilla movement in his country. Everyone was too busy, and the task was given to me to turn it in to a film. I had never edited a film on my own and knew next to nothing about Latin America. I remembered that Robert [Kramer]—who I had known from grade school and college—had recently been travelling on his own in Latin America. An intelligent narration needed to be written, and I knew he could write well. We finished the film—called *FALN* after the initials of the guerilla group—and perhaps somewhat melodramatically, took pseudonyms as credits (Robert Kramer inverted became Robert Remark, while I opted for my middle name: "Peter David") In retrospect, the film tends to swim in youthful romanticism for what we later learned was a politically marginal group; Robert however, always proudly listed it as the first film in his filmography." This recollection comes from the second annual *Nation* Hollywood issue where Gessner wrote about the late Robert Kramer. Gessner now lives in San Francisco where he is at work on a book about his second career as a private investigator.

SOME HALF-DOZEN FILMS produced by the National Liberation Front of Vietnam are making their way around the country, shown for the most part in poor screening conditions to limited audiences. According to recent reports in the New York press, at least one film has been shown to local high school audiences, drawing indignant protests from suburban parents. Despite the difficulties imposed by a sound track loaded with hyperbole and slogans (the English narrations have all the literary grace of a pamphlet), and despite the deteriorated physical condition of the films which makes many of these screenings little more than mysterious lantern shows, the very existence of these films merits attention.

As a record of the face of the war in Vietnam, and even more as an indication of what the film makers want "us" to know about them, the NLF films are a humbling experience to the viewer. In one (dated 1965), there is a brief sequence in a Vietcong-held village where, during a lull in the fighting, a Western-style ballet is performed within a ring of watching guerrillas. Even the hardened view which says that such things don't happen spontaneously, that they are arranged for the visiting camera, must cope with the fact that these people, the Vietcong, engaged in a brutalizing struggle, have thought it important to include dance in the midst of footage of a vicious guerrilla war.

If this instance indicates that the Vietcong's vision of itself in some sense includes an awareness of the human implications of the kind of war it is forced to fight, its interpretation of events in the United States appears to be filtered through the prism of ideology. For example, one is saddened by repeated references throughout these films to the "progressive American peoples" linked to shots of domestic anti-war demonstrations. Rather than realistically assessing the size and shape of current anti-war sentiment in this country, the film makers seem to have chosen to plug in the appropriate ideological platitude. It may be that, as James Cameron put it in his recent series of articles in The *New York Times*, "too many officials speak an English or French that was actually learned in slogans"; one also suspects that the twenty-year heritage of civil war brings with it a certain hardening of thought, an impatience with the niceties of language and distinction-making.

Once the narration is peeled away, and the images themselves are allowed to live for what they are, the texture of life in Vietnam forces its way through. Another film contains an extended sequence about captured equipment which begins as an apparent ode to self-sufficiency, only to move in a quite unexpected direction. From neatly stacked piles of guns and machinery, the camera turns to people making candleholders from what seem to be spent shells, to still others cutting jeep tires into sandal patterns. For a moment, the gulf between these people and a civilization which, even in peacetime, has managed to institutionalize the notion that *things* wear out, seems to loom larger than any logistical speculations about how the Vietcong supply themselves.

Of the six or so films now making the rounds, only one seems to go beyond the momentary revelatory glimpse to create a more whole impact. It was produced, probably by the NLF or a militant wing of the Buddhists, sometime after 1963 (there is no more precise internal evidence), and deals with the wave of demonstrations which followed the Diem government's suppression of the Buddhists.

It begins with what is a prologue of almost abstract battle footage: a montage of swooping planes, machine-gun rattles and barbed wire, not unlike Lewis Milestone's *All Quiet on the Western Front*. Abruptly, we are swept into a slow processional of Buddhist priests going out into the streets of Saigon to demonstrate for what, to Americans, would seem to be the most basic of liberties—the freedom to worship. Great bales of barbed wire are unrolled in front of them by soldiers; the younger priests, whose faces strangely recall those of the early civil rights workers in the American South, quietly place their hands around the wire as the soldiers begin to try to cordon them off. A tear-gas grenade lunges across the street, streaming white smoke like some kind of mythic Oriental paper beast.

The Diem soldiers, in camouflaged battle dress and holding shields which resemble the tops of garbage cans and which they seem to use to ward off objects thrown at them by the crowd, begin to move against the priests; at this point, the film takes on the qualities of an ominous pageant play. Oddly incongruous Western symphonic music replaces the English narrator (who, with good sense, has kept quiet throughout most of the demonstration sequence), and an unpredictable concordance of sound and image occurs: stock movie music joined with startling images raises the film to an entirely new level, toward a totality of emotion quite difficult to describe precisely. It is one of those rare moments in motion pictures when one plus one equals three. (Something of the sort happens in Luis Buñuel's *Land Without Bread*, a 1932 documentary of an impoverished region in Spain, in which Brahms's *Fourth Symphony* is used throughout the film *not* as a handy contrast but rather in an almost architectural way to provide a vaulting, an unattainable ceiling of emotion which hovers over the sordid level of human action.) Generally, the NLF film makers do not employ music in such ways; the music in other films is of an indeterminate martial nature, used conventionally to fill in behind the narrator.

The Buddhist film, in many ways the most successful of the NLF group, seems to have received less circulation than what is perhaps the most widely seen but unfortunately the least interesting of the lot. This picture, dated 1965 and bearing the title "Foreign Correspondents Visit the National Liberation Front" (at any rate, something like that), records *Humanité* correspondents Wilfred Burchette and Madeleine Riffaud eating and singing with happy peasants. The film is almost completely uninformative and comes close to being embarrassing—Mlle. Riffaud is more than effusive in her desire to kiss and fondle young Vietcong guerrillas. The quality of the print is mercifully poor and a good portion of all this is practically invisible.

In addition to these films of the war in the South, there is one from the North which depicts recent preparations for air defense. It has an untranslated Vietnamese narration, and does not appear to have been widely seen in this country. The film seems to have been made in 1965, after the start of bombings in the North. Perhaps half the footage deals with preparatory and actual antiaircraft drills, ranging from heavy guns to small arms. An extended and well-put-together sequence begins with telephoto shots of what appear to be United States swept-wing jets returning again and again over an indeterminate target. Small-arms fire is put up from the ground with what seems to be pathetic intensity, but Chris Koch, formerly of WBAI-FM radio, witnessed such drills by students during his recent trip to North Vietnam and, upon returning home, called the Department of Defense to inquire whether small-arms fire could bring down an airplane. He was reportedly told: "Hell yes! During World War II we used to do that all the time." Evidently, massed gunfire forms a kind of super-shotgun spread which can imperil fuel supply tanks, rockets, or other vulnerable parts.

What comes through from this film, and indeed from all the NLF films, despite their monothematic crudeness and technical imperfection, is something of the brute level at which the Vietnamese people, North and South, seem prepared to resist an increasingly destructive and degrading war. The master image might be one of a wounded, angry fox facing the striking force of a mailed fist.

Although the NLF movies draw unexpectedly large audiences (mostly students) wherever they are shown, their net effect is ambiguous at best. They seldom exploit the motion picture as a particular form of communication, nor do they explore the special qualities that set it off from pamphlets or slide shows. The films do not achieve a sense of the camera's own participation in events, a sense present in the footage of volunteer cameramen for the Spanish Republic (*To Die in Madrid*). Judged by the standards we apply to works of art, or even against the more vague measure of some kind of immediacy of feeling, the work is crude and conventional. One responds with something of the suspicion Trotsky felt, perhaps unjustly, for the work of the poet Mayakovsky: "[he] shouts too often where one should speak; and so his cry, where cry is needed, sounds inadequate."

Reports from some of the Vietnam teach-ins have indicated that one of the principal difficulties in raising discussion with students is that cold-war structures of thought have so conditioned people that they do not think of Vietnam in terms of the aspirations, indifferences, antipathies of its people, but rather as a "plot"—vast numbers being manipulated. This writer and a small group of independent film makers—a loosely federated cooperative with no political or aesthetic manifestoes to proclaim—have undertaken to produce a film whose subject will be the very nature of this dilemma (the project has received the support of various organizations, including the Artists and Writers Committee to End the War, and Students for a Democratic Society).

The film is to be directed at those who have remained indifferent to the war or actually support the Administration's policies in Vietnam. It is not to be a work of "propaganda," which seems useless now, but a film which sets out an encounter with all that we know about the war and the American response to it. Selections from the NLF films discussed above will be combined with domestic newsreel sources and extensive shooting in this country. The film will juxtapose footage from Vietnam with official policy statements; it will seek interviews with those in power, with returning soldiers, and perhaps with former French colonials; it will attempt to find and elucidate the visual correlatives in this country which underlie and support the American response to the war. It will attempt to do all this without making ex cathedra statements of its own; rather, it will seek to embody a complex of thought and feeling in the language of film. The film project has received support and offers of advisory assistance from several independent film makers, including Hilary Harris and Leo Hurwitz. In addition, an offer of an original music score has been made by Morton Feldman and other contemporary composers.

JUNE 25, 1983

FICTIONALIZING THE TRUTH IN LATIN AMERICA

Ariel Dorfman

•

Ariel Dorfman is a Chilean playwright, critic, novelist, and screenwriter whose play *Death and the Maiden* was filmed by Roman Polanski. His books include *Widows, Konfidenz: A Novel, How to Read Donald Duck* and the recent memoir *Heading South, Looking North: A Bilingual Journey*. He teaches at Duke University.

The horrors of the past are comfortable. There is nothing we can do about them except remember.

ON MAY 5, A group of mothers whose children are missing came from Guatemala, from Chile, from El Salvador, from Argentina, to Washington. The idea was simple: if these women could not be with their offspring because they had been kidnapped, because their governments have refused to acknowledge that they had been kidnapped, at least they would not be alone on Mother's Day. In the presence of Representatives Pat Schroeder and Barbara Mikulski, one mother after another stood up to tell her story.

Few Americans heard about this extraordinary, perturbing, emotional meeting. Colman McCarthy of *The Washington Post*, acting on his own, wrote a column, but the major media, which had devoted hours and hours, pages and pages, to the survivors of the Holocaust just a few weeks before, ignored it (the same major media that had virtually ignored the Holocaust when it was happening, forty years ago). They did not send one reporter, one camera, one crew. I know. For two weeks I lived on the phone, asking people, begging them, to come, to cover the story.

They did not come. They were not interested.

Forty years ago, Hitler conjured up the technique of making people disappear. He ordered French *résistants* to be deported to the *Nacht und Nebel* of Germany, to be executed. There was a twisted, demoniac logic to such repression: the *résistants'* unmarked graves could not be used as rallying points or memorials. And their friends and relatives were condemned to uncertainty about the fate of the ones they loved. Now, decades later, Latin Americans are refining this technique of demoralization. The armies that are committing these crimes are not foreign, though they treat their own people like a conquered populace. They speak the same language and laugh at the same jokes.

How can this horror be communicated to Americans?

In the last year and a half there have been two films that enabled US audiences to experience vicariously the drama of the missing persons in Latin America. Both are based on true stories. One, *Missing*, tells the story of Ed Horman, an American businessman who went to Chile in 1973, soon after the coup that ousted Salvador Allende, to search for his disappeared son, Charles. He did what all relatives of missing people do. He went to hospitals, questioned witnesses, badgered the authorities. Finally he wound up where so many of them wind up: at the morgue. The other film is *Jacobo Timerman: Prisoner Without a Name. Cell Without a Number*, which was made for television and shown in prime time. It concerns the disappearance, torture and survival of Timerman, editor and publisher of Argentina's most influential daily newspaper.

Both pictures work because they infuse the characters with an aura of familiarity. At the most superficial level, we feel that it is not Ed Horman sweating it out but our own Jack Lemmon. Nor is it some foreign journalist being prodded with electricity till the TV screen wants to faint; it is Roy Scheider, the star of *Jaws*. Their dilemmas have also been made recognizable to Americans. The stories may be set in faraway Chile or Argentina, but there is nothing remote about what is happening to the characters.

In *Missing*, the central figure is someone with whom most Americans can identify. The father, who lost contact with his son long ago, now must face the fact that he is dead. The film touches people in the United States most directly when it deals with the generation gap that the Vietnam War created, and with the pain of closing that gap. *Prisoner* also gives Americans a character with whom they have become well acquainted through endless media exposure. He is an amalgam of two stock figures: the Jew as victim and the heroic journalist who is punished because of his fight for the truth. And there is a confrontation between a rugged individualist and corrupt authorities to warm viewers' hearts.

The screenwriters of the Timerman film went out of their way to Americanize the Argentine protagonist. Suppose this man was your husband, went the NBC promotions. And the audience has no difficulty going along with that supposition. His family life, his accent, his professional habits, his snappy answers, his children who raid the refrigerator and need their report cards signed, all have an American ring. Everything exotic about the real Timerman has been weeded out. Indeed, the true aliens, the real foreigners in the picture are the military and the secret police. They are portrayed as stereotypical Nazis, gangsters and Latino bandits. It is easy for Americans to see what happened to Timerman in terms of the ultimate suburban nightmare, in which the average American family is under siege. Half the film is devoted to the trauma of being locked in your own bedroom while men with guns plunder your kitchen, steal your wardrobe to give to whores, take your pillows and censor your mail.

This over-Americanization is rather distasteful, at least to me. The sitcom-like situations weaken the film and make it less compelling than Timerman's book, on which it is based. At the same time, I am not one to argue against esthetic methods that allow millions who would otherwise remain ignorant to become familiar with the human rights abuses suffered by people in many Third World countries. It is an extraordinary and amazing event when American TV screens show scenes of unremitting terror and brutality committed by governments that the Reagan Administration not only embraces but would like to wed and bed.

But both films do more than convey information about dictatorships. They allow Americans to travel with the central figures on the road leading from innocence to knowledge. In the beginning, both protagonists have high standards of living and the typical prejudices of their class. They feel relatively comfortable with the system—as do many viewers. And they believe themselves to be invulnerable, or at least protected by society. Viewers share their shock at the degradation and violence that suddenly strike them, and learn with them the painful lessons of their experiences.

Scheider/Timerman learns that unless you are prepared to surrender yourself to it totally, you cannot applaud a military takeover without eventually becoming one of its victims. He comprehends that nobody is beyond the reach of governments that are beyond the democratic control of the people. And he learns that his commitment to humane ideals is strong enough to sustain him during his imprisonment, when he had no name and no number.

Lemmon/Horman also changes—from a staid, conservative businessman who believes in the American way of life to a man who accuses his country of having engineered or at least tolerated the murder of his son. The screenwriters (Costa-Gavras and Donald Stewart, who won an Academy Award for their script) exaggerated the hostility and harshness that the real Ed Horman felt toward his son's idealism. In the book by Thomas Hauser on which the movie is based, Horman says that while he did not completely approve of his son's trip to Chile, he "understood and was able to accept what they were doing." The generational conflict is played up in the film. "He must have been doing something, to get into all this trouble," Horman says. Later he remarks, "If he had stayed where he belonged, this wouldn't have happened."

Charles was killed because he rebelled against his father's values, but paradoxically that punishment transforms Ed Horman. To recover his boy he must understand the younger generation's point of view, and he must also *uncover* his country. He eventually comprehends that the military men who executed his son were defending American business interests, and he reacts to that knowledge by killing his former self—and his ideals about his country. "What is the matter with this world?" he demands, once he realizes that unarmed civilians are being exterminated. "You sound just like Charles," his daughter-in-law answers.

In order for Timerman and Horman to find themselves, they must lose their countries. Timerman must explore the depths of evil in his adopted land: not only the anti-Semitism but the antihumanity as well. He must strip off his illusions, painfully, layer by layer, until he understands that he is a foreigner in the land to which he and his parents immigrated. His departure is only the last step in a distancing that began with the first kick in the genitals.

Horman also loses his country. It is his tragedy that the two things in his life that represent the future, his son and his country, are sworn enemies. History has dictated that he cannot keep either one of them. At the end of the film, official America shakes the hand of the dictator, and his son lies dead.

Audiences are moved by witnessing these men make that characteristically American mythic journey, the journey from innocence to experience. But if they have made that trip, it is because others made it before them. Jacobo Timerman was jailed because he asked questions about the *desaparecidos* and published their names in his newspaper. He became a victim because he refused to remain silent about other victims. And Ed Horman's son preceded him on that trip. He and so many others went to places like Chile to give themselves to a cause, breaking with the ruling values of their country, with what that country stood for in the eyes of the poor abroad. They were driven by another American vision; they were continuing the march, not westward but inward, toward a different frontier, an ethical one. They believed America should export democracy and equality rather than weapons. Charles Horman was killed—like American layworkers and nuns in Central America—by soldiers trained by the United States, armed with U.S. guns, in a country kept afloat by U.S. loans or aid.

American audiences can identify with Jacobo Timerman, the successful man made a victim, and with Ed Horman, the father who has to stand in his son's shoes. But can they understand what motivated them, what transformed them? Can they comprehend that their tragedies happened because of vaster, more unrelenting tragedies all around them?

Those tragedies are only hinted at in the films. There is something missing from these films about the missing: the people of Latin America.

At one point in *Missing*, Ed Horman visits the infamous Estadio Nacional, the open-air stadium where thousands of prisoners were herded together to await interrogation and torture. A prisoner, whom he confuses for "one glorious moment" with Charles, speaks an extremely significant line. He shouts at Horman: "My father cannot come to get me at the stadium." Then he turns to Colonel Espinoza, who is in charge of the stadium, and sarcastically asks if the prisoners might have ice cream with their supper.

The scene is touching but implausible. No prisoner in his right (or even wrong) mind would dare lift his voice in mockery against an ordinary soldier, let alone the commander of a concentration camp. One month after the coup, we Chileans had already learned how to bow our heads and mutter yes; we had learned to communicate by insinuations, allusions and jokes, and to avoid looking anyone straight in the eye.

Even if that scene is factually incorrect, its thrust is clear. It presents another point of view, that of those who are in danger but have no privileged immunity. Having pronounced that shocking truth, the prisoner vanishes from the film.

What about him? What about the son whose father could not go to the stadium to search for him?

What about the eye peering out of the peephole of the cell across from Timerman's, the eye that blinks at him urgently and keeps him company, like a lover's lamp in the night? What about the body to which that eye belongs, which we do not see? What about the millions of other bodies we never see?

On October 7, 1973, three days after the real-life Ed Horman arrived in Chile, a group of *Carabineros*, the Chilean police, paid a visit to Isla de Maipo, a small agricultural community some twenty miles west of Santiago. There they arrested Sergio Maureira Lillo, a 47-year-old peasant. They also took his four eldest sons: Sergio Miguel, 29; José Manuel, 25; Segundo Armando, 24; and Rodolfo Antonio, 22. The other family members never saw them again.

While Ed Horman was getting the runaround at the American Embassy and being driven by a chauffeur from one dismal place to another, the Maureiras were going from police station to police station. They would spend the next five years just as Ed Horman spent his month in Chile, just as Risha Timerman spent the days of her months, asking for news of her husband. In November 1978, thirteen bodies were discovered in an abandoned mine in Lonquén. Among them were those of the five Maureiras.

The assassins were pardoned under a "general" amnesty, which excluded from retribution those who had tortured, while leaving in jail or in exile those who had been tortured.

One year later, about the time Jacobo Timerman was released from house arrest and boarded the plane that took him to safety in Israel, the Maureiras were finally given permission to bury their dead. A few days afterward, however, that permission was revoked, and the corpses were thrown into an unmarked grave. Since there was no tomb to visit, the

Maureiras made what they called a "pilgrimage" every Sunday to the mine where the bodies had been discovered.

One day, the owner of the mine had his workers blow it up with dynamite, as though he believed that a disappearance must continue after death. It must be shown that these people had never existed, that they had never fed others with their work or looked into the eyes of their loved ones. They must be denied a history.

What about them? They are missing because they lived in places that are themselves missing—missing from conceptualization, missing from vision, almost missing from humanity.

The Maureiras made the mistake of being born in a miserable, insignificant country. They compounded their mistake by wanting to live with dignity. They were missing before the police came for them. They did not appear on prime-time TV.

The Maureiras are absent not only from television and movies. They are also absent from speeches and policy. I have attended countless meetings and seminars in Washington. Over and over, I hear the same statistics and abstractions. Rarely is there a glimpse of the people behind all the maneuvering and speculation. When they do appear, when they do rebel, when they do answer back and make their own judgments, when they defeat an army or ambush a policy, then the politicians and the spies and the analysts and most of the professors seem genuinely amazed. Where did they come from, these people who are not part of the scenario?

Americans can identify with Ed Horman and Jacobo Timerman. But can they go further? Can the compassion they have for Ed Horman be transferred to his rebellious son, and from there—and this is the decisively difficult step—to those who died with him, those anonymous people whom, in a sense, he died for? Can they see Timerman not from the eye of the camera but from the swollen, lost eye across from his cell?

Each person who saw *Missing*, who saw *Prisoner*, was given a message, a message about his own responsibility in the tragedy of the invisible and unnamed Maureiras. He can discard the message without reading it or he can pass it on. He can become a messenger.

It can be risky. Messengers in ancient times who bore bad tidings were sometimes put to death.

But that did not happen only in ancient times. Both Jacobo Timerman and Charles Horman learned some dangerous news. And rather than run the risk of silence, they decided to run another sort of risk and tell the world what they had discovered.

JANUARY 17, 1994

GATT AND THE SHAPE OF OUR DREAMS

Daniel Singer

•

Daniel Singer, *The Nation's* European correspondent, was *The Economist's* Paris Correspondent from 1958 to 1968, when he left after the student-worker upheaval in May 1968. He is the author of *Prelude to a Revolution, The Road to Gdansk, Is Socialism Doomed?* And, most recently, *Whose Millenium: Theirs or Ours?*

MAASTRICHT, NAFTA, GATT. . . . As the complex struggle over the globalization of the capitalist market proceeds, the debate surrounding it gets more tortuous and the linguistic hypocrisy defies even Orwell's imagination. Freedom to work means the right to be exploited, and internationalism is identified with the movement of capital in search of profit and universality—with the reign of merchandise throughout the world. The result is not so much strange alliances (these would have happened in any case because of the multiplicity of the interests involved) as a dangerous confusion. Thus, resistance against the expansion of big business may well be taken for narrow nationalism. The only remedy for this is to put each action in its context and explain its motive and the vision of society by which it is inspired. But doing this is not always easy.

How difficult it is to clarify matters is illustrated by a fierce fight during the recent GATT negotiations, a struggle over money that is insignificant in its immediate effects yet may be crucial in the long run, as it will shape our dreams, our thoughts and, therefore, our acts. The battle is over Europe's insistence that it continue subjecting American movies and audiovisual materials to quotas and other restrictions—the so-called "cultural exception." In the European, and particularly the French, press the issue was portrayed as being largely a fight by greedy Hollywood producers for a heftier share of foreign film revenues. This clashed with the US version, which was that hypocritical, elitist Euros are protecting a dying industry from more popular US products. But behind such silly contradictions there is a serious question. To put it succinctly: Should culture be treated like any other commodity?

Imperialist! Protectionist! Joan of Arc! The right of people freely to choose! When such high-sounding words are tossed around—often to conceal less exalted interests—one is tempted to paraphrase: "When they hear the word culture they reach for their checkbook." In fact, a great deal of money is involved. What is at stake is the removal of obstacles hindering the export offensive of the mighty American film industry. Not that Western Europe is now a Zhdanovian fortress tightly protected against the wicked products of Hollywood. Last year, US audiovisual exports to the European Community (with films, TV, and videotapes accounting for about one-third each) amounted to roughly $4 billion. They have much more than doubled in the past ten years and dwarf shipments in the opposite direction, estimated at around $250 million.

The dominant position of the US media industry is even more striking if one looks only at the subject of greatest controversy, the cinema. Out of the total film revenue earned within the EC, nearly three-quarters now goes to American companies, the proportion ranging from about 60 percent in France to 90 percent in Britain. Last fall, as Federico Fellini's coffin was lying in state in a Cinecittà studio, people were really mourning the virtual death of the Italian cinema. They could have extended their rites to Western Europe's film industry as a whole. France, with its 150 or so movies a year, provides the only quantitative exception. The French, not surprisingly, were also the main inspirers of the campaign to keep film and television out of GATT negotiations, a crusade fought with great passion by European directors, actors, writers and technicians.

Which obstacles do the Americans want removed? Essentially two: film subsidies and quotas for television. For the first, let us take the

French example. France has a National Center of Cinematography, which levies a tax on cinema tickets (11 percent), TV revenue (5.5 percent) and videotapes (2 percent). From this it raises nearly $80 million a year, which it plows back into the trade, notably through credits to filmmakers as an *advance* on their future earnings. About a third of French films get such credits, which provide for a substantial portion of their budgets; without such aid many quality films would not be made. The French say the levy is an internal matter of the profession. The Americans retort that it is state sponsored and that, though foreign films are taxed, only the French ones get credits.

The TV quota system is, potentially, a more serious hurdle. It is based on a community directive known as "television without frontiers," which stipulates that, in principle, a majority of the programs shown on each TV station must originate within the EC (Actually, the proportion is not supposed to fall below the level of 1988, which was 60 percent.) The French have made an additional stipulation: At least 40 percent of the programs must be produced in a Francophone country, Such quotas, if they persist, will set a real limit on American expansion. The proposed extension of GATT rules to cultural products would not involve the immediate removal of barriers, but through such devices as the most-favored-nation clause (which would mean that, say, American films must be treated like German or British ones), it would spell their destruction in the not-too-distant future. The EC first asked that the "specificity" of cultural goods be recognized, then, under French pressure, that they be "excepted" from the GATT talks altogether. The French view prevailed in the final stages of the negotiations. The battle is far from over, but the American offensive has been temporarily contained.

The facts and figures confirm that what is being questioned in this trial of strength is not the dominant position that the American film industry has already acquired in the European market. It is Hollywood's inexorable drive toward a quasi monopoly, with European companies reduced to the marginal role of suppliers for special-interest audiences or subsidiaries of American giants. Régis Debray, ex-revolutionary in Latin America and later an adviser to President François Mitterrand, argued against such an outcome, quoting the words of a Time Warner executive in conversation with the head of Arte, a Franco-German cultural TV channel: "You French are best at making cheese and wine, or in fashion. Filming is our specialty. So let us get on with filmmaking and you keep on with the cheeses." In other words, comments Debray, "Let us shape the minds and you stick to stomachs."

Not so fast. Our collective stomachs are financially too precious to be left to France, as was shown in the bitter GATT battle over agriculture. On the other hand, the control of our minds, or to put it more prosaically, the monopoly of the image, may well be a prize awarded to the dominant power.

In the early days of the cold war, Arthur Koestler provoked an outcry when in a magazine story he imagined Moscow occupied and *Guys and Dolls* being performed at the Bolshoi. How distant that indignation seems today, when Rambo Umpteen is being splashed all over China, when recent American soap operas and sitcoms dominate the screens of Western Europe, while earlier versions are dumped in the poorer half of the European continent. If this trend is allowed to continue, we will be sentenced to a sinister uniformity of heroes and models, metaphors and dreams. Mastery of the image may well become both the instrument and the symbol of leadership in the new world order.

The ambiguity of the discussion springs from the duality of cultural goods, conceived potentially as both creative works and as merchandise. GATT has no such preoccupations. It deals with the free flow of commodities, and it so happens that the United States is better at manufacturing, packaging, advertising, and selling cultural goods. It has advantages in size and scope, in language and experience. The difference was driven home in October, when *Jurassic Park* opened in France, amid the usual ballyhoo, in 450 of the nation's 4,402 cinemas. *Germinal*, the French blockbuster based on Zola's novel, had been launched a couple of weeks earlier on 370 screens. The French product had cost $28 million, the American double that amount. So far so good. French critics, however, were quick to point out that by the time it had reached Paris *Jurassic Park* had already pocketed $327 million in the United States and, together with revenue from merchandising, may well top a billion dollars by the end of the year. Income from foreign sales should be as astronomical. Commentators seized this occasion to explain less exceptional examples of American advantage, notably the mass-produced TV programs that, having covered their costs at home, can be dumped abroad at prices the local competition is unable to match.

What should the Europeans do to fight back? Concentrate, streamline their operations, dub their films into English and then improve the sales of their slicker wares? The remedy looks worse than the disease, judging by some of the European co-productions aimed at the lowest common denominator and recorded in English so as to broaden the market. Yet even if the Europeans did overcome their linguistic and national differences and manage to produce films or soap operas as successful as the American ones, this, far from solving the problem, would simply worsen it. Our increasingly Americanized TV screens, whatever the origin of the programs, make the conclusion obvious. What is at stake is the nature of the product, not its language or the nominal nationality of the producer. After all, Universal, the maker of *Jurassic Park*, is owned by Matsushita, Columbia by Sony, Fox by ex-Australian Rupert Murdoch and MGM by Crédit Lyonnais. And vertical concentration in the world of electronics and the media is increasing: The German publisher Bertelsmann and the Dutch telecommunications conglomerate Philips-Polygram also plan to invest in Hollywood. Yet all this will not fundamentally alter the extent of American cultural domination.

Herein lies the misunderstanding surrounding the recurring campaigns against American "cultural imperialism." Clever European merchants may occasionally use that slogan to favor their business—but not many of them and not the really big ones. *Sua Eminenza* Silvio Berlusconi, the Italian king of commercial television, who recently revealed his neo-Fascist sympathies, and Martin Bouygues, whose father, with money made on public works, bought TFI (the biggest French TV channel, with about half the national audience), know only too well that if they launched an offensive against the whole system they would be undermining their own position within it. The so-called anti-imperialists are not taking aim at American art. They are attacking the commercialization of creativity, the imposed uniformity, the manufacturing of culture, which American big business has raised to a fine art but of which it is not the only practitioner.

Fortunately, some artists have always been able to overcome social obstacles and create against the odds. This is less difficult for writers and painters than for filmmakers because less initial outlay is required. Yet there are such creators in all forms of art; they are as numerous in the United States as in Western Europe and, far from being resented by the "anti-imperialists," they are hailed by them. Toni Morrison, who on her recent European journey was feted here on Arte, and Woody Allen are among many recent examples. Yet whatever their success, real artists go against the trend of the machine of commercial mass culture, which codifies our desires, stifles our dreams, shrinks rather than widens our consciousness. The "anti-imperialist" battle thus knows no frontiers. It is, in fact, our common struggle against commercial conveyor belts and culture treated as a commodity.

This, in turn, suggests the only way for Europe's genuine resistance, though it is not an easy battle. Since culture will not cease to be a commodity in a world of merchandise, in art as well as in politics the road to independence seems to lead through a radical transformation of society. That implies the painful search for a world in which artistic creation will no longer be dominated by the tyranny of the market but will not be subjected to the dictatorship of the state either. The provision of guarantees against the latter development has become an imperative since the dreadful Soviet experience.

Let us not kid ourselves. We are not there. We are not even moving in that direction. Indeed, for the immediate future the prospect is gloomy. With the expansion of cable, the spread of satellites and Europe's continued deregulation, we are actually going the other way. All we can do at this stage is to multiply pockets of resistance, islands of free creation. We can organize holding operations, using such pretexts as the conflict over "exclusion" to slow the advance of the commercial juggernaut of cultural conformity. In this rear-guard action we may rely on our gut instinct against GATT culture, that is to say, the resistible reign of merchandise.

OCTOBER 13, 1997

FREEDOM AND THE DREAM FACTORY

Marcel Ophuls

•

Marcel Ophuls is the Academy Award winning director of *A Sense of Loss, The Sorrow and the Pity,* and *Hotel Terminus: The Life and Times of Klaus Barbie.*

THESE DAYS, ALL the way from "Deal Beach" in Malibu, we can often hear the clarion call: "Give me liberty or give me dollars!"

Earlier this year I received a call from our friends at the Human Rights Watch Committee here in my semi-retreat, at the foot of the lovely French Pyrenees. They asked me to add my signature to a prestigious list of Hollywood names urging the Chinese bosses—those freshly recruited disciples of trickle-down economics, those glorious conquerors of their own people—to let the Bill of Rights prevail in Beijing. How could I refuse? How could anybody refuse? Not only did I feel indignantly righteous—I also felt flattered.

As a postscriptum to my signature, however, an afterthought to our common fight against totalitarian censorship, I suddenly felt compelled to fax just one quibble of dissent: "even though Walt Disney is not my favorite multimedia enterprise, and Oliver Stone is not my favorite director." Remember what word old, crotchety Voltaire sent from his retirement in Ferney, a stone's throw away from the Swiss border, where he had settled so he could hightail it to safety in case of sudden trouble from his royal French masters in Versailles: "Even though I disagree with you," etc, etc. Well, these days, just in case of a National Front election victory next year, I live fairly close to the border myself.

But back to Malibu beach: I've already forgotten if it's Disney CEO. Michael Eisner who wants to tell the world about the Dalai Lama's sufferings and Oliver Stone who has produced one more of his epic biographies, this time about Chairman Mao, or whether it's the other way around. What I do remember is that when I last visited Tinseltown to receive one of those "lifetime awards" from my fellow documentarians in the Academy of Motion Picture Arts and Sciences, I found myself scared to death, standing on a podium, surrounded by giant golden Oscars, quite spontaneously denouncing the company town I grew up in and the industry that once produced the likes of Frank Capra, Ernst Lubitsch and John Ford. "Thank you very much for inviting me" is approximately what I said, "but I think your current bosses, ladies and gentlemen, are largely responsible for what is happening in Sarajevo and a good many other places." (Don't take my word for it. You can look it up in *The Hollywood Reporter*, which wrote up my comments on the violence suffering films today, so much of it that we are all being brutalized, and the real, brutal murders taking place in the former Yugoslavia and elsewhere cannot compete for an audience.)

Biting the hand that feeds you, I'm afraid, can sometimes be the only way to resist in these dark and bitter days, the only way to preserve some measure of individual freedom in the face of intellectual corruption, general cynicism and the collaboration of greedy conformists.

Once, many years ago, while working for ABC News as a staff producer, I embarked upon an ambitious project called *Company Town*. It was at the time of the infamous David Begelman affair. Does anyone still remember that former president of Columbia Pictures who died not long ago? He had been caught signing other people's names to checks to recover some minor gambling losses in Las Vegas. Those whose names he used were all dependent for their professional survival on his power as a captain of the film industry. While out in LA, filming with a small crew, I went to see my friend François Truffaut, who was staying at the Beverly Hills Hotel, as he did most every summer, reading film books at poolside while waiting to pay his respects to Renoir and Hitchcock. At 9 o'clock that morning, while we were filming, he was in his suite watching a golden oldie, *The More the Merrier*, on the local TV station. "Marcel," he said, "all our lives, we've been fighting censorship, and rightly so. And in our eyes, of course, the worst form of censorship has always been self-censorship. But lately I've begun to ask myself. Just what is the difference between self-censorship . . . and a sense of responsibility?" Well, my film was never finished because I got fired, and Truffaut died just a few years later.

So nowadays, I ask myself every once in a while what a fellow filmmaker like Oliver Stone and I still have in common. He's a director, it seems to me, whose approach to reality is severely tainted by cheap sensationalism, a steady barrage of halftruths and a totally paranoid view of contemporary history. This, unfortunately, seems to appeal greatly to the narcissistic, collective self-pity of entire generations of post-Vietnam college kids. But even worse, what in God's name do I still have in common with Michael Eisner, who continued to deal out millions of the green stuff to his former friend Michael Ovitz, when the two, after a year of executive, "creative" razzle-dazzle together at Disney, no longer saw eye to eye? What interests do I share with men who ask for the sacred freedom to export their merchandise to Beijing, while denying *droit moral* and authors' right to the real filmmakers all over the world? These particular decision-makers keep voting big fat bonuses to themselves while blighting entire regions of the beautiful French landscape with stupid "theme parks," where underpaid hirelings wander around like lost souls in Dante's *Inferno*, wearing monstrous Mickey Mouse heads for the amusement of imbecilic children fed on video games.

It's not that I'm opposed to the rich and powerful on principle. Even though I'm neither rich nor powerful, I recognize that somebody has to be. By this time, I've become fairly well resigned to the fact that in order to make movies, one must woo these people and convince them to open their purse strings for us. As a matter of fact, I'm looking for a fairly large sum of money right now.

But what on earth should move me to any kind of solidarity with this fellow Eisner, a man who, a day after his takeover of ABC, my former employer, appeared on *Good Morning America* and in reply to the talk-show host's timid and slightly worried query about what effect an entertainment giant might have on TV news, just flashed him a smile as gentle as a shark's: "Aren't you proud to be working for Walt Disney?"

It so happened that many of the names I found on that petition I signed in favor of freedom of thought in China reappeared shortly thereafter on a self-righteous and completely idiotic document, a full-page advertisement purporting to teach German Chancellor Helmut

Kohl, his government and all the rest of those nasty, nasty Germans all about American Democracy. By rushing to the defense of the Church of Scientology, the same Oliver Stone and other freedom-loving Hollywood celebrities did not shy away even for one moment from comparing to the Nazis a democratic, freely elected government that, after all, was co-responsible for, among a good many other things, bringing down the Berlin wall, thus helping to deliver millions of its own citizens from the totalitarian clutches of a police state.

It's still a wonderful life. But *O tempora! O mores!*, O Capra, O Lubitsch, where are you now? Paraphrasing what "Concentration Camp Ehrhardt" said to Jack Benny, in the great Ernst's valedictory hymn to politics, the spirit of resistance and the world of make-believe, the immortal *To Be or Not to Be*: "What they're doing to the culture of Shakespeare, we're doing now to Poland."

JANUARY 31, 2000

THE LAST UPRISING

Carl Bromley

•

Carl Bromley is the editor of this anthology. His interest in film and politics was stoked by an adolescence consuming violent "video nasties" which had been banned by the British government. While his parents despaired at his viewing habits he claimed that they were essentially political and therapeutic. It was an uncle of his who weaned him off such violent fare by exposing him to his Betamax collection of French new wave and Italian neo realist cinema. His articles of film, politics and literature have appeared in *The Nation, In These Times*, and *Cineaste*. He is planning a PhD thesis about Hollywood as a global superpower. This piece is a review of *The French New Wave* by Jean Douchet and *Truffaut* by Antoine de Baecque and Serge Toubiana.

THE FILM CRITIC and writer Peter Biskind has observed that every bygone age is lit by a retrospective glow of nostalgia, for American film-makers like Francis Ford Coppola, Martin Scorsese and Paul Schrader, the New Hollywood of the seventies was a golden age, "the last great time." So it is with those who witnessed the arrival of the first movies made by Jean-Luc Godard, François Truffaut and their colleagues from the French *nouvelle vague* in the early sixties. David Thomson, in a column whose headline—"Sit Down, Child, and I'll Tell You About Jean-Luc Godard"—indicates how distant we are from that time, reflected, "If you are 35 or less, even if you've heard of Jean-Luc Godard, you won't appreciate the aura he had in the early 1960s."

When Hollywood set its attack hounds on the French film industry during the last GATT round, we were reminded of this distance. Rallying filmmakers like Scorsese and Steven Spielberg to the call of "artistic freedom," Jack Valenti's Motion Picture Association of America, with the help of the Commerce Department, tried to bully France into removing the French film industry's remaining protectionist mechanisms. Hollywood's actions helped clarify a tribute paid to Truffaut, in the wake of his untimely death from a brain tumor in 1984, by Jean-Luc Godard, who declared: "Now we have lost our protection." How prophetic. Big Hollywood would have undoubtedly behaved similarly if Truffaut were alive; it is questionable, however, whether the MPAA would have been able to engage Scorsese and Spielberg. The New Wave had an electrifying effect on these young filmmakers. Moreover, it was Truffaut, as the New Wave's international diplomat, who did the most to cultivate and befriend this community, to the extent that Spielberg cast him in *Close Encounters of the Third Kind*.

Though France prevailed during the GATT quarrel, the consensus was that Hollywood was winning the war. Irrespective of a tariff here or there, Tinseltown held dominion over the international film industry with an 80 percent market share. And both critics and supporters have pointed to a malaise in French cinema that the GATT round illuminated; an industry heavily subsidized, losing market share to Hollywood and becoming internationally insignificant. Morever, a range of voices in France and the United States accuse the French New Wave of nurturing the forces that corrupted French cinema.

The auteur theory, first popularized in the fifties by Godard and Truffaut while employed as film critics for *Cahlers du cinéma*, proposed that true films of distinction bear the mark of their director. The theory is blamed for enthroning a director-as-king ideology in which everything else, including audience, is secondary. The epithet *nombriliste*—navel-gazing—has been flung at French art cinema by many in France. David Puttman, the English producer of *Chariots of Fire* and *The Mission*, devotes two rather shrill chapters in his recent book *Movies and Money* to charging that the New Wave's legacy was "dangerous artistically as it was damaging commercially." Even from the left, the upstart Danish filmmaker's collective Dogme 95 has called the New Wave a political failure hopelessly compromised from the start, "a ripple that washed ashore and turned to muck," its slogans of freedom and individualism, and the auteur concept itself, "bourgeois romanticism."

So much for the Black Book of the New Wave. The New Wave, like so much else from the sixties, if it isn't recommodified, is invoked as a dangerous place where youngsters ought not to prowl. Two recent books, however—Antoine de Baecque and Serge Toubiana's *Truffaut* and Jean Douchet's lavish study *The French New Wave*—rescue it from caricature and what E. P. Thompson called "the condescension of posterity," bringing us closer to its retrospective glow, retrieving and illuminating what Godard described as the "last uprising." A cinematic social movement of sorts emerges; perhaps that's what agitates the New Wave's detractors, many of whom would be only too glad to sign manifestoes championing the rights of studios' accountants and shareholders.

What we now know as the New Wave was a relatively short-lived affair. A close-knit group of filmmakers who had been France's most precociously brilliant film critics in the fifties had, by decade's end, graduated to filmmaking. Nineteen fifty-nine was the watershed: Truffaut's *The 400 Blows* and Godard's *Breathless* catapulted the group to international attention. The box-office bonanza that this new streetwise, low-budget cinema generated, with its infectious yet bitter-sweet romanticism, youthful swagger and asphalt-aimed, handheld camera, enabled others from the entourage, like Claude Chabrol, Jacques Rivette and Eric Rohmer, to share the limelight. A thousand gardens bloomed, and innovators outside the immediate *Cahiers* circle who had toiled in making documentary shorts—Chris Marker, Alain Resnais and Agnes Varda—were also given greater exposure.

And then by 1962 it was all over. A series of box-office flops had removed the spring in their step. Then a libel suit filed by Roger Vadim against Truffaut, after Truffaut had accused him of breaking the auteur's moral code on the set of his friend Jean Aurel's movie, created a sensational atmosphere that delighted the New Wave's enemies. When Vadim won, the pundits were describing the New Wave as "dead and buried." Godard noted how the camaraderie had gone: "We've each gone off on our own planet, and we can't see each other in closeup anymore, only in full shot. The girls we sleep with separate us each day even more, instead of bringing us closer."

The contours of this story are well-known. Through some critics have described *Truffaut* as "workmanlike" (admittedly, we don't get the full scoop about him and Catherine Deneuve; neither is it a particularly interpretive or innovative work), it offers up a fascinatingly full account of the filmmaker's life. From this raw material we can reconstruct Truffaut's political and artistic trajectory and show how important the Nazi occupation, postwar Gaulism and the vigorously Stalinist and nationalist French Communist Party (PCF) were in shaping his and the New Wave's politics and aesthetics.

Douchet suggests that the young *Cahiers* cinephiles embraced American cinema because the French industry was involved in a state-sponsored abandonment of reality: "French film confined itself to the studio and wallowed in a pessimistic and morose vision of daily life." The major films about the French Resistance projected a national, collective fantasy designed to hide a "sense of hidden and burning shame," promoting a national policy of reconciliation that was designed to absolve French society of its wartime collaborationist tendencies.

Because it had a few skeletons of its own to hide, the PCF largely subscribed to these myths; but its involvement in the film world alienated many *Cahiers* intellectuals. As the cold war solidified, the PCF's intellectual rigidity and hysterical anti-Americanism spilled over into its growing influence in the French Federation of Cinema Clubs. The trade paper *L'Ecran francals*, which it once controlled, expelled Andre Bazin, Truffaut's surrogate father, from the paper for being a "Catholic leftist."

Cahiers critic Jean Domarchi sketched the Stalinist position: "What is Soviet is good, what is American is bad. Note nevertheless one deliberate distortion of the postulate: French cinema, although bourgeois, has the right to every kind of accommodation." The PCF and its attendant organizations, far from posing a revolutionary threat, had accommodated to the corporatist structures of Gaullist France. In the film industry the PCF embraced and enforced this arrangement through its trade union allies, who were a junior social partner in an "umbrella of government control and bureaucratic mechanisms" that was established by the state-directed Centre National du Cinéma (CNC).

The CNC developed a financial structure that monitored box-office sales and plowed the taxes from foreign films back into the French industry. The system had its obvious strengths: Market forces were contained and a measure of job security was created, along with an "elitist journeyman" system, in which only those judged competent by other film professionals could work in the industry. On an artistic level, however, Douchet claims it had unwanted consequences: "The system, especially the work card, quickly became a constraint, for it restricted creativity by promoting academic repetitiveness and a sense of imitation that would conform to professional standards of ability." To direct one had to endure a lengthy system of apprenticeships "that enslaved [the apprentice] to an aesthetic that was at best popular, and at worst reactionary. The process produced neither revolutionaries nor resistance fighters, simply artisans, occasionally good ones, but rarely artists."

Within this system it was the screenwriter, not the director, who was king. As Truffaut noted impertinently, "When they hand in their scenario, the film is done; the *metteur-en-scene*, in their eyes, is the gentleman who adds the pictures to it." As opposed to this studio-bound and rather theatrical cinema, the *Cahiers* crowd championed the work of such French mavericks as Jean Renoir, Jean Cocteau, Robert Bresson, Jacques Tati, and Max Ophuls, real "men of cinema," who imposed their creative vision on their work, irrespective of source material, subject matter or genre. Scandalously, the *Cahiers*, crowd also looked to America's dynamic studio system and to directors no one had given the critical time of day before: Alfred Hitchcock, Howard Hawks, Nick Ray, filmmakers who transgressed "the artificial vision of the world offered by Hollywood" and imposed "a point of view about the truth of that world."

The official French left hated the *Cahiers* group and the New Wave, branding them as petit-bourgeois dilettantes who fetishized individualism, unpatriotic provocateurs who defended Hollywood movies, cultural dandies who "challenged the Marxist, and Marxist-oriented, left-wing culture subscribed to in intellectual circles." The company young Truffaut kept cannot have endeared him either: upper-class, conservative patrons who delighted in his insouciance; former Nazi-sympathizing film critics exiled in Franco's Spain. Even his fellow editors at *Cahiers* had to caution him about the sexist and homophobic turn of some of his writing.

But Truffaut was contradictory as well as contrary. When he was charged as an army deserter his prosecutors described the company he kept as "anti-militarists, Communists and homosexuals." Truffaut was friends with Jean Genet and—importantly—Bazin, a deeply committed Christian socialist who probably believed that Truffaut's extreme views were weakly held. If anything, Truffaut had a "mistrust of all forms of proper, decent, righteous, official discourse."

The New Wave's reaction to corporatism was a "cinema of poverty" made outside the system and, in the case of Chabrol and Truffaut, funded from the fat of their wives' dowries. This was a cinema that finally allowed Paris to breathe, engaging with a young consumer culture. It was apolitical, yet the political would find it. As Douchet—a member of the New Wave crowd from the beginning—observes: "It was inevitable that the joyous spontaneity of 1958 would one day have to confront politics. And this is exactly what occurred ten years later, when the streets were again full."

At first the political was confined to the question of cinematic form. As the Godard aficionado says to a skeptical Marxist friend in Bernardo Bertolucci's New Wave-ish *Before the Revolution*, "A dolly shot is a style and a moral fact." Though Godard's second film, *Le Petit Soldat*, was banned by the Gaullist censor because it dealt ostensibly with the taboo subject of the Algerian war, arguably, with its spies armed with cameras roving throughout Geneva, it is more an autocritique of the New Wave's obsession with cinematic truth than an act of political engagement. But Godard's films began to develop a political consciousness of their own. A Brechtian influence can be detected. As Susan Sontag suggested, language and image collide in his work—signs, texts, stories, monologue and interview undermine the flow of images, distancing us emotionally, especially during moments of pathos. We never forget this is cinema (or its end, as Godard proposes in *Weekend*).

Godard's protagonists are often drenched in American pop culture; its cinema, books and cars obsess them, to the extent that Godard probably spoke for a generation when he suggested that *Masculin-Féminin* could have been retitled *The Children of Marx and Coca-Cola* (a description that resurfaced during May '68). Other dichotomies—cultural and musical, political and racial—persist throughout his work, but his films are primarily activated by sexual tensions in which resolution is rare.

Gunshots are heard throughout *Masculin-Féminin*—usually offscreen, almost as musical accompaniment. They gesture to the toxic state of sexual relations (two men are shot dead by women in the film), but they are also a premonition of a radical political culture that was beginning to challenge the prevailing sterility of consumer culture. Almost all of Godard's films from *Les Carabiniers* onward refer to this rupture: In *Weekend* it reaches apocalyptic pitch with its hippie-guerrilla-cannibals, but *La Chinoise* a remarkable film about a cell of young Maoists, anticipated May '68 and the PCF's complicitous role in bailing out de Gaulle, even though at the time of its release the characters' plans to close down the universities was dismissed as fantastical.

The February 1968 rallies outside the Cinémathèque Française protesting the ouster of director Henri Langlois, a New Wave mentor in many respects, were, as Truffaut's biographers suggest, the "first taste of territorial struggles waged against the administration and the Gaullist government" that would culminate in May '68. It was also a New wave reunion. Truffaut, Godard, Rivette, Chabrol, Pierre Kast—they were all there, united again, scuffling with the police. Truffaut, whose career was going through a lull, found the whole experience rejuvenating. The protests were the answer to a question he had once agonized over: "Is cinema more important than life?" It was then, but life, and the injunction to change life, would return with a vengeance three months later.

Although authority figures are challenged in Truffaut's films, his movies are more obsessive about the physical, emotional and literary dimensions of love, and hence his output was never directly political in the Godardian sense. Truffaut moved recognizably to the left when he began to direct films; he put his career on the line by joining the likes of Sartre and de Beauvoir in signing the Manifesto of the 121 in 1960, a "Declaration on the right to insubordination in the Algerian war," which many regarded as treasonous. It certainly cut him off from the right-wing company he used to keep. And in May '68 he was instrumental in closing down the Cannes film festival.

Truffaut could never bear the pious "good conscience of the left," though, and he shunned the official, Communist trade union-sponsored marches in May. He did take part in the last major student demo of the period in Paris's Latin Quarter, and his comments reveal how its festive and unofficial nature dovetailed with his traditional dislike of orthodoxy:

> What moved me about the students was that they were returning the blows they'd received from the police. I followed their entire movement; I even marched, though I had never marched before. I feel an enormous admiration for young people who are capable of chanting "We're all

German Jews!" I never thought we'd ever see intelligence, humor, strength, justice in the street at the same time. That is what stirred me.

But when May '68 passed Truffaut returned to his vocation: Cinema was still cinema for him and not an ideological state apparatus, as many on the left saw it. In many ways Truffaut's work in the immediate, post-'68 period was his best—*The Wild Child*, *Day for Night* and the magnificent *Two English Girls*. His work insulated him from the disillusioning experience of defeat many of his more radical colleagues, who wanted to rid cinema of its "reactionary structures," had to endure. They had to grapple with the question Robin Wood posed: how to "nurture a radical voice within a culture that doesn't want to listen to it." *Cahiers* was temporarily transferred into a rather dreary Marxist film journal that asked all the right questions about class and ideology but shed the love of cinema that had once made it so essential. For Godard, the struggle continued, even though there are few takers these days for the films he made with the Dziga-Vertov group. "He feels that since May '68 it's impossible to make the same kinds of movies and he resents people who still do," Truffaut observed. The Brechtian street theater of *Tout va bien* (starring Yves Montand and Jane Fonda!) attempted to link the unofficial, shop-floor strikes of that period (1972) with May '68: While rank-and-file workers undoubtedly still faced intransigent bosses and dozy PCF trade-union officials; while intellectuals were enjoined to start from zero and rethink what it meant to be a leftist intellectual, it probably isn't a stretch to suggest that Jean Eustache's *The Mother and the Whore* was far more representative of the milieu of the post-'68 generation, its post-revolutionary sadness consumed as it was with cynicism, lechery and suicide.

In Godard's recent self-portrait *JLG/JLG*, scenes from *La Chinoise* flicker on a distant television set while Godard mourns that he and his leftist colleagues hadn't realized that the injunction to make "two, three, many Vietnams" would result in the creation of "two, three, many Americans." His recent films strike a similarly plaintive tone: Godard enjoys a Prospero-like existence in his Swiss hideaway while he observes that the profane world of material objects is challenged by the natural and spiritual world. These films are beautiful, difficult, and immeasurably sad.

While time simply passes in these films, in Douchet's gorgeous book the past and present converge. Its content, really a scrapbook of reflections on the New Wave, is animated by the book's thick coffee-table format, with bold, splashy stills that recall the color and rich, tragic sensuality of films like Godard's *Contempt* and Varda's *Le Bonheur*, Belmondo's rough, exuberant physicality in *Breathless*; Anna Karina's furtive wink in *A Woman Is a Woman* and her unforgettable and much imitated dance in *Band of Outsiders*. But Douchet's book isn't just eye candy. As he retrieves what has been lost, he suggests that "it is the same today as it was for the directors of the New Wave": Where the American cinema of the postwar years "liberated the tastes, vision and the the imagination of the young rebels" and pointed to the sclerosis of French quality cinema, "today, it is American film that is diseased, and filmmakers from all countries, Americans included, must struggle against it." For nearly a generation our leaders have told us there is no alternative, as American's free-market ideology becomes a world ideology. The same could be said of world cinema.

In lieu of radical challenge to this, in an environment where immediate commercial success is the sole criterion of judgment and where, as Douchet puts it, in the name of competition "one must submit to the rules established by an enormous [commercial] machine designed to pulverize," any attempt to impose contrary cinematic visions—whether auteurist, collective agent provocateurist, or even within the system—is more than just a necessary evil, it is an imperative.

10

Late Hollywood?

Or: Forward to the Military-Industrial-Entertainment Complex!

•

This final thematic selection of articles from the last two decades of the magazine returns to the question of the intersection of entertainment and politics.

APRIL 18, 1981

"It Must Have Been______"

Sidney Lumet

•

Sidney Lumet is the director of *Daniel, The Verdict, Prince of the City, Equus, Network, Dog Day Afternoon, Serpico*, and *Twelve Angry Men* and the author of *Making Movies*.

I HAVE JUST finished a movie called *Prince of the City*. It's a long, complex film and one of the most difficult and satisfying movies I've ever made. It's about a cop informing on other cops, and I was drawn to the theme for very personal reasons.

In the early 1950s I was a young, hot-shot director at CBS. I had two very successful shows on the air: *Danger*, a melodrama series on Tuesday nights, and *You Are There*, which was not only getting awards right and left but was even *sponsored* on a Sunday evening in the 6:00 to 6:30 time slot. The sponsor of *Danger* was a marvelous man, Mel Block, who made Ammident toothpaste and Pycopay toothbrushes. As blacklisting spread through CBS, he became more and more disturbed. And when I was "named" in the *American Legion Magazine*, Mel was determined to fight. He asked me to go see Dan O'Shea to get CBS off his back. O'Shea was a captain of industry, a leading Catholic who raised and gave lots of money to the Church, and whose job it was to clear people employed by CBS. He was also gentle, intelligent, warm, and felt that his job was "to save as many of you as I can."

O'Shea's first words as I came through the door were, "Please don't come in with your hands up." I had come in angry. I was angry at myself. I felt that *any* questioning of my beliefs was a violation of everything this country stood for. So why was I there? Because I wanted to keep working, of course. To be wiped out without a trace for an unknown reason was intolerable. Just not working was intolerable.

The only hint of why I'd been accused came when he asked me if I'd been a member of the Communist Party. I answered, "Never," hating myself as I did it. I had just taken a step I didn't want to take. There was already enough knowledge of where this led. Many accused persons had come in indignantly and had wound up a week or a month or a year later doing the unspeakable: naming names. Was I now on the same path? I had no names to name, as I had not been a Communist, but there were people I knew who had already been blacklisted, and about whom I would be asked down the road. If one hoped to be cleared, the only thing that worked was showing your good faith by answering anything about anybody: informing.

We chatted a while longer on a "Dan"-"Sid" basis. As I left I turned to him and asked, "How can you do this job?" I'll always remember his answer: "Better one of us, than one of them." This civilized, liberal man was doing the zealots' work for them.

After about a month, Mel Block's brother Stuart came to see me. He was embarrassed and apologetic. He said they had finally traced the source of my being named. It came from Harvey Matusow, who later became notorious and was prosecuted for recanting much of the testimony in his book, *False Witness*. Matusow was in the hierarchy of our government's professional anti-Communist informers. He claimed to have been a C.P. member, found God one day and was now atoning for his sins by testifying, in case after case, against former members. Stuart Block said that Matusow had seen me at some C.P. meetings. Would I meet with Matusow and Victor Riesel, a Hearst columnist, at Mel Block's apartment to see if this could all be straightened out? Both he and Mel would understand if I refused; it sickened them to even propose it, but Mel had fought as hard as he could and hoped I would come. I said yes. Mel had done something then considered herculean: he had gotten the information and set up a meeting.

The next two weeks were a nightmare of confused feelings: self-loathing for going at all, elation at the idea of confrontation, gratitude to Mel Block for having traced the accusation to its source. There was the chance to be heroic and true to myself, the dread of no longer working, the abyss of the end of a career. And the knowledge that, when this ordeal was over, clearance was only possible by taking that last step: informing.

I walked up Park Avenue in a turmoil. The hope that a speeding cab could settle the conflict occurred to me. As I rode up the elevator I didn't know whether I'd be Tom Paine or crawl to save myself. I had no idea what I was going to do. I knew only the basic thing that I still believe today: that in truly critical situations advance planning doesn't work. One responds to the moment. The elevator opened into the apartment. I walked across the thirty-foot living room. Riesel didn't get up, but Matusow did to shake hands.

I started what felt like a diatribe: how dare you, what kind of people are you, what right do you have, don't you know the meaning of this country, etc. Much to my astonishment and terror, I was behaving "well." Matusow raised his hands and said, "Don't get yourself in a fit, you're not the one." I stopped. Everything that had been racing at ninety miles an hour suddenly had no place to go. Matusow then said to Riesel and Block, "He's not the one. It must have been ______," naming someone I'd never heard of. There was a minute of chitchat and the meeting broke up. Matusow and I rode down in the elevator together. He asked if I needed a lift.

Perhaps it was the dim memory of this experience that informed my reading of Robert Daley's book, *Prince of the City*; I knew immediately that I wanted to make a movie of it. Briefly, it's the true story of Bob Leuci, a New York detective in the Narcotics Division. He is assigned to a new team, the Special Investigative Unit, with seventy other detectives, New York's best, to crack the hard core of dope in New York City. They are the elite. They have no one to report to, no assigned precinct, no time cards, no paperwork. They are asked only to produce results: arrests.

It is 1971, the time of the Knapp Commission hearings. The air is crackling with investigations of police by other policemen. Bill Phillips and Frank Serpico are about to testify about police corruption. Leuci is questioned by city investigator Nicholas Scoppetta as a normal part of the commission procedure. A relationship develops between them. Scoppetta suggests that Leuci go underground for them. Leuci refuses, saying he will not fink on other cops. Eventually he comes over because, among other reasons, he's convinced that bail bondsmen, lawyers and judges are integrally involved in dope traffic. They are the truly corrupt ones. Leuci lays down one primary condition; he will never wear a wire or testify against his friends or partners, anyone he has worked with. The government agrees. He becomes the classic informer.

He has also set in motion the classic tragedy of the man who knowingly steps into a situation feeling he can control the circumstances, only to find that the circumstances are controlling him. For by the time his six years of work are over, more than fifty detectives in S.I.U. will be indicated for corruption, two will commit suicide, one will go insane and Leuci will turn in friends *and* partners. He will also confess to being just as corrupt as those he turned in and will escape prosecution only because of his government work as an informer.

Prince of the City is not only about informing, however. It is also about cops and the complexity of their lives. I've known a lot of cops, most of whom join the force with a good deal of idealism. They wind up with the highest suicide and alcoholism rates of any profession. In Leuci's life, the circumstances of informing added even more pressure.

Leuci has often talked about what the informer's life does to the psyche. All emotions were disguised, turned into something else. He was in constant danger of being killed. But fear was the first thing to hide because its detection would have been a dead giveaway, literally. So lying became a way of life. He reached a point where he himself didn't know whether or not he was telling the truth about the simplest thing. Improvision, inventing, not really answering, he became a whole other person in his own skin.

Working out my own feelings about an informer was probably the biggest single problem for me. My own experience at CBS had left me a lot more compassionate about them. I kept thinking of that elevator ride to Mel Block's apartment, not knowing which way I'd go. In *Prince of the City*, I did my best not to prejudge this issue—to let the conflicting tensions speak for themselves. But I am too close to *Prince* to know how much of my ambivalence has found its way into the movie. As work progressed, I found myself moved more and more by Leuci.

For looking back, it is now clear to me there was one essential difference between Leuci's experience and mine. People who named names in the 1950s, as much as I feel for them, were violating themselves and injuring our democratic institutions. Bob Leuci was trying to break dope. He didn't succeed, but he put a big dent in organized police support of it. Whatever his reasons, he tried. So for me he's a hero. Informing in criminal activity is very different from informing in the political sphere.

MAY 13, 1991

THE NEW CUSTERISM

David Seals

•

David Seals is executive director of Black Hills AIM, secretary of the Bear Butte Council, poet and author of *The Powwow Highway* and *Sweet Medicine. The Powwow Highway* was filmed in 1989.

WHEN KEVIN COSTNER was shooting *Dances With Wolves* in 1989 in South Dakota, where I live, a full-blood Lakota elder gave me a copy of the screenplay to read. David Bald Eagle lives way the hell out in the middle of the South Dakota prairie on the Cheyenne River Reservation, home of the Minneconjou and Sans Arc and Two Kettle Lakota Sioux, about as far from Hollywood as you could get, culturally, and still be in the same country. He ranches on about 600 acres leased from the tribe and lives in a ramshackle house built of scrounged lumber from the nearby town of Sturgis (only eighty miles away, that's considered close out here) and the reservation ghettos of Cherry Creek and Red Scaffold. It's a desolate, beautiful landscape without trees or much water, but Dave loves it. So do I. We sit out on his porch in the total darkness and peaceful silence, with no street lights or traffic or sirens roaring, and watch the fireflies and talk about the Spirits of our ancestors scaring the hell out of somebody all the time and how things are "all fucked up" on the reservation with the booze and no jobs and phony-baloney medicine men and women putting curses on people because they're jealous or some damn thing. It's the damnedest mess. But mostly we laugh about it and people come over to visit all the time and we cook up a pile of food and maybe watch something on the VCR with the kids. There's always a pack of kids around, abandoned sometimes by their parents off on a drunk somewhere, playing with the goats and horses and cats and dogs, looking for snakes and birds' nests and gold.

Dave is over 70 and has the handsome Lakota features of classic popular conception, and he's worked in a number of movies over the years as an actor and cultural consultant. He just shakes his head recalling the day a helicopter landed out by his place, bringing the script of *Wolves* for his perusal and assessment. He was flattered by the attention, but not too much. It was mostly pretty funny. He wouldn't say anything more about the script except that it was a typical Hollywood deal, and maybe I should read it to see what I thought, since he, like many Indians around Cheyenne River, thinks I know something more about movies than most people, owing to the fact that my book *The Powwow Highway* was taken by Hollywood.

I hunkered down on his big old comfortable couch discovered in an alley in town, with the kids and goats outside screaming, and read about the good old days in the 1860s when a wounded and disillusioned cavalry officer came out West to escape the horrors of the Civil War. He was a man of better sensibilities than most of us, appreciative of the wide open solitudes and beauties of nature, and a heroic warrior too. Quite a guy. Just as he was meeting up with some Indians—maybe they were the Sioux or maybe the Comanche, I couldn't tell—a few carloads of Indians piled in the door on some errand or other and we proceeded to drink coffee and discuss the possibilities of getting some work in this new movie. Dave was mad because the tribe still hadn't gotten out to his place, after ten years of pleading, threatening, and cajoling, to dig a well, so he still didn't have indoor plumbing or anything. He has to haul his water in barrels in the back of one of his pickups—which are always breaking down out on the bumpy rutted dirt roads—from a faucet at the new Takini High School a few miles up the gravel road.

Now, you have to understand the peculiar government-to-government relationship of the United States of America to the Great Sioux Nation. According to the 1868 Ft. Laramie treaty—which followed an 1851 treaty, and presumably reflected the turmoil and conditions leading up to it at just about the same time and place our *Dances With Wolves* paean occurs—the Sioux under Red Cloud had kicked

General Sherman's butt all over Wyoming and the Americans were suing for unconditional peace on the Bozeman and Oregon Trails. In a mood of great conciliation and general patriotic national pride, the Sioux and Arapaho agreed to a cease-fire if the Americans would abandon their forts and go away forever; in turn, the victors would allow them to have their roads to the golden Elysian fields of California and Oregon and Montana. Sherman agreed to the terms, promising what later became all of western South Dakota from the east side of the mighty Missouri River to the Wyoming border to the Indians as their sovereign national territory; plus, they got for unceded hunting territory parts of Wyoming, North Dakota, Nebraska and Montana.

It was a great empire. Of course, Red Cloud didn't like the fact that other chiefs were sitting around challenging his claim to leadership, like Sitting Bull and Crazy Horse—who both refused to sign the treaty, by the way, smelling a rat—so he went to Washington wearing a big top hat and shook hands with President U.S. Grant. Grant and the Congress ratified the treaty and it became law.

Anyway, all this was being set up while the story of *Dances With Wolves* was going on right in the middle of it, but I couldn't discover any of that as I went back to reading the screenplay by Michael Blake. There were some very poetic and nature-loving Indians all over the place, and a beautiful white babe who had been captured as a pioneer child—her whole family butchered by them sneaky Pawnees—but nowhere were there any of the complex intratribal feuds going on or whiskey traders and railroad men and land speculators who were everywhere out here. Mostly what we got was some pretty thoughts about living in harmony with nature and each other. That's OK, I figured, what the hell, it's at least pro-Indian and might bring in a few jobs for the troops.

But I had a lot still stuck in my craw about Hollywood making Indian movies too, after my experience. It requires backing up a little to understand, about like what it takes to even begin to grok the history of European-indigenous relations on the broader political and social and religious scales. It's probably a lot like the complex Arab–Israeli mess, and may be just as difficult to untangle.

Just about everybody would probably agree that the *image* of a culture is as important, especially in this high-tech world of instant global telecommunications, in the perception of it or of a race of people as whatever lies in the *actual* truth of that culture. Indians have often been victims of stereotyping—Custerism, I call it—and this reduction of the image of a people kills as surely as any real-life, Wounded Knee-type massacre. What is this Custerism? The celluloid residuals of Manifest Destiny, played out as emotional climax.

The blatant racism of the "Old Custerism" as exemplified by Ronald Reagan's portrayal of General George in the 1940 *Santa Fe Trail* must surely be obvious to anyone who hasn't already prejudged Custer and his American cavalry as the good guys and Crazy Horse and his Indians as the bad guys who wantonly butchered Our Troops. The parallels of a Hollywood actor becoming a Washingtonesque semidivine President-Protector-King are insidiously apparent, and betray a nationalistic cant in the film industry that can only be characterized as propagandistic. The usage by US generals recently of the term "Indian Country" when referring to Iraqi-occupied Kuwait brings what many people might consider the harmless nature of the entertainment business into the deadly arena of politics. (The May *Esquire* blows its bugle about the "Surrender in Indian Country" too.)

The Old Custerists rounded up Un-Americans in Hollywood and New York in the late 1940s, about when John Ford was cranking out so-called classics like *Fort Apache*. In that little gem we hear Colonel Henry Fonda complain to Captain John Wayne that they have little chance for "glory or advancement," because while some of their fellow officers are "leading their well-publicized campaigns against the great Indian nations—the Sioux and the Cheyenne—we are asked to ward off the gnat stings and flea bites of a few cowardly digger Indians." The Duke replies, "Your pardon, Colonel, you'd hardly call the Apaches 'digger Indians,' sir." (If only Hank Fonda had known how valuable the Apaches would become as attack helicopters!) The nauseating thing about Ford's endless litanies to racism, like *The Searchers* especially, is that they are apologized away as being exposures of racism! *Cheyenne Autumn* made author Mari Sandoz sick to her stomach when Ford butchered it into a white love story instead of the truly tragic odyssey of the Cheyennes from Oklahoma to Montana in the 1870s.

We're not even talking here about the obvious crap like *The Last of the Mohicans* or all the Hiawathas and the thousands of spectaculars and cartoons and shows like *F Troop* that are still flooding cable TV every day, poisoning every new generation. I'm trying to point to what is called the best of American moviemaking, the Oscar-worthy (if not winning) films of high artistic merit. *Broken Arrow* and *Shane* and *Red River* fall into this category. Why, in what are otherwise wonderful works that I love too (I'm from the West, born and bred), must they always throw in the flaming arrows coming out of the dark from the sneaky subhumans, the unspeakable implications of things done to Our Women, the truncated grunts and groans of people thereby depersonalized because they don't talk, can't talk, English?

Things got better in the wake of the sixties, we are told. *Little Big Man* was another watershed, like *Broken Arrow*, portraying a decidedly pro-Indian point of view. It was like a breathing spell between the Old Custerism and the New Custerism, which we'll get to shortly. While it still had the all-important requisite of a white man as the central protagonist, it tried mightily to understand the rather mysterious ways of the strange people living in tents. It had a cute chief in it, who cracked jokes and spoke poetically and was really a Human Being for a change. This was progress! Custer and Our Boys were shown slaughtering innocent women and children in bloody scenes. *Soldier Blue* showed the unbearable savagery of racism too. But these films were still set in a historical context, distant, almost irrelevant, and white people were always the characters in the central focus.

Then *Billy Jack* exploded on the scene. Ah, finally, a modern Indian in the middle of the worst redneck cowboy towns. I liked Pauline Kael's comments in *The New Yorker*; she found herself watching with a sympathetic smile, because even where the writing was terrible, the instincts were "mostly very good." It was sappy and melodramatic, with lots of lost white runaway kids trying to find a better society by living with the Indians, and one-dimensional white racists foaming like mad dogs, but golly, there were real Indian actors playing our songs and speaking articulately too! It was cool. They talked about treaties, and it was a box office hit and spawned a sequel and some Skins got some work for a while actually talking about the Bureau of Indian Affairs and dealing with some real and complex problems.

But the revolution sprouting on the bloody television images of Vietnam faded as the war ended, at least for the Americans, and Gollywood went back to romantic historical epics like Charles B. Pierce's things. I can't even remember the names. Richard Harris danced through one sequel after another of his masturbation fantasies as A Man Called Horse, a great warrior who comes to save the poor Indians who can't save themselves. We got books like *Hanta Yo*, purporting to tell the authentic story of the Sioux, which caused some Skins to swear they'd kill author Ruth Beebe Hill if she ever showed her face in Sioux Country. ABC rushed to produce a five-hour miniseries about it titled

Mystic Warrior. Many Indians kind of enjoyed blue-eyed Trevor Howard being a cute old Chief in *Windwalker*, but for every one of these halfway-sincere attempts there were ten Charles Bronson or Chuck Connors–type flicks fulfilling noble savage fantasies.

In the 1980s the Custerism, like everything else, just got worse. We were treated to Larry McMurtry's Pulitzer Prize–winning *Lonesome Dove*, with Frederic Forrest as the half-breed maniac Blue Duck slaughtering and scalping everything and everyone he could get his hands on. *Young Guns* converted the village of Cerrillos, New Mexico, into an authentic replica of Billy the Kid's exciting and adventurous world of yore. To top it off, some film crew was also nearby in New Mexico about then shooting something they called *Powwow Highway*, which they claimed was based on a novel of the same name that I wrote.

To back up a little on this yarn, but without running over you with too much detail, I had indeed optioned my soul to the devil, and made $10,000. I was tired of outhouses and walking to the grocery store because I had no car, and stealing food too. My 7-year-old son Sky even got a part in the movie. He had fun, flying first-class up to Sheridan, Wyoming, where they were shooting, and staying in the Holiday Inn. He liked his fellow stars A Martinez, of soap opera *Santa Barbara* fame, and Gary Farmer.

But a disturbing story later filtered out about the film company's shooting in South Dakota, on Bear Butte, a mountain sacred to the Cheyenne and Sioux. They had protested the film company's being there, so it left. Gary Farmer dismissed the incident with disgust. No one else could tell me anything. About a month afterward, in Denver, a full-blood Tsistsistas Southern Cheyenne elder, Richard Tall Bull, told me, "Three Indians died because of your movie." Huh? "They were struck dead by lightning. They had passed themselves off as spiritual leaders and got some money from that film crew. They were winos." He was madder at the Skins than at the film company or me.

What does all this have to do with Custerism in the cinema? This whole experience revealed to me not only the frightening political dimensions of the entertainment industry but also the cultural onslaught of insensitivity. I had prayed on Bear Butte a month before the movie option ran out back in July 1987, and gone through a terrifying ordeal in a courtroom as a politically suspect AIMster, and my prayers to the Goddess Wohpe for help for the people were, in my superstitious heathen estimate, answered when funding came in for the movie. There really is a mysterious world existing beside this one, a parallel dimension that can perhaps be explained not as much by physics or electromagnetism (yet) as by the symbolic poetry of mythology. It is the world where lightning strikes those whose intentions betray greed and self-importance. It is the perspective elders like Tall Bull and Bald Eagle give when death and life intermingle as parts of our political and economic survival.

Dave Bald Eagle was eager to rush out and get a job on *Dances With Wolves* because that was an economic necessity, but he also saw the foolishness of the thing and joked about how he always tried to stay in the background in the crowd scenes so maybe no one would notice him in the movie. Other full-blooded Lakota elders in it, like Dave Yakima Chief, told me the same thing. They were of course flattered by Kevin Costner's invitation to be in his movie, and by all accounts he is, as Vincent Canby remarked in his *New York Times* review of the movie when it came out in late 1990, "a foursquare kind of guy." But many Indians are disturbed that, although such movies help pay a few bills for a little while, they are not as harmless as they might seem: They are part of a system that routinely throws around millions and millions of dollars while tens of millions of people in this country, in chillingly high proportions people of color, don't have much more than a box of macaroni in the cupboard.

How has Kevin Costner helped us? His movie has reaped over $150 million and Dave Bald Eagle still has to use an outhouse. Dave Chief doesn't even have that much—he is homeless at age 63. These two pointed out to me what is at best a questionable cultural call in the making of *Dances With Wolves*: The men generally speak Lakota in the feminine form; the screenplay's dialogue was translated by a woman, who also served as the primary linguistic coach. Many elders around here, including Grampa Bill Horn Cloud, are mad about it. (Imagine if Costner and his baseball buddies in *Bull Durham* had spoken as if they'd stepped out of *Little Women*). This in a movie lauded for its "authenticity"—which was more closely achieved when it came to props: Joe Flying By and the Pipe ruling elders' council, and even the Pipe Keeper himself, Arvol Looking Horse, preferred that Costner and his Hollywood Indian Floyd Westerman not represent the Pipe in the movie. The Pipe is the sacred Canupa of White Buffalo Calf Maiden, who founded the buffalo culture nineteen generations ago; but they went right ahead and smoked it anyway.

This is the New Custerism—General George sporting velvet gloves and so-called liberals are the New Custerists, torn between their cultural guilt and self-interest. It goes beyond James Fenimore Cooper's good intentions into stuff that does indeed pave the road to hell. It encompasses not just trampling on what might be sacred but a hidden Victorianism as well, which has to clean up my dirty beer-can-strewn highway or its historical equivalent, keep us at a safe remove, make us Good Indians again, like Costner's and Blake's syrupy noble savages. Books or movies like this neutralize real action, the possibility for social or political reform that might arise from truly stimulating literature or drama. (This idyll takes place, incidentally, in landscapes where the David Bald Eagles can't leave their homes untended or drunks will sweep in to loot them; and the filmically perfect village of tipis *Wolves* shows at one point is perched on a Belle Fourche River that is undrinkable and polluted from gold mine tailings.

Instead of creating a great new multicultural paradigm, *Dances With Wolves*, by its huge success, is spawning more of the same old clichés. Where the Old Custerists didn't mind blatantly stereotyping Indians as savages, for New Custerists the sentimentality and romance must not be sullied. *Son of the Morning Star* rushed into production and was seen for four hours this winter on ABC, striking while the iron was hot. Not even the Uncle Tomahawks who have rejoiced ad nauseam about the glories of Costner & Co. liked this latest paean to G. A. Custer, who was after all really a complex kind of guy and not just a blood-and-glory murderer but a good husband and mostly a foursquare Joe. The *New York Times* rejoiced about *Son of the Morning Star* and said that maybe Indians will be the social cause célèbre of the Gay Nineties.

Wolves was up for twelve Oscars and won seven; Costner decided he liked bows and arrows and moved on to *Robin Hood*. The Skins in the trade have gone with Uncle Tomahawk: They're shooting another remake of *The Last of the Mohicans*, if you can believe it, though there are a few modern-day films in the works. Robert Redford is doing a Tony Hillerman mystery in Arizona, and I'm hearing conflicting stories from the Navajos and Hopis about it. Some of them are protesting it because of purported trespass on sacred areas. A Hopi friend of mine, Hartman Lomaweima, from Second Mesa, says the movie company has wandered into a local feud about a gravel pit. He laughs about it; others, like a Pueblo lawyer I know, say it's a serious cultural travesty again. (John Nichols, who wrote *The Milagro Beanfield War*, which

Redford directed on the screen, told me, "It was the worst experience of my life. They used such a picturesque backdrop that you forget how difficult it is to live a life of poverty.") And *Young Guns* veterans are doing a thing around Wounded Knee and Leonard Peltier here in South Dakota, produced by Robert De Niro. Redford has also funded a Peltier documentary—its director was seen cruising around here last summer in a Mercedes limo—though Steve Robideau, Peltier's cousin and the director of a defense committee for him, probably the most knowledgeable and earnest man in the world regarding Leonard's call for a new trial, says he hasn't been contacted about it. What's more, Ted Turner's got features planned for cable TV, and the rumor mill has it that others are thinking of a series to be called *Lakota Moon.* We wait to see if we get anything more than moonshine.

JANUARY 6/13, 1992

JFK AND *JFK*

Alexander Cockburn

•

Alexander Cockburn is *The Nation*'s "Beat the Devil" columnist, a column named after his father's novel of the same name which was filmed by John Huston in 1954. Some of Cockburn's essays on film, on Ian Fleming and James Bond, and *Top Gun*, are found in his collection *Corruptions of Empire*.

WHETHER JFK WAS killed by a lone assassin or by a conspiracy has as much to do with the subsequent contours of American politics as if he had tripped over one of Caroline's dolls and broken his neck in the White House nursery.

Of course many people think otherwise, reckoning that once it can be demonstrated that the Warren Commission was wrong and Oswald was not the lone killer, then we face the reality of a rightist conspiracy engineered to change the course of history. (The idea of Oswald as a leftist conspiracy of one or more has perhaps fortunately never had the popularity one might have expected.) This is the view taken by Oliver Stone, who has stated in interviews, such as one in *Spin*, that "Kennedy was really moving to end the cold war and sign a nuclear treaty with the Soviets; he would not have gone to war in Southeast Asia. He was starting a backdoor negotiation with Castro." Instead of which good things, there was "the first coup d'etat in America."

In *JFK*, Stone leaves no doubt about the coup's sponsors. A sequence in grainy black-and-white, presumably designed for extra *vérité*, shows L.B.J. planning the assassination with the Joint Chiefs of Staff. This is a $40 million equivalent of *MacBird*, though Stone's model is another Shakespeare play.

The core of this vision of history is put by Kevin Costner in his role as New Orleans District Attorney Jim Garrison:

> We have all become Hamlets in our country, children of a slain father-leader whose killers still possess the throne. The ghost of John Kennedy confronts us with the secret murder at the heart of the American dream. He forces on us the appalling question: Of what is our Constitution made? What is our citizenship—and more, our lives—worth? What is the future, where a President can be assassinated under conspicuously suspicious circumstances, while the machinery of legal action scarcely trembles? How many political murders disguised as heart attacks, cancer, suicides, airplane and car crashes, drug overdoses, will occur before they are exposed for what they are?

Stone wrote those words himself (and at one point even planned to have the ghost of JFK appear to Garrison as he stood in his kitchen making a chicken sandwich while watching news of Bobby Kennedy's assassination). It's an important passage, for in its truly fascist yearning for the "father-leader" taken from the children-people by conspiracy, it accurately catches the crippling nuttiness of what passes amid some sectors of the left (admittedly a pretty nebulous concept these days) as mature analysis and propaganda: that virtue in government died in Dallas, and that a "secret agenda" has perverted the national destiny.

With this demented optic, left ultimately joins hands with right, as happened during the Gulf War when the para-Birchist Craig Hulet won an enthusiastic following amid radical circles for his conspiratorial account of the Bush regime's policy even though anyone with half a brain could see after about thirty seconds exactly where he was coming from. Out the window goes any sensible analysis of institutions, economic interest and all the other elements constituting the open secrets and agendas of American capitalism.

The Ancestry of *JFK*

The psychic bloodlines of *JFK* may be traced at least in part to Ellen Ray, who met Oliver Stone in an elevator in Havana and placed a copy of Garrison's *On the Trail of the Assassins* in his hand. Along with Bill Schaap, Ray had published Garrison's book and, as I vividly recall from several conversations, has long felt that history did a U-turn for the worse when conspiracy laid JFK low. Why the publishers of *Covert Action Information Bulletin* and *Lies of Our Times* should take this position I'm not sure, unless we take a biographical approach and argue that maybe it all goes back to Ellen's Catholic girlhood in Massachusetts, with an icon of JFK on the wall. But then lots of other people including Bill didn't grow up as R.C. Mass.-based Jack fans, so the reasons probably lie elsewhere.

Intellectual ancestry for the assertion that JFK would have pulled the United States out of Vietnam can be traced back to an essay by Peter Dale Scott, "Vietnamization and the Drama of the Pentagon Papers," which appeared in Volume V of the Senator Gravel edition of the "Pentagon Papers," published by Beacon Press in 1972. This volume, edited by Noam Chomsky and Howard Zinn, offered critical commentary designed to put the Papers in perspective.

Scott, now a professor of English at UC Berkeley, attempted to prove by philological analysis that whereas the official editors of the Papers working in the Pentagon—headed by Leslie Gelb and reporting to Robert McNamara—wanted to show there was continuity of policy between JFK and LBJ, the opposite was the case. Scott's focus was on National Security Action Memorandum 273 and on shifts in the verbal expressions of policies that occurred between the Honolulu conference of November 20, 1963, attended by JFK.'s top advisers, and LBJ's November 24 policy meeting on Vietnam, the first in the wake of JFK's murder and including the same advisers, which led to the adoption of NSAM 273 immediately thereafter.

Scott lays enormous weight upon minute textual alterations, signaling these with urgent italic. Thus, on October 2 the Kennedy position was "The security of South Vietnam *is a major interest of the United States as other free nations [sic]*. We will adhere to *our policy of working with the people and Government of South Vietnam to deny* this country to communism and to suppress the *externally stimulated and supported insurgency* of the Viet Cong as promptly as possible. *Effective performance* in this undertaking is the *central objective* of our policy in South Vietnam."

Such, in Scott's yearning interpretation, was the language of benign intent, as contrasted with the NSAM 273 language of November 24: "It remains the *central objective* of the United States in South Vietnam to assist the people and Government of that country *to win* their contest against the externally *directed* and supported communist *conspiracy*. The effectiveness of their contributions to this purpose."

To the sensible eye, those differences may be credited to the determination of an uncertain Johnson White House, following the assassination, to show the world its resolve, as opposed to the more anfractuous approach of a Kennedy White House trying to steer a path through the Buddhist crisis, the impending coup against Diem, the discontent of some liberals at growing involvement and the rage of conservatives that not enough was being done.

There was, however, no change in policy, and the measure of Peter Dale Scott's fantasizing may be gauged by his claim later in the same essay for the "overall Kennedy strategy for movement towards international relaxation of the cold war and conversion to a full-employment civilian economy at home." Military spending was slowing near the end of Kennedy's term for exactly the same reason it slowed near the end of Ronald Reagan's season in office. The largest and most rapid military buildup in the peacetime history of the United States had been accomplished. JFK had doubled the number of Polaris nuclear submarines; increased Minuteman purchases by 75 percent, tactical nukes in Europe by 60 percent and the total number of weapons in the strategic alert force by 100 percent.

Kennedy, having fought the 1960 election partly on an imaginary missile gap, then acted as if this missile gap were genuine. In his vivid account in *High Priests of Waste*, Ernie Fitzgerald suggests that the military spending surge of the Kennedy years definitively undermined all rational standards of productivity and cost control achieved in the preceding seven decades (though an old auto worker from the Chrysler plant in Newcastle, Indiana, once remarked to me that such declines could be traced back to the cost-plus contracts of the Second World War). The idea that Kennedy was methodically tilting toward a full-employment civilian economy is preposterous.

Scott's essay has had a pertinacious half-life, and one of those paying tribute to it is a military historian named John Newman, one of Stone's advisers on the film. Newman's *JFK and Vietnam* first came into the offices of Sheridan Square Press, Ray and Schaap's publishing house, whence it was passed on to Stone, who assisted in its dispatch to Warner Books (part of the conglomerate backing *JFK*), which is publishing the book in February.

JFK and Vietnam is a serious book with two curious features. One is the absence of any substantial evidence for the author's frequently repeated claim that by February or March of 1963 JFK had decided to pull out of Vietnam once the 1964 election was won. Newman's only sources for this are people to whom JFK would, as a matter of habitual political opportunism, have spoken in such terms, such as Senators Mike Mansfield and Wayne Morse, both of whom, particularly the latter, were critical of JFK's escalation in Vietnam. Against their recollections may be placed the accounts of those to whom JFK spoke out of the other side of his mouth, such as Dean Rusk or even RFK.

The other curious feature is Newman's inference that the assassination should be re-examined in the light of his conclusion that LBJ reversed JFK's stance on Vietnam. Perhaps he wrote this late section of the book after association with Stone had commenced. The *ciné vérité* of LBJ hatching the coup with the Joint Chiefs was but a short step, and Newman was on hand for the press briefings on *JFK* in Los Angeles in mid-December, ready with scholarly backup.

THE JUNKYARD OF HISTORY

Oliver Stone looks upon the assassination as the coffin of all the bright hopes of the early sixties. To get a truer insight all you have to do is go to a junkyard or an auto museum and look at the colors. Bright hopes were really being born in the mid-fifties, with Detroit palettes of desert rose, aqua, even paisley. By the time of the New Frontier the colors had darkened into the dreary greens, tans and drab blues of combat. With their prophetic three-year lead times, the colors told the story. Kennedy had betrayed the hopes of people like Stone before he had stepped off the inauguration stand.

"Get a life," Captain Kirk once told some Trekkies. Get some history too. Critics of *JFK* like Tom Wicker have fretted that "in an era when mistrust of government and loss of confidence in institutions (the press not least) are widespread and virulent, such a suggestion [i.e., that representatives of the ruling elites murdered JFK] seems a dubious public service." In fact the dubious public service is to suggest that JFK himself was not a functional representative of those elites.

The real JFK backed a military coup in Guatemala to keep out Arévalo, denied the Dominican Republic the possibility of land reform, helped promote a devastating cycle of Latin American history, including the anticipatory motions of the coup in Brazil, and backed a Baathist coup in Iraq that set a certain native of Tikrit on the path to power. He presided over Operation Mongoose, inflicting terror upon Cuba. At the very moment bullets brought JFK's life to its conclusion in Dallas, a CIA. officer operating firmly within the bounds of Kennedy's policy was handing poison to a Cuban agent in Paris, designed to kill Castro.

Lawrence J. Bassett and Stephen Pelz wrote in the 1989 collection *Kennedy's Quest for Victory* that "by putting American advisers in harm's way . . . he helped to engage American patriotism in a war against the Vietnamese people. By arguing that Vietnam was a test of the West's ability to defeat the people's war strategy and a test of American credibility in the Cold War, he raised the costs of withdrawal for his successor." JFK sent in 16,000 advisers, sponsored the strategic hamlet program, launched napalm and defoliation upon the South and covert terror and sabotage upon the North. He never entertained the idea of a settlement as advocated by J. K. Galbraith when the latter was Ambassador to India.

Thomas Paterson, editor of this volume, put it well. Only out of respect for history "emerges unpleasant reality and the need to reckon with a past that has not always matched the selfless and self-satisfying image Americans have of their foreign policy and of Kennedy as their young, fallen hero who never had a chance. Actually, he had his chance, and he failed."

APRIL 6, 1992

THE TIE THAT BINDS

Nora Ephron

•

The journalist and novelist Nora Ephron is the writer of *When Harry Met Sally* and the writer-director of *Sleepless in Seattle* and *You've Got Mail.* This piece originally was a contribution to a Town Hall symposium on *JFK* organized by the Nation Institute in 1991.

I AM NOT here to talk about *JFK* per se, but about what it is like to have written a movie based on something that happened. Nine years ago, Alice Arlen and I wrote the screenplay for *Silkwood*. It was a carefully annotated script, meticulously researched, and we kept scrupulously to what we determined were the key historical facts of the case. In Karen Silkwood we wrote a character who was considerably closer to whoever Silkwood was than to the person who had been written about in journalistic accounts—most of which had tended to whitewash Karen and gloss over certain less-than-perfect aspects of her character. In fact, what drew Alice and me to Karen Silkwood's story were the less-than-perfect aspects, and what we tried to write was not a movie about a heroic woman who did something heroic but rather the story of a complicated and interesting and flawed woman who quite unexpectedly did something heroic. We were extremely proud of the job we did and of the movie Mike Nichols made from it, and we were completely unprepared for what happened when it came out, which was first, an article in the Arts and Leisure section of The *New York Times* that focused completely on comparing the "facts" in the movie with the "facts" of the Silkwood case; and second, about two weeks later, a *New York Times* editorial denouncing the movie as a "docudrama." A docudrama, in case you don't know, is a movie The *New York Times* disagrees with the politics of.

The point I am trying to make here is that it doesn't matter whether you are good little girls like Alice and me or big bad boys like Oliver Stone. The *New York Times* is going to pound you into the ground.

They will not bother, of course, if your movie is *Out of Africa*, or *GoodFellas*, or *The Pride of the Yankees*, or *Bugsy*, or *The Glenn Miller Story*, or *Lawrence* of *Arabia*—to name just a few of the wonderful movies that have done what any movie based on something that actually happened must do: *which is to impose a narrative.* So no one really objects that Denys Finch Hatton didn't really see Isak Dinesen on a train on her way to Africa, or that Tommy De Simone was actually very tall, or that Mrs. Lou Gehrig looked nothing whatsoever like Teresa Wright. These things don't matter, because they . . . don't matter. For something to matter it must be political—or more important, ambiguous, deliciously ambiguous, unresolved, mythic. The very thing that attracts a filmmaker to a project is the thing that guarantees his life will be hell once he makes it.

Because suddenly, the filmmaker has ventured onto forbidden turf, and on this turf is a big sign that says Keep Off the Grass. In the case of *JFK*, the attack is that much worse because the press is one of the reasons we still don't know what happened in Dallas, and whenever you write something that implies that the press is not doing its job, or has not done its job, you get into trouble with journalists because you mortify them. (Incidentally, this happens with books too, not just with movies. It happened with *All the President's Men* and *The Final Days*, to name two books that were mortifying to the press, and I would suggest that the recent gang rape of Robert Caro on the ground that he was wrong about Coke Stevenson was actually inspired by the mortification he caused the press by discovering things about Lyndon Johnson, particularly about the source of his fortune, that had lain around undiscovered by the press for years. But I digress.)

So. You venture onto the grass. But no one says, Keep Off the Grass. That would give the game away. What the press say as a rule is not that they mind your being on the grass but that they object to you methodology. What they say is that they have no problem with your making a movie of this sort as long as you stick to the facts. Now this is a fairly comical notion, because it implies that having the facts correct means that the story you tell is correct, as we all know the number of times we have read things that were correct on the facts but just plain wrong. In the case of *JFK*, the most commonly objected-to of Oliver Stone's methods was the combining of documentary footage with film footage. But the truth is that Stone could have done without all that, and in addition he could have changed Garrison into the flawed human being he actually was—and why didn't you, Oliver? oh never mind—the point is you could do any number of things and the press will still find something to object to. They will point to a silver fork that was actually stainless steel, or a breakfast that was actually a dinner, or some character you have made a composite of, or some event you have telescoped—something that proves that you have got it wrong. And they will fall on this like a fumbled football and wave it in the air to show that you have distorted the truth. All of this is nonsense; that's what I'm trying to say. Because what the press is truly objecting to are not your techniques but that you're there at all, that you have a political agenda and—and this is the important part—that you are imposing a narrative. Or put more simply, that you are telling a story.

Now it is a writer's obligation to impose a narrative. Everyone does this. Every time you take a lump of material and turn it into something you are imposing a narrative. *It's a writer's obligation to do this.* And, by the same token, it is apparently a journalist's obligation to pretend that he never does anything of the sort. The journalist claims to believe that the narrative emerges from the lump of material, rises up and smacks you in the face like marsh gas.

A couple of years after *Silkwood* was attacked in The *New York Times* I found myself at the New York Bar Association on a program on docudramas with Max Frankel. Frankel was at the time the editorial page editor of the *Times*; he is now executive editor of the paper. And I want to tell you what he said when it was his turn to speak. He said that he was wearing a tie, which indeed he was, and he held his tie up for all of us to see. He said that he had put the tie on that morning and that it had special meaning for him, it was a gift of enormous sentimental value—he went on at some length about the tie, although never being much more specific than that, so we never did find out what was so special about the tie, or who gave it to him, and I don't even remember what it looked like. When I called him about this a couple of days ago, he not only didn't remember what it looked like either but he didn't even remember the story, although he did say that it sounded like the sort of thing he might have said (which I assure you he did). Here's what he went on to say: He said that if you put an actor into a movie playing him, giving a speech at the New York Bar Association, wearing an identical tie, it would not be the truth because you would have no way of knowing what that tie meant to him. Now I love this story. I love it because it's so honest. And I love it because it's right out there: Max Frankel honestly believes there's only one version of the story, and it's his. But I just told you my version, and I promise you it's just as good.

I said to him that night, Max, you mean we can't even make *Dr. Ehrlich's Magic Bullet*? And he said, That's right. He was quite cheerful about it. By the way, when I called to check the story with him the other day, he continued in his merry way by ending the phone call with me by saying, And congratulations on your recent success in fiction.

Fiction and nonfiction. Is that all there is? Or to put it in the opposite way, as Edgar Doctorow did in an essay a few years back: "I am thus led to the proposition that there is no fiction or nonfiction as we commonly understand the distinction: there is only narrative."

Edgar Doctorow brings me to another story. Years ago, Doctorow wrote a novel called *The Book of Daniel*. It happens to be a masterpiece. It is a novel that was clearly inspired by the historical fact and ongoing myth of the Rosenberg case, and is an improvisation on it. (I always feel that someone should mention the Rosenbergs at any event sponsored by *The Nation* in Town Hall.) The characters in the book are named the Isaacsons, and when it was published, it received splendid reviews. Some years later, Sidney Lumet made a movie based on the book, called *Daniel*. And when the *New York Times* Arts and Leisure section put out its hit on the movie—an article that, it will not surprise you to hear, compared the events in the movie with the facts of the Rosenberg case—it actually said that Mandy Patinkin was playing the part of Julius Rosenberg. So here we have the case of a writer who removed something from fact, who never pretended to be telling the story of the Rosenberg, but they nailed him for it anyway.

Having said all this, let me speak to the topic as I understand it, which is what the obligations of film are to history. As someone who was trained as a journalist, I have strong feelings about this that I suspect are slightly more rigid than the average screenwriter's. I believe that you have to hit the marks, whatever the marks are. The marks differ from project to project, and there's no way to make a simple rule about what they are. In the case of *Silkwood*, as I explained, one of the primary marks was Karen's character, which we believed we had a moral obligation to convey, warts and all. There were, in addition, a number of episodes that, it seemed to us, had to be conveyed as accurately and with as little dramatic license as was possible. When we got to areas where it was not known what happened—like when Karen Silkwood's urine sample was contaminated with radiation—we did not depict anything in connection with that that wasn't known at the time. At the time, we did compress things; we made up the characters of the people Karen worked with, et cetera. We made a movie that was our version of what had happened. What we believed was that we had written something that conveyed—not the truth, but what it was like, sort of, maybe, and what it was like in a way that ordinary journalism couldn't come close to.

It was clear to me when I saw *JFK* that I was seeing Oliver Stone's version of the story. And I didn't object to it, any more than I object to the 601 books that have been written about the assassination. One of the problems with the movie *JFK* is that it is more ambiguous and brilliant than its defenders, but that shouldn't be held against the movie, which in its own way is not just a wild and wacky look at the assassination but manages to capture thirty years of Kennedy assassination madness and recapitulate it in a way that seems to me practically ontological (I hope I'm using that word correctly). What intensified this even further was Oliver Stone's splendid performance as himself, a performance that was genuinely inspirational to those of us who were bewildered and cowering in the same circumstances. Unfortunately, though, there are very few directors who want to make a movie and spend the four months after it opens with Ted Koppel. On the contrary: Most directors will look at a similar sort of movie and say to themselves, life is too short.

There are people who say that movies have a special obligation in this area, that for instance young people will see *JFK* and think that the Joint Chiefs of Staff killed President Kennedy. But I don't know why they think this any more than I did. And what if they do? Eventually they will grow up and figure it out for themselves. Or else they won't. It's not the issue and it's not the filmmaker's responsibility.

The real danger is not that we might have an inaccurate movie—which, by the way, never hurt anyone. The real danger is that the wholesale, knee-jerk objection to movies based on things that happened might result in something far worse, which is a chilling effect on the creation of works of art.

May 18, 1992

Exchange

Oliver Stone

•

A Stone's Throw

Santa Monica, Calif.

Former Warren Commission assistant counsel Wesley J. Liebeler's defense of his résumé-building work is almost refreshing in its transparency ["Beat the Devil," March 9]. Abetted by Alexander Cockburn's total ignorance of the subject at hand, he improvises, freely associating sources and figures, and offers his opinion that the Warren Commission did a great job, except they got "the entrance wounds in the wrong place." They had the murder on film and some three dozen medical personnel examined the body—but they never did pin down exactly where those wounds were. There goes the whole case: Without knowing where the entrance wounds are, there is absolutely no way to substantiate the lone-gunman thesis.

What we see in the interview is a merging of the far right and the far left for entirely different agendas. Liebeler's operating principle is fairly simple and human: Cover your ass. Cockburn's is philosophical. His dialectic view of history precludes the possibility of individual choice affecting the outcome of events—thus, the very thought that Kennedy might have betrayed his capitalist upbringing by halting the war in Vietnam is unbearable. As Cockburn puts it: "The effect of *JFK* is to make people think that America is a good country that produced a good President killed by bad elites." While that is exactly what I believe, it's a veritable nightmare for Cockburn, who clearly is convinced that a democratic country cannot be good, and could not elect a leader who wasn't merely another link in the inherently evil system.

The Nation joins in the fray with its marvelous illustration of the single bullet theory, a crude drawing swiped in toto from a January 19 article in *New York Newsday*. Poor Governor Connally is squatting in a mysterious hole (or perhaps on the floor of the limousine), a sitting duck for the überbullet heading downward into his armpit. That's an odd configuration, especially in light of the facts: (1) the extensive photographic record of the motorcade shows that Connally's seat was at the same approximate height as Kennedy's; and (2) if, in fact, the bullet did enter Kennedy's back and exit his throat as Liebeler et al. claim, the bullet would have had an *upward* trajectory upon leaving Kennedy. The *Newsday*-cum-*Nation* drawing turns the preposterous single-bullet path into a straight downward line through the two men—a lot more palatable, even believable, but showing something that never was. This is a tactic we usually ascribe to CBS and *Time*, and we expect *The Nation* to correct the record. Not so this time out.

Instead, we get the Dan Rather school of journalism: It is because I say so. With what would be a good title for his memoirs, Cockburn shrugs off his factual errors in his original *JFK* column: "I thought it was true when I wrote it." In journalism, in history, in criticism and in publishing, it is not enough to "think" something is true. Nor should it be necessary for the readers to call Cockburn on his errors; that is *The Nation's* job. It doesn't matter that Cockburn is a columnist with a considerable following and a penchant for provoking controversy. As a selling point, controversy helps, but please, don't misinform the public in the name of commerce.

The public is not stupid. As the polls show, a strong majority know the evidence does not support the fantasy that a lone nut shot and killed the President of the United States. Journalists (like Cockburn) and journals (like *The Nation*) should be our protection against official untruths. But in this unique instance, the media have bought wholesale the lies and distortions passed down from Washington. *The Nation* and Cockburn trivialize the event of November 22, 1963, by dismissing it as nothing more momentous than an accident. That will not do. As the record shows, Mr. Cockburn, JFK did not trip on Caroline's doll. He was murdered—and history changed—by parties still unknown.

•

COCKBURN REPLIES

Petrolia, Calif.

STONE'S ADMONITION TO me not to "misinform the public in the name of commerce" is matchless effrontery. The film from which he stands to make millions is undoubtedly one of the most willfully error-riddled pieces of "historical reconstruction" in the history of cinema. Like all demagogues Stone is now a fullblown megalomaniac given to such sentiments (announced grandly at a Nation Institute symposium at Town Hall) that "Even when I'm wrong, I'm right." As his ludicrous mistake about the illustration I included in my Liebeler interview shows, he is wholly ignorant of the basic forensic, evidentiary and historical record, and is dependent on compliant "researchers" who tell him what he wants to hear. Any fact inhospitable to his preposterous überconspiracy is blandly denied. Example: In *JFK*, David Ferrie confesses to his involvement in the conspiracy. No such confession was made, as is clear even from Garrison's book. Aha, said Stone at the Town Hall event, the confession was made to one of Garrison's assistants. Ed Epstein, author of books on the Warren Commission and on Garrison, called this assistant, who said that Ferrie had done nothing of the sort and that the story was nonsense from start to finish. So far as historical scruple goes, Stone makes Cecil B. De Mille look like Braudel. One of the most squalid aspects of the whole affair is that Time-Warner plans to distribute "documentary materials" about the assassination to schoolchildren.

In tune with the fascist aesthetic of his movie, Stone now mounts the traditional fascist defense: He, like Kennedy, is victim of a gigantic conspiracy, and "the media have bought wholesale the lies and distortions passed down from Washington." Passed down by whom? Let's have precision here. In *The Nation's* case, exactly who pulled together myself and four other writers variously critical of Stone's version of history and "passed down" to us the necessary "lies and distortions"? It's one thing—not uncommon—to extract money from the public under false pretenses. It's another, à la Stone, to whine all the way to the bank.

ALEXANDER COCKBURN

JULY 5, 1993

Out in Hollywood

Paul Rudnick

•

Paul Rudnick's screenwriting credits include *Isn't She Great? In & Out, First Wives Club, Jeffrey* (based on his play), *Addams Family Values, Sister Act*, and *The Addams Family*. He also writes a monthly satirical film review column for *Premiere* magazine under the name "Libby Gelman-Waxner."

WHENEVER A MOVIE star is asked by, say, Barbara Walters if he or she would ever play a gay character, the reply is almost always, "Of course! If it's a good role, I'd play an ax murderer!" Stars tend to equate gay characters with extreme, antisocial types; they will occasionally add the cautionary footnote, "You don't have to be an ax murderer to play one, you know. You use your imagination." Stars approach gay roles as if they require a second language and De Niro–caliber research; "I have gay friends," they will confide, "and I met with them."

Hollywood has treated gay issues and characters with both abject fear and too much respect. The fear derives from Hollywood's sole motivation for any decision: marketing. Gay movies do not make money, say the studios. This statement should be amended to read: Dull earnest and impossibly sincere gay movies do not make money. Industry stalwarts usually lunge at 1982's *Making Love* as a test case for the public's rejection of gay material. This was a terribly well-meaning film, in which Michael Ontkean played a hunky, sensitive doctor married to the perky, extraordinarily naïve Kate Jackson; Michael finds himself attracted to his rugged, if somewhat footloose, patient, Harry Hamlin. Michael eventually leaves Kate for Harry; many tears flow, but everyone ultimately behaves well and Michael and Harry prove that gay commitment is simply a matter of sharing conditioner. This film, for all its political perfection, is numbingly trite; the two men never even ask Kate if she felt similarly overshadowed by Farrah Fawcett and Jaclyn Smith on *Charlie's Angels*. The movie lacks any real characters, let alone any style or wit; it is a single-issue film, and one longs for Kate to confront Michael by howling, "He's prettier than me, isn't he? It's the hair thing, isn't it? Well, I hope you're both just too happy, with your Lacostes and your Levi's and your goddamn free-range brunches!"

Such mundane gay torment also befouled the seemingly more exotic *Kiss of the Spider Woman*, in which William Hurt's swishy, imprisoned window dresser pouted and fantasized and ultimately Became a Man only by taking a bullet. Hurt's performance was boldly amateurish, with each frame insisting, "I'm not really like this." Hurt's miscasting was breathtaking—he seemed to be a flaxen-haired Greenwich stockbroker taking a community theater fling at the title role in *Mame*. Real, ravishing gay style can be found in Michael Serrault's work as Albin, the matronly drag queen in *La Cage aux Folles*, and in almost any of Pedro Almodóvar's films (*Law of Desire*, *What Have I Done to Deserve This?*). Mere homosexuality is never the subject of *La Cage* or the Almodóvar films; the scripts assume a great gay diversity and explore more subtle issues of gender and obsession instead. The gay characters in these films are more than just gay, although they giddily exploit the resources of camp, irony and homoeroticism. In Hollywood, if a character is gay, that's usually all he or she is. To be fair, if a character is straight in a Hollywood film, his or her emotional range is even more restricted. In *The Producers* director Mel Brooks's gay caricatures, the epicene director/choreographer Roger DeBris (Christopher Hewett) and his goateed secretary, Carmen Giya (Andreas Voustinas), are helplessly funny as they model the bustled Victorian gowns they have selected for "The Directors and Choreographers Ball" and demand that Gene Wilder "Be brutal—*they* will." Brooks has a truly bizarre attitude toward gay men, finding them both terrifying and comic, sort of satanic maître d's; still, his arched-eyebrow stereotypes are allowed more oomph than, say, your average Tom Cruise role.

("Tom Cruise" is such an inspired name for a gay porn star that it seems wasted on such a shiny-cheeked boy scout.)

Woody Allen, whose work often chronicles upscale Manhattan, has almost never written gay roles; even the superb satirist Paul Mazursky is hamstrung by such characters as the awkwardly conceived gay teenage son in *Down and Out in Beverly Hills*. Steven Spielberg portrayed the lesbianism in *The Color Purple* as a form of counseling for abused wives; Spike Lee has for the most part avoided the presence of gay characters in his panoramic films of African-American life. These major directors seem either confused or paralyzed by the notion of gayness; they fear giving offense, either to watchdog gays or mass-market conservatives.

The solution to all this bigotry and PC muddle may very well lie with gay filmmakers. Spike Lee and John Singleton, among others, have brought an authentic minority vision to the screen, complete with wild irreverence; perhaps only a gay director can afford the freedom to depict gay life without creating a pious plea for tolerance, or a mincing *Three's Company* cartoon. An American Almodóvar is required; candidates include Gregg Araki, who wrote and directed *The Living End*, an all-male, HIV-positive *Thelma and Louise;* Todd Haynes, whose output includes *Poison* and the contraband *Superstar: The Karen Carpenter Story*; and Gus Van Sant, whose *My Own Private Idaho* starred teen throblets Keanu Reeves and River Phoenix in a kind of gay grunge valentine. My money leans more toward Jennie Livingston, the director of *Paris Is Burning*, a documentary on vogueing and drag balls that was so intelligent, so resonant and so entertaining that it managed to be attacked by both brimstone fundamentalists and concerned liberals alike. John Waters is also a peculiarly American genius, with a kitschmeister's appreciation of filth and glitter; the late Bill Sherwood struck a more realistic, slightly soapy tone in *Parting Glances*, a Woody-tinged investigation of Central Park West butcher-block guppiedom.

Of course, gay life can be equally available to straight directors, when they just stop quivering. Stephen Frears did handsomely by the gay romance in *My Beautiful Laundrette* and Mike Figgis used Laurie Metcalf as a no-big-deal lesbian police detective in the Richard Gere thriller *Internal Affairs*. Other gay-themed projects on the horizon include *Interview With the Vampire*, the film version of Larry Kramer's *The Normal Heart* and numerous depictions of the Stonewall riots; Daniel Day Lewis is often proposed as possible casting for all of these films. In Hollywood, quality English acting-gay; the accent allows the stars to seem sufficiently distanced, nonthreatening and nonsexual, so that Aunt Prudence in Des Moines can claim, "Oh, he's not gay—he's British." Hollywood is also holding its collective breath over Jonathan Demme's upcoming *Philadelphia*, in which Tom Hanks plays a lawyer with AIDS; the success or failure of this film is seen as another litmus test for the commercial potential of gay subject matter, as if any one film or star could provide conclusive findings. In the gay community, the movie is thought to be Demme's apology for the seemingly gay serial killer in his Oscar-winning *Silence of the Lambs*; I think Demme might also buy each gay person on the planet a nice Rolex or maybe a stole.

Hollywood is riddled with gay studio executives, moguls, writers, actors and directors; most of them, like their heterosexual counterparts, are profoundly untalented, only with better shoes. Along with high-toned gay films, gay viewers might also demand big-time gay schlock: Jean-Claude Van Damme kickboxing gay-bashers, or any of the Sheens as a rebellious gay detective who won't play by the rules, in a thriller titled *Get Her. Three of Hearts* was a decent step toward lesbian romance pulp, and Sharon Stone's bisexual murderess in *Basic Instinct* at least had a wardrobe. We need unwatchable gay musicals and James Belushi vehicles from Disney, and even Schwarzenegger or Stallone as an evil gay robot from the future, sent to Earth to eliminate framed botanical prints and baseball caps worn backwards at the gym.

Gay people need to see their lives on-screen, gay kids need role models and the straight audience needs to accept gay characters without retching or crying depravity. While all of these are admirable goals, they could and will result in cinematic PC pablum, in the multiplex equivalent of *Heather Has Two Mommies*, a children's book so consumingly correct that the kids in it compete to see who can claim a family member in a wheelchair. Art, or even entertainment, exists on the whimsy of talent, not agenda. Great gay films, or films with great gay characters, will succeed if they are marketed by great gay promotion departments and are publicized via McDonald's Happy Meals with condoms tucked inside. Of course, there is one other sure-fire route to satisfying both gay and straight audiences simultaneously, but it is tragically out of reach; I speak, of course, of more Joan Crawford films.

JULY 21, 1997

GET THEE BEHIND ME, DISNEY!

Katha Pollitt

•

Katha Pollitt's "Subject to Debate" column appears every other week in *The Nation*. Pollitt has also written essays for *The New Yorker, The Atlantic, The New Republic, Harper's, Mirabella, Ms., Glamour, Mother Jones*, and the *New York Times*. A collection of her writings, *Reasonable Creatures: Essays on Women and Feminism*, was published in 1994.

THE SOUTHERN BAPTISTS have been on the wrong side of just about every issue since their founding in 1845 as a pro-slavery splitoff from the regular Baptists: mixed dancing, racial segregation, equality for women and, my personal favorite, converting the Jews. Ever since that project was announced last year, I've waited for the missionary to knock at my door with all the ardor of the spider for the fly: You'd be surprised how hard it is to get a real theological disputation going in these ecumenical times. It may be some time before the Southern Baptists get around to the Upper West Side, though, because at this year's convention delegates decided to boycott Walt Disney and all his works—even ESPN, the sports channel, which must be quite a sacrifice—for being too gay-friendly. Making a measurable dent in the profit of the Disney corporation is bound to be even harder than persuading the Chosen People to wash in the blood of the Lamb. This time, though, they don't need to ring my doorbell. I'm already on their side.

I tried to like *The Little Mermaid*, which struck me for reasons that now elude me as less monolithically sexist than *Cinderella* or *Sleeping Beauty*, the Disney movies of my youth. I enjoyed bits of *Beauty and the Beast* and *Aladdin*: the funny sidekicks and comic show tunes, the inventive visuals (the fabulous dancing dinner in the Beast's ruined mansion), the amusing repartee. But when you go to these movies with a small child, as I always did, your judgment is skewed by the fact that the alternative is going mad with boredom at the playground or spending a rainy afternoon crouched on the floor playing with plastic horses. With my daughter now 9 and off at camp, I went to see *Hercules* by myself. Big mistake.

The ancient Greeks get a lot of criticism these days for being dead white men and all, but you have to give them credit—they knew how to tell a good story. The myth of Heracles may lack a certain grandeur—even the ancients seemed to regard him as a jolly buffoon, and some of those famous twelve labors involved activities that would have been taken as humorously degrading, like cleaning up manure or wearing a dress. But it's still a rich and evocative, if not entirely coherent, tale, with motifs that turn up in stories as apparently different as Gilgamesh (friend seeks to rescue friend from underworld), Christ (child of mortal mother and divine father wins immortality through earthly struggles) and fairy tales (impossible tasks, dragons and giants, enemy stepmother/queen, golden apples, western journey, poisoned shirt). Bits of the Heracles myth appear in writing from Milton to of all people, Stalin, who saw in the hero's antagonist Antaeus—a giant whose strength depended on remaining in contact with his mother, the Earth—a metaphor for the party cadre's putative connection with the working class.

The myth of Heracles is about a lot of things, I am trying to say, but among the things it is not about is a lonely adopted child who "will go most anywhere to find where I belong," a son with a crush on his powerful benevolent dad, the corrupting influence of celebrity, or the redemptive powers of romantic love. Of course, every generation retells the old stories in new ways—but these particular new ways are already stale, a hyped-up super-glitzy version of a thousand old B-movies. The only truly funny character is Hades, who talk like a Hollywood studio head; his sidekicks, the demons Pain and Panic, who talk like stand-up comics, are basically the hyenas from *The Lion King*, another Disney stinker. The rest are clichés: Hercules' tutor, a satyr named Philoctetes, or Phil, is the tough-talking boxing trainer with a heart of gold; his girlfriend, Megara, or Meg, is the tough-talking "dame" with a heart of gold. The movie is incredibly knowing about show business, its real subject: It mocks both the old Hollywood of film noir and the new world of multimillion-dollar celebrity athlete tie-ins and endorsements (Here has a theme park, a sandal deal, his picture on a thousand tchotchkes and hordes of screaming fans and would-be groupies). But it offers no alternative to the values of those worlds; the sentimental being-a-good-person-is-what-really-matters conclusion is to the rest of the movie what the Jean Hersholt Humanitarian Award is to the Oscars. In real life *Hercules* merchandise is the new tie-in at McDonald's.

Why do we feed our children this dreck? Why do grown-ups feed themselves this dreck? Over and over, I hear parents complain that their kids don't like to read, that the boys are obsessed with sports and the girls are already superconscious—at 8—of their looks and their weight and their clothes. But where do children get a different message about what's important? In *Hercules*, being strong and destructive is the *summum bonum* for all the men and being beautiful, thin and sexy is the basic requirement for all the female characters, from Hera (Hercules' mother, in this version) and Meg to the Muses, downsized for some reason from the traditional chorus of nine to a black gospel quintet—four glamourpusses and one short, fat frump.

I'm not sure exactly why it's *Hercules* that's brought home to me the totalizing power of the corporate media. Maybe it's the gratuitous know-nothing way Disney puts the myth through a blender, not just free-associating all sorts of story elements (Hera his *mom*?) but destroying its very essence, which has to do with the testing and acknowledgment of limits, both human and divine. Or maybe it's the mediocre music and dialogue (Thebes is the Big Olive), the long repetitive stretches of rock-hurling and pillar-shattering. Or the general feeling of immense amounts of money and skill expended to impress upon our children that they live in a world entirely processed by the same corporate forces that brought them this movie.

The Southern Baptists will surely lose their fight against Disney. In today's America, the Mouse beats Christ hands down. But if the Baptists, with their intact belief system, their organized and politicized community, their intensely felt (if bigoted) convictions, cannot mount a successful challenge to corporate mass culture, the rest of us clearly have a task ahead worthy of Heracles himself.

JUNE 15/22 1998

CULTURE WATCH: ALIEN NATION

John Leonard

•

John Leonard, a *Nation* contributing editor, is TV critic for *New York* magazine and the media critic for *CBS Sunday Morning*. He has been *The Nation*'s literary editor, editor-in-chief of the *New York Times Book Review*, a columnist for *Esquire*, a TV critic for *Life* and *Newsweek*. His latest book is *When the Kissing Had to Stop: Cult Studs, Khmer Newts, Langley Spooks, Video Drones, Author Gods, Serial Killers, Vampire Media, Alien Sperm Suckers, Satanic Therapists and Those of Us Who Hold a Left-Wing Grudge in the post-Toasties New World Hip-Hop*.

FORGET *SEINFELD*, A cheese doodle of urban fecklessness in which, to every penis joke, the whitebread slackers wore a prophylactic smirk. The truly momentous occasion on pop culture's social calendar is the June 19 opening of the big-screen *X-Files* movie. The paranormals who started lining up the morning after the last episode of the fifth season of the Sunday night Fox TV series are as worried about Agent Mulder as Agent Scully is. Scully, a red-haired forensic pathologist, used to doubt Mulder's theories of alien abduction, which is why they were paired by the FBI in the first place. But that was before Scully herself was raptured up to a Mother Ship, hickeyed with biochips, and maybe even diddled in her Irish Catholic DNA. While Mulder has lately begun to wonder if his sister's body-snatching is a false memory implanted in him by a shadowy government/"syndicate" cabal of chain-smoking Cancer Men, Scully barely escaped torching on a suspension bridge by orifice-impaired golems who may or may not be "rebel" aliens opposed to the colonizing of planet Earth by shape-shifters, viral-like oil slicks, and killer bees.

If you don't know what I'm talking about, you haven't been paying attention. THE TRUTH IS OUT THERE, *The X-Files* explains as it scrolls its credits. And that truth, from Roswell to the Grassy Knoll to the Christic Institute, is paranoid—a serial embodiment of Don DeLillo's intuition in *Underworld* of "some deeper meaning that existed solely to keep him from knowing what it was." Personally, I enjoy those episodes of *The X-Files* devoted to a self-contained Rod Serling woo-woo more than those that elaborate the eschatology of UFO, invasion—for instance, the one about the serial-killing translator of medieval Italian poetry who met lonely women in chat rooms on the Internet, parked with them in big American cars in bereft municipal spaces, secreted a membrane of gastric juice that smothered even better than a baggie and then fed on their fatty tissue: Vampire liposuction! On the other hand, I was also abducted by Calista Flockhart.

But so alert has *The X-Files* been to every fitful conniption of an epileptic culture that it is now received wisdom, or at least Established Lore—with its own Web sites, a product line of mugs, caps, T-shirts, comic books, prosthetic limbs and gels, and a ten-city "*X*-Po" road show in hangars like the Javits Center in Manhattan. It even makes jokes, not only about what Mulder calls "the military-industrial-entertainment complex" but about itself as well: How, it wondered recently, could the same bungling government that gave us Amtrak and the Susan B. Anthony dollar possibly sustain a conspiracy to suppress evidence of an invasion by saucer-borne polliwogs who have been sucking our sperm and snatching our eggs ever since the Pyramids? (GOVERNMENT DENIES KNOWLEDGE is another of the program's bumper stickers.)

I will explain everything in a minute, but first be advised of some ground rules and flimflam. I call *The X-Files* and like-minded cinemas "paranoirs." Those regressive hypnotherapists who buy into alien abduction, as they buy into a satanic-ritual abuse, I call "psyclops." And those academics who insist on publishing monographs about such phenomenal I call "Cult Studs"—for their piratical boarding, under a black flag of Lacan and Foucault, of pleasure craft on the pop seas; their swashbuckling style; and their slaughter of the innocents. You may ignore these terms. Years ago nobody paid any attention either when I sought to characterize a new species of lit crit—so fixated on the dirty little secrets of genital organization in dead writers that it neglected to notice the language with which they transformed their experience—as "Bed Pan."

Now, then: Crop circles! Cattle mutilations! Anal probes! Mind scans! (How come these aliens are so seldom interested in stealing our *brain* cells?)

> I have described something I myself witnessed, and I have reported something which I was told by someone else, but someone I believed as thoroughly as if I had witnessed the scene myself. I will now add something which I have read about.
>
> (St. Augustine, *City of God*)

Fifty-one years ago next week, or maybe the month after—anyway, sometime in June or July 1947—a flying disc crash-landed near Roswell, New Mexico, littering the scorpion-riddled landscape with hairless, earless, four-fingered ETs whose dead bodies were whirlybirded by black helicopters to "Area 51," a secret military compound in the Nevada desert, where they have been covered up ever since except on the Fox network, the Sci-Fi, A&E and Showtime cable channels, dozens of movies, an equal number of lurid Web sites, thousands of magazine and supermarket tabloid articles and almost as many books, including last summer's *The Complete Roswell UFO Encyclopedia* from the folks who'd earlier brought us *The Official X-Files Magazine*, just in the nick of a *Time* magazine cover story on Rosewell's own fiftieth anniversary celebration, Encounter 97, which included a flying saucer Soap Box Derby, a UFO. belly dancer and a speech by Charioteer-of-the-Gods Erich von Daniken.

On the Tuesday before Encounter 97, the Air Force held a televised press conference, not to discuss Agent Orange in Vietnam, or uranium bullets or retarded bombs in the Gulf War, but to release a 231-page report on all things Roswellian. According to the AF., those weren't aliens; they were weather balloons and crash-test dummies from parachute drops. About Area 51, it had no comment. This inspired the funniest column Maureen Dowd has yet written for The *New York Times*, suggesting that Dick Gephardt and Janet Reno must be aliens, and that Bob Bennett, Dick Armey and Brian Lamb had obviously been saucerized and fiddled with.

Oddly, the Air Force probably told a partial truth. Phil Patton explains in *Dreamland: Travels Inside the Secret World of Roswell and Area 51* that the real Roswell story indeed involved military balloon projects like Moby Dick and Mogul— spying on Soviets instead of the weather. It can't be accidental that the 509th Bomb Group, the special unit that vaporized Hiroshima and the only unit capable in 1947 of using atomic weapons, was in charge at Roswell. And we know for sure that Area 51 is the top-secret military reservation where Lockheed Skunk Works developed its U-2; the CIA, its SR-71 Blackbird drone; and the Pentagon, its F-117 Stealth fighter, which—along with other "black" aircraft like the robotic Aurora, the titanium-alloy Orient Express, the batlike Black Manta and the whale-shaped flying Shamu, plus the usual red darters, orange orbs and green magnesium flares dropped by test pilots to decoy heat-seeking missiles and the usual MIG Ferrets picked up at an Israeli swap meet—are likely to be what ufologists have actually seen in the desert night sky, when they aren't just stoned on crystal meth. But I'm getting ahead of myself, and *Dreamland* won't even be published until August.

Whereas, according to Jodi Dean in *Aliens in America: Conspiracy Cultures From Outerspace to Cyberspace*, 27 percent of Americans told Gallup they believe aliens have visited; 17 percent told *Time*/CNN they believe in alien abduction, 65 percent that a U.F.O. crashed in Roswell, and 80 percent that the Feds are covering up what they know; and another 2 percent told Roper they had been abducted themselves, which translates into 3.7 million adults—and since many claim multiple kidnappings, we are talking about an air-traffic control nightmare. I'd like to know more about these people. Are they mostly male/female; whiter than black, Asian, Latino; Catholic, Protestant, Jewish, Muslim; likelier to have graduated from high school or college; watching paranoirs; left-handed gun-owning pro-life Perot voters; previously therapized; lactose-intolerant? Dean says the UFO community "combines a reasonable replication of the demographics of the United States (tilted toward the white middle class)," but the footnote to which she directs us concedes: "At present, I can't provide solid evidence for this statement." She also asserts that "a common (though mistaken, classist, and elitist) view is that people who believe in UFOs are poor, uneducated, white, and usually American. Poll data suggests otherwise." But for this assertion there isn't even a footnote, much less poll data.

Never you mind. Dean is a Cult Stud at Hobart and William Smith Colleges who has gone to waterbed with a scrum of psyclops and seen in the flickering light "apocalyptic modes of truth." At least she's upfront in believing what the abductees say—about those missing minutes, and "absence [that] itself marks an alien encounter," the tracking devices and the sex crimes. Cult Studs usually hide their cards behind their patter, as if what they really believed about the data they massage were less important than the flashdance of their minds at play among riotous signifiers. This was Carl Jung's game when he was quizzed on flying saucers in 1958. He wrote a little book, *Ein moderner Mythus: Von Dingen, die am Himmel gesehen werden*, in which it mattered not at all to Carl whether the "archetypal circles in the sky" were real or "symbolical rumors"; he just maundered on instead about "the shape of the center," icons as "weightless as thought," mandalas, rotundums, "lenticular" galactic shapes and God's watching eyeball. The man was his own cave, inside of which it is impossible to distinguish the Swiss cuckoo from the fascist tom-tom.

Still, Dean tricks up belief with obligatory buzz: "Advocating these alien experiences as worthy of serious attention is effected by appropriating the discourse of therapy . . . [Therapists] access the production of those feelings and experiences, pointing to a truth beyond the witness." This truth is, naturally, postmodern and "consensual," based on "the intensity and authenticity of the emotions a person expresses while hypnotized and the consistency of the person's memory with those of other abductees." It stands in principled opposition not only to the "governmental-juridical discourse" and "the dominant rationality" of "elite, official 'arbiters of reality' " but to what John Mack at Harvard calls "the Western scientific paradigm." Moreover, since "various Marxists, feminists, and multiculturalists have stressed the importance of knowledge gained at the margins; the importance of the standpoint of the oppressed as epistemologically superior to the falsely disembodied, disconnected view from nowhere," the very stigma attached to belief in UFOs "enables the alien to function as an icon for some difficult social problems"—like illegal aliens (from, of course, Third Worlds), alienated labor, AIDS, NASA, the New World Order, anxieties about breeding, miscegenation and hybridity, repressed sexualities, silenced subjectivities, boundary breakdowns and border transgressions associated with "end-of-the-century culture" and "end-time strangeness."

Perhaps I'm falsely disembodied, but the view from my nowhere is that real oppression is a lot heavier than not being believed when you go on *Ricki Lake*, while still selling thousands of copies of your book about what they did to your Bermuda Triangle in the Teilhardian noosphere. Even if the S/M script the hypnotherapists write for "abductees" does less damage to our neighborhoods than the Black Mass fairy tales they sanction about tortured tots and bloody bunnies at the local daycare center, I still wonder which films these psyclops go to, which comic books they lip-read and whether it's ever occurred to them that "the intensity and authenticity" of an emotion no more warrants our respect than liking hip-hop and hating breakfast; says even less about why we get up in the morning; and says *nothing* about whether the individual experiencing these emotions is confused or bonkers—headed to an abductee support group or, in Nike sneakers, to Heaven's Gate.

Mark Seltzer, a Cornell Cult Stud, has just published a jazz riff similar to Dean's, except on the Sons of Sam among us instead of the Whitley Striebers. *Serial Killers: Death and Life in America's Wound Culture* doesn't belong in this particular body bag, but Seltzer's notion of "the pathological public sphere" is as vivid as it is instructive:

> shock and trauma; states of injury and victim status; the wound, the disease, the virus, and epidemics of violence; disaster, accident, catastrophe, and mass death; the abnormal normality of paranoia and psychosis; the pornography of mass-mediated desires and other forms of addiction and artificial life. The subject, on this model, can experience the social only as an intervention or invasion from without . . . Along these lines, history and psychology, reality and fantasy, change places.

If one picks among sample populations who've been stigmatized, oppressed and "reinscripted"—and chooses to ignore old-fashioned categories like women, blacks, Latinos, gays, the downsized and immune-deficient—*why not* serial killers instead of alien abductees? Or nuns, bulimics, performance artists, computer illiterates, sanitation engineers, surfer bums, White House interns, Deadheads and Camille Paglia? Smokers, vegans, drag queens, mimes, the firstborn, the lastborn, the adopted or the cloned? Pop goes the pomo weasel.

> There is an old bon mot sometimes ascribed to Sir Hamilton A. R. Gibb of Oxford . . . that every Arab word has its primary meaning, then its opposite meaning, then something to do with a camel, and lastly something obscene. Similarly, it was said at Harvard, when I was there in the

'60s, that every Sanskrit word means itself, its opposite, a name of God, and a position in sexual intercourse.

(Wendy Doniger, *The Implied Spider*)

Why saucers? That's easy. Patton reports in *Dreamland* that on June 24, 1947, a pilot near Mount Rainier in Washington saw nine objects "as shiny as mirrors" flying at tremendous speed in a "boomerang" formation, and later told an Oregon newspaper columnist that they "flew like a saucer would if you skipped it across the water." The Associated Press picked up the story, and in its version the objects changed from flying like a saucer into "saucer-like" objects, and then into "flying saucers."

Why polliwogs? Whence this recent consensus that the long-distance Other is, to quote Dean, a "hairless, chalky-colored creature with large black eyes," looking like a froggy preborn fetus? It is certainly the dominant trope of the paranoir, as well as TV commercials for air fresheners, skateboard accessories, Volkswagens, Diet Coke, Kodak film, AT&T cell phones, Milky Way candy bars, Rice Krispies and Stove Top stuffing. Dean links this Fetal Chic less to obsessiveness about abortion or Spielberg's 1977 flying-harmonica movie *Close Encounters of the Third Kind* than to "anxieties around reproduction, mothering, and the capacity to protect one's children," as well as to Christa McAuliffe's death in the 1986 Challenger explosion, which "opened cultural imaginings of space to the sacrifice and victimization of women." In fact, as Thomas Disch tells us in *The Dreams Our Stuff Is Made Of: How Science Fiction Conquered the World*, the hairless androgyne is as old as Poe's "Mesmeric Revelation" ("you will have a distinct idea of the ultimate body by conceiving of it to be entire brain") and later elaborated by H. G. Wells, whose Martians in *The War of the Worlds* were "heads—merely heads. Entrails they had none." Natural selection got rid of everything except the brain.

Reverse this evolutionary torque, and what we get swimming up the phylogenetic ladder is at first fishy, then froggy and finally Frankenstein. Factor in punk rock and skinheads, not to mention Sinead O'Connor doing her Vatican rag. (I won't get into the needy mother in Sigourney Weaver's *Alien* movies or the missing father and lost child in Spielberg.) Aliens in the TV paranoirs are either white and bald, or black and buggy, unless they're angels. I'm reading Disch because he traces the origins of Whitley Strieber's bestselling "nonfiction" traumatic seizures—the latest of which, *Confirmation*, is full of hard evidence of Whitleys among us, all of them on a diet rich in Striebers—back to remarkable prefigurations in his earlier fantasy fictions that hardly sold at all, much as another second-rate sci-fi novelist, L. Ron Hubbard, would only make a bundle when he started a religion. While Disch's real business is a witty and cranky ramble through the pulp form—sex, drugs, rock and roll and J. G. Ballard— with digressions on right-wing politics, an overindulgence of Heinlein, a back-of-the-hand to Ursula Le Guin and a once-over-far-too-lightly for Frank Herbert and cyberpunk (no Pat Cadigan, no Neal Stephenson!), he is briskly dismissive of Roswell as the Atlantis, Mu and Oz of UFO believers. He also reminds us just how banal the aliens are that we meet in abduction scenarios, compared with the aliens in sci-fi. This accords with my own instinct that visitors from, say, Sirius the Dog Star won't look like anything we're capable of imagining; that we'll *know* they are alien because they'll *look* it—not even insecticidal or reptilian, but maybe enzymes, crystals or bacteria; a Trekkie Borg-like Hive, a Net-scape bot, a waste-product virus or a few hummed bars of dodecahedral music.

Why abduction, and all that hanky-panky with eggs and sperm? We are warming up for the Apocalypse. We've got the millennial jitters. Not only from Daniel in the Old Testament, and Revelation in the New, but from The Second Book of Esdras, the Syriac Apocalypse of Baruch, the Dead Sea War Scroll and the William poems of Blake and Butler Yeats—we dread unsealed books, lakes of fire and Judgment Day. Each troubled age embodies its own worst fears in devil worship or demonic possession; in Lilith, Grendel or Caliban; in Gog, Moloch and Minotaurs; in cannibals, vampires, furies, centaurs, gorgons, hellhounds, Norns and Hydras; in the dragon, the mermaid and the Sphinx. The difference in the past was that the image of this dread was propagated in the temple or the asylum, instead of mass-merchandised by the hypnotherapeutic media.

There used to be fairies, goblins, trolls, pooks, gnomes, snow maidens, munchkins, sylphs and hobbits who seized and transported us to other dimensions, where time got funny. There used to be saints, Christian or Sufic and variously possessed by Clouds of Unknowing, Uncreated Light, ecstasy and automatic writing. There have always been freaks—Wild Men and Missing Links, wolfboys and zombies, witches and geeks. (See the dwarf in the art of Raphael, Mantegna, Velázquez, Carreño, Carpaccio, VanDyck, Veronese and Goya.) Manticores, hippogriffs and the seven-breasted Black Diana of Ephesus! You needn't be a Steven Marcus to have noticed that repressed Victorian sexuality caused lots of ghost stories. When the 509th Bomb Group dropped Big Boy on Hiroshima, we got Godzilla, the first radiation mutant—after which, a cold war full of bad-seed aliens, of Triffids, Pods, Blobs, and Body Snatchers, man-eating dandelions, meteoric slimeballs, blood-sucking carrots and collectivized Bolshevik killer ants. Why not, then, just in time for the Second Coming, a spectral regiment of the Unborn—a Casper the Hermaphroditic Ghost? Fearing (and desiring, too) to be Possessed, we get the Dracula we deserve.

> Leopards break into the temple and drink to the dregs what is in the sacrificial pitchers; this is repeated over and over again; finally it can be calculated in advance, and it becomes a part of the ceremony.
>
> (Franz Kafka, "Leopards in the Temple")

What Phil Patton brings to this groaning board is a brilliant book in which nothing is as it seems, while everything has a rational explanation, and yet, even so, the "rational" is its own sort of Dracula. "You know," he is told by a droll acquaintance, "trailer parks cause tornadoes. It's a scientific fact." To which Patton replies: "And maybe deserts cause UFOs?" But it is the military bases and secret research facilities located in those deserts—"the presence of all that strange and frightening weaponry"—that disposes people to see discs and lights.

His Dreamland, although an episode of *The X-Files* removed it to Utah, is in the Emigrant Valley of southern Nevada, "the Shangri-La, the Forbidden Temple of black, or secret, aircraft . . . set inside 4,742 square miles of restricted airspace and four million acres of bomb range—a space as big as a Benelux nation. It would come to be called by many names: Groom Lake, Watertown, Paradise Ranch, Home Base, Area 51." He also calls it "Pentagonia," a "junction of the twin ideologies of nuclear power and air power," whose "invisible culture" casts "a great shadow" on the reciprocating "culture of ufology—the antimatter of the matter."

At its perimeter—from Bald Mountain or Freedom Ridge—both sides are looking at each other through nightscopes and scanners. Inside are the military drones and their black engineers. Outside, uneasily complicit, are the "youfers" (the saucer-heads) and the "stealthies" (hoping for a glimpse of the latest "silver bullet" that will render America invincible to its many enemies).

For the youfer, Dreamland is Area 51, Hangar 18, MJ-12 and Level 5;

gravity waves and Zeta Reticuli; secret bases on both moon and Mars, plus "genetic interventions"; "omnibeams," "etherians" and Ashtar; igloo-shaped ships and space-women with names like Lyra; the planet Clarion, the voice of A-lan, the lost continent of Lemuria and beautiful Venusians mating with apes; gray robots in serfdom to preying mantises, hybrids incubated for their vital enzymes, surveillance orbs the size of basketballs and "Dream Police"; not to dwell on the manufacture of time-warp saucers by escaped Nazi scientists in league with the alien "Serpent People" at the center of a hollow earth.

For a stealthie, this "secret city" is where all the spy planes come from; only as alien as our government is to its citizens; no more peculiar, really, than sister installations in an archipelago of Pentagonias, of nuclear labs, ballistic-missile ranges, spy-satellite consoles and radar test stations from White Sands and Los Alamos to China Lake and El Mirage, from Tikaboo and Tonopah to the Blue Cube of Sunnyvale; a "black-budget" world of ramjet engines and nuclear cannons, waste spills and weapons accidents, fallout, cancers and white spots the size of silver dollars on dead deer; walking tanks, robot planes, laser light, Darkstar, Black Yak, Teal Rain, Have Blue, Project Grudge—and no more singular, either, considering the existence abroad of similar warrior mindscapes like Machrihanish, Kapstan Yar, Tyuratum, and Lop Nor.

Patton, of course, is a stealthie. He likes some of the youfers, but he grew up a childhood nut about airplanes, and knows what he sees in the night sky, and never met an angel or an alien (that "huge fetus or hungry child, with big Keene kid eyes . . . an echo of Munch's *Scream*—the very face of modern angst!") or bought into the eighties craze for abduction (with "its sexual and personal obsessions—I was taken because I was special, I was abused—tied in with talk-show psychology"). And although his well-furnished mind is more at home with the poems of Wallace Stevens and the Edo prints of Hiroshige than joysticking with the Stealth pilots as they practice-bomb America in the dark (Minnesota boat docks, Denver highrises), what really riles this wonderful writer and civilized man—and what all of us, including Agent Mulder, ought to be worried about more than E.T.—is the kidnapping of democracy by black budgeteers in a shadow republic, who even now spend $40 billion a year on secret weapons for a stealthy Star Wars wet dream.

After the Gulf War, you'll be happy to know, the Air Force let Annie Leibovitz snap a shot of a Stealth for *Vanity Fair*. And in the twilight zone of Area 51, where citizens are not allowed, the desert tortoise has made a comeback, and the western snowy plover and long-billed curlew, the kit fox and the mountain lion, four species of bat and six kinds of rattlesnake.

JULY 6, 1998

BULWORTH AGONISTES

Patricia J. Williams

•

Patricia J. Williams is a *Nation* columnist and professor of law at Columbia University. In 1993, Harvard University Press published Williams's *The Alchemy of Race & Rights* to widespread critical acclaim. Her most recent book is *The Rooster's Egg*.

I RARELY GO to the movies. I get panicked in echoey, dark places filled with crunching, slurping strangers while flat figures thrash and shout on a giant screen. All the more remarkable that I've gone to see Warren Beatty's political farce *Bulworth* three times now, trying to figure out what I think about it. For flat figures, some of the characters are pretty provocative. For a popular medium, it's pretty radical. And for a polemic about PACs, it's both unusually pointed and howlingly funny.

I know, the movie has its shortcomings. It's true that Beatty does black people only marginally better than anyone else in Hollywood, but he knows power, if not the ghetto, and this movie is effective precisely because it takes on the issue of power. And I'm not as concerned as some that there aren't more middle-class black people in it—yes, I'd like to see more of us boogie types in films generally, but, to be fair, *Bulworth* isn't about race alone; more specifically, it's about racism's intersection with America's deep, and growing, class divide. And, yes, similar social statements by black filmmakers haven't got a quarter of the attention or, more likely, haven't got made at all, but that's a larger problem of the movie industry's production choices, not a criticism of Beatty per se. Indeed, *Bulworth* parodies Beatty's own privilege in this regard relentlessly and quite cleverly.

Nor am I as concerned as some that Beatty's rendering of rap music is a white appropriation of black youth culture—he's far too over the top to be just another Ace Ventura. "Damn," says an amazed black child in the film, struggling for descriptive precision, "Is that how white people rap?" No, not really, not even, not hardly. Bulworth, as mad Homeric hip-hop soothsayer, is beyond appropriation, beyond mere parody. Watching him play the pagan naïf with second sight, one is reminded that some scholars hypothesize that the Delphic oracle was located atop rich deposits of natural gas. Beatty as Bulworth is sui generis, a Jabberwock wiffling off to do battle with frumious bandersnatches, a bizarre life form unto himself.

For all that, I guess I kept going back because I am amazed by a movie this overtly left wing, fearless and eccentric; or maybe I just went to hear the words "universal healthcare" spoken out loud. In any event, *Bulworth* is a smart, funny, hopeful movie, filled with the possibility of reform. The ambivalent, tremulously human side of even the most untoward characters shimmers just beneath the surface. It's downright refreshing to see anyone in Hollywood take such stands, such risks.

Yet despite the range of *Bulworth*'s controversial aspects, the most-discussed issue in the media has been not its take on healthcare or the insurance industry or campaign finance but the interracial relationship between the sixtyish Bulworth and the balefully beautiful and very young flygirl played by Halle Berry. Most editorializing about the movie has treated Berry as though she were Beatty's own black Monica Lewinsky. For a while I kept getting calls from reporters asking, Isn't it novel! exciting! touching! revolting! I kept wanting to reply with the same question that one of the black characters asks a crowd of reporters at the very end of the movie, when the two kiss publicly: "What's the matter, haven't you ever seen this before?"

Bulworth is a wild dream of a movie, a *West Side Story*–ish allegory, a collage of symbols and telescoped meanings. Perhaps its limitation is that the image of social unity as miscegenation, while well and good as metaphor, is rendered a bit too literally for an American audience, and thus never escapes the paradigm of sexual politics parading as *Realpolitik*. Berry's role never quite rises above the most ancient of clichés: Tragic Mulatta as bridge between black and white; between hope and despair, good and bad, sane and insane; the positive and negative divided by two, multiplied by sex. (I will concede, though, that Berry is rather less wilted a gardenia than your average tragic mulatta: "Nobody's going to kill you," she soothes like a gentle mother as she removes from the folds of her tooled leather garb a hunk of sci-fi weaponry with a barrel the approximate size of a grandfather clock.)

If I were writing the ending to *Bulworth*, I'd embellish that stuff where he sputters on about how insecure he is as a white man and she has to reassure him that he's her "nigger," and then the next thing you know he gets shot by the corporate lobbyist. I'd add on a little coda in which she shyly—no, coyly—confesses her insecurity about being politically disenfranchised and he rushes to reassure her that he's her ever-lovin' honky mentor. Then he'd get shot. Probably faster than before. (But that's why I'll never be writing screenplays for anyone but *The Nation*: My mushiest moments of romantic longing are all about access to resources rather than sex.)

I guess this is why I was disappointed to hear Beatty quoted in a number of publications reducing his own movie to the literal proposition that "fucking everyone until they're all the same color" will eliminate racism, echoing, I suppose, Arthur Schlesinger's earlier and somewhat more academic pronouncement that "we can count on sex and love to defeat those who would disunite America." Fine, if it's true. But much of the self-congratulation around this issue is too frequently a diversion from confronting the hard facts of complicated political fragmentation. Take Lani Guinier, for example, dubbed, drubbed and mocked by the media as our very own "quota queen." Where was the celebration of her existence as the glorious product of an interracial union—a black father and white mother—the melded hope of a future beyond race? When it comes down to the nuts and bolts of political trench warfare, in other words, "procreative racial deconstruction," as Beatty calls it, means diddly.

But I digress. It's a pity there isn't room left to discuss that little matter of universal healthcare. Oh, well. Hollywood can do only so much. Real love, real politics, all that is up to us.

NOVEMBER 16, 1998

THE CLINTON-DOUGLAS DEBATES

Christopher Hitchens

•

Christopher Hitchens, a longtime contributor to *The Nation*, has been a columnist for the magazine since 1982. He is also a columnist for *Vanity Fair*. His latest book is *New York Times* bestseller *No One Left to Lie To: The Triangulations of William Jefferson Clinton*. He once wrote and presented a television show for Britain's Channel 4 titled *J'Accuse: Spike Lee*.

SPEAKING TO AN audience on Martha's Vineyard a few days after ordering the destruction, by a volley of cruise missiles, of a factory in Khartoum, Bill Clinton was at his huskiest. Worse, he was at his most confiding:

> I was here on this island up till 2:30 in the morning, trying to make absolutely sure that at that chemical plant there was no night shift. I believed I had to take the action I did, but I didn't want some person who was a nobody to me—but who may have a family to feed and a life to live and probably had no earthly idea what else was going on there—to die needlessly.

At the time, I remember being both nauseated and impressed. Nauseated by the mock-compassionate and pseudo-humanitarian bilge that the man was uttering. (It was around the thirty-fifth anniversary of Dr.

King's celebrated address to the March on Washington, so he was milking his famous "comfort level around black Americans" on top of the usual lip-biting horror show. How better to commemorate Dr. King than by committing random mayhem in Africa and then blubbering to African-Americans?) And impressed, almost as never before, by the absolute contempt he shows for his listeners, and the pathetic transparency of his mendacious devices. Glance at the above sentences and you will see a President and Commander in Chief essentially saying that the Al-Shifa plant in Khartoum must have been a chemical-weapons facility because, among other reasons, it wasn't even guarded at night.

Now Rob Reiner tells a mutual friend that he remembers what Michael Douglas says, while attempting to get Annette Bening to disrobe in that forgettable movie *The American President*. Seeking, as who indeed would not (we all do it, all Presidents have done it, well almost all, let's have no sexual McCarthyism, it's no big deal, how would *you* like to be asked about this stuff?), to get into the underwear of a female lobbyist by exposing his human and thoughtful and reflective side, Douglas tells her:

> Somewhere in Libya right now, a janitor is working the night shift at Libyan intelligence headquarters. And he's going about doing his job because he has no idea that in about an hour he's going to die in a massive explosion.

When Ronald Reagan did this sort of thing, recycling lines from bad movies to justify policies—like Star Wars—that were wicked as well as fantasy-driven, there were expressions of polite concern. But that was then. As a matter of fact, a huge appropriation for a Star Wars program was contained in Clinton's much-ballyhooed budget deal, but I notice that subject, too, has been dropped by the intelligentsia.

Actually, one poor and anonymous man was randomly killed in the rocketing of Sudan. I don't suppose that the President has lost a wink of sleep over him, although he may well have had a family to feed and undoubtedly a life to live and most certainly had no earthly idea what was going on, or indeed what had hit him. Moreover, a very large number of people going to die, or are dying now, as a direct result the destruction of a poor nation's chief product medicines and agricultural pesticides. And everyone knows how this works in an underdeveloped country; it is the children and the old people, and those who are already sick who die when the medicines and the antibiotics and even the analgesics fail to show up. I look at Bill Clinton's face—I can force myself to do it—and ask: "People are put to death to save *that*?"

This is, as far as I know, the only time in recent history when a President has made war on civilians for a contemptibly obvious personal and political motive and escaped without any protest from the traditional stage army of the good. And it's not as if, as in precedent cases, the ghastly truth only emerged after a leak, lapse of time. Four of the five members of the Joint Chiefs of Staff were excluded from the hurried decision to bomb, and as Seymour Hersh, who has tried brilliantly to ventilate the subject, put it recently, those men "had an explanation for why they were cut out." They were cut out because they would have said 'no.' "

Most of the evidence for their doubts was in plain view right away, and quite a few ordinary civilians were so "ironic" and "cynical" that they even gaily mentioned *Wag the Dog* on the day of the bombing itself. But irony and cynicism, as people have an interest in forgetting, are not mere mannerisms, or "coping skills" for dealing with the post-modern. They originate in hard won and dearly bought experience. What if, dear sir or ma'am, your apt cultural reference to a recent clever and weightless motion picture turns out not to need those smirking "air-quotes" you are so goddamned fond of? What if you are speaking, or have come upon by accident, the literal truth? As soon as the implications of this question became plain, individuals who had seldom got anything so right in their whole lives dropped the ironic act and went back to being obedient citizens who didn't like Ken Starr, either, and wanted to move the country forward or at any rate to "move on."

The presidential "approval ratings" actually went "up" a bit after Cruise Missile Day. ("A bounce," we were coldly assured, is the customary reward for such operations, and no more or less than the President deserved.) I have become intrigued by these same ratings. People tell me confidently that the "numbers" express satisfaction with the economy, and also dissatisfaction with moral conservatism. The collectors of these numbers must be jolly good at their "job." I sometimes wonder what it would take to bring them down (the numbers, I mean). People were unmoved, we were told, by the campaign finance scandal as well. They were unmoved by Bosnia, too. But they must have like something about Clinton of Khartoum, or they wouldn't have awarded him any extra points. Myself, I have concluded on no better evidence that the masses look upon politics as a private matter. Why shouldn't they? Meanwhile, it's not *Wag The Dog*, stupid. It's *The American President*.

APRIL 5/12, 1999

LOOKING FOR MR. RIGHT

WHO'S RUNNING THE CONSERVATIVE CLUB IN TOWN?

David Corn

•

David Corn is the Washington editor of *The Nation*. He is the author of *Blond Ghost: Ted Shackley and the CIA's Crusades* and a novel *Deep Background*.

"I AM IT."

So says sixties-radical-turned-eighties-conservative David Horowitz, with a chuckle, when asked to describe conservative political activity in Hollywood. It's a boast and a lament. A decade ago, Horowitz took it upon himself to challenge the political atmosphere of this stronghold of liberalism. For years, he had been decrying The Left—in his mind, a well-oiled, coherent and influential movement deserving capital letters—and its power in the media and academia. Setting his sights on Hollywood, as if a right-wing *nudzh* could alter the tenor of Tinseltown, was a mark of Horowitz's hubris. But he has had a dash of success. There is now an organized, if small, conservative outfit in town. It has no discernible influence on the product of Hollywood, no noticeable impact on electoral or issue-oriented politics. But about once a month, Horowitz pulls together a couple of hundred right-of-center people from the entertainment industry and elsewhere to hear a speaker from the world of politics—say, George Will or Newt Gingrich. This group gathers at a fancy hotel, schmoozes and listens. It does not raise money or agitate for conservative causes or candidates. It merely offers a haven for Hollywooders who don't fit the liberal Democrat stereotype. In a community where only a few actually bother with politics and fewer do anything that can be considered right of center, the 60-year-old Horowitz has created a cell of his own—with cocktails.

To open the Hollywood front in his crusade against The Left, Horowitz formed the Wednesday Morning Club, a group that now has about 170 members. The group was established the morning after Bill Clinton's victory in 1992—hence the name—but its origins stretch back to 1980. That year, Lionel Chetwynd, an accomplished screenwriter (*The Apprenticeship of Duddy Kravitz*), was working with the Ronald Reagan campaign and hosting meetings where Reagan boosters talked up their candidate before Hollywood denizens. After a session featuring supply-side guru Arthur Laffer, Stanley K. Sheinbaum, a prominent LA liberal, chastised the attendees for flirting with Reaganism. "Sheinbaum pointed his finger and said, 'You are consorting with people who ran the Hollywood blacklist. I know who you are and I know where you work,' " Chetwynd recalls. "It was chilling. No one came back. A lot of people said, 'I'm with you, but don't tell anyone.' " (Sheinbaum vaguely remembers the event but does not recall being openly hostile.)

After that, Chetwynd, who was born in Britain and raised in Canada, backed away from electoral politics. Following the 1987 release of his film *The Hanoi Hilton*, a movie about American POWs that conservatives embraced, Horowitz sought out Chetwynd. It took Horowitz several years to persuade Chetwynd to saddle up for his effort to break The Left's hold on Hollywood. After Clinton won in 1992, Chetwynd was willing to take another stab at corralling Hollywood's cons. "I had had nightmares about the Sheinbaum episode," Chetwynd, 55, says. "But I felt that if we cannot have an alternative view here, it's bad for the Republic. We create the popular culture here, and there's no political debate in Hollywood? That cannot be healthy."

The two set up the Wednesday Morning Club in the office that houses Horowitz's think tank, the Center for the Study of Popular Culture. (In 1997 the center received $500,000 from right-wing billionaire Richard Mellon Scaife.) Horowitz and Chetwynd recruited actor Tom Selleck, entertainment power-lawyer Bruce Ramer (who represents Steven Spielberg) and writer-producer Bob Gale for the steering committee. Soon the club was drawing A-list politicos, mainly Republicans, as speakers. Occasionally a star or two were present at the events, but sometimes Pat Sajak was the most recognizable face. Last April, Texas Governor George W. Bush spoke at a club breakfast before 500 people. He assailed "moral decay" in America but steered clear of Hollywood-bashing. "I advocate abstaining from sex until you find your right life partner," he remarked. Senator Orrin Hatch appeared before the group and gripped, "When I come out here [for a fund-raiser] I get about $30,000. For Gore, it's about $2 million."

In January of 1998, Newt Gingrich addressed the club but ducked the hot-button, entertainment-related issues. (It had taken Horowitz three years of badgering to convince Gingrich to visit. "He felt Hollywood was a Democratic town, and the Republicans couldn't pick up any money here," Horowitz explains.) In March, more than 200 gathered at a club dinner at the Beverly Hills Hotel to hear journalist/pundit Chris Matthews. When he slammed Clinton and the "Vichy Democrats," the crowd applauded. When he referred to the "innate goodness" of his friend Al Gore, audience members hissed.

This is not hard-core politics. At the Matthews event, several participants said they valued the club because it allowed them to hobnob with like-minded individuals. "People come here for the enjoyment," one non-entertainment lawyer noted. "It's mostly social," said Midge Elias, a nutrition writer.

Horowitz claims only modest intentions for the group. "Lionel and I did not aim to change the Hollywood culture," he explains. "We have tried to end the McCarthy-like treatment of people in Hollywood who do not subscribe to the line of the liberal left. It was set up not to carry out a political agenda but to normalize Republicans." Horowitz's vision of Hollywood is harsh: "Republicans are treated like Communists during the cold war. Republicans are seen by The Left as indecent, lacking in compassion. . . . The atmosphere in Hollywood is as bad as it was in the McCarthy period. True, there are no Congressional committees [pursuing conservatives] and no blacklist maintained by the studios, but a lot of people lose jobs daily in this town [because of their conservative beliefs]. Nobody can show you the proof of that for the obvious reason that no one wants to lose more work. The power in Hollywood is all on The Left. There's a graylist." And apparently this keeps conservative celebs from speaking out. "If there were a Susan Sarandon or Alec Baldwin of the right," Horowitz argues, "The Left would severely punish that person."

Can the power of The Left in Hollywood be that awesome? After all, Elia Kazan, who snitched on fellow Communists in the fifties, was voted a lifetime award by the Oscar pooh-bahs over objections from remnants of the old Hollywood left. "That the award would pose a problem," Horowitz says, "is an index of the power of The Left."

LEFT OUT?

Not all of Horowitz's compatriots feel besieged by an oppressive leftism haunting Hollywood. "People have been asking me for thirty-five years if I was losing jobs because of my conservative politics," says Charlton Heston. "I've never felt that was the case." Neither does Rob Long, a successful, 34-year-old sitcom writer and club member. "It's never been tough for me," he remarks. "The default position in this town is liberal. But they don't run you out of town if you're not. The worst I've gotten for being conservative is bemused indifference. That's not so bad." Long notes that he has never heard of anyone not being hired in Hollywood because of politics. "I've read many film scripts from conservative writers. They're god-awful and deserve not to go anywhere. It's much easier, though, to lull yourself to sleep at night saying I'm not being hired because of my politics." On the set of *Cheers*, Long worked happily with two of the town's most notable lefties: Ted Danson and Woody Harrelson: "They were interested in talking issues with me. They were incredibly respectful and thoughtful."

Actor Kurt Russell, a registered Libertarian often misidentified as a conservative or a Republican, says that a few times he has been told that someone in the industry did not want to work with him because of his presumed politics. "I was surprised it would make any difference," he comments. "But I don't pay much attention to it. The bottom line here is the color green. And, in the end, they will find a way to shut their ears or eyes to make money in this town, and I'm very much for that." Edgar Scherick, a veteran mini-series producer and a Wednesday Morning Club steering committee member, recalls that in his decades-long career, he has seen "one or two occasions when a writer was deemed too conservative to get a job, but they got it because I stood up and said, it's ridiculous." And Chetwynd, who frets about liberal groupthink in Hollywood, acknowledges that his own career has not been hindered by anticonservative bias: "My political views are tolerated because I'm a good salesman and I do my job well."

Although Horowitz insists political discrimination is rampant and ideological intolerance rules, he maintains that his Hollywood campaign strives for no more than "to restore dialogue in the entertainment community. We've established a civil place." He wants to be a "bridge-builder" who engineers "honest debate."

This is the kinder, gentler David Horowitz, an author and jouster otherwise known as a fierce ideological warrior. Last year, after Steve Wasserman, editor of the *Los Angeles Times Book Review*, sliced in half a brief commentary Horowitz had written on *The Communist Manifesto* for a forum in the review, Horowitz sent a scorching letter to the publisher asserting that "Wasserman has an agenda in defending Marx." (Months earlier, Horowitz had praised Wasserman as a "fair-minded" fellow who had "improved" the book section.) At a recent talk at Harvard, Horowitz declared, "Inside every Leftist lurks a totalitarian" (not much bridge-building there). He assailed author/academic Cornel West as "an empty intellectual suit, he's not that smart, and he got his place because of the scramble for black faces in the university." Horowitz recently bought an ad in *The New Republic* that announced he intends to out The Left. The ad claims The Left is absent from "the radar screen of American politics." Thus, under the headline "Who is Left?" he produced a *j'accuse* list pronouncing Hillary Rodham Clinton, Marion Wright Eddman [*sic*; he meant Edelman], Sydney [*sic*] Blumenthal and—what a shock!—Senators Paul Wellstone and Ted Kennedy as national figures of The Left. He "exposed" the causes of The Left: prison reform, affirmative action, a living wage. He also ID'd Senator Robert Torricelli, a devoted anti-Castroite, as a leftist. "We think," the ad shouted, "it is time to . . . identify the political left."

Is such simplistic pink-sheeting the work of a man who yearns merely for civil and honest exchange? "I have various incarnations," Horowitz explains. "On campuses, I'm confrontational. In Hollywood, I'm not confrontational at all. I defend this town. Oliver Stone has been to my events. I have participated in Alec Baldwin's events."

Nonsupporting Actors

Horowitz is lucky; he has no competition. In a company town, where thousands of people vie for each job, no one else is looking to be the Mr. Right who leads Hollywood's conservatives. Not even NRA president Charlton Heston, the elder statesman of Hollycons, attempts to recruit other film celebrities for the right. "I don't proselytize," he says. The vacuum Horowitz was able to fill existed partly because the heavies most often fingered as conservatives or Republicans—Bruce Willis, Arnold Schwarzenegger, Tom Selleck and Kevin Costner—have engaged in little overt political activity. Their politics, erratic or lacking coherence, have not been those of the committed.

In 1988 Willis attended a fundraiser for a Democrat running for Senate. The following year, he and Demi Moore worked with radical-to-legislator Tom Hayden to shut down a nuclear power plant in California. In a *Playboy* interview near that time, Willis sounded like the stereotypical Hollywood lib. Citing water pollution and ozone depletion, he moaned, "We are literally destroying the planet." He blasted Reagan for dubbing the Soviet Union "the evil empire." He said military corporations had killed the Kennedy brothers and were "setting up [Vice President] Bush to be the next President." Willis argued that "this country needs a leader who can say, 'I want to help the people.' " Who did he have in mind? Hayden, the darling of LA's left. Then, one presidential election later, Willis was at the Republican National Convention in Houston—backing Bush. In last year's *Armageddon*, Willis is first seen driving golf balls at a Greenpeace ship protesting oil drilling—a self-mocking reference to his politics but also a reminder of his dramatic flip-flop.

"He's 'Get off my back, I don't like taxes,' " says Horowitz. "It's basically leave-me-alone politics. He's not involved in anything." The same is true for Mel Gibson, who is known for opposing abortion rights and being critical of gay rights activism. "I've never even met him," Horowitz notes.

Kevin Costner is frequently cited as a celebrity Republican, although he no longer is. He did socialize and golf with President Bush, and in 1992 the Bush re-election campaign leaked word that he would appear in a commercial for the President. Costner, then a registered Republican, had no intention of aiding Bush, according to a close associate of Costner. He was a Clinton supporter. "We had to tell the Bush campaign to stop saying he was going to do ads," the associate says. Before the 1996 election, Costner switched his registration to Independent. He gave $5,000 to the Democratic Party and attended the Democratic convention. Still, he continues to receive invitations to GOP fundraisers, and in February the *New York Times* referred to him as a Republican. "He's not a particularly political guy," says the associate.

In the early nineties Tom Selleck shot a commercial for the conservative *National Review.* But in 1992 he made a $1,000 donation to the presidential bid of Democratic Senator Paul Tsongas. Five years later, *New York Times* columnist Maureen Dowd reported that Republicans were urging Selleck to run for the Senate in California—a story Selleck quickly shot down. His political profile has been low ever since. However, Heston reports that Selleck has agreed to do an ad for the NRA. "He's not a Republican," says an actor who knows him. "He's an independent." In assessing Selleck's politics, a former producer points to his last major role: a gay television reporter in the gay-friendly film *In & Out*. "That was not a role or a movie to please social conservatives," she observes.

In 1997, after undergoing heart surgery, Arnold Schwarzenegger quipped, "We made, actually, history, because it was the first time ever that doctors could prove that a lifelong Republican has a heart." But as a longtime GOPer, Schwarzenegger has provided little tangible support to his party. In recent years, according to federal campaign records, he made one measly contribution of $1,000 to the Republicans. "He campaigns occasionally for the national Republican ticket, but he doesn't make a big deal out of it," says an LA publicist. In 1992 Schwarzenegger joined George Bush in New Hampshire and asked voters to "send a message to Pat Buchanan: *Hasta la vista,* baby." When Jesse Ventura, who has appeared in two Schwarzenegger films, was sworn in as Minnesota governor, Schwarzenegger attended the inauguration, as a friend.

Kurt Russell is irritated that he gets tagged as a Republican and conservative. "Republicans will call me [soliciting contributions], and I'll say, 'Sorry, fellow, I'm not a Republican.' " Instead, he has bonded with the libertarian Cato Institute in Washington. Recently, he hosted a Cato dinner in Los Angeles with José Piñera, a labor minister under Chile's General Pinochet in the seventies. Piñera, who pioneered the privatization of Chile's retirement program, has been a crucial player in Cato's attempt to privatize Social Security. Russell votes for Libertarian candidates, but he does not provide financial or PR support to the party. When Gingrich appeared at the Wednesday Morning Club, Russell, who considers Gingrich a friend, introduced him. But Russell, who has not otherwise participated in the club, made sure to declare, "I'm not a Republican, I'm a Libertarian."

Alone in the Desert

There is only one conservative celebrity in Hollywood committed to serious partisan activism: Charlton Heston. Each election, he slogs along the campaign trail for GOPers across the country. Last year he aided a dozen Republicans, eight of whom won. He has his own political action committee, which in 1998 raised $168,000. (He has solicited donations at fundraisers by reciting the Ten Commandments.) Heston realizes he is one of the few Hollywood stars who devote themselves to the heavy lifting of politics. "Most people in the film community don't really understand what being politically active means," he says. "They think it is just doing interviews." And that includes Hollywood liberals: "I'm content that the Hollywood left thinks being a political activist means riding Air Force One and hanging out with the President."

But Heston doesn't let politics interfere with work. He has been cast in Oliver Stone's next film, and he just finished acting in a Warren Beatty movie. "We had a lot to talk about," he says of Beatty. "We agreed on a few things." Such as? "Beatty is nontypical of Hollywood liberals," Heston replies. "He thinks Clinton is an idiot." And many prominent liberals in the film industry, he adds, "are hunters, skeet shooters, or gun collectors, or keep a handgun because of their public prominence. It is not widely known that one of the finest gun collections on the West Coast is Steven Spielberg's. He shoots, but very privately."

Apart from Heston, the Hollywood right is not that right. Most folks associated with Horowitz's club are pro-choice. At the Chris Matthews event, several participants said the Republican Party had to go moderate to rebuild. Steering committee member Edgar Scherick noted that he "hates zealotry"; he was put off by House impeachment manager Bob Barr and opposed removing Clinton from office. Sitcom writer Rob Long concedes there may be a legitimate reason for right-leaning Hollywooders to eschew public identification with the GOP: "The Republicans can be kind of weird . . . Arnold Schwarzenegger has to worry that at any moment the Republicans will issue a platform calling for all gay people to be exterminated, and it would be very difficult to do business in this town if people think you believe that. If you look at Hollywood Republicans, you'll find pro-choice, country-club Republicans."

The Horowitz Gang is also at odds with the national conservative movement in the culture wars. Not surprisingly, Horowitz and his comrades do not wail about the culture manufactured by the hometown industry. "Hollywood deals in basic archetypes that are fundamentally conservative," Horowitz asserts. "The great empowering American myth is the individual against the system. That's *Star Wars*. It's a conservative message. I'm rather sanguine about Hollywood's product." One of his favorite films is *Pulp Fiction*; he claims he enjoys *South Park*, a raunchy animated cable show. He has urged self-appointed values-czar Bill Bennett to lower the volume on his public attacks against Hollywood. "I'm not in sympathy with ratings, the picketing of films, attacks on films," Horowitz explains. "The bottom line is what consumers want. If they like garbage, garbage will reign." Indeed, the Hollywood right can be downright liberal when it comes to content. "Nobody should tell anyone else what to produce," says Scherick. "That's the end of democracy. It's what Hitler did." Rob Long roots against the censors of the right: "I am a loyal Republican, but I don't want to see a show I'm working on lambasted by someone in my party." And even Heston, perhaps the only Hollywood rightist in complete sync with the social conservatives, dismisses efforts to control Hollywood's output. "I'm not going to be the monitor of my colleagues' choices," he remarks. "I have enough enemies as it is."

Eyes Are the Prize

What institutional Hollywood cares most about is putting eyeballs in front of televisions and backsides in theater seats. "Obviously, people interested in politics go to Washington, not Hollywood," Chetwynd observes. But for decades there has been a connection between the capitals of politics and entertainment. There's money in the showbiz community for candidates—mostly Democrats, but not exclusively. (Last October the Center for Responsive Politics noted that in the 1998 election cycle, movie, television and recording studios had so far donated $6.5 million to federal candidates and parties, with two-thirds going to Democrats.) A small number of stars speak out on issues they may or may not know well. Infrequently, a movie or TV show will handle a social or political issue. So the politics of the entertainment business attracts more attention than that of the paper-products industry. Yet, as Horowitz notes, "98 percent of the people in Hollywood have no politics to speak of, or their politics are an inch deep. People do what they have to do to get ahead in this town."

In Horowitz's script, that means they kowtow to The Left. But at least he has provided a chat group for those who don't. "We have created a platform in the entertainment community where a Henry Hyde can come and get a warm welcome and respectful hearing," says a justifiably proud Chetwynd. "The group is respectable. In that sense, David Horowitz has accomplished what he set out to do." The next frontier, Chetwynd reports, is to show the world—meaning Hollywood—that all conservatives are not the same. "Bill Clinton and his minions in Hollywood," Chetwynd explains, "have been successful in grouping conservatives as a monolithic band of extremists." Think of a mirror image of Horowitz's view of The Left. "We now have a social burden," Chetwynd continues. "I have to be allowed to be a conservative without people imagining I dress up in a bedsheet to have dinner with Bob Barr. People have to be able to believe you can be a conservative and still be a good person."

In Hollywood, that is the battle conservatives believe they are fighting. It is a skirmish unlikely to affect what occurs in Washington (or Sacramento), or what happens on the campaign trail, or what is coming soon to a theater near you.

April 3, 2000

Inside Indiewood

The Best of Times, the Worst of Times

Peter Biskind

•

THE NATION ASKED seven prominent members of the independent film community, including several filmmakers who released major films this year, to take the temperature of the movement at this moment of flux. Participating are Allison Anders (Sugar Town); Alexander Payne (Election); Kimberly Peirce (Boys Don't Cry); John Pierson, former filmmakers' rep and author of the bible on independents, Spike, Mike, Slackers and Dykes; David O. Russell (Three Kings); Kevin Smith (Dogma); and Christine Vachon, a producer of Boys Don't Cry, Happiness, Velvet Goldmine, and many other films. The interviews were conducted and edited by Peter Biskind.

Q: Historically, independents have defined themselves against Hollywood, but last year the studios made several movies that displayed many of the characteristics of independent films. Meanwhile, more and more independent directors are working within the studio system. What's going on here?

Allison Anders: *American Beauty* is not my idea of an independent movie. What was the budget on that? Like $30 million or something? And you've got these huge stars, Kevin Spacey and Annette Bening. Come on. That's the same scale as *The Graduate* was back in 1967. It's a studio movie for thinking adults, you know? It's a screenwriter's vision, not a director's vision. This guy [director Sam Mendes] is from England, doesn't know American culture. It's not like the Coen brothers where they're sitting there writing the script and cracking each other up and putting in fucking crazy-ass music and stuff. [Mendes] was a director-for-hire. My film *Sugar Town* opened the same weekend as *American Beauty*. If you have a choice between seeing an independent with [actors] you don't know and seeing *American Beauty* with stars in it, then you're like, Well, maybe I'll go see that. Which is what happened to Sugar Town.

John Pierson: Hey, look, David O. Russell is like my hero right now because here's a guy who made a no-budget film, *Spanking the Monkey*, and then made a midlevel Miramax screwball comedy, *Flirting With Disaster*, that seemed to me to be still very personal and really hilarious, and then *Three Kings*, making probably the most political film of the year—inside the studio system, like a termite. Putting George Clooney in the film and getting Warners to pay for it, that's great.

Q: So now it's OK for independents to work for studios?

Kevin Smith: Independent cinema is a myth. It was always kind of weird when people went, Yeah, you're an "indie." With the exception of *Clerks*, I've always made studio films—*Mallrats* for Universal, *Chasing Amy* and *Dogma* for Miramax, which is now a studio.

Christine Vachon: I'm wondering if "independent" ever really did mean anything, you know? When I started producing ten or twelve years ago, an independent film was essentially a movie that you managed to finance by conning your friends and relatives into giving you money for [it], and all the so-called independent films I worked on were some kind of permutation of that, like *Parting Glances* or the first film I produced, *Poison*. I guess independence was supposed to mean free from any kind of creative control. But it's very rare these days that any money is "free." Whether it's the studio telling you that you have to put a star in or an equity financier telling you that you have to put a star in, they're still both saying it. So what difference does it make if that money is coming from New Line or if its coming from Paramount or if it's coming from Joe Blow? Somebody wants to get their money back.

Q: What happens to independents when they end up in the belly of the beast? David, how did you land at Warner Brothers, traditionally one of the most conservative studios, known for mega-budget Kevin Costner vehicles, the *Lethal Weapon* series and so on?

David O. Russell: When I made my first two films, which could be considered classically independent, the studios would all meet with me and say "Come make a movie here." It was interesting to me to take them up on that hunger with a very subversive large film. To answer, "Will you really?" And keep saying "really" until they said no. But they never said no.

They showed me this straight-ahead action script about the Gulf War. I started doing some research and thought: Boy, this could be interesting. Take an action picture and put all these politics in it and a subversive attitude. I told them that, and they said, OK. I said, I don't want to do this and bring it back and have you freak out. They said, No, no, we've made these films with Oliver Stone and Martin Scorsese. The week I handed in my script there was an article in the *New York Times* lambasting Warner Brothers, saying it had bombed with dumb picture after dumb picture with very generic formulas and they need to work with more exciting filmmakers. I think that gave a lot of the young executives in the company hope. You know, they wanted to shake it up. Lorenzo di Bonaventura [of Warner Brothers] said to me at one point that if he couldn't take risks like this, he didn't want his job anymore.

There was one person at the studio who tried to stop me. He thought, "This movie is not a studio movie, and it should not be made." And he appealed to George Clooney, saying, "The politics of this film are going to make your life dangerous and you're going to come under a lot of heat. From both patriotic Americans and patriotic Muslims." But George stood up for the film, said to the executive, "I don't believe you."

Q: So what's happened? Are we seeing the greening of the studios?

Smith: I think it's the Miramaxization of the studio system. Like five years ago, would a studio have made *American Beauty*? Never! Would a studio have made something like *Three Kings*? Not nearly as quirky as David made it. It would have been a pretty much straight-down-the-middle war movie.

Russell: I think something has changed. I think the Sundance culture has definitely had an impact on the audiences of the United States—they've become more sophisticated—and also the studios. Ten years ago *Three Kings*—a war/action movie—or *Election*—a high school movie—would have been *Heartbreak Ridge* with Clint Eastwood, or—name a high school movie from ten years ago. Look at *The Talented Mr. Ripley*. On the face of it, it's a straight thriller, but at another level it's so dark and homosexual, you know, for a movie of that scale. But there are executives who yearn to work with independent-minded filmmakers and make the film that is different from the run-of-the-mill "product." Maybe I have a somewhat warped view, but I see plenty of that. My feeling is that many of them would be very happy to work with any of the directors in this forum, happy to make films like *Election* or *Boys Don't Cry*. Studios want to find that *Good Will Hunting* audience.

Pierson: Well, it's an astonishing development. I think they'll do more. With caution. But let's not get carried away.

Vachon: We certainly had the experience with studios that have been anxious to work with us and then have looked at how we actually make our movies and have basically said, You're crazy, we can't make a movie like that. It's not like we're such insane guerrilla filmmakers who are out there on the seat of our pants. It's just like with *Boys Don't Cry*, you're banking on a director that has virtually no experience. You're putting in as your star a kid who has only been on a television series. What studio in the world would have allowed that to happen? None of them!

Q: Kimberly, you got blown off by MGM, didn't you?

Kimberly Peirce: I showed *Boys Don't Cry* to MGM, and they got totally excited. They said, "We're green-lighting it." And I'm like, "Are you sure? Because if you green-light this picture I'm gonna quit my job." So I gave notice, flew out to LA, bought all these new clothes because you have to for the meeting, go in there, seems fine, but they just kind of dick around. It's no skin off their back because I'm nobody, right? Christine Vachon, who was my producer, she followed up, and it was like, "It's green-lit, well, maybe it's not green-lit," and then I'm like, "Well what color is it? Red? Is it off, is it on?" Meanwhile I'm back in New York and my bills are piling up. I did get my job back.

Q: Traditionally studios have been interested in skimming off the cream of the independent crop, but what often happens is that once they get them, they hamstring them. Did that happen to you, David?

Russell: They were most comfortable with the more traditional elements of *Three Kings*, the action elements. But we were always in a money fight, because they knew the film was dark and so they tried to keep the budget down, which was around $47 million. The first thing they went after was, "Well, you don't need to go inside the body and you don't know if it's going to work anyway." That's the kind of thing you're hanging on to by your fingernails and running off to the side with the cinematographer to do. They said, "If this body-cavity thing doesn't test well, we're going to try to get you to take it out." Fortunately, audiences liked it. I do want to credit Warner Brothers. I think it is the Steve Ross tradition over there. They're very loving to filmmakers.

Q: So, is your next film up going to be a studio film?

Russell: Having been through this hybrid experience, I'm not in a hurry to repeat it. I found it stressful, combining the Hollywood genre pressures and budgets with independent-minded ideas, which you do have to fight for. I guess in this case it was just the sheer undertaking of it that wore me out. I just hated the size of the crew, it was so big and unwieldy. I looked at the set and I said to myself "What am I doing here?" In the future, I'd be happy to work on smaller-scale, character-based pictures. At least for a few movies. I suspect I would be left alone more on a smaller film because the investment is smaller.

Q: Anybody else?

Pierce: I'm doing my next film with a mini-major. You're with a studio whatever you do. If I don't accept any money and I write this script and then sell it to Hollywood, it's the same difference. The real question is, What are the terms? My deal gives me final cut. I write the script, and they look at it and give me notes. I don't have to take them, [but] if they're good notes I will.

Q: What's the downside?

Vachon: The kind of movies we make will never really "test well." And having to go through that process is always frustrating. Todd Haynes is always going to make movies that are extraordinary and unlike anything else you've ever seen, whether you like them or not. So try and fit his kind of round peg into a square hole, and it makes me feel horrible. We test-screened *Velvet Goldmine* at Miramax's insistence, and it was difficult. I mean, the two movies aren't comparable, but if you'd test-screened *2001*, it would have bombed.

Russell: I don't think the majors have figured out yet how to market these pictures. I don't think they knew how to market Alexander's movie [*Election*] or *Rushmore*, which is a film that I liked a lot. Or my movie even. There's no greater heartbreak for a filmmaker than to find yourself in the hands of a big marketing machine that has been doing *Conspiracy Theory* with Mel Gibson or that sort of thing. It's frightening.

Alexander Payne: The unfortunate thing about the cinema today is that the presence of marketable elements is far more important to distribution divisions than the quality of the film. Even in script stage, marketing will say, If this film had such and such a star, or if it got into the story more quickly and easily, or if it were such and such a genre, or the ending were changed in such a way, or if this character were made more sympathetic, we could market it better. Have them change the content of the film. Egotistically speaking, I'm in the genre of Alexander Payne films, and I love the idea that my films are difficult to categorize. The mistake they made with them was putting a happy face on what are considered in today's market dark films. I feel that dark merely means realistic, films that don't buy into these prettifiedmyths of how people live, and who people are, that we've been fed for the last twenty years.

Q: Aren't big studios more sensitive to pressure groups, so you get potential censorship situations where they dump controversial pictures like *Happiness* and *Dogma*?

Pierson: It's not just about the politics or the protest or the aesthetic. It's a calculation, like, what will I do for this return? *Happiness* is not going to be a breakout, top-grossing movie, so it's like, OK, we got this much trouble to make this much money. It's really about the money.

Q: So if the historic differences between studios and independents are increasingly blurred, does the term "independent" retain any meaning at all?

Smith: My definition of independent used to be any film that couldn't be made through a studio. So I guess at the beginning of the millennium, independent really seems to mean films that surprise people when they actually do any business!

Peirce: Am I still an independent based on this new deal I have, the same way I was when I sat in my New York apartment for years, unpaid? I don't know. I mean I'd like to think so. I'd be naïve to think that the money and the power that I'm getting doesn't at least pose a temptation of change. I'd never had need for an agent, and then suddenly my life was unmanageable without one. The gifts start coming, you're getting the champagne and you're getting the calls while you're in the shower. But the main thing is not to think about stars, not to think about Sundance, not to think about distribution, just think about who these characters are and what's going to bring them to life.

Pierson: I think that you can still use budget levels as a fair criterion. Anybody who is making a film for less than $100,000 is an independent filmmaker. When it's applied to a film like *Pulp Fiction*, people can go back and forth. But by the time you get to *Good Will Hunting*, it's just not worth the breath. It's like, "Oh, come on now." It's the oh-come-on-now factor.

Payne: You know what? Just because I only spent $150,000 on this film, that doesn't suddenly ennoble me with this great independent voice. The thing is, the budget of a film does not matter; who is in a film, the stars, none of it matters as long as we're allowed to exercise our authorial voice.

Anders: To me it means the director is the auteur. This is his or her personal vision. It was not a director-for-hire kind of thing, it was not made by a committee. There can be big stars in it, but an actor didn't take over and kick the director out. A studio didn't come in and take over.

Q: In this context, does "selling out" mean anything anymore?

Smith: It used to be easier to go, This is a fucking sellout. Now, it's a bit nebulous. I've heard that *Chasing Amy* was a sellout, and I'm like, really? I mean I don't have the checks to show for it. I've heard *Dogma* was a sellout because I had stars in it—[but] it would have been so much easier and so many fewer headaches had that movie never gone into production. So the selling-out thing, you don't take it very seriously. It's usually hurled at you by 17-, 18-year-olds on the Internet.

Q: Suppose Jerry Bruckheimer came to you and said, Kevin, I want you to direct *Armageddon*. You're my guy. Would you do it?

Smith: See, I would never do *Armageddon*, but not because, hey man, I wouldn't make a piece of shit like *Armageddon*. I just don't have the talent to pull it off or the patience. [*Armageddon* director] Michael Bay lives, breathes, and eats that kind of filmmaking. I barely live, breathe, and eat the kind of filmmaking that would get a student a B on his film thesis project at film school.

Q: Maybe it gets down to: Would you take big money to direct a film you weren't interested in?

Smith: *Holy Man* was offered to me to direct, with a pretty hefty price tag, too. They said, You can rewrite it and direct it for blank. And blank was more money than I've ever seen in my life. More money than I've made with directing fees on all my films combined—for making one movie. Which, you know, would be a very cushy job. But I just couldn't do it, because it's not really what I want to do, and I didn't write it. So therefore I don't know what it should look or sound like. The idea of taking a paycheck to do something that I don't really have a passion for and could easily be replaced by somebody else, that to me is selling out, because that's just being really inauthentic to yourself as a quote-unquote artist.

Q: Do any of you consider your films political?

Peirce: Yes, not because that was my intention, but because *Boys Don't Cry* is coming out of a cultural wound, a crime against identity, against gender. Our culture destroyed Brandon Teena. He kind of aspired to be a Montgomery Clift or a James Dean. He wanted to get the girl just as much as any of those guys, and did it in Hollywood style, you know, bar fights and car races, and now he's joining the legacy of Hollywood stars in a way. It was so moving to me when I saw Hilary Swank as a form of Brandon walk onto the Golden Globe stage to get that award. It was like "My God, Brandon's arrived. How did the culture let that slip by?" Because I think people were saying, I love Brandon, and not judging him, and that was the point, to give him a kind of acceptance after his death that he couldn't get in his life.

Q: Look at *Election*. Even though it came out almost a year ago, if you put it against the template of the primaries, it's a contemporary political satire: Tracy Flick is Gore, bred from birth to robotically run for president; George W. is Paul Metzler, the dumb but sweet jock; and McCain is the third-party dark horse, Tammy Metzler, sans lesbianism.

Payne: I have no idea. In writing it we always thought Paul Metzler was sort of Reaganish, just a nice guy who smiles a lot and everything good happens to him. But politics is not something preconceived. It's something that just emerges.

Q: What about you, Kevin? John Pierson once quoted you in his book saying, somewhat enviously, that Spike Lee could write politics and you couldn't. But *Clerks* is on one level full of class commentary, and *Chasing Amy* has a lot to say about gender issues. It's just not explicit.

Smith: Yeah, I guess it depends on what your idea of politics is. For me, when I watched *Do the Right Thing* many years ago, it was like, Never in a million years would this story occur to me. How could it? I don't have a black perspective. But the stuff I do know about is being a white guy. I worked in a convenience store, and I guess there are some politics attached to that. But if I had known that going in, it would have been very obvious and not nearly authentic. And probably would have corrupted the whole thing. Because I started out not knowing what the hell it was; I just wanted to write the story.

Q: Alexander, you once made a provocative statement: "Being a young American film-maker is worse than making films under Communism, because the commercial and ideological exigencies are so strict that they suppress creativity." What did you mean by that?

Payne: I mean you always work under cultural and ideological constraints. Under Communism the workers are always good, the capitalists are always bad. How is it different here where the lead character has to be sympathetic, by page 30 such-and-such has to happen. If it's a couple who are apart, they have to come back together; if there's a crime, it must be punished. Someone recently said to me, Well in *The Talented Mr. Ripley*, he gets away with it. There are just assumptions about how things should be that outrage me. And that even extends to how films are lit. As a director you have to fight that. Why is that smoke there? What's that light source coming from over there? Why is this actress so pretty? Why is this actor's hair combed so nicely given the circumstances? Why are all the cars clean? What is this anal thing about everything in a movie having to be clean, pretty and beautiful? Like the typical American family, it's upper middle class with a big open kitchen, and they all have Range Rovers. Who are these people? I'm tired of it. [Hollywood conventions] are more rigid because you could at least make art under Communism. I think if I lived in an oppressive country I might become a truly great film-maker.

Q: Because you'd be forced to use indirection?

Payne: Of course. You saw it in so many Eastern European directors under Communism, and now you see it in films from Iran. Scorsese talks correctly about the film director as smuggler.

Q: In *Mean Streets* and *Taxi Driver*, he appears as a criminal. Director as killer.

Payne: The grenade thrower. I just hope that we are entering an age more where films do throw grenades, where they question, not support, the dominant ideology. Because that's what we used to have, films throwing grenades. I lament that we have so many movies and so many TV stations that film may have lost power to shock and challenge. I didn't get one single protest letter from *Citizen Ruth*, not one.

Q: There were an unusual number of women at Sundance this year.

Anders: It's not making the first film that's so difficult for women; it's making the second one and building up a body of work. A lot of things have stopped women from moving forward. One is the mythology of the young male independent filmmaker, the new Orson Welles. It's like everyone is looking for this Orson Welles. You want a guy who walks off his second movie and goes to Mexico and doesn't finish it and the studio recuts it. Why is that myth so powerful? I'm to the point where I wish he had never been born.

Vachon: I have to disagree. I hate hearing—like, "My movie is not getting made because I'm a lesbian, or it's not getting made because I'm a woman, or it's not getting made because I'm black," because a lot of those scripts come to me and I can tell you exactly why they're not being made, and it's not because of that person's gender or sexuality. It's because they're lousy. Or the director is insisting on an unknown. Or the budget is $10 million when it could get made for three. Or because the idea is so inherently anticommercial that it's better to do it for $200,000 on digital. I honestly believe that great work wins out in the end. And I have to believe that. Because otherwise it's just like, why bother?

Q: If it's true that women find second films so hard to finance, why is it true?

Anders: The first film, you are making it no matter what. You're just plowing ahead doing all the things that you have to do despite someone in one of the women's issues in *Premiere*—she should be hung—who said, "I don't think any woman would make a film like Robert Rodriguez did, he really sacrificed a lot to make his first movie." I did phone sex to make my first movie. How dare she! I know a girl who's a stripper to make money to make her film. What happens with the second movie is that you think that you now are going to be courted, and you are being courted to a certain extent, but they're also courting these young white males that they have seen at the festival, and that's where their money is going to go. The support just isn't there. The fact that Kimberly Peirce hasn't been nominated for an award herself—why not? They are nominating her actresses, which is great, but why, if people loved her direction so much, is she not nominated?

Q: Are women better off in the independent world than in the studio world?

Anders: I think we are a bit worse off in the independent world. The independent film companies are looking for the men just as much as [the studios]. I really turn to the black filmmakers for my model because there's always something out of Spike Lee's mouth that helps me get perspective on our place in the industry. Some journalist once asked him "Are you encouraged now that so many black filmmakers are working?" Of course, there were about five. And he said "No, I'll be encouraged when we're getting the same budgets. I'll be encouraged when we're getting the same opportunities." Women are too grateful when we get to make a movie. While I think gratitude is a very nice spiritual trait to have, enough already. It is time to move into action because gratitude alone never got women anything, and certainly it didn't get us the vote and everything else that we've accomplished. Kimberly's movie is almost a metaphor for this—like, "Well, I'll just pretend I'm a boy and hope no one notices I'm a girl." And you know, I just got to go look at what happened to Teena in the end. I don't want to be there. I'm a girl, and I've got a voice, and I'm going to make a movie as a girl.

Q: The other striking metaphor for female film-makers appears in *The Blair Witch Project*, where the director is a woman, and she's not only killed, she's humiliated, the arrogant know-it-all who got them into it.

Anders: Right. It's almost like they got killed for supporting her vision. You followed this crazy person.

Q: How do you size up the revolution to come in digital production and distribution?

Payne: You know what? Certainly the digital thing makes the means of production accessible to everybody, which is interesting, but it doesn't solve the film-maker's problem of what's the script, what's the story and what are you going to do. The same thing happened thirty years ago with 16 millimeter and Cassavetes starting to make films. We've seen it before. I still like 35-millimeter film in theaters. It's the only thing I think about.

Q: So, is it the best of times or the worst of times?

Pierson: I hate the idea that it's become easier for anybody with a first-time success to now parlay that into additional films. If the wrong people get those opportunities and keep churning out what's obviously a glut of films right now, that begins to clog the arteries for first-time talent trying to come in the traditional way, making a movie that goes to a festival and gets released in a theater.

By the same token, in this twenty-year cycle that we've had, I think a lot of ground has been covered, so it's increasingly hard for those people to be truly original. And now marketing is king. Anything that can begin to succeed will succeed at a far higher level than ever, and that's because audiences—even the smart audiences—enjoy being marketed to, and so they flock to the one film instead of spreading out the vote among dozens.

Vachon: When I first started making movies, if a film like *Poison* did $1 million worth of box office, that was seen as great success.

Everybody got a little bit of money in their pockets. Then the bar rose. Some people have blamed *Pulp Fiction*. I don't know if that was it, but there was a feeding frenzy about these movies, suddenly a sense that they could potentially make real money. *Safe* was the kind of movie that should have sat in a theater and become the movie that people talked about at cocktail parties, but it didn't have time. It came out just as that was all shifting, where if you didn't deliver the numbers in the first week or two, you were out. The kind of movies I was making, which could be targeted to the gay audience and not lose money because of their budgets and the low cost of distributing them, all that has gone out the window now. To do a genuine theatrical release for a film is much more expensive than it used to be. I think the p&a [prints and ads] budget on *Poison* in 1990 was something like $80,000. On *Velvet Goldmine* in 1998, it must have been somewhere between $5 million and $10 million.

Q: So it's becoming a first-weekend business, just like with studio films?

Vachon: Exactly. And on *Boys Don't Cry*, we were huddled by our phones that whole weekend. Are they buying tickets? Are they going? Because I knew my movie's fate rested on that.

Pierson: The key to me is that indies still think they are fighting studios, and clearly they're fighting each other. I counted 175 indie releases in New York last year, or 180. Over 175. You can't even remember 100 of them.

Q: Another way of asking this question is, If *Clerks* came along today, could it break through the way it did in 1994 at Sundance?

Smith: If we'd made *Clerks* today, I doubt it would have gotten into Sundance—Well, maybe. It wouldn't have gotten into competition, that's for sure. And Miramax would not have touched it with a ten-foot pole. Too small. Far beneath them. We were the last in a long line of small American independent films that they really pushed, that they made their name on.

Q: So, it's the worst of times?

Pierson: Not necessarily. A big plus now is that very talented people like Kevin Smith and David Russell can step inside the system but leave the door open so they can step back out. And filmmakers who made their names on first features can actually have sustained, ongoing filmmaking careers.

April 3, 2000

War Games

The Pentagon Wants What Hollywood's Got

James Der Derian

•

James Der Derian, who teaches international relations at Brown University and University of Massachusetts, Amherst, was one of the first international relations theorists to popularize the use of popular culture and film in the study of International Relations. His books include *On Diplomacy, Anti-Diplomacy, The Virillio Reader*, and the forthcoming *Virtuous War*. In this article he sketches a possible future for cinema.

LAST AUGUST PROMINENT political leaders, military officers and representatives from the computer and entertainment industries gathered at the University of Southern California to announce the opening of a new "Institute for Creative Technologies" (ICT). The innocuous title concealed a remarkable joint project: to produce state-of-the-art military simulations by pooling expertise, financial resources and the tools of virtual reality. Onstage for the signing ceremony and press conference were Steven Sample, president of USC; Louis Caldera, Secretary of the Army; 'Rocky' Delgadillo, deputy mayor of Los Angeles; Rick Belluzzo, CEO of Silicon Graphics; and Jack Valenti, president and CEO of the Motion Picture Association of America. Even Governor Gray Davis made an appearance, virtual and gargantuan onscreen via satellite link from the Capitol. The front rows of the auditorium were sprinkled with uniforms and suits, the military's top computer war-gamers swapping stories with executives from the entertainment industry. Toward the back of the room the major network and print media, including CNN, had installed themselves to broadcast this new alliance to the world.

After some opening remarks, USC president Sample introduced the featured speaker, the Army's Louis Caldera. Caldera mapped out the purpose and potential of a "very exciting partnership" that seemed to include just about every major LA player in high tech, higher education and high-as well as lowbrow entertainment. "This $45 million contract will fund joint modeling and simulation research and has high-value applications for the Army as well for the entertainment, media, video game, film, destination theme park and information-technology industries that are such a key part of the California economy . . . This partnership will leverage the US national defense and the enormous talent and creativity of the entertainment industry and their tremendous investment in cutting-edge applications of new technology." Having stroked the local powers, Caldera addressed the needs of his own constituency, in the now-common military language that makes *Neuromancer* sound like an out-of-date Army field manual. "The ICT will significantly enhance complex interactive simulations for large-scale warfighting exercises and allow us to test new doctrines in synthetic environments that are populated with intelligent agents in future threat challenges." The speakers who followed parroted the press releases in simpler language. "Synergy" and "verisimilitude" popped up with cue-card frequency; everyone was keen to dance on the "cutting edge."

But while the soldiers and politicians vied for media attention, the guy who made it all happen hugged the auditorium wall. The only evidence of his affiliation was a government pay-scale suit, a loud haw-hawing at the speakers' jokes and a slight rolling of the eyes at questions asked by the press. The ICT is the brainchild of Mike Macedonia, son of one of the Army's best war-gamers, graduate of West Point and now chief scientist and technical director at STRICOM (Simulation, Training and Instrumentation Command), the newest and probably the most unusual command post in the military. Thirty miles northeast of the pink arches of Disney-world in Orlando, Florida, STRICOM looks like a research park pretending to be a military base. Steel and glass corporate buildings, owned by Lockheed Martin, Silicon Graphics, Westing-house, SAIC and other military industries, encircle the various headquarters of the Army, Navy, Marine Corps and Air Force. Charged with providing the military with a "vision for the future," STRICOM leads a combined military and industry effort to create "a distributed computerized warfare simulation system" and to support "the 21st century warfighter's preparation for real world contingencies." Its motto is telling: "All But War Is Simulation."

Under the auspices of his boss, Michael Andrews, deputy assistant secretary of the Army for research and technology, Macedonia brought STRICOM to LA after he realized that the commercial sector—in particular the film, computer and video-game industries—was outstripping the military in technological innovation. Where trickle-down from military research on mainframe computers once fueled progress in the field, civilian programmers working on PCs could now design video games and virtual environments that out military simulations to shame. Macedonia came to Hollywood to find the tools and skills for simulating and, if necessary, fighting wars of the future. As the blood and iron of traditional war gave way to the bits and bytes of infowar, netwar and cyberwar, he saw the ICT as a vehicle for integrating the simulation and entertainment industries into this much-heralded "Revolution in Military Affairs."

Macedonia's initiative draws on a long tradition. Ever since nineteenth-century chemists began to fix images on film made with the same nitrocelluloids found in explosives, the military and the movie industry have been in a technology relay race for seeing and killing the enemy while securing and seducing the citizen. Gun and camera became a single calibration with the mobilization of Hollywood during the Second World War. At the start of the war, military-preparedness documentaries were quickly re-edited to produce propaganda movies like *To the Shores of Tripoli*. Famous Hollywood directors soon joined the cause, contributing feature and training films like Howard Hawks's *Air Force* (1943), John Huston's *The Battle of San Pietro* (1945) and Frank Capra's series *Why We Fight* (1943–45). The War Department supplied manpower, equipment and funding, and Hollywood provided actors, directors and, for the most part, the talent. Between 1939 and 1945, close to 2,500 war movies were made.

After such extensive collaboration, the opening of the Institute for Creative Technologies might appear to be another case of incest, just further proof that LA has never had much of a purchase on reality, rather than a cause for alarm. But there is a difference. By its very task and potential power to create totally immersive environments where one can see, hear, perhaps even touch and emotionally interact with digitally created agents, the ICT is leading the way into a brave new world that threatens to breach the last firewalls between reality and virtuality.

Set in the larger technostrategic scheme of things, ICT matters—very much. The diplomatic and military policies of the United States have become increasingly dependent on technological and representational forms of discipline, deterrence and coercion that might be described as "*virtuous war.*" At the cyborg heart of virtuous war is the technical capability and ethical imperative to threaten and, if necessary, actualize violence from a distance with virtually no casualties.

On the surface, virtuous war cleans up the discourse of conflict. Fought in the same manner as they are represented, by real-time surveillance and TV "live feeds," virtuous wars promote a vision of bloodless, humanitarian, hygienic wars. This is not to say—and this point requires emphasis—that virtuous war is any less destructive, deadly or bloody for those on the short end of the big technological stick. One needs only to note the skewed casualty rates of prototypical virtuous wars like the Gulf War (287 Americans lost their lives—many by accidents), the Mogadishu raid (eighteen Americans killed) and the Kosovo air campaign (a remarkable, casualty-free conflict for the NATO forces). We seldom hear about the other side of the casualty list: Post-Vietnam, the US military studiously avoids body counts of the enemy.

Unlike other forms of warfare, virtuous war has an unsurpassed power to commute death, to keep it out of sight, out of mind. In simulated preparations and virtual executions of war, one learns how to kill but not to take responsibility for it; one experiences "death" but not the tragic consequences of it. We now face the danger of a new kind of trauma without sight, drama without tragedy, where the lines between war and game, pain and pleasure, fact and fiction do not blur: They pixelate in hyperreal detail on the same screen. In this context, when the Pentagon and Hollywood announce a new collaboration, we best tune in.

At the closed luncheon following the press conference, the writer and director John Milius (*Apocalypse, Now, Red Dawn*) told war stories to an audience dining on chicken breast and "whipped goat cheese yukons." He spoke, half-jokingly, of how he wanted to put an end to the alienation between the military and the movie industry by setting up a production team for the Army that would make *Wag the Dog* look tame. That brought to mind Eisenhower's famous 1961 farewell address, when he warned of the "danger that public policy could itself become the captive of a scientific-technology elite." What would he have made of this addition of new media and entertainment industries to his "military-industrial complex"? Of new technologies of simulation being built at universities to create a high fidelity between the representation and the reality of war? Of the human mimetic faculty for entertainment and gaming joining forces with new cyborg programs for killing and warring? He'd probably not have let it get it in the way of his golf game. By the end of the visit, I was left wondering, *pace* Eisenhower, if the Military Industrial-Media-Entertainment network had just gone online.

Six months after the fact, I'm not so sure. My effort to find out just what was in the works at ICT produced more promissory notes than any actual project developments. The reasons given for not going on record were ongoing negotiations and imminent signing, with "one of the best-known directors in Hollywood" and some of the "best computer graphics guys on the planet." The only names dropped were Randal Kleiser (director of *The Blue Lagoon* and *Honey, I Blew Up the Kid*) and 3D Realms, makers of the video game Duke Nukem (motto: "The only good alien bastard is a dead alien bastard").

One person willing to talk on the record was Mike Zyda, chairman of Modeling, Virtual Environments & Simulation at the Naval Postgraduate School, chairman of the original 1997 National Research Council report that gave cause and code for the establishment of the ICT (*Modeling and Simulation,* http://books.nap.edu/catalog5830.html) and, not coincidentally, chair man of Mike Macedonia's 1995 computer science PhD dissertation committee. Zyd originally envisioned the ICT as a place that would act as coordinator and broke for the most imaginative and technically advanced modelers and simulators. "The Defense Department," he says, "has spent millions and still can't match SimCity." ICT shouldn't be chasing Hollywood, says Zyda. It should target off-the-shelf video game technology, like Sony Playstation2 Capable of generating 66 million polygons per second, it leaves platforms like Silicon Graphics in the dust. Commercial video games could be redesigned to test the intellectual aptitude and psychological attitudes of potential military recruits. Spin-off technology would be used to help kids at risk explore potential career paths.

Richard Lindheim, who was eventually appointed director of ICT, has a different vision. After a long career at NBC, Lindheim went on to become executive vice president of the Paramount Television Group, producing *The Equalizer* and taking charge of the later *Star Trek* series, *Next Generation, Deep Space Nine* and *Voyager*. I caught up with him at STRICOM, where he was preparing for a series of Washington briefings. His previous employment probably best explains why *Star Trek's* total-immersion simulation, the Holodeck, kept popping up in our conversation (as well as how Herman Zimmerman, the art director of *Star Trek*, was procured to design the ICT's office space). "The ICT is on a quest to envision and prepare for the future," and, says Lindheim, "our Holy Grail is the Holodeck." Lindheim invoked writers like Jules Verne, who popularized the idea of the modern submarine and inspired scientists to turn unreality into reality; *Voyager* could do the same for ICT. By the end of our conversation, I realized that the Holodeck was not just a metaphor; it was the endgame for ICT.

The Holodeck and the Holy Grail notwithstanding, the Institute for Creative Technologies is unlikely to save (or destroy) the world. It is not yet evident that it can run a project or a battlefield simulation, let alone an intergalactic war. However, cutting edge or opening wedge, the ICT does look to be Hollywood's—and the Pentagon's—premier laboratory for virtuous war. Will this new alchemy of brass, celluloid and silicon produce a kinder, gentler, sexier cyborg, like *Voyager*'s Seven of Nine? Or will the simulations of Creative Technology turn on their creators, like Frankenstein's monster? Either way, the ICT warrants public scrutiny.

11

Our Critics Speak

THE PATH OF THE MOVIES

Gilbert Seldes

•

The article below was one of a series of three devoted to cinema. Seldes was the author of an influential study of popular culture, *The Seven Lively Arts*.

IT WOULD BE idle to undertake a commentary on the moving picture without suggesting, beforehand, some of the prejudices with which twelve years of observation have fortified me. I hope to check those prejudices and to verify their relation to actuality, thus preserving my integrity as a critic; but I cannot toss them out of the window. I can only place them conspicuously, so that no one will be misled.

First of all, I agree entirely with the movie men who, about 1914, began to insist that the moving picture is an art. It is also a mechanism and it is also a business; so is the symphony orchestra. We have heard of symphony orchestras which, having become great business organizations, were able to become almost perfect instruments, yet slumped seriously as providers of aesthetic pleasure. The case of the movie is a little different. The producers insisted that their work be called an art, but they were themselves unwilling to submit to the discipline, the mental strain, which the creative life requires. From the first day they struggled to perfect the instrument; from the second, to organize the business. So far as they thought of art at all, they conceived it childishly and vulgarly. Some of them, without thinking, produced work of an extraordinary aesthetic interest, work in which the creative energy communicated itself by appropriate methods.

If the moving picture is an art it must have something to do with the creative impulse; it must have control of its mechanism, and it must use materials adaptable to that mechanism to say that the movie must be thus and thus; yet these are specific requirements. And my whole basis of criticism of the movies lies here, because I hold that the movie is better entertainment when it is good movie. Apart from the pictures of natural phenomena and of current events, you cannot make an interesting picture without sound principles of art.

Briefly, I believe that the contemporary feature picture, the body of the average program, is a failure because the producers are on the wrong track, trying to do things better done elsewhere, neglecting their own mechanism and the things they ought to be doing with it, using unadaptable material, attaching themselves deplorably to the stage and accepting from it a system of acting totally inappropriate to the screen.

These are not the things you think of when you see a dull movie. You think that the taste of the director is bad or that the motives of the characters are muddled or that the situations are incredible or that the actors are hams. The ineptitude and stupidity of the movies were not discovered by intellectuals; read the fan letters in the movie journals, criticizing details in the pictures, and you will understand how obvious these faults are. It is probable that the producer's instinct is frequently wrong; it is certain that the instinct is not checked by sound theory. (The instinct remains in most cases what it was in the beginning—to make money.)

I believe that all these unhappy things would gradually disappear if the movie returned to the right path. I say "returned" because at the outset, without theory, the producers did what they could, using whatever came first to hand, and often hit on the best of all possible materials. The serial thriller, the melodrama, the fantastic movie and the spectacular were all good movie (they were "cinema") even if they were not in every case good movies. Supremely the slapstick comedy as it developed in Chaplin was pure moving picture. All these were presented simply for their value as entertainment; they were crude and awkward, but they were not offensive. Except in the comedies the creative imagination was rudimentary; ingenuity took its place. The mechanism was only beginning to develop. Yet they were on the right path, leading to imagination, fantasy, and a free play for creativeness.

The dominating producing company of today began its career by promising "famous players in famous plays"; by "players" the phrase meant actors, and the "tie-up" with the stage was complete. Readers of Mr. Terry Ramsaye's history of the movie will recall that Mary Pickford became far more important to Famous Players than any famous actor or actress they could import; they will also be aware that neither Chaplin nor Griffith was a great stage star. But the stage influence, utterly alien to the movie, has never been shaken off; even the spectacle film has not been able to overcome the great dramatic feature film. Nor has the single success of Chaplin in creating a method of playing which is not stage-acting persuaded the directors that the moving picture must create its own type of playing. The extraordinary merit of Mary Garden in her field is due to her sense of the relation between playing and music, a relation far removed from that between playing and speaking; and similarly the merit of Chaplin, as a player, is that his expressiveness is related to the screen and not to the spoken word. There is a rhythm in his playing which is appropriate in his medium. There was that, too, in the playing of Werner Krauss and Conrad Veidt, the two chief figures in the almost legendary *Cabinet of Dr. Caligari.*

The moving picture is further astray in thinking so much of its relation of photography. As a result it prides itself on reproductive accuracy instead of an imaginative power. It should, of course, be much closer to painting (and not purely representational painting, in which the only pleasure is in the accuracy of the likeness) and to sculpture and to music. It has absorbed in plot (derived from the stage) and in realism.

Apply these things for a moment to *The Last Laugh,* recently shown in New York to an unexpectedly numerous and appreciative series of audiences. *The Last Laugh,* the work of Murnau and Mayer, is the exact opposite of almost all American moving pictures. In the first place it banishes altogether the aid of subtitles. Everything which needs to be expressed is transposed into visual images. This ought to seem about as revolutionary as saying that a painter has worked in oils instead of in coffee beans to paint a picture of a coffee plantation. The endless application of the camera to stage plays and spectacle has not taught the American director what his camera can do. Secondly, *The Last Laugh* has a story but no "plot"; a hotel-doorman is demoted to be lavatory attendant and an ironical happy ending restores his prestige in the society in which he moves—that is all. Further, the picture is both imaginative and ingenious, more ingenious and less imaginative than *Caligari* but notable in both respects. Its materials are extremely commonplace, yet it is not at all a realistic film; it reproduces actuality for a definite purpose and in a definite design. It has, again less so than *Caligari* but again notably, a rhythm and a life of its own—a life at a tangent to ours, recognizably possible to us if we found ourselves on the screen with the people already there.

That America as a whole and D. W. Griffith in particular have failed to produce hundreds of such films is shocking. (I gather that *Isn't Life Wonderful?*, made by Griffith, has unusual quality; I missed it, and now Mr. Griffith has joined Famous Players to make Marie Corelli's *Sorrows of Satan*.) There are American methods which Murnau could have used to advantage in *The Last Laugh*; but these are as nothing in comparison with the artistic rightness of the German film—a quality, I hasten to add, which is not German but universal.

MARCH 22, 1933

King Kong

William Troy

•

William Troy was a regular contributor to *The Nation* and for many years taught at Bennington College. The critic Allen Tate wrote "I, for one, rate William Troy among the handful of the best critics of this century."

AT LEAST ONE of our national characteristics is illustrated in the RKO-Radio production of *King Kong* which loomed over the audiences of both Radio City movie-houses last week. It is a characteristic hard to define except that it is related to that sometimes childish, sometimes magnificent passion for scale that foreigners have remarked in our building of hundred-story skyscrapers, our fondness for hyperbole in myth and popular speech, and our habit of applying superlatives to all our accomplishments. Efforts to explain it have not been very satisfactory; the result is usually a contradiction in which we are represented as a race that is at once too civilized and not civilized enough. If Herr Spengler interprets the extreme gigantism of the American mind and imagination as the sign of an inflated decadence resembling that of Alexandria and the later Roman Empire, others discover in it the simpler expression of a race still unawakened from childhood. At Radio City last week one was able to see the contradiction pretty dramatically borne out; an audience enjoying all the sensations of primitive terror and fascination within the scientifically air-cooled temple of baroque modernism that is Mr. Rockefeller's contribution to contemporary culture.

What is to be seen at work in *King Kong* is the American imagination faithfully adhering to its characteristic process of multiplication. We have had plays and pictures about monsters before, but never one in which the desired effect depended so completely on the increased dimensions of the monster. Kong is a veritable skyscraper among the apes. In his own jungle haunts he rules like a king over the rest of the animal world; and when he is taken to New York to be exhibited before a light-minded human audience he breaks through his chromium-steel handcuffs, hurls down two or three elevated trains that get in his way, and scales the topmost heights of the Empire State building with the fragile Miss Fay Wray squirming in his hairy paw. The photographic ingenuity that was necessary to make all this seem plausible was considerable, and in places so remarkable as to advance the possibility of a filming of certain other stories depending largely on effects of scale—*Gulliver's Travels*, for example, and possibly even the *Odyssey*. But, unfortunately, it was thought necessary to mitigate some of the predominant horror by introducing a human, all-too-human, theme. "It was not the guns that got him," says one of the characters at the end, after Kong has been brought to ground by a whole squadron of battle planes. "It was Beauty killed the Beast." By having Beauty, in the person of Miss Wray, lure the great monster to his destruction, the scenario writers sought to unite two rather widely separated traditions of the popular cinema—that of the "thriller" and that of the sentimental romance. The only difficulty was that they failed to realize that such a union was possible only by straining our powers of credulity and perhaps also one or two fundamental laws of nature. For if the love that Kong felt for the heroine was sacred, it suggests a weakness that hardly fits in with his other actions; and if it was, after all, merely profane, it proposes problems to the imagination that are not the less real for being crude.

JANUARY 22, 1938

SNOW WHITE AND THE SEVEN DWARFS

FAIRY TALE IN FIVE ACTS

Mark Van Doren

•

Katrina vanden Heuvel wrote in her anthology *Nation: 1865–1990*: "No story about *The Nation's* 1920s can be told without mention of the Van Doren dynasty—brothers Carl and Mark, and their sisters Irita and Dorothy. From 1920 to 1922 Carl ran the book section. He was succeeded by Irita, who later became literary editor of the *New York Herald Tribune*. Mark succeeded Irita. And Dorothy, who later became a successful novelist, was associate editor from 1919 until 1936. First and always a poet, Mark edited the magazine's book section from 1924 to 1928. His "First Glance" column ran from 1925 to 1928." Apparently Van Doren was tickled pink about the idea of being paid to watch movies and he would go and see movies almost every night. However he finally quit in 1938 due to the sheer volume of films he had to watch. Van Doren went on to win the Pulitzer Prize for poetry and was a much-loved teacher at Columbia University.

THE QUESTION WHICH everybody must have asked in advance about Walt Disney's *Snow White and the Seven Dwarfs* was whether it would justify its length. Not only was the film to be many times longer than anything Mr. Disney had done; it was to tell a story which he could be imagined as telling in the accustomed time. A fairy tale like an anecdote is by definition brief, and its form helps its content to be credible. We can believe three things that are done in three paragraphs when one of them alone, drawn out to epic length, would be preposterous. The question then was whether Mr. Disney had lost any of his secrets abandoning his form.

The fact that everybody likes *Snow White* is not necessarily an answer, though it has its importance. Thousands are trampling one another to get into the Music Hall; but the question still is whether the good thing they are there to see could possibly be better, I am not sure that it could, and yet in view of the future which the film opens up I am sure that the matter should be argued. Mr. Disney has both expanded his story and contracted it. He has added animals; he has differentiated and named the dwarfs; and he has elaborated the wicked stepmother in her role as magician, giving her a laboratory with monster retorts and a long-legged raven to scowl in the corner. On the other hand he has suppressed two of her attempts on Snow White's life—the tight lacing and the poisoned comb—and he has stopped short of Snow White's wedding. The wedding is perhaps not missed, but my guess is that the queen should have had more things to do and less time in which to do them. She was the only one of Mr. Disney's creatures who even approached being tiresome.

Mr. Disney's other developments are all to the good, and indescribably delightful. The animals, for instance—I can remember, no finer moment in any film than this one when at. Sunrise in the forest the banks of eyes which have looked so sinister all night turn out to belong to rabbits, fawns, chipmunks, bluebirds, and turtles. The transition is from shadowy evil to the clearest and most blithesome benevolence. The antics of these charming beasts vary henceforth between the beatific and the absurd; the pride of the baby bluebird in his voice, the ticklish turtle offering his belly for a washboard when Snow White starts housecleaning for the dwarfs, and the squirrels undoing cobwebs with their tails are but understatements of the very touching love for Snow White which they share with a helpless audience. Then there are the dwarfs—in their seven foolish ways as irresistible as the heroine, and of course no less devoted to her than the animals are; though one of them, Grumpy, remains a misogynist almost to the end. Mr. Disney's triumph with them, like all his other triumphs, is one of understanding. His technique, about which I know little, must of course be wonderful; but the main thing is that he lives somewhere near the human center and knows innumerable truths that cannot be taught. That is why his ideas look like inspirations, and why he can be good-hearted without being sentimental, can be ridiculous without being fatuous. With him, as with any first-rate artist, we feel that we are in good hands; we can trust him with our hearts and wits.

APRIL 26, 1940

CITIZEN KANE

Anthony Bower

•

Anthony Bower, who was formerly the film critic for *The New Statesman* in England, wrote a fortnightly letter from Hollywood which combined industry news and film reviews in the early 1940s before he was drafted into the Army. He returned briefly as a film critic after Agee's resignation in 1948 but had to return to Europe "for an extended stay" and was replaced by Manny Farber.

Hollywood, April 18

CITIZEN KANE HAS probably had more advance publicity of one kind or another than any other picture yet produced. Practically everybody connected with the production has been reported on the verge of a lawsuit. Some have said that all this uproar was nothing but exceptionally well-handled publicity, while others have sworn that William Randolph Hearst was determined to prevent the picture's release. Finally it was announced that the picture would definitely be released in the near future, and the press assembled at last week's preview in a state of great expectancy.

Many would probably have rejoiced to find producer, director, actor, and part-author Orson Welles's ambitious first effort in Hollywood not an unqualified success: after all, the man had had no previous cinema experience, and if reports were true he had walked into the studio and produced on a very low budget a film which was a masterpiece.

It must be stated here that no amount of advance publicity or ballyhoo could possibly ruin the effect of this remarkable picture. It is probably the most original, exciting, and entertaining picture that has yet been produced in this country, and although it may lack their subtlety it can certainly be placed in the same bracket as the very best pre-war French productions.

The film may not have been inspired by the life of William Randolph Hearst, but the story of Charles Foster Kane, as unfolded in the picture, certainly bears a remarkable resemblance to Hearst's career. The incident concerning the Spanish-American War, the vast collection of useless antiques acquired by Kane, and certain details such as the picnic, with the guests compelled to spend the night under canvas, are familiar parts of the Hearst legend; and the castle of Xanadu, Kane's retreat from the world, with its endless acres and private zoo, is more than reminiscent of San Simeon. If Mr. Hearst decides, as many others undoubtedly will, that the film is only the most thinly disguised version of his life story, he will perhaps be favorably impressed with the sympathy and understanding with which the subject has been treated, and may even be delighted to have provided material for a drama of almost classical proportions.

The film opens with the death of Kane, a very old man, alone in the colossal, ugly monument to his wealth and power—Xanadu. A sort of March of Time dealing with Kane's life is then presented. The producers of this short are dissatisfied, finding it too superficial and impersonal, and are determined to obtain more intimate details of the man's personal history. The remainder of the picture deals with the information on Kane's life and character obtained respectively from his guardian, his chief assistant, a dramatic critic who was once his best friend, his second wife, and his butler. This technique of unfolding the story necessitates five separate flashbacks and creates a certain amount of confusion which is more than compensated for by the powerful effect obtained by the gradual illumination of character, until with the click of the final switch he is fully revealed—empty, lonely, and unhappy, a victim of his own personal power.

This excellent cinematic material Welles has embellished with brilliant directorial, pictorial, and dramatic touches. He breaks, with the greatest effect, practically every photographic rule in the business, employing very few close-ups, playing whole scenes with the faces of the performers in shadow, using lighting to enhance the dramatic value of the scene rather than the personal appearance of the actor. He is, in fact, one of the first Hollywood directors really to exploit the screen as a medium, and it is interesting to note that in doing this he has used an entire cast with no previous screen experience.

The acting both of Welles and of the rest of the Mercury Theater cast is excellent. Dorothy Comingore as Kane's second wife, whom he forces to sing in opera to gratify his ego, is particularly effective; so is Joseph Cotten as the dramatic critic, Welles himself gives an amazing performance as Kane, equally convincing in youth, middle age, and senility. The photographer, Gregg Toland, has achieved some wonderful effects, particularly the scene in the projection room of the newsreel company.

The picture has made a tremendous impression in Hollywood. Charlie Chaplin is reported to be prepared to back any venture that Welles may have in mind. Perhaps when the uproar has died down it will be discovered that the film is not quite so good as it is considered now, but nevertheless Hollywood will for a long time be in debt to Mr. Welles.

NOVEMBER 8, 1941

DUMBO

Siegfried Kracauer

•

Kracauer was the author of a number of classic studies on film including *From Calagari to Hitler, A Psychological History of German Cinema*, and *Theory of Film*. During the Weimer Republic of the 1920s he pioneered the critical study of mass culture and modernity, work that had great influence on the likes of Walter Benjamin (Kracauer was his editor) and The Frankfurt School. His essays and journalism from *Frankfurter Zeitung* from this period are collected in *The Mass Ornament* and his short book *The Salaried Masses: Duty and Distraction in Weimar Germany*. The following review was published the year he emigrated to the United States.

THE NEW MODEL brought out this year by the Walt Disney studio is a flying baby elephant. He comes to life in the film that bears his name, *Dumbo*, a charming picture filled with marvelously conceived episodes. Despite this, Disney continues in it a development the problematic nature of which has grown more and more apparent since "Snow-White."

In "Plane Crazy," Disney's first Mickey Mouse cartoon (1928), a little auto is changed through the power of the cartoonist's pen alone into an airplane, which takes flight with Mickey at the controls. In *Dumbo* a similar miracle occurs: the baby elephant suddenly spreads his ears and volplanes through the air like a Pegasus or a bomber. Here, however, the miracle does not result simply from the fact that the film is a cartoon film, but originates in the psychological effect of a "magic feather" which Dumbo's friend, a little mouse, has elicited from some insolent crows. This tiny difference betrays a structural change in the Disney films. Through a long period Disney spurned the traditional notions of reality and created his own laws for the elements of our visible world: in "Plane Crazy" Mickey's girlfriend uses her petticoat as a parachute, and the Skeleton in "The Skeleton Dance" (1929) employs his thigh bone to play upon a xylophone made from the bones of his skeleton friends. These metamorphoses come out of the observed relations between shapes or movements; the more ruthlessly they destroy familiar connections, the more they are justified—the more they manifest the artist's power over his material. Is the cartoonist dependent on fabulous princes, wizards, and magic feathers in order to defy the laws of nature? By including such fairytale beings more and more Disney has unnecessarily overburdened his films.

In addition, *Dumbo* clings to camera reality and even, deals with imaginary things on the same plane. There is no doubt that Disney intends here to imitate the technique of the realistic film; but it must be acknowledged, too, that this intention turns against the principles on which Disney's classic short cartoons are based. In them he sought to build a world which had as little to do with ours as Mickey with a living mouse; his creatures strolled through a cartoonist's space in a time which, like the space itself, spread or shrank to his liking. In *Dumbo* Disney treats not only imaginary objects as real, but more, he combines them with human figures and does things which could as well have been done in the studio, and thus threatens the true interest of his medium. The cartoon film tends toward the dissolution rather than the reinforcement of conventional reality, and its function is not to draw a reality which can better be photographed.

The turn to a realistic style is fostered by the full-length cartoon which requires a story. One is reminded of the old comedies; they too have suffered from their extension to feature length. Film comedy and cartoon coincide in that they do not aim at the development of plots but rather at the exposition of particular incidents. For both kinds of film the whole "story" is just a gag or a series of gags. Hence they should be brief; for only on this condition can the plot keep its quality of a thread that holds together the pearls of the gags. The nature of the incident in both comedy and cartoon influences the nature of the plot. Thus the genuine cartoon would scoff at the idea of machinery ruling mankind and, like the comedy, select as its hero the weak little creature who must assert himself against the stupid and evil powers of our world. It is to their own disadvantage that Disney's feature films do not follow this line, but submit too readily to current social conventions. Significant in this respect is the conclusion of the present film: young Dumbo, instead of flying off toward some unknown paradise, chooses wealth and security and so ends as the highly paid star of the same circus director who once flogged his mother Jumbo. Is no better solution possible? However questionable the illustration of absolute music may be, *Fantasia* proved, at least, that feature cartoons are not necessarily dependent upon a "story." One could wish, too, that Disney would stop animating fairy tales into conventional everyday life, and, proceeding like Chaplin, develop everyday life into fairy tales through his cartoons. As to the methods of representation, he might be able, after the example of great painters, to transform *both* real and imaginary objects in his art and thus bring it to a new level.

Dumbo shows that Disney has already an inclination toward such a transformation. Hopes are raised by such scenes as the erection of the circus tent—a sequence in which reality is transferred to a strange, exciting sphere. Most fortunately, too, Disney's artistic instincts frequently prevail against his artistic intentions and thrust aside the disturbing story to bring in such happy inventions as the gang of crows, the beautifully developed play of the champagne pearls, and many others quite as delightful.

The Curse of the Cat People

James Agee

Dwight McDonald, who was an old friend of Agee's, wrote about his film reviews: "Agee brought to film criticism some qualities not as common in the trade as they might be. The most distinctive one I have already mentioned: He fell in love with movies at an early age and the affair didn't cool off—on the contrary! Although he never actually brought her off to bed (i.e., made a movie), love makes one observant of subtleties and nuances. Agee's reviews are suffused with intimate understanding." Readers are directed to the new paperback edition of Agee's collected film writings, *Agee on Film: Criticism and Comment on the Movies*, published by Modern Library which includes Agee's entire output as a film critic for *The Nation*.

TARDILY, I ARCH my back and purr deep-throated approval of *The Curse of the Cat People*, which I caught by pure chance, one evening, on a reviewer's holiday. Masquerading as a routine case of Grade B horrors—and it does very well at that job—the picture is in fact a brave, sensitive, and admirable little psychological melodrama about a lonely six-year-old girl, her inadequate parents, a pair of recluses in a neighboring house, and the child's dead, insane mother, who becomes the friend and playmate of her imagination. Since you have probably heard about it already from other reviewers, and since it is the sort of picture anyhow which deserves to give one the pleasure of personal discovery, I will not do more than say that dozens of the details are as excellent as the whole intention. Certain confusions in the plot—especially one scene in which the imaginary playmate, by pinning a gift to her gown, momentarily seems to categorize herself as a mere studio wraith—suggests that the people who made the film worked out two versions, one with conventional supernatural trimmings, the other, the far from conventional story they got away with. I was rather pleased than not, incidentally, by the trick, or accident, or both, which kept me and the audience uncertain, clear to the end, whether the ghost was a "real" ghost or the far more real fantasy of the child. In the same way I liked the ambiguous melodrama about the daft old actress and her tortured daughter, in the sinister house; though here I would have liked even better the much purer, quieter realism which they would have achieved if they had taken their key from the wonderfully chosen house itself. I wish that the makers of the film, and RKO, might be given some special award for the whole conception and performance of the family servant, who is one of the most unpretentiously sympathetic, intelligent, anti-traditional, and individualized Negro characters I have ever seen presented on the screen. And I hope that the producer, Val Lewton, and the rest of his crew may be left more and more to their own devices; they have a lot of taste and talent, and they are carrying films a long way out of Hollywood.

Even so, they have things to learn. This had every right to be a really first-rate movie; but good as it is, it is full of dead streaks—notably the writing, directing, and playing of the parts of the parents and the kindergarten teacher—and there are quite a few failures of imagination and of taste. The people with whom I saw the film—a regular Times Square horror audience—were sharply on to its faults and virtues. When the Ideal Playmate (Simone Simone) first appeared to the imagination of the infant in a dress and a lascivious lighting which made her façade look like a relief map from What Every Young Husband Should Know, they laughed their heads off. They laughed again, with tender and perceptive spontaneity, when, confronted by snobbery, the little girl caught her shoulders into a bewildered, instinctively pure shrug of distaste. And when the picture ended and it was clear beyond further suspense that anyone who had come to see a story about curses and were-cats should have stayed away, they clearly did not feel sold out; for an hour they had been captivated by the poetry and danger of childhood, and they showed it in their thorough applause.

That is, I grant, a specialized audience, unobstreperous, poor, metropolitan, and deeply experienced. The West Times Square audience is probably, for that matter, the finest movie audience in the country (certainly, over and over, it has proved its infinite superiority to the run of the "art-theater" devotees—not to mention, on paper which must brave the mails, the quality and conduct of Museum of Modern Art film audiences). As long as such an audience exists, no one in Hollywood has a right to use the stupidity of the public for an alibi; and I suspect that a few more films as decent and human as this one would indicate that there is a very large and widely distributed audience indeed for good films.

DECEMBER 23, 1944

NATIONAL VELVET

James Agee

•

FRANKLY, I DOUBT I am qualified to arrive at any sensible assessment of Miss Elizabeth Taylor. Ever since I first saw the child, two or three years ago, in I forget what minor role in what movie, I have been choked with the peculiar sort of adoration I might have felt if we were both in the same grade of primary school. I feel I am obligated to this unpleasant unveiling because it is now my duty to try to review her, in *National Velvet*, in her first major role.

So far as I can see on an exceedingly cloudy day, I wouldn't say she is particularly gifted as an actress. She seems, rather, to turn things off and on, much as she is told, with perhaps a fair amount of natural grace and of a natural-born female's sleepwalking sort of guile, but without much, if any, of an artist's intuition, perception, or resource. She strikes me, however, if I may resort to conservative statement, as being rapturously beautiful. I think she also has a talent, of a sort, in the particular things she can turn on: which are most conspicuously a mock-pastoral kind of simplicity, and two or three speeds of semi-hysterical emotion, such as ecstasy, an odd sort of pre-specific erotic sentience, and the anguish of overstrained hope, imagination, and faith. Since these are precisely the things she needs for her role in *National Velvet*—which is a few-toned-scale semi-fairy story about a twelve-year-old girl in love with a horse—and since I think it is the most hopeful business of movies to find the perfect people rather than the perfect artists, I think that she and the picture are wonderful, and I hardly know or care whether she can act or not.

I am quite sure about Mickey Rooney: he is an extremely wise and moving actor, and if I am ever again tempted to speak disrespectfully of him, that will be in anger over the unforgivable waste of a forceful yet subtle talent, proved capable of self-discipline and of the hardest roles that could be thrown it. (I suggest it jealously, because I would so love to make the films rather than see them made; but if only a Studs Lonigan for the middle period could be found—the two I will mention might conceivably overlap it—and inter-studio entanglements could so be combed out that both Rooney and James Cagney—from whom Rooney has learned a lot—were available, they could find in Farrell's trilogy the best roles of their lives; and those novels, done as they should be, could become three major American movies.)

There are still other good things about *National Velvet*: the performance of Anne Revere as the girl's mother and of Donald Crisp as her father (except for their tedious habit of addressing each other as "Mr. Brown" and "Mrs. Brown," and some conventional bits of business which I suspect were forced down Crisp's throat); the endearing appearance (I don't suppose one can really call it a performance) of Jackie Jenkins; and a number of gently pretty "touches," mainly domestic, which may have been Clarence Brown's, who directed, or may have been in the script, or for that matter in Enid Bagnold's novel. And there are few outright blunders, like the silly burlesquing of one adolescent love scene.

Yet in a sense—the sense of all the opportunities, or obligations, which were either neglected, with or without reason, or went unrealized—almost the whole picture is a blunder mitigated chiefly but insufficiently by the overall charm of the story and affectionateness of the treatment, by Rooney's all but unimprovable performance (I wonder only only about his very skillful but stylized use of his hands in his impressive drunk scene), and by a couple of dozen piercing moments—which may have transfixed me exclusively—from Miss Taylor.

The makers of the film had an all but ideal movie: a nominally very simple story, expressing itself abundantly in visual and active terms, which inclosed and might have illuminated almost endless recessions and inter-reverberations of emotion and meaning into religious and sexual psychology and into naturalistic legend. But of all these reins, all of which needed so light, hard, clear a hand, they seem to have been conscious only of the most obvious; and they have bungled even their management of those. Far from understanding and valuing their story for all it is worth, they don't even tell its surface half well enough.

To take just two samples of this: the sequence during which the horse is trained for his race gives you little more than generalized pretty-pictures instead of a précis of the pure technical detail which must have deeply excited, instructed, and intensified the girl, and so could and should have done the same for the audience. As for the race and the immediate preparations for it, they are only the more sadly flunked because, again in a secondary, generalized way, they manage to make you half forget the fact by being quite fairly exciting. If the audience could have experienced what the girl experienced, with anything like the same razorlike distinctness of detail and intensity of action and of spirit, they would have been practically annihilated. But they not only never have a chance to identify themselves with the girl or her horse; they hardly even get a good look at them, during the whole course of the race. The jockeys, moreover—and again their horses—are not only not characterized, and play none of their professional tricks on each other or the amateur; by some horribly misguided desire to enhance the contrast between their mature masculinity and the heroine's frightened nubility, they are selected to look less like jockeys than like guards on All-American. Such neglect amounts to a dereliction, not of art, if Hollywood fears and bridles at the word, but of the most elementary common sense, which amounts to the same thing. If a man wrote a piece of music so full of chowf-chowf, people would hardly bear to listen to it (unless it were given some such title as "The Four Freedoms," or perhaps "The Seven Against Thebes"). But that is not going to make a flop of *National Velvet*. I expect to see it again myself, for that matter.

JULY 5, 1947

ZERO DE CONDUITE AND *L'ATALANTE*

James Agee

•

IF YOU REGARD all experiment as affectation and all that bewilders you as a calculated personal affront, and if you ask of art chiefly that it be easy to take, you are advised not to waste your time seeing Jean Vigo's *Zero de Conduite* and *L'Atalante:* go on back to sleep, lucky Pierre, between the baker's wife and the well-digger's daughter, if you can squeeze in among the reviewers who have written so contemptuously of Vigo's work. If you regard all experiment as ducky, and all bewilderment as an opportunity to sneer at those who confess their bewilderment, and if you ask of art only that it be outré, I can't silence your shrill hermetic cries, or prevent your rush to the Fifth Avenue Playhouse; I can only hope to God I don't meet you there. If, on the other hand, you are not automatically sent either into ecstasy or catalepsy by the mere mention of avant-gardism, if your eye is already sufficiently open so that you don't fiercely resent an artist who tries to open it somewhat wider, I very much hope that you will see these films. I can't at all guarantee that you will like them, far less that you will enjoy and admire them as much as I do, for they are far too specialized. I can only be reasonably sure that you will find them worth seeing.

Zero de Conduite is a forty-minute movie about a French boys' boarding-school. It is hard for me to imagine how anyone with a curious eye and intelligence can fail to be excited by it, for it is one of the most visually eloquent and adventurous movies I have seen. But its fullest enjoyment depends rather heavily, I believe, on subjective chance. I happen to share a good deal of Vigo's peculiar kind of obsession for liberty and against authority, and can feel this in particularly clear emotional focus, as he does, in terms of the children and masters in a school. So the spirit of this film, its fierceness and gaiety, the total absence of well-constructed "constructive" diagnosis and prescription, the enormous liberating force of its quasi-nihilism, its humor, directness, kindliness, criminality, and guile, form for me as satisfying a revolutionary expression as I know.

On one seeing, anyhow, the film is quite bewildering, even if you understand its main device, as I was slow to do; but if you know the device, and accept it, the bewilderment itself becomes essential to the poem, and to your pleasure in it. As I see it the trick is, simply, that Vigo gets deeper inside his characters than most people have tried to on film, is not worried about transitions between objective, subjective, fantastic, and subconscious reality, and mixes as many styles and camera tricks, as abruptly, as he sees fit—always, so far as I can see, using the right style at the right moment, and always using it with force, charm, and originality. I assume that he intended, as one of his main points, to insist that these several levels of reality are equal in value, and interpenetrative; and I would accept this aesthetically for its enrichment of poetic perception, metaphor, and device, even if I rejected it intellectually.

It seems clear to me that on the wild level of *Zero*, and on levels less adventurous, the unprejudiced eye could learn its way around such intricate treatment as naturally as it learned to link the many disparities which make up the basic vocabulary of conventional movies. Most movies, including many of the best, have been made timidly and under great handicap, with fragments of the movie alphabet which were mostly shaped and frozen by around 1925. In an important sense Vigo is far from "unconventional"; he is merely making much of the rest of the alphabet available. He has gone as far in this, I think, as Eisenstein or Dovzhenko—in a very different direction, of course—and a great deal that he has done in this film, bold as it is, should be regarded less as inimitable experiment than as the conquest of more of the full ground on which further work can be done. It is as if he had invented the wheel. Many others were fumbling at it; some still are; but nobody of anything remotely like his ability is trying to find further uses for it; and one is sure to be branded as a solemn snob, incapable of "enjoying" movies, if one so much as dares to speak in favor of these elementary devices by which enjoyment could be enlarged.

The boys in *Zero* are seen as they see each other; the audience is one of them. Although they are much the hardest, most happily perceived children I have seen in a movie, in one sense they are sentimentalized. They have the aloof, dangerous beauty of young, wild preying animals; whereas some of the schoolboys I knew were merely unnoticeable, others were sick, others gentle or timid, and still others were safe-playing, sycophantic dolts from the day they were born—faculty members already. I wish they had been shown in this variety, however it might have complicated Vigo's child-worship and his anarchic fury. The teachers, however, are perfect. Seen as the boys see them or hope to see them, they are masterpieces of caricature, mainly ferocious, one coldly compassionate, one in the hyperboles of admiration. The sympathetic teacher who inspires them to revolt is a sort of lay Chaplin; another, an inspired epitome of the snoop, suggests Groucho Marx or, still more, a tiptoeing lobster dressed in an undertaker's suit; the headmaster is a pompous, murderous, shrieking midget.

There are so many wonderful scenes that I can mention only a few: the silent, mysterious opening, in which two boys in a railway compartment play out the most beautiful white-magic I have ever seen, with toys, tricks, and suggestions of competitive vice; a blood-slowing capture of paralysis of time on a Sunday, and on the carpet of the headmaster's office; a dormitory riot and procession, bearing a crucified teacher through a slow-motion storm of pillow feathers, which combines Catholic and primordial rituals and as an image of millennial, triumphal joy has only been equaled on film, so far as I know, by newsreel shots of the liberation of Paris. Vigo does some beautiful things, too, with subtly *slurred* rather than slow motion; and the stripped, mean sets and the occasional glimpses of pure naturalistic action are grim and firm as stone outcrops. Maurice Jaubert's score seems good but nothing extraordinary as music, but fitted with the film I like it as well as any outside Dovzhenko's *Frontier*.

(*To be continued*)

JULY 12, 1947

Of the two films by Jean Vigo at the Fifth Avenue Playhouse, *Zero de Conduite*, which I commented on last week, seems to me all but unblemished inspiration, moving freely and surely in its own unprecedented world from start to finish, one of the few great movie poems. I admire *L'Atalante* less; it is only the best French movie since the best of René Clair. *Zero* seems to have been made, as all the best work has to be, from the inside out; *L'Atalante*, on the whole, is put together from the outside inward. It is very good, spasmodically great poetry applied to pretty good prose; a great talent trying, I judge, to apply itself so far as it can stand to, conventionally and commercially.

The story, which Vigo adapted rather than invented, could almost be one of those pseudo-simple, sophisticated-earthy things which several French movie-makers handle gracefully, to the delight of cultivated Americans who will despise Vigo's work; the sex life of a jealous barge captain and his restive peasant bride; the crawling of the claustrophobic, ironically christened barge along the Seine; a couple of weird flirtations; estrangement; reunion. But Vigo's treatment shows up the French movie "classics" of this sort for the genteel literary exercises they really are. The old familiar "civilized," "Gallic" smirk is strictly outlawed;these are horribly serious, instinctual, brainless people, presented with a naked directness that is beyond patronage or gentle laughter up the sleeve, beyond even any particular show of sympathy. The "atmospheres" which in later films of this sort are sketched in so prettily are not pretty here but gravely monumental, and all-pervasive. The ordinary clever use of props in French films is here no tender exhibition of naive trinkets before the comfortable but a solid drench of inanimate objects, passionately, all but mystically, respected for what they are, and mean to their owners.

At its best *L'Atalante* is sensuously much richer and more beautiful than *Zero*—in spite of the somewhat damaged prints it is clear that Boris Kaufman's camera work in both films should have an article to itself—and once in a while the picture breaks free into Vigo's half mad, strangely majestic kind of poetry. The bridal procession from church to barge, which opens the film, is a great passage, forlorn, pitiful, cruelly funny, and freezingly sinister; Dita Parlo (the bride) is the fullest embodiment of sub-articulate sex that I have seen; the trinket salesman with whom she flirts is an astonishing crossbreed of slapstick with a kind of jailbird Ariel; and Michel Simon, as a pre-mental old man, is even more wonderfully realized as a poetic figure, a twentieth-century Caliban. Vigo was a more experienced director by the time he made *L'Atalante*, and the picture shows gifts fully as great as those shown in *Zero de Conduite*. But for all its quality *L'Atalante* suggests the strugglings of a maniac in a strait-jacket; whereas in *Zero* he moves freely, and it turns out that he is dangerous only to all in the world that most needs destroying.

It is clear that Vigo picked up a good deal from German films of the early twenties, from Clair and Chaplin, and from the whole creative brew of the Paris of his time. On a foggy day, indeed, or with a prejudiced eye, it would be possible to confuse his work with the general sad run of avant-garde movie work, as several reviewers, including some whom I ordinarily respect, have done. But Vigo was no more a conventional avant-gardist than he was a Hollywood pimp; he was one of the very few real originals who have ever worked on film. Nobody has approached his adroitness in handling reality, consciousness, and time on film (in *Zero*); or has excelled his vivid communication of the animal emotions, the senses, the inanimate world, and their interplay (in *L'Atalante*); nor have I found, except in the best work of the few masters, a flexibility, richness, and purity of creative passion to equal his in both these films.

Here is the little I know about him. He was the son of a Basque revolutionist, and learned to walk in the prison in which, as Vigo put it, his father was suicided. Perhaps that helps explain why he never so much as tried to learn to put his best foot forward. He began his career as an artist in a photographer's studio in Nice. He became an assistant movie cameraman, helped organize a film society, and made *A propos de Nice*, which was, I gather, a short and extremely sardonic film, nominally in the "documentary" manner. In Paris he made *Zero de Conduite* in 1933 and *L'Atalante* in 1934. He planned several other films, including one about tennis (with Cochet) and one about the French penal colonies; but all arrangements for financing these schemes fell through. When Paris censors saw *Zero* they forbade its release; even at a press screening it caused a near-riot. He was luckier with the more conventional *L'Atalante*. The miseries of dying, of tuberculosis, at the age of twenty-nine, with most of his abilities still unused, were exacerbated in Vigo by his knowledge that now that he was helpless to interfere, movie tradesmen were making little improvements on the picture.

Today, according to the Hollywood *Quarterly*, from which I got most of this information, both films are playing the French neighborhood theaters. It is not said whether they are popular.

MAY 7, 1949

FIGHT FILMS

Manny Farber

•

Manny Farber's book *Negative Space*, recently reprinted in an expanded edition, deserves a place on every film lover's shelf. His essay "White Elephant Art vs. Termite Art" is part of the common vocabulary of film writing. Farber, a champion of low-budget "termite cinema," the action film, the B-movie against the dread Hollywood middlebrow cinema, revolutionized the practice of film criticism by bringing his wit, painter's and art critic's eye to his film writing. He was a film critic for *New Republic* and then *The Nation* from 1949–1954. Dwight McDonald said Farber was "as perverse and original a film critic as exists or can be imagined," Farber is also an accomplished painter whose work has had retrospectives at the Museum of Contemporary Art in Los Angeles, Pittsburgh's Carnegie Museum, and the Rose Museum at Brandeis University.

THANKS TO ROCKY Graziano's infamous fame, and the box-office killing made last year by *Body and Soul*, the studios have been turning out fight films as fast as they could steal each other's material: though tightly humorless and super-saturated with worn-out morality, they remain pure fantasy in so far as capturing the pulse of the beak-busting trade is concerned. You go to this type of movie expecting to see plenty of good prizefighting and the atmosphere that surrounds the trade. You come out on the street feeling like a sucker, having been frustrated by a jittery camera man who is always in the wrong place, doublecrossed by editing that switches you continually away from the fight, tricked by actors who couldn't fight their way out of a subway rush. These actors, with bodies attuned by years of acting to comfortable, easy, relaxed movement, foolishly try to ape a trade they may have studied for a month, instead of relying on their own imaginations to convey boxing technique. Occasionally an aggressive actor turns up, like Cagney or Mickey Rooney, who loves to act and move in his own way, which results in a style as unique and worth watching as the technique of the average pug.

The scenarios seem to have been written by a gossip columnist—they concentrate on spanking the hero for the un-Christian way he breaks training by smoking, the mean treatment he accords his friends, and, most of all, his crude, ugly approach to women. He goes with disreputable females, mistreats his mother and the girl back home waiting for him; but the fact of the matter is that he, more than any other movie hero, is swamped by a prize collection of boring, freakish women. While the gangster, cowboy, ballplayer are lauded, the boxer is never presented as anything but a bad nickel.

The romanticism of the script is quite restrained compared to the peculiar business that goes on in the ring. Whereas real fighters actually hit each other about one-sixth of the time, the fearless "phenoms" of the cinema are hitting every second—and never anywhere but flush on the chin or in the stomach; in spite of this, the hero is usually looking around the audience for someone he knows. Hatred can propel a fighter who looks like a spent, squashed herring to heights that always surprise his opponent. There are no decisions, fights are never stopped, there are plenty of foul, which the hero is above recognizing even when a blow tears his knee half off; it seems incredible that in-fighters, counter-punches, "cuties" are never characterized—only one type is presented, a creaking version of the mauling club-fighter.

The two latest fight films, *Champion* and *The Set-up* return to the movie-for-movie's-sake technique of pre–1935 B films, but they are dehumanized by an effort at newsreel realism and a compulsion to grind away at a message. Attempting to describe the sadism of the ring, the directors exaggerate the savagery inherent in prize-fighting dragging in enough peripheral mayhem to scare the officers of Buchenwald. The basic quality of these scripts seems to be a pure, imaginative delight in the mangling of the human body: tired fighters inhale with the frightful expression that leaves one with the feeling the air is filled with needles rather than oxygen, while outside the arena people are thrown from trains, smacked by canes, bricks, and blackjacks—in *The Set-up* this builds into the overwhelming impression of a nightmare. What results is a double distortion—the effect of over-smearing brutality and the lust for ultra-realism—which strangles the actual movement. The action, mimicking reality, moves too fast to convey its meaning through the medium of the camera; unless realistic pace is transformed into the slower rhythm that movies can handle, it tends to jumble action. The hard, crassly clear photography of *Champion*, which aims at spotlighting reality, actually produces a metallic stage set, while the bitter moral realism which *The Set-up* aims at produces another type of overstatement which has the flavor of lurid melodrama.

Champion is hung on the weariest formula in boxing films—the success story. In the original Ring Lardner version success is only a minor strain in a theme devoted to depicting a morosely malevolent pug; the movie reverses the emphasis so that the hero (Kirk Douglas) exhibits above all things a flagrantly lucky, talented, bewitching adaptation of Hollywood's pet ideal that all amoral, egocentric behavior possesses an endurable charm and fascination. Douglas, as a windmill of activity on the screen, portrays a hard, quartzlike, malevolent show-off, yet maintains a smooth inner serenity. The movie's voltage is chiefly a tinny, quick wit displayed through the virtuosity of Douglas's performance and the director's (Mark Robson) flexibility with the medium. In an unbearably moving death scene, in which the hero throws himself over the moon of emotion, and the camera spills on oatmealish atmosphere around him, the style is a cross between Howard Hawkes and Euripides, the visual details magnificent. Except for this cinematic episode *Champion* pivots on a vaudevillish technique which consists of strategizing scenes to the last detail before the actors go before the camera, thus saving the time and money that go into excessive reshooting. They rely on the self-sufficiency of their characters for movement rather than on expensive movement from locale to locale. Actors appear, as in no other film, loaded with material and perfectly trained. The result is a new aesthetic in which every effect is the $64 one, perfectly executed, and dehumanized.

The Set-up—its prizefighters aren't champions but the derelicts, beginners, old men who fight four-rounders in arenas that have more trash on the floor than seats—is a shocking movie, not only because it is often good but because it is the grimiest, most brutal film in years. Its direction schizophrenically moves from puerile overstatement to its opposite in every scene. The movie's honesty comes from the static performance of Robert Ryan as a thoughtful preliminary fighter one punch away from punch drunk, and the same kind of performance from this fighter's wife, Audrey Totter. Their inflexible, singletrack approach to acting is this: don't act, move a muscle, or smile, it looks insincere.

JUNE 4, 1949

JOHN HUSTON

Manny Farber

•

HOLLYWOOD'S FAIR-HAIRED BOY, to the critics, is Director John Huston; in terms of falling into the Hollywood mold, Huston is a smooth blend of iconoclast and sheep. If you look closely at his films,* what appears to be a familiar story, face, grouping of actors, or tempo has in each case an obscure, outrageous, double-crossing unfamiliarity that is the product of an Einstein-lubricated brain. Huston has a personal reputation as a bad-boy, a homely one (called "Double-Ugly" by friends, "monster" by enemies), who has been in every known trade, rugged or sedentary: Mexican army cavalryman, editor of the first pictorial weekly, expatriate painter, hobo, hunter, Greenwich Village actor, amateur lightweight champ of California. His films, which should be rich with this extraordinary experience are rich with cut-and-dried homilies; expecting a mobile and desperate style, you find stasis manipulated with the sure-handedness of a Raffles.

Though Huston deals with the gangster, detective, adventure thriller that the average fan knows like the palm of his hand, he is Message-Mad, and mixes a savage story with puddin'head righteousness. His characters are humorless and troubled and quite reasonable so, since

***The Maltese Falcon* (1933), *In This Our Life, Across the Pacific, Sap Pietro, The Treasure of the Sierra Madre, Key Largo, We Were Strangers*.

Huston, like a Puritan judge, is forever calling on them to prove that they can soak up punishment, carry through harrowing tasks, withstand the ugliest taunts. Huston is a crazy man with death: he pockmarks a story with gratuitous deaths, fast deaths, and noisy ones, and in idle moments has his characters play parlor games with gats. Though his movies are persistently concerned with grim interpersonal relationships viewed from an ethic-happy plane, half of each audience takes them for comedies. The directing underlines a single vice or virtue of each character so that his one-track actions become either boring or funny; it expands and slows figures until they are like oxen driven with a big moralistic whip.

Money—its possession, influence, manufacture, lack—is a star performer in Huston's moral fables and gilds his technique; his irony toward and preoccupation with money indicate a director who is a little bitter at being so rich—the two brief appearances Huston makes in his own films are quite appropriately as a bank teller and a rich, absent-minded American handing out gold pieces to a recurring panhandler. His movies will please a Russian audience: half the characters (Americans) are money-mad, directly enriching themselves by counterfeiting, prospecting, blackmail, panhandling.

His style is so tony it should embarrass his threadbare subjects. The texture of a Panama hat is emphasized to the point where you feel Huston is trying to stamp its price tag on your retina. He creates a splendiferous effect out of the tiniest details—each hair of an eyelid—and the tunnel dug in a week by six proletarian heroes is the size of the Holland Tunnel.

Huston's technique differs on many counts from classic Hollywood practice, which from Sennett to Wellman has visualized stories by means of the unbroken action sequence, in which the primary image is the fluid landscape shot where terrain and individual are blended together and the whole effect is scenic rather than portraiture. Huston's art is stage presentation, based on oral expression and static composition: the scenery is curiously deadened, and the individual has an exaggerated vitality. His characters do everything the hard way—the mastication of a gum-chewing gangster resembles the leg-motion in bicycling. In the traditional film life is viewed from a comfortable vantage-point, one that is so unobtrusive that the audience is seldom conscious of the fact that a camera had anything to do with what is shown. In Huston's you are constantly aware of a vitaminized photographer. Huston breaks a film up into a hundred disparate midget films: a character with a pin head in one incident is megacephalic in another; the first shot of a brawl shows a modest Tampico saloon, the second expands the saloon into a skating rink.

The Huston trademark consists of two unorthodox practices—the statically designed image (objects and figures locked into various pyramid designs) and the mobile handling of close three-figured shots. The Eisenstein of the Bogart thriller, he rigidly delimits the subject matter that goes into a frame, by chiaroscuro or by grouping his figures within the square of the screen so that there is nothing else to look at. He is a terror with a camera where there is hardly room for an actor to move an arm: given a small group in close quarters, around a bar, bonfire, table, he will hang on to the event for dear life and show you peculiarities of posture, expression, and anantomy that only the actor's doctor should know. The arty, competent Huston would probably seem to an old rough-and-ready silent film director like a boy who graduated from Oxford at the age of eight, and painted the Sistine Chapel during his lunch hours.

Aside from its spectacular evidences of his ability to condense events and characterization, the one persistent virtue of Huston's newest and worst movie, *We Were Strangers*, is Jennifer Jones, who wears a constant frown as though she had just swallowed John Garfield. Garfield acts as though he'd just been swallowed.

JUNE 18, 1949

FRENCH MOVIES

Manny Farber

•

THE WEARIEST MYTH of critics tabs Hollywood for the formularized movies and foreign studios for the original ones; actually the worst Hollywood B has more cinematic adrenaline than most English or French movies, and no one is more electric than the English director Olivier, reactionary than the Frenchman Pagnol, victimized by easy sensibility than the Italians De Sica and Rossellini. The art of these prize-plastered directors washes like a waterfall over their movies so that you feel common for paying only $1.50 for your ticket to culture; they are more dispiritedly indebted to pre–1935 Hollywood technique than Sturges, Huston, or Korda. The decadence of the French film, dominated by pooped-out aesthetes, is somewhat belied by *Devil in the Flesh* which has almost the weight and fulness of a *Madame Bovary* (more than can be said for the Radiguet novel on which it is based). This film's decadence—its novelistic approach; the smooth, velvet finish of ten-year-old MGM films; time-worn images like fire for passion, raindrops on water for sadness—does not keep it from being the best movie condemned by the Legion of Decency since *Monsieur Verdoux*.

The love affair in *Devil in the Flesh*—a restless, bored young wife (Micheline Presle) bed-locked with an unstable charmer (Gérard Philipe) who doesn't yet shave—is a staple as old as the French novel but never realized so well on film. This disastrous affair moves with an inexorable logic the love film hasn't had since psychiatry took over Hollywood; the inexplicable last shot (sky breaking into V-formations of airplanes) is a minor disturbance.

Director Autant Lara creates a tapestry of unemphasized details; density and depth, currently ignored by directors in favor of the one-thread effect, are produced here by some old-fashioned ideas of what makes a beautiful movie. Trying as Griffith did for the serenely articulated image drenched in sentiment, he sinks his actor into a perfectly ordered environment emptied of discord (sunlit scenes glow without heat, rain is soft and warm, family scenes are as unhectic as a Childe Hassam canvas). The impression of profusion comes from the bounfitul detailing of each shot and of the central characters; like the treatment of the Chaplin figure, these two roles are loaded with expression and gesture and seen from all sides. The attempt to imbed the story like a pearl in a period (World War 1) and a milieu (suburban Paris) results in the use of some banal devices: figures are back-lit with halo-like contours, viewed obliquely behind grillwork, lace curtains, flowers; the last shot of a scene is cemented in time by a lingering camera. But the overall effect is of being submerged in and idling through a self-contained world.

The solidity of this movie, as of current French films, is partly a gift from the past gods of art. In a Hollywood movie each event is seen for itself, without cultural overtones; events in Lara's movie are unconsciously burdened by the painting, literary, and movie tradition of the preceding century. Both in subject and treatment (boating scene, François's home) this movie recalls Seurat and Manet; the movie would not have been so laden if Proust had not created such a dense atmosphere; with decades of precedent to draw upon, directors like Pagnol, Lara, Clouzot do impeccable funerals and walks through the streets with their eyes shut and both hands behind their backs. The wry treatment of incidental people, waiters, school teachers, mothers, is an old snobbery that should have been given up before it was started. It would be nice to see a French movie free of its academic albatross.

Gérard Philipe, a new, momentous figure in European films, is an original actor, so absolutely the ill-starred creatures he plays—the glum, impudent adulterer in this, an over-sweetened but near-perfect Myshkin in the excellent *The Idiot*—that his performances are less magical for being so real. French movie actors (Raimu, Barrault) have tried for an absolute naturalism based on theatrical expression, and the spectacularly gifted Philipe is the $64 end-product of this tradition. The average player presents a threefold personality—the script character, the type he represents in the public mind, and his private-life personality. Philipe presents one whole different character in each movie, no carry-overs. His François—arrogantly sensitive, disaffected, histrionically bad-tempered, a social sneerer but indolently dependent—seems to have walked into the movie from an art-colony garret bringing no acting baggage with him. His performance is as rich a characterization as any in Tolstoi and one bound to amuse people who think of the boudoir hero in terms of physical beauty and bourgeois virtues; François lies, tricks, wilts at the tiniest obstacle, flees, and is generally a whirlwind of unsavory attitudes. Philipe seems to live on the screen rather than perform; he manages to be three-dimensionally in action so that the cubistic effect is of seeing from all sides. Compared with this fresh, realistic performance, the Boyer-Cooper-Stewart lover seems to be built out of the old nuts and bolts of romantic acting.

SEPTEMBER 23, 1950

SUNSET BOULEVARD

Manny Farber

•

SUNSET BOULEVARD—THE story of Hollywood movies draped on a depressing sex affair—is an uncompromising study of American decadence displaying a sad, worn, methodical beauty few films have had since the late twenties. Its creators—pseudo-sophisticated Charles Brackett and Billy Wilder, a mean director with telescopic eyes—are dispassionate observers rather than artists who dig inside their characters, and they make the melodrama even shallower by top-casting it with the superficial Gloria Swanson. My guess, though, is that this contrived but essentially uncorrupted journalism will live longer than a "great human" job like *The Bicycle Thief*, a film that hides the worst type of cheating sentimentality beneath its "untouched" surface.

The story, parading an unadmirable hero (William Holden) through ugly affairs with his best friend's fiancee (Nancy Olson) and a rich neurotic of fifty (Swanson), amounts to morbid liaison world between the "talkie" and silent film world, with Swanson doing a lot of ear-bending with a voice like a hollow stone wall, while Holden does an unemphatic version of the best silent-film pantomime. The tragedy inherent in his gigolo setup with the ex-star is largely muffed because the Brackett-Wilder combination—vague about the sunset period of an actress's life—entwines Holden with a cliché of the frustrated middle-aged artiste and drenches them both in gimmicks and weird atmosphere. Holden occasionally escapes into a more accurately observed world of young Hollywood talent, before the Swanson character clobbers him with three incredibly well-placed bullets which skillfully nudge him to his final floating place, the swimming pool recently dredged for the body of Alan Ladd, the late star of *Gatsby*.

The cold, mean *Sunset Boulevard*—a beautiful title, though I suspect it was shot on another boulevard—is further proof of the resurgence of art in the Hollywood of super-craftsmen with insuperable taste. American filmmakers have suddenly learned how to make movies work as plastically as Mondrain paintings, using bizarre means and gaucherie, with an eye always on the abstract vitality produced by changing pace, working a choppy sentence against a serene image, extravagant acting against quiet. In this gimmick-ridden *Sunset* a corpse talks. The improbability bothers me less than the fact that he over-talks, explaining action—when Holden is delicately beached by the cops—that explains itself with a morbid realism about American scene. But his lines—spoken with a nice, trapped, Midwestern twang—work as wise-guy counterpoint to scene, building up each audience perception like a good tailgate trombonist. Study the silent closeup of Holden being needled by a lecherous clerk, and you must respect skill that compresses so much of the kept man's malaise into a fraudulent secondary bit. This scene, with its lingering focus on a nauseated countenance, is a small horror movie that not only starts with an improbable, hammy cruelty by the clerk but uses it to magnify Holden's unhighlighted anguish. The upsetting fact about craftsmanship that always finds a way to outmaneuver criticism is that it is putting movies beyond the tastes of an audience that heretofore has judged films for elements—morality, sociology, message—no longer primary in such form-conscious art.

Save for one devilish axis, this would be a stiff, obsessively detailed record of corruption. Holden is one of the most quietly charming hard-luck guys a movie ever watched for his pinpoint reactions, which give the film its endless silent perceptions of the way an average studio worker thinks, moves, worries, daydreams. As the murdered narrator, he spreads a dense poolroom pallor over the imagery (his lines operate like silent film titles), but the Hollywood tone of his tight gestures and pantomime—the bound-in floridity, jumpiness, and showy crispness—is what gives this movie its virulent snap. The load is entirely upon him because the other portraits, while blistering, run from good comic strip (Fred Clark's safe-playing producer) through soggy urbanity (DeMille playing himself) to stereotyped abandon (Swanson).

The movie is stultified by spectacle, novelistic development, and a slow dismemberment of the human beings that are strictly from Von Stroheim's day. It is hard to find any logic or life in Swanson's grotesque because the director is too busy building baroque furniture both her and her ménage. The illogicality of her mausoleum-like mansion, moldering outside while one butlet keeps the inside jungle of rococo spotless, is less stultifying than the eclectic worship of forebodingly cluttered shots and dated insights about contaminated life. Where John Huston cuts a face into a mosaic of analytic shots, *Sunset*, without any short cuts, standoffishly views a butler descending eighty stairs, crossing acres of beefy carpet, to open a door. Just as laborious and frightful is the old single-alley focus on character. Save for one poignant, relaxed scene in bed, Swanson stays exactly as directed, and very like Theda Bara, within a nasty stereotype: she sinks talon-like fingers in her lover's arm, telephones his other girl with a voice dripping demoniac evil, piles up straight gestures and exclamations that are the stock notions of the undersexed neurotic. This dated technique would sink the movie under minutiae if Wilder's inveterate meanness didn't turn every shot into a shocking, mad, controlled chewing of assorted twentieth-century cuds.

JULY 28, 1951

STRANGERS ON A TRAIN

Manny Farber

•

A STATE OF uncertainty, generally accompanied by a feeling of anxiety or fear; indetermination; indecision." This, according to Webster, is the meaning of suspense—probably the best single theme for movies in an anxious era like this, when we are all sweating out something—from A-bombs, bullets, or furloughs to pregnancies, ironclad marriages, or high prices. But this theme has been misconstrued and bastardized by both Hollywood and its critics. One director in particular has made his living by subjecting the movie audience to a series of cheap, glossy, mechanically perfect shocks, and for this he has been hailed as the High Boojum of Suspense. The name of this artist is, of course, Alfred Hitchcock—who has gone farther on fewer brains than any director since Griffith, while cleverly masking his deficiency, and his underlying petty and pointless sadism, with a honey-smooth patina of "sophistication," irony, and general glitter.

Having vented this long-pent-up gripe, I hasten to add that Hitchcock's latest film, *Strangers on a Train*, is fun to watch if you check your intelligence at the box office. It is too bad that this director, who has the observing eyes of a Dos Passos and the facility of a Maupassant, does himself the disservice of intercutting rather good naturalistic scenes with so much old hoke. His forte is the half-minute visual uncertainty—a murderer's hand straining through a sewer grating for a symbolically decorated cigarette lighter. Hitch not only shows the fingers straining forward with slow, animal cunning but throws a white, metallic light over them, thus turning a dirty black hole into Grauman's Chinese on opening night. The whole thing is done in a boxed closeup, so that one can't help feeling the camera man could have cut the nonsense short by handing the Ronson up to the villain. The late-twenties Hitchcock, devoted to the fairly credible style of John Buchan and Belloc Lowndes, would have rejected all such intrusive, romantic, metronome-timed schmalz and no doubt fired the script writer for lifting the gesture and locale from a film—*The Third Man*—made by his former shadow, Carol Reed. However, like so many transplanted foreign aces who consider American audiences more childish, gullible, and slow-witted than those in the Marshall Plan countries, Hitchcock has gone so soft that he makes even the average uninspired native director look comparatively noncommercial. His only really punchy Hollywood job was *Lifeboat*. *Strangers on a Train* ranks somewhere between that effort and mushy gab-fests like *Sabotage*, *Under Capricorn*, *Spellbound*, and—though it had its merits—*Rope*.

Because chases and homicides and Pearl White escapes clutter his pictures, no one notices the general emasculation Hitchcock has perpetrated on the thriller. Brittle, soft-cheeked, petulant pretty boys (Dick, Dall, Todd, Donat, Cummings, Granger) are projected into high melodrama. These characters seem to disappear like clothes dummies within their tweedy, carefully unpressed Brooks Brothers jackets and slacks, thanks to a director who impregnates costume and décor with so much crackling luster, so much tension and latent evil, that the spectator expects a stair corner or tie clasp to start murdering everyone in sight. Hitchcock did a lot of harm to movies by setting off a trend toward investing backrounds, architecture, and things like cigar bands with deep meaning. Finally, he takes all the bite out of his stories by whipping quickly but delicately down various "artistic" detours. In *Strangers on a Train* he cuts away from a brutally believable strangulation to the concave image cast up by the lens of the victim's fallen spectacles. At once the onlooker loses interest in the murder as such because he is so entranced with the lush, shadowy choreographic lyricism with which Hitchcock shows the life being squeezed, fraction by fraction, out of a shallow, hateful nymphomaniac.

The movie, by the way, is built around the travestied homosexuality of the murderer. Robert Walker provides the role with a meatier, more introverted, unhealthier savor than the stars usually give a Hollywood production. This is partly the result of Hitchcock's mechanical and spurious use of the new closeup style of camera work, which is evidently aimed at fetishists who like to study pores. Here he has given Walker an oily, puffy face and made him skitter his tiny eyes back and forth horizontally until it appears that the actor looks at everybody as if he were reading a book. But somewhere in the past two years Walker has picked up an aggressive jump style of acting; so that he seems to bull his way through the action—even when quietly waiting around a carnival for the sun to go down—like a thoughtless, savage two-hundred-pounder about to plunge for a touchdown. The heavy blanket of twisted melancholia which Walker spreads over this film is beautifully counterpointed by the work of Laura Elliott in the role of the victim. She seems to swish up into the picture like a sexy bespectacled baby whale. All the best things in *Strangers* have to do with the playing of these two.

SEPTEMBER 1, 1951

JERRY LEWIS

Manny Farber

•

THE GRIMMEST PHENOMENON since Dagmar has been the fabulous nationwide success of Jerry Lewis's sub-adolescent, masochistic mugging. Lewis has parlayed his apish physiognomy, rickety body, frenzied lack of coordination, paralyzing brashness, and limitless capacity for self-degradation into a gold mine for himself and the mannered crooner named Dean Martin who, draped artistically from a mike, serves as his ultra-suave straight man. When Jerry fakes swallowing a distasteful pill, twiddles "timid" fingers, whines, or walks "like Frankenstein," his sullen narcissistic insistence suggests that he would sandbag anyone who tried to keep him from the limelight. Lewis is a type I hoped to have left behind when I short-sheeted my last cot at Camp Kennekreplach. But today's bobby-soxers are rendered apoplectic by such Yahoo antics, a fact that can only be depressing for anyone reared on comedians like Valentino, Norma Shearer, Lewis Stone, Gregory Peck, Greer Garson, Elizabeth Taylor, or Vincent Impellitteri.

That's My Boy has to do with the transformation of an inept sissified bookworm (Lewis) into a halfback as sterling as glamour-boy Martin, a man who nonchalantly slaps off tacklers the way most of us shoo away mosquitoes. (For his part, Martin has modeled him self so carefully on Crosby and Como that he seems to jiggle like a mannered skeleton inside his heavily padded suits.) The film is almost saved by Eddie Mayehoff, a lantern-jawed bruiser with practically no mouth and a funny way of overemphasizing his role of an ancient Bronco Nagurski; I figure him for a terrible-tempered ruskless mastodon who never actually went to college but knows enough to despise this puerile TV-style pigskin parody. If I am right, he supports my opinion that the American public is now ready to laugh at lepers and gas-chambers.

Almost every Italian film trickling into the "art" theaters these days has been awarded a prize by a foreign film festival. They also have in common a flux of odd-angled shots of thighs and heaving bosoms; a quantity of daring propaganda against such ogres as warmongers, pimps, non-leftist priests, prison wardens, Lesbians, and petty government officials; and an all-around frenzied unkemptness in cutting, lighting, make-up, and underlying purpose. Such a movie is *Women Without Names*, a detention-camp melodrama which won the Selznick award in Venice and will probably play here to an almost solidly male audience—aesthetic to the core—drawn in by such ads as "women trapped by intrigue . . . and the heartless passion of ruthless men!" Not to mention stills like the one of Simone Simon languishing in bra and shorts on a mattress of hay in order to tease the fat pervert who sits nearby, ogling her in a torment of frustration. With sharp Italian sense of irony and realism, the director has struck a donkey into one corner of the frame and scoured the brassiere industry for a spectacular zebra-striped number—just what you'd expect a prisoner to wear on off-hours in the camp stable. The story behind this sly scene is that a gold-hearted hoyden is trying to seduce a fruity ice-cream vender into marriage so that she can promote herself and her pal, Valentina Cortesa, out of this corral for women without passports. The plan fails; the pal dies in childbirth while the camera, by way of no change, dollies down a line of sulky, dowdy onlookers. In Cortesa, my favorite actress of the moment, the film has at least one undebatable asset: no tricks, quiet grace, and a sensitive beauty which must have seen and lived wisely and well.

Just in case you've run out of sodium amytal for the weekend, here are a few substitutes with which I've just caught up. They've been floating around for some time. *Fabiola*: Christian tribulations in the time of Constantine. A two-hour chaos of disconnected sequences snipped more or less at random from a much longer French production. English dubbed in; livestock by Barnum; male and female costumes by Claire McCardell; lighting by Mr. Moon. *Tony Draws a Horse*: Cecil Parker and all the gang in a sophisticated British psycho-comedy. Very intelligent movie in which the heroine swaths her head in a bandana, pulls her dress over her head, and then takes the bandana off. Perhaps, this is the English way of distracting your attention from obvious cheesecake. *The Secret of Convict Lake*: Battle between the sexes, somewhere north of Carson City in 1871. Five escaped convicts drop in on eight temporarily unattached lady pioneers of the sort you might meet in Lord and Taylor's any day now: Gene-Tierney, Ethel Barrymore, Richard Hylton. A grotesquely overcivilized Western larded with small talk about decency and indecency, peace of mind, kindness.

Force of Arms, the only likable film I saw last week, deserves a longer review than I can give it here.

OCTOBER 20, 1951

A STREETCAR NAMED DESIRE

Manny Farber

•

EVERYTHING THAT KEPT the Broadway *Streetcar* from spinning off into ridiculous melodrama—everything thoughtful, muted, three-dimensional—has been raped, along with poor Blanche Dubois, in the Hollywood wood version, so that the drama takes place completely in the foreground—all clamor, climax and Kazan. The movie opens characteristically with cabs zooming in an arc toward the camera and then cutting sharply into the New Orleans depot. With "impact" thus established, Warner Brothers takes us into the station for an artistic tip-off on what's to follow: a herd of crinolined bridesmaids jounce gaily off the Seaboard Limited while away to the side the shabby-genteel figure of Blanche (Vivien Leigh) emerges through a cloud of engine steam. A chirpy sailor interrupts his whistling long enough to give Miss Dubois directions to her sister's house. A streetcar named DESIRE, in white block letters a mile high, lunges in another vicious arc before our eyes, and there we are in Stanley Kowalski's serene, sexful, squalid little flat in the French Quarter. From here on, the story proceeds as Tennessee Williams first wrote it, except that all the frankest—and most crucial—dialogue has been excised and the last scene has been churned disastrously to satisfy the Johnson office but confound the spectator. These changes bothered me less than the fact that screenwriter Williams thought he could turn his play into a movie by merely running the cast "outdoors" to a bowling alley or waterfront cafe whenever the dramatic structure of the original work permitted such a maneuver.

However, if the author surrendered without firing a shot, the actors and directors certainly did not. Marlon Brando, who on the stage gave a revolutionary head-on portrait of the rough-and-ready, second-generation American Joe, has upped the voltage of every eccentricity by several thousand watts. The performance is now more cinematic and flexible, but the addition of a lush physicality and a show-off's flamboyance to the character of Stanley makes him seem like a muscular version of a petulant, crazily egotistical homosexual. Brando, having fallen hard for the critics' idea that Stanley is simply animal and slob, now screams and postures and sweeps plates off the table with an ape-like emphasis that unfortunately becomes predictable.

As the ex-school-teacher-harlot-belle in this study of social-sexual disintegration, Miss Leigh injects a bittersweet fragrance and acrobatic excitement into the role, but the effects are freakish, too ambitious and endless. All this inchoate electricity helps sustain Kazan's record of directing nothing that is boring or insipid. The morning bed scene with wholesome Mrs. Kowalski (Kim Hunter) shows her as smug and contented as movie wives usually are in that situation. But Kazan gives the audience a rough shove with his candid view of the lady's legs widely spread under a disheveled sheet that never saw the inside of a laundry. Still, by activating all the characters to a pitch where they seem one comic-opera step away from lunacy Kazan has obliterated William's more delicate gradual revelation of the fact that Blanche is a rotten old Dixie apple fated for squashing by that raw, instinctual, 100 percent industrial American, Stanley Kowalski.

MAY 17, 1952

SISTER CARRIE

Manny Farber

•

HOLLYWOOD FILMS WERE once in the hands of non-intellectuals who achieved, at best, the truth of American life and the excitement of American movement in simple-minded action stories. Around 1940 a swarm of bright locusts from the Broadway theaters and radio stations descended on the studios and won Hollywood away from the innocent, rough-and-ready directors of action films. The big thing that happened was that a sort of intellectual whose eyes had been trained on the crowded, bound-in terrain of Times Square and whose brain had been sharpened on left-wing letters of the thirties, swerved Hollywood story-telling toward fragmented, symbol-charged drama, closely viewed, erratically acted, and deviously given to sniping at their own society. What Welles, Kanin, Sturges, and Huston did to the American film is evident in the screen version of Dreiser's *Sister Carrie*, which is less important for its story than for the grim social comment underscoring every shot.

You first see Carrie Meeber, rural and naive (Jennifer Jones), rushing to get off a daycoach while a drummer tells her she is making a mistake: "South Chicago? That's the slums." The remark which makes a 1909 masher round like a 1952 social worker, is full of meaning that the movie audience by now is wise to, and the writers need only touch on Carrie's first threadbare months in the city. The next few scenes are also immersed in social significance and accomplish the same kind of half-implied storytelling. One of them shows a crabby foreman driving Carrie so relentlessly that she runs a needle through her finger and loses her job as a shoe-stitcher. Since the foreman is played by a spidery bit player always typecast as a mean "pinch-penny," and since his dialogue runs to sentences like "Here's a dollar, a whole day's pay," the spectator has picked up a quick course in non-union labor in no more than two minutes of screen time.

The most important aspect of all this social significance is its prejudice against Americans, who are being ridiculed in films as completely as they were in the writings of Mencken. In this movie, the bias is managed, Mencken fashion, by treating people as "national" or "local" types rather than ordinary figures, and then casting the roles with actors who love to over-act uncharming traits. Carrie's first amour is played by Eddie Albert, whose portrayal of an American "go-getter" consists of flashing a big, lopsided grin, twirling a heavy gold watch and using his voice like a loud musical instrument. Somehow the heroine, whose strong point is her essential gentleness, puts up with this caricature who opens every conversation with either a belch or a couplet: "Charley's the name, charm's the game!" When Carrie and her second lover, the sleek restaurant owner Hurstwood, skip to New York with his partner's money, they are tracked down by a detective from the Western Bonding Company. The acting of this leering, gum-chewing slob is rendered by Ray Teal, who has a penchant for using one eye as though it belonged to a cruel pig and working a rich, sneering sound into his voice. Hurstwood's decline takes him into a Third Avenue hash house run by the sort of confident, ruthless Irishman Barry Kelley has been enacting since he entered films. The cameraman helps with floor-shots that exaggerate his huge belly and the lazy, tyrannical way in which he lolls in a chair. And finally, Hurstwood's wife, rich shrew that she is, turns up near the end to trade him a divorce for the rights to their Chicago home. Miriam Hopkins plays the scene by holding her mouth in a single grim line and keeping a rigid, buzzard-like look in her eyes.

One of the cardinal elements of the Times Square technique introduced in the era of *McGinty*, *Citizen Kane*, *A Man to Remember*, and *The Maltese Falcon* was the use of very close, snarling presentation which put the actors practically in a nose-to-nose relationship with the movie spectator. The entire production of *Carrie* is thrown at you in shallow scenes, the actors arranged parallel-fashion and statically on the front plane of the scene so that their physical presence is overpowering. The film was fortunate in having Laurence Oliver as the high-powered Hurstwood, all delicacy, intelligence, and high style up to his last weakened whispers on the Bowery. But after an hour of close views Olivier becomes less a figure than a formidable mustache, a mouth that has a tendency to flap, and poignant hands that sometimes mimic the gestures of madonnas in medieval painting. In one of the last views of the pitiable Hurstwood his ravaged face is exposed to Carrie as she turns a lamp on it. The fact that Hurstwood is ashamed to show himself seems next to ludicrous after an hour spent watching his face disintegrate over most of the screen.

Carrie is also fortunate in having a handsome production all around, but in the deliberate and magnified style to which Hollywood has turned, lightness of touch is impossible. When the camera dollies slowly over the cubicles of a flop-house (the big "art" scene) one has the feeling that the director is working with material that is as heavy and dignified as a Steinway grand inlaid with precious stones.

JULY 4, 1953

TIMES SQUARE MOVIEGOERS

Manny Farber

•

IT IS A custom among professional pipe smokers to offer romantic estimations of American moviegoers. The latest evaluation appeared in the *New Leader*—a tongue-in-cheek description of the action-movie fans who attend shabby theaters west of Times Square. It was a classic case of what happens when a critic turns sociologist. Mr. Markfield found that the largely male audience for action and horror pictures was made up of a desperate crew—perverts, adolescent hoodlums, chronic unemployeds, and far-gone neurotics—who possessed an impeccable taste in good, unpretentious off-beat films. These moviegoers shuddered or tittered, snored or shrieked obscenities. But somehow, while unable to control their bodies and emotions in the slightest degree, they were movie critics who simply couldn't be fooled by the expensive or pretentious. "Marvelous" was the word used to describe the infallible instinct of this *Lumpenproletariat* which causes Hollywood to shake in its assorted beach sandals.

It is a dangerous thing to lump a whole audience under general labels. The writers who did this in the twenties—during the era of Griffith, Sennett, and other silent-film "greats"—convinced a world-wide reading public that American moviegoers had low standards of appreciation and were to be treated like unintelligent children. Today, it has become fashionable for intellectuals to pretend to the same level of responses as the average member of the average audience. Every day another intellectual goes "popular" with a poetic, gaga dissertation on Mickey Spillane, "Moon Mullins," Ray Robinson, or Teresa Brewer. People everywhere are now encouraged to consider the audience for pop-artists infested by aesthetes looking like roughnecks and behaving like slobs.

As a steady customer in male-audience houses, I've never seen anything odd or outstanding in the clientele. Finding interest and excitement in almost any type of film filled with brawny men, destruction, and fights, a steady procession of people fill most of the seats from midmorning until almost dawn, lapping up the bad with the good, the merely pretentious with the unheralded realistic gems. My reason for citing a difference with Mr. Markfield's illusions is to encourage moviegoers to look at the screen instead of trying to find a freak show in the audience.

The Moon Is Blue is a small comedy that seems to sparkle, sound monotonous, look machine-made, and appear smartly guided at the same moment. For a while it merely irritated me. A blatantly calculated actress named Maggie McNamara trades jokes with a miscast William Holden in the observation tower of the Empire State Building. The girl is supposedly a wittily open-minded ingenue actress being picked up by a "terribly sweet" and personable young architect. They both talk in empty little sentences that suggest only the psuedo-teenage characters in popular magazine romances. After hearing innocuous things like "Oh, this is terrific" or "You're nice, I like you" in an observation tower that has been used to death by moviemakers there seems little reason to expect anything daring or smart from *The Moon Is Blue.* Nevertheless, when the pair shift to the young man's bachelor apartment, the dialogue shifts to a steady drumbeat of better-than-average epigrams, and though people come through doors and answer phones as constantly as in television comedy, the movie seems to get more flexible and interesting. How this happens is a little intangible, but it may be because Miss McNamara looks natural acting a proper little pop-off and because the director, Otto Preminger, can set up a modern apartment scene that seems as shrill and phony as Broadway living actually is.

While its sex is strictly antiseptic, this Preminger project has been tagged as too "blue" in story, action, and dialogue by Joe Breen's industry-censorship department. Everybody remains idyllically pure, but the risqué lines caused the Breen office to condemn the picture. It will therefore be kept out of several thousand theaters.

AUGUST 8, 1953

3-D Films

Manny Farber

•

IT WOULD BE silly to underrate Hollywood's current battle with stereoscopic film technique. The conversion to 3-D or its alternative, the wide screen, is not any overnight occurrence dreamed up as a counter-attack against television. Hollywood's move toward "giant screen" effects and a three-dimensional look about the actors has been going on in earnest since the period of "The Best Years of Our Lives." In fact, it has been the chief drive in the work of every important American director except De Mille, who never changes, and Huston. The basic objective in "new vision" films seems to be the same as that of "flat" films—a more accurate and natural image.

What you usually see on the new aluminized screen is a picture in which the actors' contours are extremely sharp and there is little building up of the figure with dramatic light effects. The 3-D director, in order to make you aware of the depth factor in a scene, tries to lead your eye quickly past the actors. Along with sharpening the outline of bodies, there is an effort to clarify the "feeling" of negative spaces—the spaces in a composition that are more or less unfilled. One of the most overworked images in the new 3-D's is a view through a frame made of an animal's legs, the boughs of a tree, or the opening between the wheels of a wagon. The frame intensifies the feeling of space behind it, making a sort of hole between the front plane of the screen and whatever is seen in the background.

The result of this three-dimensionalism is a more exact impression of masses. Flat cinema tended to put so many pounds on the actors that the rarest sight in a Hollywood film was a small wiry figure. Now for the first time a lot of lean or close-knit shapes are showing up in films—such as those of Guy Madison and Frank Lovejoy in *Feather River*—and some actors who were getting too bulky for the screen, like Mitchum, seem to have suddenly shrunk.

Unfortunately, working in a 3-D film does not seem to improve the acting of stars. *Second Chance* the first 3-D with stars in the leading roles, amounts to a sort of hurried tour through Cuernayaca and Taxco. The characters are all chasing one another and fleeing from some dreadful thing in the United States. Jack Palance, an incredibly hardbreathing gunman, is trying to get as far from a crime investigation as possible, Linda Darnell is trying to shake Palance along with her past as a famous gun moll, and Bob Mitchum, also pursuing Darnell, is a prize-fighter drifting down hill from a fight in which he killed an opponent. These unhappy expatriates are not far from the characters in any Hemingway short story, but the actors, except Palance in his familiar "burning coal" performance, drift through the story as if it were a bad dream. Darnell's one effective scene is the product of a carefully planned shock—after thirty minutes of being clothed to the neck in black she is suddenly sprung on the audience in a gay, low-cut job. The three-dimensional expanse of Technicolored flesh is all but dazzling. Mitchum always shows good sense in his self-consciously indolent portrayals. He acts unpretentious as a celebrity in a Mexican town, is frankly lascivious the moment he sees Darnell, and manages to look agile and crafty in the prize ring. But that prizefight scene is the only one in which he seems to be awake.

The actors apparently lose heart when they are shrouded in bad to fair photographic effects. Every actor before he operates must be placed in an awkward composition that carefully defines the front, middle, and back planes of the picture. The shot that made the greatest impression on me was the very first—the back of Palance's head coldly cutting into the bottom of the screen while one of his gangster enemies parades unknowingly before him in the foyer of a hotel. This rigid composition repeats itself almost as often as the "trick" shots—the gun blasting straight at your eyes, the rocket showering sparks on your head, Mitchum dangling Jack Pickford-fashion from a rope attached to a busted cable-car.

Something should be said about the dark, confining spectacles one wears at 3-D films, the multiple sound tracks that give the impression of voices coming from the side of the screen, and the wide screen with all the compositions "masked" top and bottom to fit. However, movies like *Charge at Feather River*, *Arena*, and *Second Chance* are mainly notable for their simple-minded stories in which there is always a chase after some prize, quarry, or goal as though movement—almost any kind of movement—were the key to depth.

SEPTEMBER 12, 1953

ROMAN HOLIDAY

Manny Farber

•

THE PARAMOUNT CREW that worked on *Roman Holiday* reminded me of expert marksmen who had made "charm" their target and seldom if ever missed it. The ancient buildings and streets of Rome are used as an unobtrusive backdrop, and I doubt whether architecture and sculpture have ever been tied in so tenderly and humorously with what the characters are doing at the moment. In the leading role of a bored princess who steals away from dull court routine for a day of street adventures with an American newspaperman, Audrey Hepburn has enough poise and looks for seven princesses. She also has an affected tomboyish delivery. But Gregory Peck, Hollywood's master of all shades of the thoughtful expression, manages by his varied throw-away movements to keep the film from stopping on Miss Hepburn's affectations. While *Roman Holiday* is too succulent for my taste, I enjoyed Wyler's switch to romantic comedy more than the heavier art style he used in directing *Carrie*, *Detective Story*, and *The Heiress*.

Wyler sometimes seems to be operating here with one eye on *The Bicycle Thief*. He is moving a well-scrubbed new movie face—Hepburn's—against the worn face of the Eternal City, and doing a lot of other photogenic things borrowed from De Sica. When his princess is pacified with a drug by the royal doctor, both the camera and Miss Hepburn start acting in an innocent-dreamy De Sica-ish way. When the heroine leaves the palazzo in the back of a laundry truck, the palace gates float up and away as though Lewis Carroll had given them life. Instead of simply crossing the street, Miss Hepburn walks into and out of a carriage and then dreamily down the street—in what *Variety* would call a boffo bit of business.

If I enjoyed Wyler's new work more than De Sica's famous comedy-drama, it is simply because Wyler is a sharp-shooting technical wizard compared to the Italian neo-tealist. Wyler is working strictly in the magically postured and timed idiom of Chaplin comedies when he starts Peck homeward with the doped Hepburn tagging behind. The main gag in this stretch is funny enough—Hepburn circling the winding stairway while Peck ascends it—but the wonderful things are the small bits of ballet work engineered by Peck and Hepburn. Peck's movement with his arm leading the sleepy girl back to the stairway is a masterful piece of grace-note acting.

Wyler does noble work getting his princess away from the inhibiting palace and into the reporter's bohemian quarters, but the adventures he arranges for the pair during the day are neither natural nor amusing. She gets a haircut, which is all to the good because of Paolo Carlini's oily-gigolo acting of the barber. After that she takes a wild motor-scooter ride, gets arrested, and escapes from a dozen plain-clothes detectives—and nothing works because it is all stock movie zaniness.

Unfortunately, the entertainment values of the picture make you constantly aware of someone's maneuverings. Miss Hepburn often startles you with perfect impressions of England's Princess Margaret Rose, even in her slow way of giving forth with a toothy, uncomplicated smile and that pale little hand wave to the crowd. You are always conscious of Wyler's cleverness—the way he times his jokes, puts sentiment into the laughs, or points up a silent stretch of story-telling with a funny photographic trick. Though I suspect the movie is aimed at an extremely gentle audience, it strikes me as a welcome, if eclectic, throwback to the beautifully acted, suavely directed comedies turned out in 1935 by Cary Grant and his zany tribe.

Laurence Olivier acts the role of an amorous, fast-moving bad man with a sort of smoldering, stuffy distinction, but otherwise Warner's has a loser in *The Beggar's Opera*. Most of the bows for the artistic failure should be taken by the technical advisers. The technicolor is made up largely of hot emerald, scarlet, and a surprising amount of black to keep the film as indistinct as possible. The story consists of a few basic items from Nelson Eddy-type operetta—a dashing highwayman having fun holding up stagecoaches, escaping from jail, falling in love—raced through in stagy, skittery fashion. Besides Olivier's swashbuckling, there are two interesting crowd scenes and some half-intelligible lyrics that sound talented and racy.

JANUARY 9, 1967

Blow-Up

Robert Hatch

•

Robert Hatch was for many years literary and then Managing Editor of The Nation during Carey McWilliams's tenure as editor. In fact McWilliams described Hatch as "one of the finest editors in New York Magazine journalism". His first editorial job was with the Office of War Information where he edited large-format news magazines which were sold throughout France and Germany. He was then film reviewer and literary editor for The New Republic and an associate editor of Scientific American. McWilliams also appointed Hatch film critic, a task he performed for nearly three decades.

CONTEMPORARY LONDON HAS won a name for being the most sophisticated of the European capital cities. It appears to occupy the position, roughly, of Berlin in the period of the Isherwood stories. Absolved of power, its rising generations have discovered again the flamboyance that always gave a hint of scarlet and lace to the gray serge of dominion. London today is gyrating to a Restoration clad in vinyl.

That, in any case, is the temper Michelangelo Antonioni has caught in *Blow-Up*, his first English-language picture and very possibly his most alluring work to date. It is a witty interweaving of dream and reality with the expectations reversed—dream being the ground on which the picture operates, reality the elusive substance for which it grasps in vain. *Blow-Up* is Gothic romance—violently picturesque and innocently wicked—recited in the Mod vernacular.

The picture proclaims Vanessa Redgrave its star, but with all respect for the attractions of her enigmatic candor and strained beauty, the billing seems more an acknowledgment of her name than of her weight on the movie. She triggers the plot, but the style, scope and mounting pressure of the film reside entirely in a young man named David Hemmings. He and Antonioni have created between them the mint image of a current Anglo-American type who makes the languorous fascinations of a Mastroianni seem country stuff. It is the con man of "in" society, the fellow who works the angles of the *avant-garde*.

The hero in this case is a fashion photographer, long-haired, tight-trousered, running on keyed-up exhaustion, coining money out of contemptuous virtuosity and a cynical instinct for what will turn the squares on. If you can imagine an Andy Warhol with sufficient vitamins, that is close.

Antonioni has devised a superb lair for this deceptive cat to prowl. His photo studio and laboratories seem to be hung as a maze of boxes and gangways on the walls of some enormous, abandoned refrigerator plant or slaughterhouse. The colors are acrylic creamy, but the angles are intimidating, and the design seems premeditated to make lay figures of everyone who works or strays within these walls except the blond, ex-slum-boy master of the place. He uses it as a huge machine, his command of its gadgetry giving him a kind of demigod's advantage over the "birds" he photographs and the females who smell him out. Part of the brilliance of Hemmings' characterization is his physical dexterity. He makes a dance of taking pictures, when he doesn't make a rape of it, and he uses cameras as though he had spent his life with them. With a camera in his hands, he is a kind of intoxicated faun; without it, he becomes a mere athlete, adept at the game of taking people by surprise.

Photography is the avocation as well as the livelihood of this aesthetic hipster. He is putting together a city picture book—one of those dissections of civic malignity—and one day in a high and windy park he finds Vanessa Redgrave with a graying lover. The sequence he shoots is to provide a conclusion to the book; but when he develops the film, far, far back in one of the frames is a pinpoint of reality which he blows up, enlargement upon enlargement (the darkroom scenes are a solo suspense ballet), into a wall-sized explosive tableau. The young man goes out to run down the facts of his discovery—but that takes him away from the studio, where he manipulates the fantasy, into streets over whose logic he has no control. What he saw in the negative is gone, if it was ever there. The jeepload of mimes who careened through the opening sequences of the picture catch up with Hemmings again at the end, and draw him into their conspiracy of the invisible event.

The film comes a clean full circle through a coolly logical extravagance of invention. The trickster is baffled, the dream prevails, and the last laugh belongs to whoever feels bold enough to utter it. *Blow-Up* is a work of wit and caustic intelligence, superbly disciplined, elegantly styled, visually astonishing and, for all that, turned out with the deceptive simplicity of perfect craftsmanship.

OCTOBER 9, 1967

THE BATTLE OF ALGIERS

Harold Clurman

•

Critic, director, producer and author Harold Clurman was *The Nation*'s theatre critic from 1953 to 1980. With Lee Strasberg he founded the Group Theatre in New York in 1931.

INNOCENT THAT I am, I enjoyed every one of the seven features I saw during the first week of the Fifth New York Film Festival at Lincoln Center. When I say that, I am not necessarily recommending them as good pictures. Some of them have glaring flaws: in some cases, a strained archness or an allusiveness bordering on the unintelligible. Nor am I particularly interested in technical devices ("pure cinematics") which preoccupy the true movie buff.

What I appreciated most of all was the relevance of virtually all the exhibits to the worlds which produced them. They are much more expressions of our day than most of the plays we see in the theatre.

We expected the festival to begin with "experiment"; it began with excellence. *The Battle of Algiers* is a first-rate picture. From the specialist's point of view this film—the work of a 35-year-old Italian director Gillo Pontecorvo—is remarkable for being an entirely convincing "documentary" of which not one foot is composed of stock shots or newsreel material. Yet one finds that one is *there* in the midst of the moment. A sense of the actual is never compromised by the taint of contrivance for effect. An expert may also admire the organizational capacity the picture demonstrates. In appearance and movement, the crowd scenes convey reality more strikingly than do the techniques of *cinéma vérité*.

The Battle of Algiers creates the impression of total objectivity. Folks with a particular political bias will contradict this. (A Parisian journalist told me that the picture was under official ban in France and that the Algerians had contributed not only their land but funds to the film's making.) The film may be "read" in various ways according to one's sentiments and convictions without our being oppressed by a feeling that a prejudiced view is being foisted upon us. Yet a specific emotion is communicated: the film is saying something. It embodies an idea without engaging in argument or special pleading.

The picture mirrors events in the Algerian uprising against French dominance of their country. At first we witness incidents in the terrorist campaign initiated by members of one cell of the National Liberation Front (the FLN). We are shown parts of the French counter-terror—bombings, etc. The Algerians kill a number of the French European policemen; the French retaliate with even greater ferocity. The Algerians then blow up several cafés and an air terminal largely frequented by the Europeans.

The French army formally intervenes through a paratroop division headed by a Colonel Mathieu. With quiet and deadly efficiency he rounds up the leaders of one of the most active of the terrorist units. Though the army code does not contain the word, torture is resorted to. When the last of the terrorists is trapped (along with his aides) the group is liquidated: the FLN rebellion is quelled. All this happens in 1954. After two years of "peace," massive and apparently spontaneous street rioting breaks out. The struggle takes on wider scope. We know the end: in 1960 the Algerians gain independence.

No matter who is being destroyed, we shudder at the terror-of the events. We take little satisfaction at the "triumph" of one side or the other in the mutual slaughter. (We even pity the poor cops.) In one of the cafés we see a crowd of Europeans (French) at their drinks and a baby licking an ice cream cone. When the place is blown up we remember that child. We are outraged at the wantonness of this "senseless murder."

We of course are equally infuriated by the French when we witness the terrible pain inflicted on the Algerian prisoners from whom their captors are determined to elicit information. The variety and ingenuity of the means employed add to the horror of the procedures. We admire the cool austerity, the intelligence and soldierly self-discipline of the French colonel but we realize that he is a killer. (He points out that he was a member of the underground against the Nazis and is thus no Fascist.) We respect the terrorist leaders for their determination, courage and steely pragmatism but they are as ruthless as the French. Even in its most violent scenes the film indulges in neither sentimentality nor delight in cruelty. It contains none of the sadism common to so many pictures presented as entertainment.

The objectivity of *The Battle of Algiers* is not indifference. We might conclude that the picture's final statement is pacifist. But I doubt that that is its intention. Pacifism is an untenable position unless one is willing to die rather than to resist evil through fighting. Only the saintly are capable of such a course, and very few of us are that.

In the context of the picture alone I found myself partisan of neither side. Some in the audience equated the struggle in Algiers with the war in Vietnam. Others thought of the more violent aspects of the civil rights movement: Watts, Detroit, Newark, and so on. Such analogies are misleading or false. The French had much more justification for the repression of the Algerian revolt than we have in intervening in Southeast Asia: they had been in Algeria for 130 years, had developed the country and given full rights of citizenship to the Algerians.

Is the picture "revolutionary" then, as we understood the term in the thirties? Not precisely. Still what it communicates is not nebulous or indeterminate in its implications. What we may gather from it politically is that ultimately no people will allow itself to be ruled by alien force. In many respects the Algerians profited from the French presence in their country and were treated better than we have treated the black man in ours. They still wanted to be free of any governing class not of their stock, language, tradition, or religion.

Even this, however, is not the picture's true import. Its content has classic and tragic dimensions beyond politics. Wars are as unreasonable as they are terrible. For it may be argued that they rarely achieve the benefits that both sides sincerely claim they are battling to bring about. (Are not many now shocked at Algeria's position in the Mideast situation?) It has been mankind's destiny to engage in internecine conflict when in one manner or another it suffers oppression. No matter how futile the effort may prove in view of the later consequences, the world bursts into flames of anger and homicide when men can no longer bear what they consider to be unspeakable injustice. This is tragic because the actual process and conduct of these conflagrations are always and everywhere "inhumanly" infernal. If this is not so then all history is a meaningless shambles. How many of us truly believe this?

War and revolutions may not be inevitable. We pray and plan to avoid them but from time immemorial they have not been avoided. In that sense they are all too human. Understanding and wisdom are impossible without an initial recognition of this tragic fact. We can accept it without condemning ourselves to hopelessness, to an impotent fatalism or to a hawkish militarism.

Much of this may be strongly contested. On another occasion I might contest it myself! That I should be impelled to say this now is simply evidence of the picture's sober eloquence, its modest power. Its acting, as well as its other elements, is in the vein of a simple and direct expressiveness.

Particularly striking in this regard are Jean Martin as the French colonel: dignified, hard, tempered, keen, and the two men of unalterable commitment and resolution who play the FLN leaders. (Are they professional actors?) The brave 10-year-old Algerian boy who is part of the rebel *equipe* is also perfectly cast and directed. All in then *The Battle of Algiers* is a film of which it may be said without absurdity that it is a masterpiece of epic realism.

My only demur relates to the musical score about which Pontecorvo was especially concerned and on which he is said to have collaborated. The music is not "bad"—it will not interfere with anyone's appreciation of the picture—but in respect to the rest it is rather conventional and not stylistically consonant with the whole.

JANUARY 4, 1971

GIMME SHELTER

Robert Hatch

•

ESSAYS PUBLISHED ELSEWHERE in this issue intimate, though they do not as yet indicate, that ours is a society at the end of its rope. It is becoming increasingly difficult to ignore such signs. They seem to occur almost daily, and if we are indeed going down, it is with a documentation unparalleled in the records of civilization's debacles. By comparison, the overwhelming of Rome was no more noticed than the fall of a sparrow.

My fragment of the record is *Gimme Shelter*, the filmed report of the Rolling Stones's 1969 American tour, which came to a dreadful climax at the free concert they gave in the Altamont Speedway, Alameda County, Calif. A free concert is a nice gesture—a present to America in exchange for the $1.5 million spent at the box offices of the other concerts—but it was not a nice occasion. It was an eighteen-hour foretaste of Hell, in which four people were killed (one on camera) and an unstated number of others were carried off to the hospital because of bodily injury or the effects of the drugs they had taken.

I mention only in passing that there was nothing free about the concert except the admission. The Maysles brothers had paid well for the right to make this film of the event, and everyone connected with it, from Melvin Belli, the West Coast lawyer/publicist, to the man who owns Altamont, was doing himself a good turn by contributing his services. It should be noted, however, that since the concert was "free," everyone was "volunteering" his aid or facilities and no one was "responsible"—for such things as crowd management or toilet facilities. What interests me more than the commercialism of hard-rock altruism, are the overtones of apocalypse that attended the occasion.

First, 300,000 people were impelled by the news that the Stones would become manifest in Alameda County to get in their cars and drive, some of them for days, to the meeting place. Second, the atmosphere they engendered was not that of an audience at an entertainment but of a hysterical congregation at a miraculous cure. Hours before the Stones emerged from their trailer, this assembly, incited by subsidiary rock groups, the hot sun, the press of bodies, the intoxication of cheap wine and I know not what drugs, was an orgiastic mass, ripping off its clothes, embracing, fighting and speaking in tongues. Third, the Hell's Angels, sergeants-at-arms for the day and night (they received $500 for their services—paid in beer) did not resemble even so much as a posse; immense in their gladiator uniforms (one leader wore the head of a puma on his shoulders), they seemed the soldier priests of some pagan mystery. They produced nothing that even resembled order, but rather a sacrament administered with fists, boots, billiard cues and that knife which one could see flashing into the shoulder blades of the slim, gun-brandishing black in the tight green suit.

At last, the Stones appeared and the ceremony of blood and sex and ectasy roared to a climax. One's eyes were on Mick Jagger, which is where they always are when the Stones perform, and he appeared here in a revealing double identity. At one moment, he was a sophisticated public entertainer, calling out shrewdly in his vulgar British accent for the crowd to "cool" it, for everybody to be "nice" so that he and his chums could play for them. It worked, after a fashion, and I supposed that the crowdwise Jagger would discipline himself to the requirements of the night. But Jagger does not seem the master of his "act"; it overcomes him and he becomes an androgynous celebrant of license. Jagger is unique in my experience—he is not effeminate but rather an obvious male who employs entirely female gestures and mannerisms. He hits the crowd with his pelvis, flings his scarf around his shoulders, jabs nervously at his flowing hair, mouths like a woman in heat, jerks with an aggressive, staccato beat that is as explicit as an anatomy chart. The ambiguity of his sex, the spectacle of raper and victim in one body, threw the witnesses into convulsions of excitement (and entitled them to the ministrations of the Angels).

After the "concert," after the Stones had been levitated in their helicopter, the crowd could be seen stumbling down the steep banks of the Speedway, falling over one another, feeling their way, with their blankets and their babies strapped to their backs, down the miles of featureless highway to their parked cars. They looked replete, peaceful, when one could see their faces; they had come to worship and, most of them, this time, had survived.

The picture is well made in the fragmented, montage, flashback, flash-forward style of contemporary pseudo-spontaneity. It employs light psychedelically, and sound to the threshold of pain. Even so, seeing Altamont on the screen cannot be more than a whisper of the real experience; but I would suppose that no one could sit through it without wondering how soon he too would be caught by the powerful tide of chaos.

AUGUST 30, 1975

JAWS

Robert Hatch

•

COMING BACK FROM vacation late in July, I expected everyone in New York to be talking about the impending bankruptcy of the city, symbolized by the hills of black plastic garbage bags that line the less affluent streets. I was right about that, but what I hadn't expected was that, in the second breath, my friends would tell me what sum of money they would not accept to set foot in salt water this summer. All of them, it seemed, had been to see *Jaws*—not surprising, since the film was, and still is, playing to packed houses in thirteen theatres of the five boroughs, plus dozens more in the nearby suburbs, and they were in a mild state of shock from having watched a 25-foot great white shark dismember bathers in waistdeep New England playground waters. Never mind that holiday crowds by the millions dunk themselves in the Atlantic summer after summer without losing so much as a toe—my friends had seen the fanged horror at his ghastly meals, or thought they had, which comes to the same thing.

Cinematic horror is not my dish—I have not, for instance, seen *The Texas Chain Saw Massacre* (partly because I own a chain saw), which played in New York some months ago and is now, I learn from a publicity release, "packing them in at drive-ins around the country." But *Jaws* appeared to be a phenomenon of considerable size, and I decided to screw up my courage and go.

It wasn't as taxing as I'd feared. For one thing, the munching scenes occupy a very small part of the picture—in all, maybe five minutes of rolling, bloody water—and for another, when you really get to see the dreadful beast, it looks very much like a marvelous piece of mechanical hocus-pocus (so marvelous, in fact, that building and operating it was the major cost of a very expensive movie). Underwater shots of pale legs dangling in the water add some moments of acute tension, and that's almost the total bill, as far as horror goes. And aside from horror, *Jaws* is a well-constructed family entertainment film, Carl Gottlieb having trimmed and accelerated Peter Benchley's reportedly rather steamy novel into a script that employs two of Hollywood's most ingratiating formulas. The first of these is the *High Noon* confrontation, in which the honest cop battles it out single-handed with the venal town fathers. In this case Police Chief Brody (Roy Scheider) pits himself against Mayor Vaughn (Murray Hamilton), a man of little scruple and less foresight who, shark or no shark, refuses to close the beaches of Amity, a fictitious town on Martha's Vineyard, when the Fourth of July weekend is at hand and the crowds are already streaming off the Wood's Hole ferry. Of course, the great fish strikes again and Vaughn becomes known on national TV as the Mayor of Shark City.

The other theme is that of the brave posse that swears to destroy the outlaw or die in the attempt. As always when this business is well managed, the avengers are a picturesque and varied lot, chosen so that everyone in the audience can identify with at least one of them. In addition to Chief Brody, a gentle, ex-New York cop who has the interesting peculiarity that he is terrified of the sea, the men on the hunting boat are Hooper (Richard Dreyfuss) and Quint (Robert Shaw). Dreyfuss (recently of *American Graffiti* and *The Apprenticeship of Duddy Kravitz*) plays a wealthy young ichthyologist whose appearance of full-bearded and somewhat didactic innocence covers a brave, peppery, and often humorous personality. Shaw, his British speech erased by an almost impenetrable New England salt-pork accent, is a shark killer by trade, partly for the money in it, but mainly to even the score for his shipmates who, during World War II, were devoured alive while awaiting rescue in the South China Sea. He it is who is consumed feet first, inch by inch, to make a kind of *Moby Dick* conclusion for the film.

All of this is exceedingly well directed by Steven Spielberg (*Sugarland Express*), a young director who handles crowds with authority, has a sharp sense of timing, knows how to capitalize on the endearing eccentricities of his characters and demands a perfection of workmanship that carries through to the last ashtray and paper cup. In particular, his staging of the hunt for, battle with, and very narrow victory over the shark is as good belly entertainment as the screen ever attains.

But basically, *Jaws* is an excellent routine movie, the sort normally made on a moderate budget and aimed at the neighborhood houses. All the big money was spent to provide the brief flashes of horror, and was gambled on the hunch that those moments—the dismembered leg sinking to the sandy bottom, the dead face in the porthole window, the fragments of a lovely girl spread out on a morgue table, the disappearance of the screaming Quint down the monster's throat—would be, as it were, bread cast upon the waters. And so it is proving; *Jaws* will be one of the historic bonanza films.

This can be made the occasion for a good deal of tut-tutting, the response to the film being offered as proof that ours is a sadly debased society which, in the absence of creative values or the opportunity for enriching goals, hungers after degrading sensation. It may be so, but in that case we are not without precedents. The Romans liked their entertainment bloody, and if that be dismissed as more evidence that vulgar times generate vulgar tastes, recall that Shakespeare resorted to instruments of torture in competition with the bearbaiting and somewhat prolonged public executions of his time. In fact, there has probably never been a time when impressive crowds could not be gathered to view pain or copulation—they are the twin dominant forms of voyeurism—to the extent that the authorities permitted. Until recently, our authorities would permit very little, so there is a large market of those who have built up no immunity to the staging of such matters. Witness the inordinate amount of excitement engendered by *Last Tango in Paris*, a conventional enough bit of rueful sentiment enhanced by several very brief scenes of *outré* eroticism. There will be imitations of *Jaws*, as there were imitations of *Last Tango* and *The Exorcist*; they will be less successful and will find their level in the shabbier houses, as the public by and large discovers the monotony in shock.

Of course, *Jaws* is a kind of pornography, in that it contrives illusions of torment that are entirely unnecessary to its narrative purpose. But pornography, of whatever sort, has the built-in weakness that it manipulates people—the characters and the audience—for the profit of the manufacturer and, after the first screams and gasps have had their turn, this proves to be rather uninteresting to anyone but the manufacturer. It is what people do, not what is done to them, that makes even the most popular theatre seductive.

Which is not to say that the new permissiveness has no lasting effects. The limits of what is acceptable have been extended and the coiners of fiction, when they feel the necessity, can make explicit what hitherto they have had to handle by innuendo. On balance, that seems to me not unhealthy—innuendo being a rather crawly device—but I will be surprised if it often proves essential, or for long profitable, to startle the audience out of its wits in order to gain its respectful attention. Grand Guignol proved to be a limited resource and *Deep Throat* is now the code name for a supernumerary in the Watergate affair.

JUNE 25, 1977

STAR WARS

Robert Hatch

•

IN THE WEEKS since *Star Wars* opened (six theatres in the Greater New York area), the stock of 20th Century-Fox, its gratified distributor, has risen some eleven points, approximately doubling its value in an otherwise sluggish market. That's the sort of cause and effect that makes criticism irrelevant. However to give you an idea—

Star Wars belongs to the sub-basement, or interstellar comic-strip, school of science fiction; *Terry and the Pirates* with astro-drive. The main participants are a princess in mortal peril, a splendid young Four-H type who is fated to rescue her, an irreverent free enterpriser with a space ship for hire, an aged mystic possessed of "the Force," and a gaggle of villains who, when they are not entirely encased in elegantly fitted plastic armor, look very much like extras borrowed from scenes of the Wehrmacht general staff plotting Hitlerian strategies. The princess (Carrie Fisher) is spunky and in both manner and hairstyle somewhat resembles the Gish sisters; the young knight (Mark Hamill) is not quite bright but adroit with machinery; the freebooter (Harrison Ford) talks with shocking cynicism out of the side of his mouth, but has an honest heart; and the old mystic, survivor of a chivalric order that combined stunning swordsmanship with the ability to transmit psychic force by telepathy, is played by Alec Guinness, which I thought the film's most remarkable surprise.

These human actors are consistently upstaged by a pair of robots—

one of them, an electronic improvement on the Tin Woodsman, seems to have derived his stilted vocabulary and obsequious manners from the servants' quarters of *Upstairs, Downstairs;* the other, shaped rather like a canister vacuum cleaner, but without the hose, is possessed (like the mind reader in *The Thirty-Nine Steps*) of the secret information that is causing all the fireworks, speaks in beeps, whistles and blinking lights and is as emotionally vulnerable as a motherless child.

This is the sort of thing that will reach one's brain, and I suspect that George Lucas (the director previously of *American Graffiti*) concocted the plot and personages deliberately to put us all in a slack-jawed state of mind suitable for maximum appreciation of his astonishing cinematic trickery. The interior accommodations of the Death Star, ultimate weapon of the wicked galactic Empire; the moment when the space ship bursts through the speed of light; the instantaneous destruction of an entire planet; the stupendous climax when the fighter planes of the freedom-loving rebels go into action against the totalitarians (don't ask what *planes* are doing in airless space)—all these and much more are impeccably engineered, often beautiful in the manner of highly machined sculpture, and by means of cumulative suspense as gratifyingly exhausting as the chariot race in *Ben Hur*.

Years from now, long after the last bucket of popcorn has been eaten at the last neighborhood showing of *Star Wars*, film buffs will be regaling one another with recollections of their favorite scenes and persons: the frontier bar patronized by the offspring of improbable matings (I liked the elephant/crocodile); the entrapment within a huge garbage compacter (courtesy of Edgar Allan Poe); the duel with cold-light swords; the bombing run down a narrow chasm to the one vulnerable spot in the Death Star; the poignant falling out of the two robots in a *Beau Geste* stretch of desert; the amiable but quick-tempered 7-foot man/bear navigator of the space ship; the bustling little brown-habited dwarfs with flashlight eyes, who sell second-hand automatons from a cave in the wilderness and, of course, Luke Skywalker, the very fair-haired boy who discovers that he too possesses the Force. All in all, it is an outrageously successful, what will be called a "classic," compilation of nonsense, largely derived but thoroughly reconditioned. I doubt that anyone will ever match it, though the imitations must already be on the drawing boards.

JULY 1, 1978

GREASE

Robert Hatch

•

I HAVE SKIPPED John Travolta in *Saturday Night Fever* because the ads display him in a discothèque *macho* pose with which I feared it might be hard to cope; and I haven't seen *Grease* during its interminable months on Broadway because the title hit me as counter-seductive. That sort of prudery no doubt disqualifies me as an audience for the screen blowup of the musical, but Paramount invited me to a preview at one of New York's biggest neighborhood popcorn houses, so I thought, what the hell.

And a kind of hell it turned out to be. First the noise: the sound track blasts away at a decibel level you might expect to encounter if trapped in an elevator with a transistor-equipped messenger boy. At that intensity, speech is intelligible only in fragments, like anxious cries flung about in a full gale, and music is not easily distinguished from the roar of heavy traffic. Not that I got the impression of losing anything very distinguished in the way of dialogue, lyrics or score.

Then the cast: we are supposed to be on and about the campus of Rydell High some time in the 1950s but the students look to be at least in their mid-20s; rather mature, that is, even for college upperclassmen. Since the dominant preoccupations of these flowers of American youth in the era of James Dean are to play doctor in parked cars and to make the zoom-zoom noises of a child obsessed by internal combustion, the effect is disagreeably one of mental retardation.

It is perhaps unfair to say so, since Randal Kleiser's direction appears to demand at all times a maximum output of undirected energy in surroundings of total confusion, but these young men and women do not seem to be conspicuously talented. They twitch rather than act, and their faces display an undifferentiated animation. They take part in dance routines based on the fling-about apache style of the film's period, but these production numbers lack shape and the individual techniques on show are not sufficiently brilliant to qualify as commercial entertainment (i.e., something you pay to see). It is not enough to reproduce a spring dance of twenty-some years ago in good old Rydell's gymnasium; you have to come up with an idea to give all that effort some point. If Frankie Avalon's camp performance as the M.C. of the evening was supposed to be that, it wasn't enough.

Though *Grease* is obviously intended to effervesce with adolescent joy of life, its unifying human characteristic is stupidity expressed in hysteria—a not very merry conceit. There is just one girl, pug-nosed and husky-voiced (I'm sorry that I cannot spot her in the cast of characters), whose eyes betray intelligence; from time to time, she throws a startled glance at the camera, as though seeking the way out.

Travolta wags his hips, combs his heavy hair and alternates between cool and uncouth; Olivia Newton-John, his co-star, is the very image (probably intended) of Disney's Snow White—until, in the final moments, she dons black satin tights and wags *her* hips along with the others. This sort of behavior may be intended as satire, but it is informed by no point of view and is therefore a mere exploitation of once-popular clichés. God knows, there is almost no aspect of American life that could fail to profit from a Swift, but *Grease* has no sting; it is an ear-splitting emollient.

JANUARY 14, 1984

Terms of Endearment

Peter Biskind

•

Peter Biskind is the author of *Easy Riders. Raging Bulls: How the Sex-Drugs-And-Rock 'N' Roll Generation Saved Hollywood*, a panegyric to the new Hollywood of the 1970s which Peter Bart, the editor in chief of *Variety*, noted was the most talked about book film in recent memory. Biskind has also edited two Hollywood special issues for *The Nation* magazine and is a contributing editor to *Vanity Fair*. Biskind was an editor at *Seven Days*, *American Film* and *Premiere* magazine.

IT'S HARD TO hate *Terms of Endearment*. James Brooks's new film is so appealing, so unassuming and good-hearred, so funny, intelligent and well crafted, that to break its spell seems churlish, like knocking Christmas. There's no way it won't sweep the Oscars, enabling Shirley MacLaine or (less likely) Debra Winger to edge out Meryl Streep (*Silkwood*) and Barbara Streisand (*Yentl*) for best actress. Then there's Jack Nicholson, a shoo-in as best supporting actor for his marvelously antic performance as the lecherous neighbor who ogles MacLaine across the hedge. But let's face it. *Terms of Endearment* is an obnoxious movie. It's a right-to-life soap opera; it does for the family what *An Officer and a Gentleman* did for the military.

Based on Larry McMurry's first-rate novel of the same name, *Terms* focuses on the fortunes of Aurora Greenway and her daughter, Emma.

Played by McLaine with enormous charm, Aurora is a caustic Texas widow who alternately tempers and terrorizes a bevy of fatuous admirers. Emma, played by Winger, is considerably more conventional than her eccentric mother. She marries a feckless graduate student named Flap (Jeff Daniels) and follows him to a teaching post in Iowa. *Terms* crosscuts between the parallel lives of mother and daughter, who keep in constant contact by phone. While Aurora is tutored in the joys of sex by the amorous astronaut next door (Nicholson), Emma, despite a romantic interlude with a banker (John Lithgow), sticks close to the kitchen and breeds like a rabbit. When Aurora suggests that Emma stanch the flow of babies with an abortion, Emma recoils in shock. But Flap turns out to be a bad investment, spending all his time reading books in the library while Emma's changing diapers in the nursery. When he is offered a position as head of the English department at a cow college in Nebraska, Emma doesn't want to go. She follows him anyway, only to discover that he's followed one of his female grad students with whom he's been having an affair.

So far, unlike any film since *The Turning Point*, *Terms* has distinguished itself by its close, sympathetic attention to the bonds between mother and daughter; it presents relationships with men exclusively from a feminine point of view and raises interesting questions about those relationships. Should men change diapers too? Should wives subordinate themselves to their husbands' careers, following them to the ends of the earth, for better or for worse, till death do them part? Should Emma leave Flap, or stick it out? We never find out the answer to that last question, because Emma gets cancer.

At this point, midway in the film, *Terms* ceases to make any serious claim on our intelligence, despite the excellent performances. The questions of sexual politics raised explicitly in the film's first half are resolved in the second half by shameless emotional manipulation. The momentum is so great that most people in the audience won't care, but while he's tugging at our heartstrings, director Brooks is getting away with murder. Before we can blink our tears away Emma is on a last fling in Manhattan, beset by career women, divorcees and victims of genital herpes. Even hospitalization is preferable to this, and Emma cuts short her trip to rush back to Nebraska General. In the New York sequence, Brooks finally lays his ideological cards on the table, and the film deteriorates into clumsy caricature. All the career women in this film are jerks, including Flap's grad student.

Not that the men are much better. They're either infantile and foolish or sex-crazed and irresponsible. Aurora always said Flap was bad news, and at the end, we see it's true. Emma's cancer is discovered right after she stumbles on his girlfriend. Are we meant to think that his affair has killed her, that male infidelity is the cancer that is destroying the family? (Emma's affair is excused because her lover isn't being satisfied by his wife—no Total Women.) More-over, Flap gives up his kids to Aurora to raise, turning *Kramer vs. Kramer* upside down. But if *Kramer vs. Kramer* attacked feminism from the vantage point of the liberal human potential movement, *Terms of Endearment* attacks it from the vantage point of the pro-life movement. Its contempt for men comes from the right, not the left. It's an expression of the deep-seated distrust of men that permeates pro-life literature, the fear that sexual equality threatens to erode the conventional constraints on male behavior by which errant breadwinners have traditionally been bound to the family. Even Nicholson's swinger is right out of George Gilder. He takes to the hills at the first whiff of commitment.

Debra Winger has made a specialty of post-feminist performances, which is to say she displays the surface characteristics of liberation—she's scrappy, direct, unglamorous—without its substance. From *Urban Cowboy* to *An Officer and a Gentleman*, the characters she plays have fought tooth and nail for equality until they're swept off their feet in the very last frame, as if to reassure anxious viewers that despite the sound and the fury, nothing much has changed after all.

Here the terms of endearment are slightly different. Emma can't be swept off her feet because Flap is too weak. But she can't divorce him either, as Aurora suggests, because that is the province of the New York herpes-infected harpies whom she detests. Under these circumstances, cancer becomes the moral equivalent of divorce. It allows her to escape from (and punish) Flap, without the stigma the right connects with dissolving the sacred bonds of matrimony.

When Emma finally dies and Flap retreats in disgrace, Aurora saves the day. The same Aurora who once had recommended abortion now embraces adoption. Since the astronaut makes a better role model than a wimpy college professor, she succeeds in transforming him into a surrogate father to Emma's oldest boy. As the dissidents fall into step, the new family takes shape before our very eyes. Will they make it legal? Hang in for the sequel.

JUNE 9, 1984

INDIANA JONES AND THE TEMPLE OF DOOM

Andrew Kopkind

Andrew Kopkind joined *The Nation* in 1982 where he was an associate editor and senior political writer until his death in 1994. While reporting for *The New Republic* in the 1960s he introduced SNCC and SDS to a national audience, as well as covering the emerging Black power movement, the counterculture and anti-Vietnam protests. He was also the *New Statesman*'s US correspondent during this period. His essays are collected in *The Thirty Years' War: Dispatches and Diversions of a Radical Journalist 1965–1994*. Kopkind was also for a time the magazine's film critic. Kopkind, who had been so clairvoyant about the coming of Second Cold War in such essays as "The Return of Cold War Liberalism," was ideally placed to review and ridicule the likes of *Red Dawn* and *Rambo: First Blood Part Two.*

WHEN WE LAST encountered Indiana Jones, he was an effective, if premature, antifascist, snatching the Lost Ark from a clutch of villainous Nazis who would use its power to defeat democracy. But times have changed; the villains have darker skins and meaner metaphysics now. The intrepid archaeologist has returned to wreak the white man's revenge on the Third World, which is using its natural treasures to obliterate the West, that region of vast wealth and limitless production values stretching oceanward from the Hollywood Freeway as far as the eye can see.

"The Hebrew god will fall," intones Thuggee high priest Mola Ram (Amrish Puri), made up to look like Bombay television's version of Louis Farrakhan. "The Christian god will be cast down. Kali will rule the world." Mola Ram's idea for *Religion and the Fall of Capitalism* involves the use of a sacred amulet of diamonds which illuminates an idol's nose: an allusion, perhaps, to the effects of the recreational drug favored on film sets. In any case, Indy vows to return the charm to a village of wretched lower peasants very much down on their luck. He has his work cut out for him.

On second thought, forget the subtext. The Lucasfilm leviathan has less on its corporate mind than meaning or message. *The Temple of Doom* is a movie about money—how to make it and spend it; and about crowd control—how to organize the 100 million or so bodies that will attend this blockbuster into orderly lines on the sidewalk, at the ticket booth, in front of the popcorn machine, at the ladies' and gents' and to the exit. It is enormously successful in both those undertakings.

Beyond that, if there is a world beyond the box office, *The T of D* is a stupendous exercise in moviemaking, and pretty amazing fun for much of two hours. The first twenty minutes are as wild and wonderful as anything committed to 70-millimeter stock: stylish mayhem in a Shanghai nightclub, semi-free fall from a pilotless plane above the Himalayas, dizzying descents over snow and water, and a perilous passage to India. The action teeters for a moment in the village of the damned, but that fulcrum is passed and Indy (Harrison Ford) is off to Thuggee GHQ. For side-kicks he has a ditsy dancer from Shanghai (Kate Capshaw) and the orphan waif, Short Round (Ke Huy Quan). Their quest will carry them over the usual obstacle course of spiders, bats, snakes, alligators, fiery pits and, thundering torrents, not to mention nauseating dinners (slop of the day: monkeys' brains in vivo), ritual human sacrifices and battles with whole divisions of bad guys dressed to the nines.

Doom happens one year earlier than *Raiders of the Lost Ark*, but George Lucas and director Steven Spielberg have suffered some unfortunate regressions in the three years before the prequel. In that effort, the woman in Indy's life (Karen Allen) was fresh, smart and tough. She ran the rowdiest saloon in Nepal with an iron glove over a velvet fist and could drink any boorish boozer under the table. This time around,

Kate Capshaw's Willie Scott is the dumbest and broadest of blondes. She shrieks at the sight of a scorpion, worries about her fingernails and her high heels and positively relishes the lash of Indy's bullwhip when he pulls her in like a stubborn heifer. Little Short Round puts her to shame. While she's tossing her Barbra Streisand curls and parading her décolletage, he's saving Indy from more than one impossible jam. It must be that boys are cool and girls are not.

Such attitudes place the movie's emotional center of gravity at about age 11, which suggests that the filmmakers have lost one year of maturity every summer since 1981. The problem seems to lie with screenwriters Willard Huyck and Gloria Katz, who bloomed in Lucastown with *American Graffiti* and can't lose its jejune sensibility. Worse, their ear is tinny, especially when they listen for Capshaw's airhead remarks. By comparison, Lawrence Kasdan's script for *Raiders* was a clever concoction of childish perceptions and adult syntax, even if the mix was good for little more than a dope rap session in his *Big Chill*. Whatever's the matter, the Lucasfilm crew had best reverse their direction. If they follow the present vectors, the next number in the Indiana Jones series will be set in a day-care center.

Before Spielberg options that idea (see my agent) he might consider the limitations of kids' stuff as projected on a giant screen. Filmmakers used to fear that such movies turn out to be merely *about* children but *for* adults; the absolute worst example of that process was Alan Parker's *Bugsy Malone*, a gangster fantasy in which no actor had yet developed secondary sex characteristics. But with Spielberg, it's the other way around: the danger is that he is making movies about adult neuroses and selling them to kids as their own.

Chief among his concerns is the problem of parental control—from mom and dad's point of view. Someone is always losing a child or two in his movies. Spidery aliens take one on board in *Close Encounters*, ghosts gobble up another in *Poltergeist*, and E. T. charms one half to death in *E. T.* We won't even talk about *Jaws*. In *The Temple of Doom*, the malevolent Thuggees make off with the entire preteen population of the cursed Indian village and put the youngsters to work in the Maharajah's mines, looking for lost amulets. The slave children are in pitiful shape, but the audience is asked to share the anxieties of their parents and to feel their relief when Indy and the 500 kids show up in peasant suburbia after a season in hell.

Because Spielberg is a grown-up, he puts grown-up notions of sex, fear, responsibility and morality into the world of the children he portrays. That is inevitable; it's the way a white filmmaker deforms black characters and male directors remake women in their image or ideology. We know that some kids demean women like Willie Scott, that they scream at spiders and bats and that some cringe when the colored races appear. But we don't know whether they would do that if parents did not inspire them, and it's arrogant of Lucasfilm to suggest that the state of childhood nature is so graceless.

JULY 7–14, 1984

ANOTHER COUNTRY

Andrew Kopkind

•

THERE IS A line in English history that runs from Marlowe through Oscar Wilde to Guy Burgess, with Heaven knows how many bends in between, and along it the legitimacy of an empire is intertwined with the politics of male sexuality. Marlowe was a rebel, an atheist, a gay bawd and a literary regicide; from his peculiar perch he threw the book at Tudor power and purpose: a finicky Faustus, a kinky Edward II, outrageous Tamburlaine. Those were hardly the noble reflections that Renaissance royalty expected to see in the theatrical mirror. Wilde was the funniest and wisest English playwright since Shakespeare, and for a while he titillated Victorian tastes. But his sexual irregularity sent him to jail, exile and disgrace, and in the moment of self-destruction he had his greatest triumph: by sad example he shattered the moral pretensions of the empire's highest society. Burgess wrote no mighty lines nor spoke witty epigrams, but he struck his own telling blow against the empire at its lowest ebb by spying for the Russians with a coterie of Cambridge comrades. Like the others, Burgess was a sexual outlaw, even as a social success. And like the others, he turned against king (or queen), country and class not because the empire was too bad but because it was mean to him. The bully who taunts the sissy gets his comeuppance in the end.

Another Country is an attempt to explore Burgess's formative years at a green and Gothic public school, unnamed in the movie but presumably Eton, and to draw some connection between his tormented homosexual existence there and his later attraction to treason. The progression is plausible, but the treatment is not entirely convincing in Julian Mitchell's sensitive screenplay (adapted from his own West End stage play). It is one thing to state the existential equation—that sexual suppression leads to social rebellion, in the presence of cold baths and a Marxist roommate—and another to make it come alive on the screen as emotional reality. Saying is not always believing.

Mitchell and director Marek Kanievska set their plot and players in that lush and languorous land of playing fields, parade drills and hymn-filled chapels which upper-class British men imagine whenever they feel compelled to sentimentalize their past. Like baseball for Americans and sexual initiation scenes for the French, public school days serve the English as a source of easy answers to hard questions about the meaning of their lives. In that other country of endless innings, idyllic affairs with older women or canings by cruel masters, they all find the motives, the reasons and the excuses for adult comportment. Or perhaps they invent them.

At least it all seemed very clear at school. The lads learn the class system in the intricate network of prefects, "gods," seniors and slaves. They practice militarism as teen-age cadets. They worship the Anglican God that favors their dormitory over all others, and they yearn to be Cabinet ministers, ambassadors and devoted civil servants in a government much like the one that rules their everyday life. They even learn how to rebel: safely by jumping the wall and strolling along the backs after hours, or dangerously by denying the legitimacy of the several school institutions. And they know the penalties for each category of infraction.

The young Burgess character—here called Guy Bennett, for this is docudrama, not history—rebels in a particularly dicey way. He falls in love with another boy, and from another house, no less. I suppose that would be like a Marine dating a Green Beret, which does not seem to be the end of the world, but it must have meant a lot at Eton. Not that the odd schoolboy crush was cause for expulsion; but serious sex and, worse, true love was considered out of the question. Bennett (Rupert Everett) not only goes head over heels for Fowler (Tristan Oliver); he comes out with his feelings, flaunts his affair and courts disaster.

The worst befalls him. He is denied election as a sixth-form god and must face a debased future without the ambassadorship to France he had once desired. But there is an alternative. Roommate Tommy (Colin

Firth) has been spouting Marx and making revolutionary noises all these years while Guy was mooning over the pretty blond boys. Perhaps communism can serve Guy as a vehicle for carrying out his personal liberation. At least it would be a way to get back at the system.

There is a moving scene in which Guy chastises Tommy for excluding sexual revolution from his laundry list of political demands, and the straight roommate immediately confesses his error and expresses solidarity with his gay friend. But it all seems too pat, and in a sense too easy, as things must be in the British Disney World of public schools. Despite the filmmakers' hopes, clear rules about the psychosexual roots of rebellion cannot be drawn. For every humiliated homosexual schoolboy who becomes a revolutionary, a thousand more lead very ordinary lives, and a few (following Wilhelm Reich's theory, not this movie's) join the humiliating class and turn their pain on victims like themselves.

As public school recollections go, *Another Country* is intelligently, even lovingly handled. Rupert Everett's young Guy (and his old one too; the actor plays the aging spy in two striking scenes) marks him as easily the best new British actor of his generation. The rest of the film work is first rate, and England's land never looked greener or pleasanter. But even fine filmmaking cannot make a point that writing fails to fashion, and *Another Country* simply is not clear enough, or tough enough, about its terribly important premise.

SEPTEMBER 15, 1984

Red Dawn

Andrew Kopkind

•

ONE MORNING IN the not-too-distant present—McDonald's has served over 45 billion burgers and Brezhnev's picture still adorns Soviet office walls—Americans wake up to find: NATO dissolved and Western Europe turned pacifist and neutral; the Greens in power in Bonn and Pershing 2s banned from West German soil; the United States and the Soviet Union locked in a de facto nuclear freeze; Nicaragua armed to withstand a US invasion; the oligarchy overthrown in El Salvador and the military crushed in Honduras; Mexico's aborted revolution successfully revived; and free showings of Eisenstein's *Alexander Nevsky* scheduled at theaters in American towns from El Paso to Butte. In other words, *The Nation*'s political project is being put into practice on a global scale.

So far so good. The premise of *Red Dawn*, which is announced before the titles in a series of punchy Brechtian headlines, may be hilariously implausible, but it's hardly worth the worry expended by liberal critics, who take director/writer John Milius too much at his word, fearing that this campy teen adventure is the first salvo of the coming fascist *Kulturkampf*. Not to worry; Milius is no Goebbels. When he hears the word "Hollywood" he reaches for his guns, but his intentions are more mischievous than murderous and his message is remarkably mixed.

Inevitably, an irksome contradiction impinges on the extraordinary scenario of world-historical events that opens the film. World War III starts when a Cuban-Nicaraguan-Soviet commando force drops into a small town in the Rockies, accompanied by an off-screen nuclear first strike against Omaha, Washington, D.C., and other expendable targets. The strange invaders land on the grounds of the high school in Calumet, Colorado, where a black teacher is in the middle of a lecture about medieval Mongolian hordes and the depredations of Genghis Khan. He's the first to get blown away. Having dispatched that irony, the commandos pretty much demolish the community and subjugate its terrified inhabitants.

The extremely fast times at Calumet High spin off the adventure plot. A small band of boys, players and fans of the Wolverines football team, escapes to the hills in a pickup, stopping at the local sporting goods store along the way for guns and ammo. Presently they are joined by two teenage girls, and the new Wolverines terrorist front swings into action. They blow up tanks with captured rockets, lure enemy soldiers into lethal ambushes and generally play such brilliant guerrilla games that a General Giap or a George Habash would be envious.

If you swivel the politics about 45 degrees to the left, *Red Dawn* begins to look more like a celebration of people's war than a horror movie about the evil empire. For all his Zen fascism, or whatever he calls it, Milius has produced the most convincing story about popular resistance to imperial oppression since the inimitable *Battle of Algiers*. He has only admiration for his guerrilla kids, and he understands their motivations—and excuses their naïveté—far better than the hip liberal filmmakers of the 1960s counterculture. I'd take the Wolverines from Colorado over a small circle of friends from Harvard Square in any revolutionary situation I can imagine.

At the same degree off center, the relationships of fish to sea, and of fish to fish, are realistically if simply drawn. The Calumet townsfolk surrender because resistance from their small urban base is impossible; armed struggle is conceivable only from the sierra. The groveling Mayor clings to his role as a collaborationist, and the resident floozies flock to the macho aggressors. Merchants try to pursue business as usual, and a few brave souls do what they can to help the guerrillas.

The imperialists behave like beasts when their power is threatened. They shoot the natives in retaliation for Wolverine raids, and they detain and execute potential protest leaders in a nice restatement of the Phoenix program used by the CIA in Vietnam. Although the

Wolverines' terrorism makes life difficult for their countrymen, the guerrillas will not repudiate their tactics. Terror is their only weapon.

The invaders argue among themselves. The Cuban captain (Ron "Superfly" O'Neal, the film's most charming and convincing character) is a veteran adviser to people's wars from Indochina to Angola, and he comes to sympathize more with the guerrillas than with the Second World commissars who oversee the occupation of Calumet. "Now I'm just like you—a policeman," he sneers at the Rasputin of a Russian officer who gives the orders. The Cuban knows all about hearts and minds, and in the end he remains the most rounded and humane warrior in the film.

The teen guerrillas have their fallings out as well. One girl rails against a male comrade for his petty chauvinism ("Did I do something wrong?" he pathetically rejoins); a boy allows his father, the Mayor, to turn him into a mole; they all have a terrible time snuffing the traitor in their midst when the deed must be done. When one young guerrillero worries, "That's what *they'd* do," another counters, "Yeah, but we live here." The territorial imperative is stronger than any doctrine. As always, the Wolverines' politics grow out of the barrels of their guns.

Guns are fun in the mountains, and the good guys handle theirs lovingly. The one clear point to the movie is that the National Rifle Association is dead right. When the invaders take Calumet, they seize the firearms registration records and arrest everyone who owns a piece, proving that guns don't kill people; gun registration does. A bumper sticker underscores the idea: "They can have my gun when they pry it from my cold dead fingers."

The rest of the politics is much more obscure than the Cyrillic-script advertisements suggest or literal-minded audiences infer. There's not much talk about ideology or economic systems, or even good guys against bad ones. A US Air Force pilot who parachutes into the Wolverines' camp tells the kids the big war started because the "two tough guys on the block" were itching for a fight. In other words, there is not much difference between the First World and the Second, and the moral high ground must be located in the Third. Communist revolutionaries may disagree, and it does seem too pat to put a plague on both big houses, but that political position is not so different from the one taken by the British Campaign for Nuclear Disarmament, for instance.

There are some other problems. The easy feminism of the guerrilla campfire hides a deeper mystification of sex and violence: the women are enigmatic animals, able to kill themselves and others with cold passion. The examples of Third World revolutionary tigresses and New Left terror queens have made their imprint on Milius's imagination. And then there's the nutty notion that Nicaragua could invade America, fair play though such a turnaround would be.

If you read *Red Dawn* as a parable of American intervention in Central America, say, or even an evocation of what might have happened in Poland if the Russians had moved in to crush Solidarity, it's not so hideous. Certainly there's nothing here that should encourage adherence to the Republican platform or a vote for Reagan. The movie cannot be seen as propaganda for a bigger defense budget; the partisans (as they're called at the movie's end) do not need Tridents or B-1 bombers. Simpson-Mazzoli—never a great piece of immigration law—gets an oblique pan: "They opened up the door down there and the Mexicans, Nicaraguans and Cubans poured in," someone remembers. But the eye and ear of the movie-goer can make of *Red Dawn* what they like. Some of it is strong stuff, but who, after watching the goings on in Dallas last month, can disagree wholeheartedly with the disembodied voice from a loudspeaker at the Calumet re-education camp: "America is a whorehouse where the ideals of your forefathers are prostituted." Maybe Milius believes that too.

A PASSAGE TO INDIA

Andrew Kopkind

•

YEARS AGO, IN a student quarter of London, there was an Indian restaurant of no great distinction other than its custom of serving a side dish, with all its meals, called Bombay Duck. This was a rank condiment of desiccated fish strips with the texture of pemmican, the salinity of baccalao and the flavor of cardboard. You don't see it much anymore, but it was a popular accompaniment in those days. The waiter would bring it as soon as diners were seated, and although the dish hardly came as a surprise to habitués of that establishment, he invariably gave a little speech of presentation. "Bombay Duck. Tastes like chicken. Use like bread. Is fish!"

As there, so here; as then, so now. There's something fishy about the epic feast David Lean serves up in *A Passage to India,* a classically conceived, beautifully constructed and exquisitely executed movie which pretends to be what it is not. It looks like an epic. We know this because it lasts for two hours and 40 minutes and contains several extremely long shots of antique trains chugging across sunset horizons. Its romantic musical score, which sometimes evokes "Lara's Theme" in Lean's bona fide epic *Dr. Zhivago*, is played by a thousand heavenly strings. It has faceless brown multitudes, colorful colonial festivities and an elephant. But if Lean came to *India* to find an epic subject, he was misinformed.

E. M. Forster's celebrated novel, published in 1924, is intimate despite its exotic locale; interior despite scenes of furious activity; intensive despite the breadth of the country it concerns and the societies it covers. Set against a historical backdrop with political props, it is about neither history nor politics, at least in the ordinary epic sense. It is a novel of crosscultural manners, psychological struggle and philosophical speculation. Forster's major characters are subtly conceived and their behavior is always ambiguous; ditto for their relationships. The period of the plot is brief; no sweep of centuries buries the business in timeless sands. If Lean were not overwhelmed by the size of the subcontinent where he filmed his movie, he might have looked to his own *Brief Encounter* rather than to *Lawrence* of *Arabia* for an appropriate model.

In Forster's story, the encounter in question takes place between Adela Quested and her passion, between her Anglo-Saxon temperament evident on the surface and a savage sexuality burning down below. Yes, that old post-Victorian chestnut falls again from the thrusting tree of English lit: middle-class British virgin (de facto or de jure) gets turned on in the Third World by native heat, art and legend, or just plain dirty talk. It must have been quite a sensitive subject in the 1920s, because the Awakening drove writers to extremes of sexual symbol and metaphor. Few modern novels are more out of control than D. H. Lawrence's hilarious *The Plumed Serpent*, in which the unfulfilled Kate Leslie gets "awakened," and much more, by a Mexican layabout who could be the god Quetzalcoatl.

Now we have Lawrence of India. Forster's Miss Quested (Judy Davis), a spiritual sister of Kate Leslie, is on her way to India to see about the possibility, or at least the logic, of marrying Ronny Heaslop (Nigel Havers), a zircon in the crown of the British raj, currently serving as a civil magistrate in the (fictional) provincial capital of Chandrapore. Ronny's mother, Mrs. Moore (Peggy Ashcroft), accompanies Miss Quested on the journey, which is heavy with portent. At dockside in Bombay we have seen already that British rule in India is doomed by its own pomposity, that imperial comfort is insupportable in the face of native squalor, and that something narsty is going to happen to Miss Quested if she doesn't mind her manners.

Both English ladies are liberal and they are easily offended by the inequality between rulers and ruled. They scorn the pomp and the polo and yearn to experience "the real India." For Mrs. Moore, a premature post-Christian, that has to do with the alternative spiritual life style expressed by Professor Godbole (Alec Guinness), the local

Hindu sadhu. For Miss Quested it is the hungry I of the sweaty, excitable Moslem physician Dr. Aziz (Victor Banerjee). Through the efforts of the integrationist schoolmaster Fielding (James Fox), another liberal Briton, Mrs. Moore and Miss Quested take tea with the two Indians, and before long most of this crowd is traipsing out to the Marabar Hills (hence, the epic elephant), on a psychosexual, spiritual pilgrimage to mysterious caves and the climax of the story. *Boum* goes the echo from the depths. *Zing* go the strings of their hearts. Atop the dusty domes Mrs. Moore loses God, Miss Quested encounters her id, and Dr. Aziz discovers that British liberalism is a mixed blessing at best.

Write like romance. Shoot like epic. Is not! Forster's India was antiromantic, impaired, *off*. Chandrapore was "scarcely distinguishable from the rubbish [the Ganges] deposits so freely." The Marabar caves were boring, empty, unholy and undecorated. Miss Quested was unattractive and neurotic; Mrs. Moore was not the saint others thought her; Aziz was tiresome and abrasive. Lean knew all that—his movie is serious, intelligent and deliberate—and he apparently wanted to be faithful to Forster's conception, but the form the director chose is always at odds with the material at hand. As a result, he had to cut and paste to restore the romance, remove the impairments, keep it *up* instead of off. Lean clears up the mystery of the cave, and thus destroys the essential ambiguity of the novel. He adds a scene in which Miss Quested comes upon a trove of Hindu porn on ancient temple ruins, thus making literal and banal what was once subtle and suggestive. He leaves out the crucial motivation for Mrs. Moore's unexpected flight from India before the conflicts are resolved. He invents a final reconciliation between Fielding and Aziz that creates a false sense of brotherhood between the British and the Indians. And he trivializes the entire colonial struggle with blimpish images of the raj and comedy-store impersonations of the natives. Guinness's Professor Godbole, in particular, is a scandalous representation. It's easy enough to ridicule a guru; the trick is to get behind the Peter Sellers routine, and Guinness manages that for just one instant.

In a week or so, *A Passage to India* will be nominated for an Academy Award, and by April, David Lean should be able to pick up his third Oscar as Best Director. He deserves a prize. For all its faults of literary license and cultural wrongheadedness, this is a striking movie-movie, perhaps the last one of the classic period that we will see. And besides, India is hot. *Gandhi* laid the groundwork. *The Jewel in the*

Crown became the middlebrow PBS *Dynasty.* Then the various assassinations, riots and industrial disasters of the past year put the spotlight on the vast nation. And as they say on *Entertainment Tonight*, there's no such thing as bad publicity.

June 22, 1985

Rambo: First Blood Part II
Birdy

Andrew Kopkind

•

VIETNAM HAS SUFFERED invasions, interventions and expeditions by every great power in this century; it has endured the visits of foe and friend, from Robert McNamara to Jane Fonda; it has survived almost half a century of bombing, mining, corruption, incineration and defoliation. All that, and now this: along comes Rambo, the ultimate weapon in humanoid form, winning with biceps and pecs the war that the mightiest nation in history lost with mere B-52s and Agent Orange. At last, William Westmoreland's dishonorable defeat has been avenged by Sly Stallone.

Rambo: First Blood Part II is at once hilarious and disgusting. It's hard not to howl at Stallone's apish ambition, the blind egomania of a lowland gorilla who looks at his reflection in a jungle pool and sees a limpid Narcissus. It is to laugh when Stallone slaughters whole battalions of Vietnamese and Soviet soldiers ("damn Russian bastards!") with crossbow, bazooka and bare hands; steals a helicopter and destroys native villages (the ones the U.S. Army missed); rescues American POWs from the Vietcong tiger cages where they have been languishing since *The Deer Hunter*. It is even worth a chuckle when Stallone finally manages to grunt out a complete prepositional clause ("for our country to love us as much as we love it") in the closing thirty seconds, even though we may have to wait for Part III for a whole sentence, with subject and predicate like they have in those European films. When Brando mumbled through *Julius Caesar*, it was tolerated as sheer Method madness; with Stallone, mumbles are the very best he can do.

But even Stallone's camp followers will have a hard time swallowing the twisted history, the racist images and the political line of Rocky's latest horror show. Its premise is that certain villains—bureaucrats, politicians, CIA operatives—sold America down the river in Vietnam and afterward, thus losing the war and preventing the return of uncounted MIAs. The lowly grunts would have won if left to their own devices, and when they were sent home the society that surrendered despised them precisely because their presence was a constant reproach. *First Blood*, which introduced Rambo, glorified the bitter and violent veteran in his struggle against cowardly authority and a complacent citizenry. In that effort, Rambo turned his wrath against small-town rednecks in the Pacific Northwest and against wave after wave of the National Guard. For the damage done, he was sentenced to a season on the prison rock pile.

Post-imperial frustration is a familiar theme in twentieth-century history: cf., Hitler after Versailles, the Tory right after Suez, the China Lobby after Mao's march. The syndrome has several phases. First blood is always drawn internally, from those at home held responsible for the unaccountable defeat. Then come the overseas revenge fantasies, sometimes enacted in terrifying reality. No doubt there are worse scenarios in store for America than the one Stallone and James (*The Terminator*) Cameron created for *Rambo,* but until the real thing comes along, we are asked to sublimate our death wishes in the Hollywood version.

Rambo is sprung by his old Special Forces colonel (Richard Crenna) and sent back to Nam. "Do we get to win this time?" he asks in a moment of foreshadowing which epitomizes the subtlety of the plot to follow. The Green Beret replies that it's all up to Rambo, but in fact the same wimps and sellouts in Congress and the Central Intelligence Agency who collapsed after Tet are setting Rambo up for failure. They want him to find no live Americans in-country so that they can continue their dirty diplomatic games of appeasement and accommodation.

Aided only by Co, the Vietnamese girl *contra* (apparently no authentic ethnic actress has succeeded France Nguyen as the all-purpose Pan-Asian heroine, so the part is played by the round-eyed Julia Nickson), Rambo has to do battle with Charlie, Ivan, a band of river pirates, assorted leeches and snakes, the CIA mission commander, the legacy of

Henry Kissinger and the ghost of the antiwar movement. It's no contest. Metamachismo carries the day. Rambo sheds only a tear when Co takes an Aka burst in the back (those damn Russian bastards always shoot you as you're running). When, dying, she implores, "Don't forget me" he merely grunts, "Uh-uh." War love is never having to say anything, and these big guys really love making war. Stallone is a Bill Broyles with muscles, but his passion for carnage is no big secret. "You're of Indian-German descent," the CIA man notes approvingly as he reads Rambo's dossier. "It's a hell of a combination." I'll say!

War and remembrance are pivotal perches for *Birdy*, but the perspective in Alan Parker's novelistic film (from the pseudonymous William Wharton's 1979 novel) is wary and wounded like a fallen sparrow's, while *Rambo*'s eye is fixed on the kill. Al (Nicolas Cage) is battle-scarred and bandaged, and when he limps from his hospital bed, he looks like the hero of *Johnny Got His Gun* miraculously on the mend. A demonic Army psychiatrist fetches him to help make contact with his old high-school buddy Birdy (Matthew Modine), another vet whom the war has scarred so profoundly that he crouches naked in a catatonic state in a dungeonlike military asylum.

Constructed intricately as a series of parallel flashbacks, *Birdy* looks for the roots of Al's bitterness and Birdy's psychosis in their working-class Philadelphia boyhood, in their dreams of freedom and flight, in their repressed emotional need for each other. Their past is imperfect, but the postwar present is impossible, and the future, for both, seems nonexistent. Symbols and signifiers swoop and crash with dizzying frequency, like a busy day at O'Hare. Cats and canaries, ecstasy and garbage, mothers and fathers; and through it all a flight motif so thick you can cut it with a bayonet.

But Parker's heavy hand hits hard where it counts: at war-love, patriotism and masculinity; and both Modine and Cage deliver wrenching if occasionally overwrought performances. Everyone involved seems to have cared about what they were doing, and their earnestness gives *Birdy* moments of astonishing truth, whereas *Rambo* is a lie from beginning to end.

APRIL 19, 1986

MY BEAUTIFUL LAUNDRETTE

Andrew Kopkind

•

COLONIALISM AND ITS discontents could become the central epic of British life in the next period, just as social class and its contradictions have dominated the insular imagination of generations past. Of course the two epics intertwine and overlap. Empire and hierarchy go together as bubble goes with squeak, as pomp goes with circumstances, as the organization of Britain's colonial system correlated precisely with the structure of its domestic society. Not surprisingly, emphasis began to shift from the consequences of class to the complications of a dying colonialism as the sun set on the Empire and flocks of imperial pigeons came fluttering back to Britain to roost. Suddenly race and caste became pressing issues in everyday life. Themes of cultural assimilation, national identity and ethnic domination—largely unexamined by the British conscience in the home islands, outside the familial context of Anglo-Celtic relations—replaced or merged with the old motifs of social mobility and privilege.

Bringing the colonial wars home has had a salutary effect on British culture, and I don't mean merely reggae music and tandoori chicken. The widening pool of available visions, emotions, habits, and ideologies has fed what was beginning to look like a veritable Sahel of sensibility, with nought but nostalgia and wrinkled self-pity to decorate the arid landscape. And if *My Beautiful Laundrette* is any indication, more rains are on the way. Seemingly slight, inconclusive, even mischievous, it is a movie that opens arguments, suggests possibilities, throws out ideas and plays with characters in a way that marks the start of a style, rather than the end of an era. It's fresh in the many senses of the word.

Written and conceived by Hanif Kureishi—an Anglo-Pakistani born in Britain—and directed by Stephen Frears, *My Beautiful Laundrette* focuses on a detail of London's demography, the neighborhoods where first—and second-generation Indo-Pakistani immigrants are digging into British life. There's a reverse archaeological element in the scene: the natives have come to the motherland to search for artifacts of the supposedly superior culture and make sense of the system that colonized them. And to dominate that system too; not since Bosworth Field has a horde from over the seas threatened to loosen British social hegemony and upset the status quo.

Kureishi produces an extended family that is neither entirely happy nor miserable, certainly not noble, but not unusually villainous either. There's Papa (Roshan Seth), who vegetates in a vodka-induced state some distance from the suffocating theocracy of his homeland and equally far from the pressures of the striving immigrant community of his exile. His son, Omar (Gordon Warnecke), is bent on making it in bourgeois Britain as a charming manipulator of lovers, relatives, and small-business deals. Uncle Nasser (Saeed Jaffrey) is the paunchy paterfamilias with an Anglo mistress on the side and a talent for capital accumulation and cultural assimilation: "I'm not a professional Pakistani, I'm a professional businessman," he boasts. More faces in their crowd belong to a drug smuggler, a sexually liberated daughter, a coven of homebound matrons and macho hangers-on, and various family fillers. Just what you'd expect: it's a group that contains in average proportion the predictable number of deadbeats, social climbers, hypocrites, romantics, waifs, naïfs, self-deluders, failed heroes, and wounded warriors. What is unusual is not their wounds or delusions, but the way those are refracted by the intense historical experience of living in Margaret Thatcher's England.

A certain amount of Paki-bashing is inevitable, but Kureishi stands even that conflict on its head. Johnny (Daniel Day Lewis), a punky baby Nazi, is Omar's old school chum, and the attraction between the two of them roughly resembles the relationship between the colonial immigrants and their former masters. It is erotic, manipulative, dangerous, unstable but continually compelling. Uncle Nasser agrees to give Omar a seedy laundrette to run, and the boy takes Johnny on as a kind of partner and servant to build up the business. Things are helped immeasurably when the lads appropriate the proceeds of a cocaine deal to refurbish the premises, which then become a pastel palace and trendy hangout called Powders.

In the meantime, Omar and Johnny are amusing themselves with a sexual affair that is part puppy love, part S&M. Aside from the fact that it is a same-sex relationship, it is no more extraordinary than the liaison between Uncle Nasser and his mistress, Rachel (Shirley Anne Field), or the engagement encouraged by the family for Omar and his sexy cousin Tania (Rita Wolf). Audiences may be baffled by the presentation of a gay relationship that is not a problem or an issue; the critic Vito Russo reported that he heard a woman at a screening ask her companion, "I don't get it. Why were they gay?" But there is no point other than the perfectly adequate explanation that it is the way things are, that some people are Pakistanis in London today, that some lovers are men, that some uncles have mistresses. The best thing about *My Beautiful Laundrette* is that it makes no small moral judgments, casts no stones of self-righteousness nor draws portentous generalizations. It is not a European movie about Asians or a straight movie about gays; more strikingly, it is not a movie of special pleading by one group or tendency or subculture for its own cause.

If that is baffling, it's because so few films have been able to make a slice of life seem true without relying on the clichés and stereotypes society imposes on it. Two very different films I've written about recently failed precisely because they were unable to develop a point of view unique to their material. *Parting Glances* was shot from deep inside the confines of New York's Upper West Side gay ghetto, but it adopted the definition of that small circle of friends from the world around it. *The Color Purple* drew beautiful and powerful cartoons of Southern black people in a bygone era, from designs that were approved by sophisticated urban white people today. Both those movies contained truths, but in a larger sense were not true; they lacked the integrity and the self-definition that *My Beautiful Laundrette* so wonderfully conveys.

Nothing is resolved in this movie, no determination is made about the success of the immigrant colonization of Britain, or the future of Omar's relationship with Johnny. The bashers come back, love falters and flares. Papa is sober and soused, business booms and busts. All that is predictable, but never dreary, thanks to Kureishi's honest insights and Frears's oblique and original vision. Life, once again, is redeemed by paradox, and Britain may yet be saved by innovation.

JANUARY 17, 1987

PLATOON

Terrence Rafferty

•

Terrence Rafferty has been a film critic for *The Nation* and *The New Yorker*. He is currently a columnist and critic-at-large for *GQ* magazine. He is the author of *The Thing Happens: Ten Years of Writing about the Movies.*

OLIVER STONE'S *PLATOON*, about a group of American infantrymen in Vietnam between 1967 and 1968, is the first Hollywood film about this country's Southeast Asian adventure that's just a war movie—and, weirdly, its straightforward genre-picture intensity makes all the other film treatments of the subject look evasive and superficial. Even leaving aside the recently popular POW rescue movies with Sylvester Stallone and Chuck Norris, which are simply macho pulp in exotic settings, Milton Caniff on steroids, American movies haven't done very well by the horrors of Vietnam and Cambodia. All the serious, films about Southeast Asia of the past ten years have been so intent on "coming to terms" with the experience that they've barely bothered to *represent* it. For all the virtues of *Apocalypse Now* no one could possibly have learned anything about Vietnam from it. Coppola stages the war as a psychedelic opera—jungles bursting into flames with the Doors' sinister "The End" on the soundtrack, copters swooping out of the sky to the music of "Ride of the Valkyries"—and the grandiose style robbed the subject of its specificity. Coppola was so caught up in creating his huge metaphoric vision of chaos (derived, in just about equal parts, from *Heart of Darkness* and Michael Herr's *Dispatches*) that he seemed not to notice the inanity of the movie's subtext: that the war could have been won if our military leaders weren't so inept and our soldiers so stoned, if only we Americans weren't so stupid and spiritually empty.

Michael Cimino's Oscar-winner, *The Deer Hunter*, also featured a hallucinated Vietnam: the war was a bad dream that his heroes, a bunch of regular-guy Pennsylvania factory workers, couldn't wake up from. Cimino meant to contrast the supposed purity of traditional American values with the war's hellish suspension of moral categories, and he wasn't fussy about how he defined his terms—not only idealizing the "clean" sportsmanship of the heroes' deer-hunting expeditions, but also inventing a Russian-roulette torture by the group's Vietnamese captors. *The Deer Hunter* was as overblown as *Apocalypse Now*, but in a different register, like an opera scored by Springsteen. It had a heavy, plodding spirit, a populist ethos verging (probably without meaning to) on the demagogic, and a defeated air that somehow managed to congratulate us on our wounded innocence, our stunned simplicity. Neither of those big-deal movies was about Vietnam at all—they were about the shape the war took in our imaginations (which is, perhaps, why they were both so muddled and unresolved). But the war was, of course, more than a bad trip, as Coppola would have it, or a child's nightmare, as in Cimino. *Platoon* gives Vietnam back some of its reality.

In *Platoon*, the war is so real that it actually sobers up Oliver Stone, who, as a screenwriter (*Midnight Express, Scarface, Eight Million Ways to Die, Year of the Dragon*), has developed his own brand of hysterical machismo. The contemporary action pictures he's written may have started out as explorations of aspects of the underworld and the drug culture, but they all wound up as lurid, wired celebrations of chaos and obscenity: uneasy mixtures of tabloid moralizing and gonzo relish, stuffed into conventional genre structures that served to emphasize the filmmakers' bad faith. *Salvador*, released early last year (and now available on videocassette), was written and directed by Stone, and made a little more sense. Its hero, a Hunter Thompson-like freelance journalist played by James Woods (with even more than his usual ferrety intensity), was clearly a kind of war junkie, traveling to Central America in search of a revolution to get high on: the character seemed an acknowledgment of Stone's own guilty pleasure in out-of-control violence and reckless, "existential" tests of manhood. Although *Sal-*

vador's politics got a bit confused and both the action and the performances were sometimes pointlessly frenetic, the movie managed, in its self-conscious way, to convey the desperate atmosphere of crisis—and without turning its background of Third World turmoil into spectacle (as Roland Joffe's *The Killing Fields* often did with its powerful and beautiful images of the Khmer Rouge takeover of Cambodia). *Salvador* was a wild, unstable movie that, intermittently, was also a vivid essay on varieties of instability, personal and political.

Stone's Vietnam movie is, surprisingly, the cleanest, simplest work he has ever done. He's not exactly an austere director, even here, but he keeps the movie focused on the day-to-day experience of his platoon through a sequence of five military actions along the Cambodian border, and he has the sense to realize that the young soldiers' fear is all the subject he needs. Stone treats the war and its participants with a strange kind of reverence, as if here, at the source of his obsession with violence and madness, he doesn't need to add anything, to jack up the voltage. In some way, the failure of earlier Vietnam movies has probably helped him. We've *had* the war as metaphor for moral chaos, and the war as rock-and-roll hallucination. Stone, who served in Vietnam in the late 1960s, must have looked at those films and asked himself if the war he'd fought was horrible because our leaders were dithering incompetents or because our soldiers were too far gone on pot or acid or Hendrix to know what was happening to them. In Stone's version, it's the soldiers who know exactly what they're doing, who kill most efficiently, like his appalling Sergeant Barnes (played by Tom Berenger, whose facial makeup transcends all previous definitions of "battle-scarred"), that are the most dangerous; and it's only the "heads"—the guys who smoke pot and listen to rock—who retain some vestige of decency and rationality. He seems to have decided that the war was awful because it was wrong to begin with, and because people were dying all around him.

This blunt attitude gives Stone's writing and direction a kind of ferocious concentration they've never had before. The fact that he's drawing on his own experience obviously helps, too. He's not scattering wild notions and off-the-wall verbal exchanges all over the landscape, as he usually does: in *Platoon*, he's too busy filling in remembered details. He adopts the classic perspective of a young soldier (Charlie Sheen) seeing action for the first time, and everything is seen here with the heightened alertness of terror: the agony of night watches; the lightning-fast mayhem of a fire fight; even the smaller, peripheral dangers—snakes, insects—that help turn simple fear into panic. It's *The Red Badge of*

Courage, without the courage. "Ain't no such thing as a coward out here," one weary veteran tells the young soldier before the climactic engagement: there are isolated acts of genuine heroism, but the only real prize this war has to offer is the sight of the helicopter that lifts you away from it for good. *Platoon* is even more narrowly focused than World War II movies were—there is (blessedly) little talk among the grunts about the girls they left behind or the candy store they're going to open up when they get back home or how the Yankees are doing—and the limitation is appropriate and powerful. The platoon Stone has created (or recreated) is a world of its own, where the business of survival drives everything else—even notions of home—from consciousness.

Stone's directorial style, which is fast, kinetic and rather literal, serves him well in the action scenes: there are few battle sequences on film as tense and frightening as these. In the intervals between skirmishes, his writing takes over, and though it's not as florid as usual, it still causes some problems. The conflict between Sergeant Barnes and his "head" counterpart, the smart, brave Sergeant Elias (Willem Dafoe), is crudely drawn and, worse yet, symbolic: the young hero, narrating in voice-over, refers to Barnes as "our Captain Ahab," and, after all the shooting is over, speaks of "Barnes and Elias fighting for possession of my soul." That dramatic hyperbole is meant to illustrate the not very original thesis that Stone saves until the last few seconds of the movie: "The enemy," Sheen's voice intones, "was in us," There is, of course, some truth in that, but there's *some* truth in almost anything we can say about that complex war—and what's refreshing about *Platoon* up to that point is that it has mostly resisted the impulse to generalize, to make the kind of statement that, like Coppola's and Cimino's can't possibly tell us any more than a fraction of the truth. At its best, *Platoon* simply shows us as much as we need to know about a small patch of the territory—Stone's own experience in Vietnam—which is probably more valuable.

It's a little ironic, though, that after his manic, hallucinated versions of *other* people's lives—the feverishly caricatured Turks, Chinese-Americans, and Miami Cubans of his previous scripts—Oliver Stone has become an honorable and scrupulous artist in dealing with the central experience of his own life. Let's hope that this strong movie isn't just an isolated episode in Stone's career, that he'll be able to carry over his new rigor and generosity from his memory to his imagination. Vietnam seems, to have made him a better film-maker—his next movies should tell us whether, in the best war-movie tradition, it's also made a man out of him.

February 7, 1987

Rendez-vous
Scene of the Crime

Terrence Rafferty

•

THE SURFACES OF André Téchiné's films are glittering and faceted; they give off a complex, spectral light. When *French Provincial (Souvenirs de'en France*) was released in 1975, its jeweled style was a bit of a shock. The previous generation of French film-makers—the famous New Wave that included François Truffaut, Jean-Luc Godard and Eric Rohmer—had, since the late 1950s been making films that exulted in the poverty of their means and found freedom in lose, digressive storytelling and natural light. Those directors were critics for *Cahiers du Cinéma*, were all lovers of the classical Hollywood film, but nonetheless shunned the studio as if its techniques were instruments of oppression they expressed themselves with the undisciplined exuberance of boys escaped from boarding school.

French Provincial, made by a member of the next wave of *Cahiers* critics, from the 1960s, seemed to announce something new. This movie, constructed as a series of vignettes from the history of a rural factory town from the 1930s to the end of the 1960s, has the New Wave icon Jeanne Moreau at its center, in a role that nearly reverses the meaning of the liberated, unconventional women she played for Truffaut and Louis Malle: here she begins as an independent-minded village laundress but becomes, over the next thirty years, a tough bourgeois matriarch. The casting of Moreau (who is wonderful in the movie) may be a comment on the history of the New Wave, which, inspired at first by the fluid and generous-spirited realism of Jean Renoir's 1930s films, had by the end of the 1960s begun to show signs of decline, of hardening into an institutional version of itself.

What's startling about *French Provincial* is that Téchiné's critique of the New Wave produces its own kind of euphoria—we feel, in every gilded frame of the movie, the director's love of the spectacle of decline, the rich efflorescence of corruption. The ravishing set-pieces of *French Provincial* seem to have been inspired by the baroque, prodigious style of Orson Welles, who was similarly fascinated by the elaborate disguises people assume in order to cheat history, by the complex self-consciousness of decadence. Téchiné's family saga often suggests a French version of Welles's *The Magnificent Ambersons*. Its abrupt, leaping continuity even pays homage, in a modernist way, to the flawed form of Welles's American provincial chronicle, which was drastically cut by the studio: Téchiné's editing has the strange effect of making his film look as if it were an abridgment of something, as if those oddly shaped scenes were the taped-together shards of an irrecoverable whole. The New Wave directors were always fond of planting little tributes to their heroes in their movies, but none of them ever did anything quite that rarefied.

Téchiné is hardly known in this country. *French Provincial* was shown at the New York Film Festival in 1975 and had a short commercial release afterward; his next film, the aptly named *Barocco*, came and went even more quickly; and the three films he made from 1976 to 1985—*Les Soeurs Brontë*, *Hôtel des Ameriques* and *La Matiouette*—have never been released here. His most recent films, *Rendez-vous* and *Scene of the Crime*, have found distributors in the United States, and although they won't win him legions of American devotees, they're fascinating—artifacts of a great but enigmatic talent, as frustrating as they are seductive. Téchiné represents the critic-filmmaker in its most extreme form. He's purely and equally both, and so he seems a perfect embodiment of the paradoxes of French cinema in the past twenty-five years, a conscious reflection of his times. His reputation may be marginal, but his dilemma is central. The French film-making who have had successes lately—Eric Rohmer (*Summer*), Agnès Varda (*Vagabond*), Maurice Pialat (*Police*)—are those who, over the years, have mastered an individual expressive style, have settled into an aesthetic identity as inevitable as the confines of the body. Téchiné's repertoire of techniques includes just about every style in the history of movies, and his critical intelligence sees all of them as moments in the history of consciousness, the pieces of which the present is constituted. He like Borges's character Funes, who's literally unable to forget anything, to whom the past is always immediate and finally too dense. Funes's body becomes a useless appendage of his consciousness, and declines rapidly from immobility to oblivion. If Téchiné's work seems, at first, wispy and elusive, it's because there's too much going on in it: too many abstract notions, too many memories of past movies and too many ghosts in every image, blurring the outlines. If we find it difficult to see his body of work clearly, it's because in some sense it doesn't exist. Téchiné's films are, rather, a spirit of work, haunting bodies that they can't quite take possession of.

Waiting for Téchiné to come into his own may prove to be futile—as frustrating as it was to anticipate a final masterpiece (or, as it turned out, any film at all) by Orson Welles. But Téchiné is still relatively young (born in 1943), and he's one of the very few directors who seem capable of a great film: if he ever found a form and a subject elegant and suggestive enough to make coherent all he knows about the way the world looks and the way it works, he could make the kind of classic that sums up an era, like *Citizen Kane* or Renoir's *Rules of the Game*. And—unlike Welles in his late years—he keeps working. *Rendez-vous* (which, although it is being released here two months after *Scene of the Crime*, is the earlier film) doesn't provide very encouraging evidence of Téchiné's progress in the years since American audiences got their last look, at *Barocco*. In fact, he appears to have picked up exactly where he left off in that delirious, labyrinthine fairy-tale thriller. He's still playing around with mirrors and masks, reflections and projections, doppelgängers and revenants—all the paraphernalia of the Romantic imagination by which identities are multiplied, confused and finally evaded. In *Barocco*, at least, this fancy intellectual footwork seems of a piece with the film's conception: with a plot full of political intrigues, double-crosses and intricate manipulations of images by the media, *Barocco* is designed as a vision of a world that's already removed from reality, a reflection of the fantasies of the powerful. It's a crazy movie—when a boxer hired to lie about a politician is shot trying to escape the deal, his girlfriend falls in love with his killer, who looks exactly like the dead man, and she flees the country with him instead—but it's beautifully worked out, a sumptuously detailed paranoid fresco, consistent with the leftist politics and the love-hate relationship with bourgeois culture in *French Provincial.*

French Provincial was Téchiné's *Ambersons; Barocco*, with its conception of history as a hall of mirrors in which bullets keep shattering images until at last they kill something real, was his *Lady From Shanghai*; following Welles, he seems to have made *Rendez-vous* as his own hasty, botched Shakespeare movie. He wrote the script very quickly (with Olivier Assayas, a current *Cashiers* writer), after several long-planned projects fell through, and shot the picture on a short schedule. They didn't come up with much of a story: a girl from the provinces (Juliette Binoche) comes to Paris to become an actress, gets involved with a shady young man (Lambert Wilson) who commits suicide halfway through, and ends up playing Juliet for a director (Jean-Louis Trintignant) who had once staged the play with her dead lover as Romeo. What came spilling out of Téchiné and Assayas, in their rush, was an endless supply of conceits—abstractions and distractions, like the suicide popping up as a ghost whenever the girl is anxious and alone in her apartment, or the director playing father figure to both unfortunate lovers. There are vast empty rooms, and about a million mirror shots, and bits of plays performed (sometimes more than once, for ironic effect) within the main action; and as brilliantly managed as all this business is, it remains essentially business. Téchiné's metaphors and paradoxes and doubles and specters seem designed to connect two simple stories—*Romeo and Juliet* and a country girl's adventures in the big city—but they never do. It's only doodling, of a particularly dense and desperate kind. *Rendez-vous* is, in a way, a look at the inside of an artist's head when he's really stuck and all he has left is a tortuous ingenuity. This is chillingly claustrophobic film.

Téchiné has fewer problems making the right connections in his latest film, *Scene of the Crime*, which has just opened in New York City. In this movie he returns to the sources of his strengths, to the elements that stimulated the rich complex of associations in *French Provincial*—a rural setting, an established film genre (in this case, romantic melodrama of the French fatalistic variety popularized in the 1930s by *Port of Shadows* and similar films), and stars with long histories (here, Catherine Deneuve and Danielle Darrieux). Oddly, he's bordering on the territory of Truffaut's weak later films, like the Deneuve vehicle *The Last Metro* and the doomed-love thriller *The Woman Next Door*, but unlike the late New Wave director, Téchiné can find ways of expressing himself fully within the limitations of the most worn-out bourgeois forms of French cinema: as in *French Provincial,* he revels in them, embellishing and subverting at the same time. In *Scene of the Crime*, Téchiné gives his story of a fortyish provincial mother (Deneuve) who falls in love with a young escaped convict the benefit of a style borrowed from an altogether different class of picture. The camera never stops moving, framing and reframing the characters endlessly, one elegant composition flowing effortlessly into another, in the manner of Max Ophüls, whose romantic tragedies of the aristocracy moved like melancholy waltzes. Playing Deneuve's mother, Darrieux—who starred in several of Ophüls's films, including his greatest, *The Earrings of Madame de . . .* —is used here as the embodiment of that high romantic spirit. At one point, during a family dinner scene, the camera pivots slowly around Darrieux's face as she tells a story, but the movement ends, somehow, on Deneuve, whose flawless beauty seems as out of place in her frumpy cardigans as Téchiné's swanky technique does in this mildly sensational provincial novella.

The director's luxurious visual choreography has the peculiar effect of pushing the romance-magazine fatalism to the brink of parody and at the same time dignifying it, elevating this Gabin-like convict and this stifled country beauty to the swirling realm of romantic myth—turning the lonely provincial cabaret where Deneuve tends bar into masked ball. Téchiné seems to have traded the helpless exhaustion of the bourgeois romantic thriller for the more conscious decadence of aristocratic fantasy, as Deneuve, in the end, chooses the confinement that results from her noble newfound love over her accustomed imprisonment within the provincial family. This would all be rather precious nonsense except for the flickers of real emotion in Deneuve's performance and the serene confidence of Téchiné's direction. This too-late-for-love story is moving because it gives Téchiné a form to explore his own deepest feeling as a film-maker—his latecomer's melancholy, his regret that the movie magic he loves had accumulated too much history by the time he learned to use it. It would be wonderful if this small, hypnotic movie proved to be a turning point for him, a therapeutic plunge into the sources of his artistic confusion which will free him, at last, to create his own grand illusions unselfconsciously.

MAY 28, 1988

WEDDING IN GALILEE
FRIENDSHIP'S DEATH

Edward W. Said

•

Edward W. Said, the University Professor of English and Comparative Literature at Columbia University, is *The Nation*'s classical music critic as well as a regular contributor on the Middle East. His latest book is a memoir *Out of Place*.

THERE ARE FEW films in international circulation that give any but the most biased picture of Palestinian life. Beginning with *Exodus*, Hollywood films have unquestioningly identified Israel with heroism, pioneering enterprise and anti-Communist antiterrorism. *Delta Force* and *Black Sunday* show the Palestinians as murderous terrorists whose only victims are innocent civilians; Sylvester Stallone is making another *Rambo*, in Israel; and CBS recently broadcast a film about a Palestinian terrorist's trial. Films produced in the Arab world, especially in Egypt, the heart of Arab film culture, have not generally been part of the international network. The only Arab director to have made a name for himself abroad is Youssef Chahine, and aside from the occasionally interesting Syrian, Iraqi or Tunisian feature, films by and for Arabs are of strictly regional importance. Egyptian comedies, and melodramas in particular, continue to delight huge Arab audiences that have still not made the switch to *Dallas* and *Dynasty*.

It is, I think, some sort of testimony to the stubborn durability of the Palestinian narrative that fascinating aspects of it have recently emerged in two radically different, and eccentric, works: Michel Khleifi's *Wedding in Galilee* and Peter Wollen's *Friendship's Death*. Both were made before the uprising on the West Bank and in Gaza totally transformed the media image of Palestinians. Khleifi is from Nazareth (in Israel proper, not the occupied territories) but has lived and worked in Belgium for a decade; his film is credited as a Franco-Belgian-Palestinian co-production, although it was filmed in Israel/Palestine. His earlier film, *The Fertile Memory*, was a lyrical documentary about two Palestinian women. *Wedding in Galilee* is a much more ambitious drama that takes place during a very long day in the life of a Palestinian village.

Khleifi's cuts between the dozens of scenes that make up his film are abrupt and, I feel, awkward. The cast is a sizable one, and the ideas operate on several levels. But *Wedding in Galilee* is nevertheless a profoundly affecting account of the Palestinian quandary, seen not exclusively as the result of Israeli occupation but also as the extension of problems endemic to Arab society in the late twentieth century. An elderly man (Ali el Akili) whose village has been punished by curfew secures permission to hold a big wedding for his son, on condition that the Israeli military governor (Makram Khoury) and his staff attend the ceremonies along with the other guests. This is not to everyone's liking, but the wedding proceeds.

Khleifi interweaves a number of strands, all of them connected to the main event, and illustrative in quite inventive ways of the central impasse in Palestinian society: the failure of continuity and of settled existence that has attended on Israel's presence. The son, Adel (Nazih Akleh), cannot consummate his marriage because of the patriarch's imposing authority; his sister Sumaya, played by the Tunisian Sonia Amar, wants out of the village, but can only visualize herself escaping as a man. A group of young men plot, but fail, to kill the Israelis; assorted relatives voice and demonstrate attitudes of loud defiance or undignified collaboration; a pair of elderly relatives wander in and out like Chekhovian retainers, casting a deepening shadow over the festivities; Tali (Tali Dorat), an Israeli woman in uniform, passes out but is revived by Arab women in a seduction scene that is dangerously close to a Pierre Loti or Orientalist fantasy.

Khleifi's method is to keep pretty much to the mundane matters in hand, a method likely to leave the impression, on most Palestinians and

Arabs, of a quaint folkloric scene. But then he brings you up short with a gesture or a sequence that rends the veil of sentimentalism. Most of the actors are amateurs, but they perform the required volte-face with conviction. Thus the old man is seen talking tenderly to his sleeping son, trying somehow to communicate a dream to him—then the boy awakens, and the old man's tone changes abruptly to sharp reproof. Or, when the Israeli commander and his crew savor the feast, one of them says without embarrassment that it is not as good as the food in Lebanon—some day, he adds with the confidence of power, you will have a meal in Aleppo.

Rituals often go awry, as when the thoroughbred mare used to transport the groom breaks out of her stall and runs into a nearby field, which has been mined by the Israelis. A disquieting sequence ensues. The Israeli soldiers hold a map of the mines' location and, firing their rifles, try to scare the animal into moving safely between the mines to freedom; the old man, petrified that his lovely mare will either be blown up or driven crazy, takes over and coaxes her out but is forced to do so under the Israelis' thumb. One is left with a remarkably reflective portrait of Palestinian life trapped inside various boxes, all of them reconfirming the present impasse. The film's affectionate frankness is indebted to Italian *verismo* and to the visionary clarity of many Third World films during the past two decades.

Wollen's work is much more self-consciously avant-garde. He is a well-known film theorist and director, whose *Signs and Meanings in the Cinema* and the more recent *Readings and Writings* have given him his reputation as a politically engaged intransigent. *Friendship's Death* is based on a short story about Wollen's sojourn in Amman during the early days of Black September, 1970. In the story, Friendship is a creature from outer space whose voyage to MIT (where he has been sent to visit Noam Chomsky, for the study of linguistics *and* peace) has been deflected, and who has ended up in Amman. The narrator is a left-wing journalist who sympathizes with the Palestinians and who is introduced to Friendship by one of the combatants. Narrator and humanoid become friends, both of them trapped in Amman as a fight between Jordanian regulars and Palestinian guerrillas rages furiously around them.

This is already enough to establish the peculiarity of Wollen's science fiction perspective—but it gets stranger. Friendship is fascinated with machines (clocks, vacuum cleaners and typewriters in particular), and of course he is interested in language. Nevertheless, his ability to comprehend earthly ideas is curiously limited (he can't understand the narrator's explanation of the Oedipus complex), and because he is a victim of sorts, he sides with the Palestinians. In doing so, he becomes "a representative, not so much of machines today, as of the potential oppressed class of intelligent machines and servo-mechanisms of tomorrow." (This is an idea not many Palestinians today will accept about themselves, but it is datable to 1970.) Joining one of the militias, Friendship is separated from the narrator, who leaves Amman just before the final defeat. Friendship, he assumes, has been captured and killed; his sadness at the Palestinian debacle shades imperceptibly into his melancholy incomprehension of Friendship's visit. He is pushed into memorializing the episode (he feels, he says, "rather like the Evangelists must have felt before starting to write, many years after the death of the protagonist"), which he does by reproducing Friendship's translation of "L'Après-midi d'un faune," a virtuoso misreading of Mallarmé—e.g. "I vault to persecute these white water-lilies" for "Ces nymphes, je les veux perpétuer."

In the film version, Friendship is a woman (Tilda Swinton) whose gender and placid beauty are perfectly suited to the curiosity, concern, oppression and wisdom Wollen wants to convey in his portrait of the victimized saintly robot. The narrator is now a tough Hemingway-like character called Sullivan (Bill Patterson), whose probing confidence is a satisfying foil for the outsider, and for the historical moment. Wollen's filmic style is understatement, although his realization of the story greatly amplifies and elaborates the narrative. Odd bits of comedy and apocalypse jostle each other. Thus Friendship comes from the period after nuclear winter; she is interested in shaving and in human hair, being hairless herself; she dreams of succulence or of impossible objects. Sullivan is fascinated by maps; rows of tombstones in Jordan point the way to the events of Beirut.

When Friendship and Sullivan part for the last time, he gives her a razor in exchange for one of her memory chips. Back home in England, Sullivan's young daughter figures out a way to decode the chip by playing it on a VCR. What ensues is Wollen's visual transposition of the Mallarmé translation left behind by the robot. The terminal sequence is an extraordinary montage of bio-mathematical symbols, geometric patterns, nuclear explosions and incomprehensible sequences. But the final effect of this articulate and calm film, so unusual and intelligent, is a melancholy almost religious in its intensity.

What makes *Wedding in Galilee* and *Friendship's Death* so extraordinary is their postmodern unexpectedness, their eccentricity, their almost tangential connection to the Palestine story. Neither goes over the well-known territory now so much in evidence during television news broadcasts, although in both films the human tragedy of Palestine has been transmuted into a quasi-mystical celebration of sacrifice and elegiac immobility. It is as if both these works of cinematic mastery, by turn witty and unutterably sad, have established a new nondiscursive medium for the Palestine story, which in one of its trajectories has gone beyond the brassy triumphalism of its military phase and settled into the travail of a difficult but far from ordinary everyday life. The other, more dominant and insurrectionary aspect of Palestinian life still awaits its Ponte Corvo or Costa-Gavras.

JULY 17, 1989

DO THE RIGHT THING

Stuart Klawans

•

Stuart Klawans received his education in cinema through a youth misspent in film societies and revival houses. Besides being *The Nation's* film critic since 1988, Klawans has contributed to the *Times Literary Supplement* ("American Notes" column), *New York Daily News* ("Museums" column), NPR (commentaries on *Fresh Air*), *The Village Voice, Grand Street, Threepenny Review, Entertainment Weekly*, WBAI (film reviews on "Soundtrack"), the *Chicago Tribune* and the *New York Times*. He is the author of *Film Follies: Cinema Out of Order*, "a history and theory of film going too far" which examines "those rare pictures that are both cinematic landmarks and monuments to a director's hubris." The book, which is an engaging detour through the world of Griffith's *Intolerance*, Erich Von Stroheim's *Greed*, Coppola's *Apocalypse Now*, and Leos Carax's *Les Amants Du Pont-Neuf*, was nominated for the 1999 National Book Critic's Circle Award.

IN THE DAYS of the Harlem Renaissance, when Langston Hughes was being attacked in some quarters for writing about black America's lower classes, Carl Van Vechten remarked jestingly to the poet, "You and I are the only colored people who really love *niggers*."

As it was with Hughes, so it has been with Spike Lee. He began his career only half a dozen years ago with the remarkably accomplished student film *Joe's Bed-Stuy Barbershop: We Cut Heads*. No one who saw it could ignore either Lee's talent or his love for the common citizens of the Brooklyn ghetto—not just the upward-striving, the politically involved, the gifted, but the whole range of street-corner society. In *She's Gotta Have It*, Lee himself portrays the fast-talking Mars Blackmon, who won't let anything so small as sexual jealousy come between him and a fellow African-American. In *School Daze*, the entire film depends on the conflict between black people who are plainly, emphatically black and those who are wannabees—that is, who want to be white. Now, in *Do the Right Thing*, you can still hear the echoes of Mars Blackmon's sentiment in the catch-phrase of Buggin Out (Giancarlo Esposito), whose standard parting line is, "Stay black."

A love like that separates loyalists from sellouts. It also animates certain troubled characters with a talent for making themselves unpopular. Jesters mock and receive favors in return; satirists love, and that seems to be Spike Lee's hard fate.

Do the Right Thing is Lee's most complex, heartfelt and disturbing film to date, a drama about racism that is more shockingly outspoken than any I've seen since David Mamet's great, and neglected, *Edmond*. Needless to say, the film depicts white bigotry with all due contempt. The best of the white characters—who seems a very good man indeed—is still ready to scream "nigger" when all else fails; the worst are willing to kill. The melanin-impaired will therefore feel uncomfortable with this film, and with good reason. But so, too, might the black community. Lee loves his fellow African-Americans, but he also portrays them as political good-for-nothings, long on talk and short on action, except when their actions are misguided. In *Do the Right Thing*, nobody does.

Set on a single block in Bedford-Stuy-vesant, *Do the Right Thing* follows about two dozen characters through a very hot summer's day, from a morning when interracial civility is already strained to a night when all hell breaks loose. The structure is episodic; brief, seemingly self-enclosed dramas follow one another rapidly, with two characters helping to frame and judge the action. The first of these is Mister Señor Love Daddy (Sam Jackson), disc jockey of an extremely local radio station, who observes the neighborhood through his living-room window and broadcasts what he sees, along with the finest in black music. The second framing character is Da Mayor (Ossie Davis), an old gentleman who rambles up and down the block all day. Da Mayor is courtly and kindhearted; he's also a drunk. To some of the younger people, he is a figure of fun. To Mother Sister (Ruby Dee), the block's reigning older woman, he is a contemptible bum. It is Da Mayor who enunciates the sentiment of the title, "Always do the right thing," in addressing his neighbor Mookie (Spike Lee). And in fact, Mookie tries hard to follow that advice. The effort he makes, and the degree to which he fails, will be the subject of debate for everyone who sees the film.

When we first see him, Mookie is at home with his sister Jade (Joie Lee), who is running out of patience with him as an unpaying roommate. As far as she is concerned, Mookie should get an apartment of his own, preferably with his girlfriend, Tina (Rosie Perez), and his infant son. Apparently, Mookie lays eyes on Tina only when he wants to do the nasty. Then, pleading the need to work, he disappears again from her life, proceeding in the general direction of his place of employment, Sal's Famous Pizzeria.

The whole neighborhood seems to meet at Sal's, and has done so for twenty-five years. In the words of Sal himself (Danny Aíello), "These people grew up on my food. And I'm very proud of that." Bearlike and bluff, Sal enjoys his business, enjoys his customers (most of them) and treats Mookie with the same combination of amused tolerance and restrained sarcasm that Mookie uses with him. There's even a grudging respect between Sal and his deliveryman—and that is a problem for Mookie. He can deal with Sal's son Pino (John Turturro), an outspoken bigot who spends the day urging honest labor on Mookie while avoiding his own work. Since Pino has declared himself an enemy of all black people, Mookie can respond in kind, with a clear conscience. But Sal is not simply the enemy. He's humane enough to command some loyalty from Mookie, who then is caught between his white boss and his black friends and neighbors.

Mookie's conflict begins with a visit from Buggin Out, owner of the fastest mouth and strangest hairstyle on the block. In search of a fresh shot of adrenaline, Buggin Out picks a fight with Sal over the pizzeria's Wall of Fame: a display of photographs of celebrated Italian-Americans. Where are the photos of black people? Has Sal never heard of Malcolm X and Michael Jordan? Buggin Out blusters; Sal boils over; Mookie gets the unhappy task of escorting his friend outside. Mookie tries to keep the incident on a personal level, complaining that Buggin Out is giving him trouble at his job. Buggin Out absolves Mookie but says goodbye with a meaningful "Stay black."

The conflict worsens with the appearance in the pizzeria of Radio Raheem (Bill Nunn). Powerfully built, inarticulate, able to peel the paint off walls with a single glare, Raheem takes his nickname from his constant companion, the biggest boom-box in Brooklyn. He stalks the neighborhood on a single-minded mission: making sure that every resident of Bed-Stuy hears the soothing tones of "Fight the Power" by Public Enemy. This is the only song he will play—in fact, the only one he will allow anyone to hear. With a heart-stopping glower and the push of a lever on his mighty box, Raheem drowns out all other music in the neighborhood. Sal threatens to throw him out of the pizzeria.

Now there are two people on the block with a grudge against Sal. A third joins their ranks when Pino gratuitously insults Smiley, the neighborhood idiot (Roger Guenveur Smith). Ordinarily, Smiley goes about preaching love and selling hand-decorated photographs of Martin Luther King Jr. and Malcolm X. Once he's been chased down the block, though, Smiley, too, is ready to take action against Sal's Famous.

Consider Mookie's dilemma. On one side, there are the protesters—his own people, even though they can't agree on what they're protesting, even though Mookie actually likes only one of the three. On the other side, there is Sal. Though Mookie *almost* likes him, he is white, he's the boss, and he is backed by a police force that's willing to kill black people. As the long, hot day comes to a boil, Mookie is given one moment to decide how to do the right thing. And that's the moment when Sal announces his own, antithetical philosophy: "You do what you gotta."

So *Do the Right Thing* comes down to an argument between morality and necessity—or rather, alleged necessity. It is a film about conflicting loyalties and evaded responsibilities; about the way our society values a white man's property over a black man's life; about the terrible gap between a community's need to mobilize itself and an individual's political acumen. To call these themes and their treatment inflammatory would be no more than the literal truth. More to the point, Spike Lee makes them lively and vivid, funny, and exasperating as well.

His style is deliberately juiced-up. The editing is fast, with dialogue sometimes crosscut on each line; the acting is often more stylized than natural. When Sal and his family first appear, for example, they seem to use three hand gestures for each spoken word. As in the past, Lee often points his camera head-on to the actors and has them talk straight into the lens. When even that method seems too oblique, he begins the shot with a fast dolly, as if the camera were a speeding Pontiac, jolting to a stop before somebody who refuses to get out of the way. Add to all this the episodic structure and the tendency of some of the characters to act out, and the film at times takes on an almost cartoonlike quality.

In other words, the style closely matches the characters' thoughts, which tend toward big, simplified outlines—the contours of a Hanna-Barbera cartoon, rather than a Disney animation. *Do the Right Thing* is very smart about portraying politics at this very dumb level. On the street, as Lee knows, there is little reasoned argument but a lot of totemism. Everything depends on which song is coming out of your radio, which photo is on the wall of your shop, which brand of sneaker you're wearing. The mere presence of a Boston Celtics jersey on a Bed-Stuy street is an insult to the residents—and if you don't know that, you obviously don't belong on the street in the first place. This, may heaven help us, is real American politics—which explains the inclusion of simple-minded Smiley in the plot and his ghastly moment of triumph at the climax.

Many of the reactions to the film, I imagine, will be on Smiley's level. Already Lee has had to explain that *Do the Right Thing* is not based on the Howard Beach case—that is, on white vigilantism—but is instead about the background to police violence. In some quarters, official murder is always alleged, never real. In those same quarters editorialists will probably call Lee's film an incitement to riot. (Sure—and racism, as Reagan informed us, is caused by civil rights leaders.) Among more open-minded viewers, though, *Do the Right Thing* will be seen as an incitement to thought. I hope the sidewalks outside the movie theaters this summer will be filled with people arguing over the rights and wrongs of Mookie's actions and the meanings of the two texts—one by Dr. King, the other by Malcolm X—that close the film.

JULY 19, 1993

JURASSIC PARK
LAST ACTION HERO

Stuart Klawans

•

IF YOU ASK Steven Spielberg for bread, will he give you a stone? Yes—and then he'll sell you a T-shirt reading, "Stones Taste Great!"

In *Jurassic Park*, the noted director of roller-coaster movies, a director whose works have in fact been *turned into* thrill rides at Universal Studios theme parks, tells the story of a showman who is about to open—a theme park. Its main attraction is a tour, via computer-controlled Fords, past real live dinosaurs. Since these creatures have been created for the film through computer-controlled animation, your experience *of* the movie is pretty closely analogous to the characters' experience *in* the movie—much as the on-screen showman is analogous to the one off-screen. To portray Hammond, the creator of Jurassic Park, the creator of *Jurassic Park* chose Richard Attenborough—another film director.

But all this self-reflexivity, this business of a snake swallowing its own tail, is nothing compared with the film's moment of truth. Coyly, ironically, as if earning the right to be crass by virtue of self-mockery, Spielberg trails his camera past a big display of items from the Jurassic Park gift shop. They are identical to the product tie-ins for *Jurassic Park*.

I think Theodor Adorno once reviewed this movie, around the time Steven Spielberg was born. By 1949–50, when Adorno resumed teaching in Frankfurt, he already had seen that there would no longer be any *outside* to our culture—no exit door through which to escape the self-advertising products that make up the inventory of our artworks, our social institutions, our very thoughts. Amid pop songs, movies and the rites of "democracy," we dwell among products that are *about* their own advertisements, that have damn little purpose except to sell themselves to us. Of course we're happy. Stones taste great!

I pick up the paper and read that *Jurassic Park* has grossed over $100 million in just two weeks of domestic release. Do I care? Is any of that money headed toward *my* bank account? But perhaps I've missed the point. From the tone of the news report, I can tell that *Jurassic Park's* success must surely be my success, too. As if in a potlatch, I can participate in the communal good fortune by offering my $7.50 to the next week's gross. To quote the ad campaign: "Be a Part of Motion Picture History!" What joy all of America must feel, as the numbers rise higher and higher! And they deserve to rise, too, because clearly *Jurassic Park* represents the forces of good—it practically says so, right in the paper. So there surely must be an opposing film, produced by the forces of evil. Here it is: *Last Action Hero*. Everyone is gratified to see it earn a mere $15 million over its first weekend in release.

Unlike *Last Action Hero, Jurassic Park* really is a hell of a piece of work, judged on a purely neurological level. Steven Spielberg wants you to jump, and you do. I suppose he could get an audience to wiggle its ears on cue. But this is all autonomic activity. The forebrain has nothing to do.

Of the dialogue that remains audible after the super-duper sound mix, only the lines spoken by Malcolm (Jeff Goldblum) suggest any wit. The screenwriters, Michael Crichton and David Koepp, have given him some cynical blather, partly about advanced mathematics and partly about his ex-wives. For a moment, the higher faculties stir; but the character turns out to have no function in the plot. Having mouthed off a few times, he's gored by a rampaging dinosaur and spends the rest of the movie lying about, shot up on morphine. At least you feel the effects wouldn't be wasted on him. He has "a deplorable excess of personality," says Richard Attenborough, sounding as if he means not the character but Jeff Goldblum himself. True enough, in this context. For the remaining cast, the film offers Sam Neill, who's been given nothing to do but some grumpy shtick; Laura Dern, who's been reduced to spunky shtick; and a couple of kid actors who are so creepily vapid they must have bar codes printed on their skulls. I should also mention the characters who have been created as dinosaur bait. They are polished off one by one, starting with the person the film-makers seem to think will be most unsympathetic to the mainstream audience and proceeding to the least objectionable: a lawyer, a fat guy, a black guy, and an Australian.

So I find myself rooting for *Last Action Hero*. Obviously, I'd be nuts to think of the picture as an underdog, considering that its reputed cost was roughly half the annual budget of the National Endowment for the Arts. Then again, that money didn't come out of *my* bank account. Besides, the movie has a few real laughs.

The story of a boy (Austin O'Brien) who is magically transported into the cinematic adventures of his favorite movie character, Jack Slater (Arnold Schwarzenegger), *Last Action Hero* already has elicited none-too-pleased comparisons to such boundary-blurring films as *The Purple Rose of Cairo* and Buster Keaton's *Sherlock, Jr.* If anything, these comparisons may be too kind. Like *Jurassic Park, Last Action Hero* is self-reflexive in the full late-capitalist, postmodernist sense. It denies the very sense of escape that Buster Keaton and Woody Allen celebrated. Then again, *The Purple Rose of Cairo* and *Sherlock Jr.* might be the wrong antecedents. *Last Action Hero* at its best plays like a megabucks version of *Airplane*! or *Naked Gun* or *Hot Shots*! (part one or *deux*).

Whereas Spielberg sells *Jurassic Park* to you with a *faux-naïf* sincerity, the makers of *Last Action Hero* are cheerily anarchic. However many objects they blow up on the screen—and anything larger than Schwarzenegger is likely to be dynamited—they take the most pleasure in exploding all sense of decorum. Some of the gags have the potential to become cult favorites—particularly the brief sequence in which Schwarzenegger demonstrates the right way to play Hamlet. ("Claudius—you killed my fodduh. Big mistake.") There are also any number of throwaway gags, which detonate in the hit-or-miss fashion of *Hot Shots*! (or, for a more venerable progenitor, *Hellzapoppin*). It seems that the young boy has been transported into something more preposterous than the average action film. He's entered a picture in which attack dogs suddenly perform circus tricks and fart jokes get dragged out for ten minutes at a stretch.

Frankly, I've seen better fart jokes. As for the action sequences, they often do far too good a job of mimicking *Blow Hard* 3, or whatever. The director, John McTiernan (*Die Hard* and other masterworks), could easily have cut twenty minutes out of the car chases and related mayhem without anybody's asking for a refund. But the most grievous sin of *Last Action Hero* isn't its bloated dimensions and lumbering pace, which sometimes put you in mind of Schwarzenegger as he'd be cast in a role meant for Cary Grant. To some viewers—especially those who write the rapt box-office reports—*Last Action Hero* is unforgivable because it doesn't pretend your $7.50 will make you part of Motion Picture History. In fact, the movie all but mocks you for having bought your ticket. That's better than rude—it's a provocation.

I said before that Steven Spielberg gets away with money-grubbing by being self-mocking about it. That amounts to saying that he justifies cynicism by being cynical. The makers of *Last Action Hero* are every bit as money-grubbing as Spielberg, and as cynical, too—but their cynicism is so blatant, so outrageous, that it succeeds at times in turning into comedy. And comedy stimulates the forebrain. It might not point to a way out, but at least it dares you to explain what you're doing at this potlatch.

To that extent, *Last Action Hero* is OK—not as good as John Woo's *Hard Boiled* (a genuinely over-the-top action thriller), but OK, all the same. And my favorite dinosaur movie? That would still be *Bringing Up Baby*.

DECEMBER 12, 1994

THREE COLORS: RED

Stuart Klawans

•

LIKE PROSPERO DROWNING his book, our modern-day wizard has gone out with a splash. A muted splash: Although Krzysztof Kieslowski's *Red* works up to a full-scale tempest at sea, the heart of its story lies in an old man's act of abnegation. It's something that can be managed quietly, both for the character in the film and for Kieslowski himself, who claims that *Red*—the final part of his magisterial *Three Colors* trilogy—is his last film, period.

The old man in the movie, a onetime judge in Geneva (Jean-Louis Trintignant), lives in isolation (if not full Prosperian exile) because of a sexual betrayal long ago. Now he spends his days eavesdropping electronically on his neighbors' phone conversations. He knows all their sins and troubles but does not act on his knowledge, either to lend a hand or to prevent others from being hurt. He does not act *because* he knows; with the network of life spread before him, he sees he cannot touch even one string without setting the whole to jangling, perhaps disastrously. I think of the grieving angel who keeps popping up in Kieslowski's *Decalogue* series, witnessing the characters' downfalls with mute, helpless understanding. I think, for that matter, of Kieslowski himself, who throughout his career has used sophisticated electronic equipment (not unlike the judge's) to track the intersections of people's lives. Ever since his early feature films such as *Camera Buff* (1979) and *Blind Chance* (1982), Kieslowski has been a connoisseur of fateful coincidences, of missed connections and unforeseen consequences. Now, upon his retirement, his screen double appears before us in the form of a judge, who at last shuts off the eavesdropping machinery and allows life to proceed without his surveillance. When does he relinquish control? Like Prospero, he does so at the moment of sending a young woman into the world.

Her name is Valentine, and she is embodied, more than played, by Irène Jacob. Her lush-lipped features are as mutable as a dream, as free of sharp edges; yet her physical presence is so strong that you can feel her tendons strain when she's at a ballet class, or sense her breath's force afterward when she guzzles a bottle of water. By profession, Valentine is a model; made insubstantial by the camera or a fashion show's runway, she is good for selling chewing gum or evening gowns. In her flesh, though, she is something else: a moral being, whose sense of right and wrong is as direct as her gait. I don't mean to say that Valentine is free of doubt. Worried over her teenage brother (a junkie) and harried by a boyfriend who is never home but always jealous, Valentine does not seem to know what to do about her situation, other than to hold on. But when, by Kieslowskian chance, she injures a stray dog, she does not hesitate. She scoops it up in her arms, lays it in her car, and drives off to find the owner. When he turns out to be the judge—a man who no longer wants to take part in the world—Valentine doesn't hesitate about him, either. She muscles her way into life.

Pared down to its essence, *Red* consists of three complex, extended dialogues between Valentine and the judge. During the first, she discovers his eavesdropping, remonstrates with him and eventually lays bare her own woes, thereby bringing a moral dilemma into his study not as electronic voices but as flesh and blood. The second dialogue takes place after the judge yields to Valentine and gives up his spying; during the third (which as a farewell scene is prelude to the tempest), Valentine finally elicits a confession on the judge's part. The construction is elegantly symmetrical—a characteristic of the screen-plays Kieslowski has written with his longtime collaborator Krzysztof Piesiewicz. And yet this skill at pattern-making, though it gives an overall integrity to *Red* (and to the entire trilogy), counts for little compared to the real thrill the film provides, which is simply the sight of the passing moment. Each action, each image, has an uncanny integrity of its own.

Valentine turns down an offer of tea; and so the judge, his eyes fixed on hers, spills the water he'd boiled for her out of the kettle and onto the floor. What a flaunting of desire, with what an avowal of impotence! What haughtiness, combined with what ramshackle despair! Another supercharged moment: The judge halts his conversation with Valentine so she can watch as the room briefly fills with light, then goes dim again as the sun moves on. How thoroughly must he know this lonely house, to be able to time that event? How keenly must Valentine, too, feel her days ticking away? And another moment, the last: The judge sees Valentine's face on television. Unlike the phone conversations he'd tapped into, this broadcast image is public property; yet it's the one communication in *Red* that bears him a personal message. Only he knows the full meaning of that closeup of Valentine, that profile set against a red background, which in one context might express a longing for chewing gum and in another might reveal terror and exhaustion. In a context the judge alone knows—the judge, and of course the audience, which is seeing the finale of *Three Colors*—that same image can suggest the reawakening of love.

I insist that the picture of Valentine is the culmination of the trilogy and not just of *Red* because I believe the trilogy is really one big movie—a point that ought to be obvious, though relatively few people have mentioned it (an exception being Dave Kehr in *Film Comment*). The facts of the production should be enough to make the case. According to Kieslowski's account, he and Piesiewicz finished all three screenplays before *Blue* went before the camera. (Zbigniew Preisner, the composer for the trilogy, contributed to the scenarios by deciding which film should be scored to a tango, which to a bolero; the musical structures worked their way into the elaboration of the plot.) Kieslowski shot *Blue* in Paris from September to November 1992. He began shooting *White* on the same day that he wrapped *Blue*, moved on to Poland (where he completed the trilogy's second section), took ten days' rest, then went to Geneva and shot *Red*, finishing in May 1993. So the parts of *Three Colors* were conceived together and shot continuously; and they were edited together, too, beginning within the first week of production in Paris.

Maybe people have overlooked the unity of this effort (and its magnitude) because the finished product has been so neatly labeled. Kieslowski, a sardonic man with a facile tongue, announced early on that the three sections of the trilogy corresponded to the colors of the French flag, which he took to signify liberty, equality and fraternity. Is there a Polish word for *blarney*? Kieslowski has now admitted that he had more in mind than slogans, however venerable; so perhaps we may dispense with the labels and look at what's actually on the screen.

What we see most vividly—no surprise—is color. Part one, photographed by Slawomir Idziak, floods the screen with blue light, which filters through water, through cut glass, sometimes through the air itself. The camera is thoroughly subjective here; as Julie (Juliette Binoche) passes through mourning for her husband and child, space seems to warp with her every mood, as if her emotions had the power to fog the air around her. *White*, shot by Edward Klosinski, is correspondingly objective. At the start, its color literally falls out of the sky onto the protagonist, Karol Karol (Zbigniew Zamachowski), in the form of a pigeon dropping; and from there on, Karol keeps getting whited out in emphatically material fashion, whether on the snowy streets of Warsaw or between the sheets with his estranged wife. *Red*, shot by Piotr Sobocinski, is of course the warmest in color but also the most dense. Its reds can be localized in objects (curtains, for example, or items of clothing), giving them a physical insistence that's lacking in the vaporous blues of *Blue;* they're also pervasive, framing the characters at every turn, unlike the isolatable incidents of white in *White*.

Three Colors invites the viewer to play at giving denotations to blue, white, red—a worthwhile game, as far as it goes. Surely blue is appropriate for its meditative heroine, suffering in well-moneyed Parisian gloom. White goes well with the clownish circumstances of its Warsaw-born hero, scuffling his way up from barber to post-Communist tycoon. So blue might be defined as a color of thought; white, as a color of hard facts; and red would be the color of the heart, as suits a film with both a hero and a heroine, who live at a geographic and economic midpoint between Paris and Warsaw. But again, this is to freeze the flow of experience into a pattern, which is fascinating and lovely but inert. Why not take color seriously—Kieslowski seems to—as a mode of perception beyond fixed meanings?

We live in a time of impatience, when people demand a paraphrasable art. In the galleries and museums—especially those that traffic in political engagement—the objects you encounter generally *read* to the viewer. They *make a statement*, as if each work were already its own translation. In bookstores and book reviews, direct address is similarly prized. John Ashbery, though eminent, is out; poetry slams are in. As for pop music, I recall an interview of a few years ago with Chuck D. of Public Enemy, who dismissed jazz as that "abstract" stuff his father listened to. It was no good because it had no words—no message.

Into this market steps Krzysztof Kieslowski, an artist who has the bad habit of meaning more than he says. His messages (as in *No End*) used to be blatant enough to get him in trouble with the Communist authorities, though not bracing enough for many of the regime's opponents. His key figure of this period, perhaps, was the title character of *Camera Buff*, who blunders into a career as a filmmaker and dissident when all he really wants is to take some shots of his daughter's birth. A provocative film; but nothing you could rally around.

Since then, the old regime has broken up, and Kieslowski has made his way West, into co-productions that must seem cushy by his former standards. Certainly he's indulged himself in a new sensuousness, beginning with *The Double Life of Véronique*; but his attitude, thank heaven, is still offensive to common sense. First he plots his movies as rationally as a diagram; then he lets the irrational pour in, trusting that blue, white and red will convey more than anything that can be said.

"To me the meanest flower that blows can give/Thoughts that do often lie too deep for tears." The age of revolution was born at the same time as Wordsworth wrote those lines, which the age of reason would have derided. (Is thought a kind of root vegetable, watered by tears?) They're nonsense; but then, the great achievement of the age of reason was to discover reason's limits. Ever since, some of the bravest thinkers and artists have mounted expeditions into the territory beyond, where the crazy beating of Wordsworth's "human heart" sometimes urges us toward resignation and sometimes toward liberation. Kieslowski's great merit as a political artist has lain precisely in his ability to remain clear-headed while venturing into the elusive, the contingent, the unresolvable. For that, all of us camera buffs owe him thanks.

JULY 29/AUGUST 5, 1996

LONE STAR

Stuart Klawans

•

MY EDITORS DISAGREE completely with the following remarks. Nevertheless: I think John Sayles gave away his game a couple of years ago in *Passion Fish*, his movie about a soap-opera star who is paralyzed in an accident—the sort of event she's been confronting five days a week on TV, and which she now faces in "real life." The suppression of quotation marks, I think, is the game. "You know the boundaries of fiction," Sayles seemed to say. "Now see how I break them down, to let in life itself."

In other films, too, Sayles has announced his triumph over narrative conventions: the self-dramatizing lore of one-time radicals in *The Return of the Secaucus Seven*, the myths of sportswriters in *Eight Men Out*, the fables of Irish patriarchs in *The Secret of Roan Inish*. To this list we may add the local legends and received histories of Texas, which Sayles now attempts to overcome in his new film, *Lone Star*.

In the border town of Frontera, in Rio County, everyone can tell a few stories about the late sheriff, tough-but-honest Buddy Deeds. One person in particular has heard all the yarns, at least a thousand times: Buddy's son Sam (Chris Cooper), who has returned to Frontera after a long absence and has been elected sheriff in his turn. One legend above all has come to obsess Sam: the tale of the night in 1957 when a young Buddy ran the previous sheriff out of town.

That man—Charley Wade (Kris Kristofferson)—was an openly corrupt, racist killer. After Buddy faced him down, Wade simply disappeared. But now, as *Lone Star* begins, a couple of officers from the local Army base stumble across a ring, a badge and a set of bones, which no doubt belong to Wade. It falls to Sam ("Sheriff Junior") to decide whether to follow Frontera custom and ignore the evidence, or to investigate and perhaps determine that his father's shining career began with murder.

While Sam busies himself debunking Frontera's rich oral tradition, a teacher named Pilar (Elizabeth Peña) is engaged in a similar struggle, this one against official history. With her support, her high school has instituted a new curriculum, to the distress of that half of the faculty for whom Sam Houston and Davy Crockett are still heroes of the white race, rather than agents of the cotton- and slave-traders. For a brief moment, Pilar's revisionism intersects with Sam's, after the town elders vote to put up a monument to Frontera's Korean War veterans, as exemplified by a sculpture of Buddy Deeds. Pilar's faction at the high school would rather see a sculpture of a Latino soldier—and so, it appears, would Sam.

But Pilar's main intersection with Sam takes place on personal grounds: their memories of having been high school sweethearts; their rancor and bafflement at having been separated back then; their present-day resumption of a relationship, carried out at a pace so glacial that it's more of a slide than a flirtation.

Once again, Sayles has set up narrative convention on one side and real life on the other, with Sam and Pilar carrying in their flesh all the truths that have been excluded from accepted history. That's the theme of *Lone Star*, and the structure, too. Pilar's perfunctory engagement in the debate over curriculum, and Sam's pursuit of the McGuffin-like killer, function almost entirely for the sake of exposition, providing excuses to introduce the information that Sayles feels the audience needs. (Like *Springtime for Hitler*, *Lone Star* is just crammed with historical goodies. Did you know that Texas used to be part of *Mexico?*) As for the climax of the film—the proof that the exposition matters—everything depends on the coming together of Sam and Pilar.

It's a well-conceived scheme, and ambitious, too (so ambitious that I haven't even mentioned a third major strand of the plot). And that, in a way, is the most damning thing I can say about *Lone Star*—because I've been able to get this far in my account without needing to discuss the *movie*.

How do characters hold themselves when they talk to one another? Are they proud of the clothes they wear, or would they dress differently if they could? When Pilar walks down the street, does Sam follow her with his eyes, or does he make himself look away? What is the camera looking at, while Sam stares at Pilar or his boots? How close does the camera stay to the characters? Does it plunge the audience into their eyes? Or does it hang back, allowing us to see people caught in the web of personal and local and national history? The life of a movie, from second to second, depends on the answers to these and a thousand other questions, none of which, unfortunately, requires comment in a description of *Lone Star*.

I'm not saying that Sayles is indifferent to these concerns, only that his direction is so slack it feels indifferent. Witness the scene in which Sam and Pilar finally find themselves alone. It's late at night in a deserted cafe. Here's Pilar, so lonely she's in danger of drying up; and here's Sam, a lean, handsome, serious man, in a town where such types are as rare as a geyser of lemonade. "You asked why I came back," the geyser says with appropriate steam. "I came back because you were here."

What does Pilar do? Does she bite off his lips? Does she perform an impromptu for percussion, using whatever beer bottles come to hand, to suggest that she won't allow Sam to screw her up again? No—although those responses might perk up the audience, they would be too soap opera—like for Sayles. Reasonably, veristically, he prefers to make Pilar hesitate in the face of temptation; he just can't figure out how she would do it. Sayles has her cross the room, walking as if she were balancing a book on her head, till she comes to the jukebox, where she pauses to comment on the antiquity of the selections; then, task accomplished, she drifts into Sam's arms and begins to dance with him. None of this action feels as if it comes from within Pilar—which is to say, it doesn't arise from any emotional exchange between Elizabeth Peña and Chris Cooper, or from any momentum generated by editing, camera placement or camera movement. It's just a bit of business, which Sayles has imposed upon the character.

It would be easy to multiply examples, but pointlessly cruel. Everywhere in *Lone Star*, Sayles's version of "real life"—let us reinstate the quotation marks—turns out to be as factitious as the conventions of soap opera, only blander. And that is often the case in his movies. When his actors are exceptional—Alfre Woodard, David Strathairn, and Joe Morton come to mind—the screen comes alive, however fitfully. When the actors can't pull off the trick, we're left with an abstract world, populated by characters who are little more than moral categories: Sayles's notions of how people ought to behave and what they ought to believe.

In past years, Pauline Kael used to amuse herself (and a few million readers) by railing against moral improvement. I would suggest she was slightly off the mark. Moral improvement has been a goal of the arts for millennia; anyone who looks forward to seeing it end had better take her vitamins. The problem, rather, lies with those moralists who are so concerned with their own virtue that they don't feel the need to perform an artist's labor, or don't know what such labor might mean. Do they define virtue in civic and political terms? All the worse; they make politics dull.

Sayles is intelligent and prolific, low in budget and high of mind. For those reasons, I have passed over his films in discreet silence till now, preferring to turn my aggressive tendencies against products such as *Twister.* If I break the silence now, perhaps it's because Bill Clinton and Bob Dole will be broadcasting their own homilies nonstop from now through November. If movies are to provide us with public space during these wan times, then let it be a space where people bite off each other's lips and smash beer bottles, where political debate entertains and romance comes complete with secretions. Better to be of the devil's party, I say, than to stand with Sayles and the angels.

AUGUST 9/16, 1999

EYES WIDE SHUT

Stuart Klawans

•

STANLEY KUBRICK'S *EYES Wide Shut* tells a story of three consecutive nights in New York City, and of the exchanges between wife and husband that punctuate them. In the wake of the first two nights, the wife reveals dreams of sexual desire, which humiliate and enrage her husband. After the third night, it's his turn to confess. Appalled at what he's discovered on the trail of his own desires, he breaks open at last, at dawn.

These events take place in late December, when nocturnal fantasies of horniness and guilt can be played out in festive surroundings. Even the low-rent den of a prostitute has its Christmas tree, radiating color in the background. Yet there's more to the film's glow of make-believe than a few holiday trimmings. New York's downtown streets have grown slightly wider. The rows of storefront are strangely tidy; the apartment interiors (except for the prostitute's) all seem to belong on Park Avenue. Fabricated by Kubrick in England, this is a dream Manhattan, which comes close to the real thing without actually touching it. When Dr. Bill Harford (Tom Cruise) walks these streets, visiting a patient's home or prowling the Village, he is not so much inhabiting a physical place as moving through a set of thoughts—thoughts that take shape in reaction to the unwelcome suggestions of his wife, Alice (Nicole Kidman).

Such rigor of structure, wed to such clarity of purpose, was uncharacteristic of the work of Kubrick, about whom I still find it hard to write in the past tense. His sudden death in March converted *Eyes Wide Shut* into a last testament—a nasty trick for fate to have played on him, since unintended, superabundant meanings were foreign to his art. The degree to which the release version itself might have seemed foreign to Kubrick will remain a subject for debate. Although he completed a cut of the film before he died, reports have circulated that the sound mix had to be finished by other hands. And then there's the issue of the alterations (defacements, rather) that were made in the US version to secure an R rating, instead of NC-17. I'll have more to say on that subject. For now, it's enough to remark that as Kubrick's Christmas fable comes before us, it is weighed down as heavily as Marley's ghost.

During the two hours and forty minutes that I spent watching *Eyes Wide Shut*, I kept longing to unburden the film, to lift the portentousness that had settled on it. And at times the weight seemed to lift on its own. In the scene of Alice's second revelation, the emotional ground shifts so quickly that gravity loses its grip. (Bill awakens her on the pretense that she was having a nightmare—an odd excuse, since she was laughing in her sleep. Yet, once awake, she agrees with him. The dream was terrible, she says, and then reveals an explanation Bill doesn't want to hear.) In other scenes, characters such as a scheming merchant (Rade Sherbedgia) and a flirtatious hotel clerk (Alan Cumming) recall the comic grotesques who have animated so many of Kubrick's films. But these moments prove to be rare. Some of the heaviness of *Eyes Wide Shut* was imposed on the film; but most of it, like Marley's chains, turns out to have been self-forged.

Proceeding at a pace that is not so much hypnotic as soporific, *Eyes Wide Shut* devotes the great majority of its running time to Bill's fantasies: his vengeful search for erotic adventure and the anxieties that ensue. Bill becomes irresistible to a grief-stricken woman (Marie Richardson), falls in with an improbably wholesome streetwalker (Vinessa Shaw) and then (in the movie's extended set piece) bluffs his way into a Long Island mansion, where men in masks and hooded capes ritualistically debauch a team of women who recall nothing so much as Vegas showgirls. In brief, Bill has a head full of clichés. Throughout his somnambulistic excursions, he treats them all with leaden solemnity—and so too, unaccountably, does Kubrick.

At one point in his career—thirty years ago, say, when he first thought of making a film version of Arthur Schnitzler's *Traumnov-*

elle—Kubrick might have directed the central masquerade to combine a *frisson* with laughter. Not any longer. "When a promise has been made here, there is no turning back," declares the master of the revels to Bill, in one of many lines that would have been better suited to a silent-film intertitle. "Go!" And Bill slinks off, with such dimwitted earnestness that he drags back the next day for more.

Who is this dolt? It's hard to say—and not just because Bill spends so much of the film behind a mask. Even without the disguise, precious little that is credible registers on his face. Those moviegoers who belittle Tom Cruise should think twice before assigning the blame to him. Remember *The Color of Money, Born on the Fourth of July, Interview With the Vampire, Jerry Maguire*, then ask yourself how that sly overachiever could have turned into the shell you see here, unless he'd been methodically directed toward hollowness.

It's a hollowness not of technique but of conception. In his later years, Kubrick seems to have forgotten that you can't have psychology without people (those inconvenient beings who demand to be listened to and watched). And so Bill comes across as a disembodied syndrome: male neglect of female sexuality. Such syndromes do manifest themselves—even on the Upper West Side of Manhattan, even in the nineties. But only in *Eyes Wide Shut* do they manifest themselves without credible human agency.

To grow rich as a doctor to people who are richer still, a man needs both charm and a sense of command. Through such traits he makes his place in the world, and can lose it at home. But since *Eyes Wide Shut* never links public life to private, we might conclude that Bill's blindness to his wife is nothing more than the error of bumptious youth. When circulating at a posh party, Bill hides behind a forced smile—except when he encounters an old medical school buddy, with whom he lapses into the playful arm-punching of a high school jock. Never once did I believe that the wealthy would entrust their lives to this man. Nor was I convinced that Bill (surely a social climber) would drink canned Budweiser; that he would discover a Village jazz club with a tuxedoed headwaiter and a last set ending at midnight; that in present-day New York, he would find a cab driver named Joe who speaks English as a first language. When a film leaves you time to notice such improbabilities, it's a sign that the fictional world before you is not surreal but sub.

As for the wife whom Bill neglects: So, too, does Kubrick. All we know about Alice is that she once managed an art gallery in SoHo (the walls of her home are covered with pictures no self-respecting SoHo merchant would touch) and that she now spends all her time caring for a school-age daughter. Such taxing unemployment may have been common among upper-middle-class women in Schnitzler's Vienna, but it would be seen as an odd in Kubrick's setting. This isn't to say that married women on the Upper West Side are necessarily happier than their old Viennese counterparts. They're just more interesting than Alice.

I think *Eyes Wide Shut* is the work of an artist who long ago stopped paying attention to the world around him. If you are someone who cares about film culture, you will want to see it anyway, perhaps more than once. Respect for the rest of Kubrick's work would demand no less. But here the final chain clanks onto the film.

Because the rating board of the Motion Picture Association of America objected to some images of crotch-to-crotch thrusting in the masquerade sequence—about sixty-five seconds' worth, according to the stopwatch of *Variety*'s Todd McCarthy—Warner Bros. altered those shots to secure an R rating. In what the distributor calls the "international release version" (that is, the film as Kubrick made it), the thrusting will still be visible. But in the "domestic version" (meaning the one deemed suitable for American eyes), Warner Bros. has inserted computer-generated figures into these shots, to block your view of the action.

I suppose I shouldn't object. Thanks to the MPAA and Warner Bros., the masquerade now has the element of risibility I'd desired. But the least one should do for a Kubrick film—even one of his lesser works—is to see it. In the United States, it is now impossible to achieve that minimum. Maybe, in making this picture, Kubrick should have kept his eyes open wider to the world around him; but there's no reason for our own eyes to be shuttered.

FEBRUARY 7, 2000

MAGNOLIA

Stuart Klawans

•

IN HIS NOVEL *A Flag for Sunrise*, Robert Stone invents this old American saying: "Mickey Mouse will see you dead." I have spent many profitable hours mulling over that coinage; and I've concluded it has something to do with our national aversion to tragedy.

American novelists have written "tragedy" into their book titles; America's playwrights, sending doomed men to center stage, have told us that attention must be paid; but the audience, after a dutiful sigh, always turns back to comedy. I don't mean just the banana-peel stuff (though we've certainly had our share of that). I'm talking about fictions that end with fresh beginnings: couples paired off, society renewed, May buds blooming over pots of gold. The comic mode rules in America, no matter the sufferings that lie in our past or the catastrophes that await, well prepared, in our future.

Perhaps the only form in which tragedy has flourished in America has been film noir—though "flourished" may be the wrong word for a mode that mushroomed at the bottom of cheap double bills and then had to be named in French. In the years when noir was fully alive, a few such films were deemed respectable and given awards, if Billy Wilder had made them; but most, like their protagonists, lived in the shadows. Noir was, among other things, a shade cast by the uneasy conscience of the people who won World War II; the grief and terror that underlay victory played in distorted shapes across the walls of grind houses.

Eventually, noir succeeded in emerging into the light; it entered the museums and film societies. And so it became an object of nostalgia, drained of a large measure of its power.

As for those recent productions known as neonoir: You can't sweat out a movie like a guilty secret when the picture keeps offering to be your guilty pleasure.

The historians who someday will define us by our stories, as we define the Greeks and Elizabethans by theirs, will note this curious gap in our imagination. But they won't be able to judge us by nonexistent tragedies; their only measure will be the comedies we've produced. If we hope to make a good showing, then those comedies had better be something more than funny. They will need at times to be deep and challenging—which is why I return to *Magnolia*.

It is a long, emotionally taxing film, one that elicited from my friend Gerald Peary a groan of, "Cry me a river!" As I noted last month, the characters in the film's intersecting stories include two men dying of cancer, two women who are walking pharmacological experiments, four abused children, and one professional misogynist. Did I mention the dead dog?

The writer-director, Paul Thomas Anderson, throws that in, too—and yet the mood at the end is comic. You can place *Magnolia* by the startled laughter that erupts at the climax, during events that are (paradoxically) both cleansing and slimy. There's comedy as well in the final reconciliations, the pardon-granting, the blossoming smile on which the picture ends.

I had hoped a film this strong might win a few critics' awards. (To date, only the Toronto group has cited it.) I also hoped it might inspire analysis and debate. But *Magnolia* is being neither honored nor much discussed; and so, rushing into the near-vacuum, I want to review it in more detail—especially now that it's in wide release, its secrets having been revealed by several critics who should know better. Those of you who haven't seen the picture and want to preserve its surprises intact should stop reading now. All others may join me in pondering how much weight *Magnolia* will bear.

Let's start with a theme that's announced in a prologue: Some coincidences, especially when they're mortal, are so uncanny as to prompt us to imagine a guiding hand. Unsympathetic reviewers have suggested that this theme is a mere ploy, meant to rescue Anderson from the banality of his individual story lines. I suspect many of these same reviewers would tag as sophomoric the whole question of randomness versus design. True enough: This is the sort of riddle posed at college bull sessions. It's also asked, in a different tone, by the middle-aged at 3:00 AM. By raising this theme, Anderson puts himself in a line that runs from the Greek tragedians—those connoisseurs of implacability—to D. W. Griffith, the first great filmmaker to cut between scenes on the basis of theme and not story.

What is montage, that basic tool of the movies, if not the construction of a pattern, devised by a godlike hand that goes unseen by the characters? Far from being a superficial ploy, Anderson's prologue goes to the heart of both drama and filmmaking. The only question is whether the film can live up to the question.

The answer begins with a whiplike montage sequence in which Anderson introduces the characters you'll be following for the next three hours. And, in a sense, he keeps on introducing them. It's not just that he gradually reveals their interrelationships: the business tie between the two dying men, for example, or the sexual loneliness that's shared by the cop (John C. Reilly) and the onetime quiz kid (William H. Macy). Anderson also tricks you into judging these characters, then smilingly changes your mind about them.

A small example: When the brilliant Philip Seymour Hoffman, in the role of a private nurse, shyly phones a convenience store for a delivery of white bread, cigarettes and three porn magazines, you will certainly guess what's coming next. But the narrative hint turns out to have been a feint; the man has an altruistic use for stroke books. A larger example: A young black kid (Emmanuel Johnson) comes across an obviously wealthy white woman, who is slumped unconscious in her open car. He rifles through her purse—and, having found her cell phone, calls for help. Finally, two glaring examples: Here are Frank (Tom Cruise), a strutting TV preacher of male supremacy, and Claudia (Melora Walters), the coke-addled, bar-trolling daughter of a quiz-show host. Talk about bad first impressions! The whole burden of *Magnolia* is to show that even these monsters—highly plausible ones at that—may conceal human hearts.

Is this, too, a mere narrative ploy? Not when so many other characters get their chance to be better than expected. A generosity of spirit, which is comic in itself, runs through all of *Magnolia*—while is fortunate, with that rain of frogs on the way.

Yes, it's time to talk about the frogs. Only the laziest movie-watcher could claim they've simply been dropped into the picture. All through *Magnolia*, to prepare you for the plague rain, you're kept informed of the changing weather. The younger of the quiz kids, Stanley (Jeremy Blackman), even asks for meteorological instruments (and has been studying a book by Charles Fort, chronicler of unexplained downpours). Three times, amid normal precipitation, characters say, "It's raining cats and dogs." Three times you see signs that read "Exodus 8:2," giving chapter and verse of the second of Egypt's plagues.

Still, who could believe that Anderson would pull such a stunt? Playing on your expectations, he begins the episode with another feint: While having you follow the cop along a midnight street, Anderson lets you think you've heard gunshots. That's what the cop thinks, too, having been fired upon earlier in the day. Now he slams on the brakes—and sees two frogs sliding down his windshield.

Suddenly, the rain of frogs becomes general. It translates the cop's personal humiliation into widespread, public calamity—something *out there*, which calls for him to do what he likes best, helping others. To Claudia, by contrast, the frogs manifest themselves as the ultimate drug heebie-jeebie. (With classic slapstick timing, they fall only when she looks away.) At the home of the dying TV producer (Jason Robards), the frogs plop down comfortably in and around a spot-lit swimming pool; a sterile Southern California "oasis" suddenly teems with life. To the producer's self-destructive wife (Julianne Moore), lying in the back of a careening ambulance, the frogs are disaster piled on catastrophe. To the quiz-show host (Philip Baker Hall) they're a judgment from on high, prolonging a life he no longer wants. To young Stanley, smiling dreamily in the grammar school library amid their drifting shadows, the frogs seem the fulfillment of a promise.

In brief, there is no single rain of frogs; there are many. And that's what makes this plague—or blessing—seem so miraculous: not the freakishness of the event but its democratic multiplicity. I could say much the same for the miracle of *Magnolia*'s performances—each flamingly intense, yet all blended into an ensemble—or for the wonder of an actor-centered filmmaking that's intricately imagistic. On every level, from its montage technique to the objects of its meditations, *Magnolia* tests to the limit the tendency of life to fall apart; and in pulling against that entropy, to gather (some of) its characters into a (mostly) happy ending, it offers a comic vision that almost does the work of tragedy.

From now on, under the legend "E Pluribus Unum," let the dollar bear the sign of a frog.

INDEX